ADVENTURES IN GOOD COMPANY

Adventures in Good Company

The Complete Guide to Women's Tours and Outdoor Trips

THALIA ZEPATOS

The Eighth Mountain Press
Portland ✦ Oregon ✦ 1994

ADVENTURES IN GOOD COMPANY: THE COMPLETE GUIDE TO WOMEN'S
TOURS AND OUTDOOR TRIPS. Copyright © 1994 by Thalia Anastasia
Zepatos. All rights reserved. No part of this book may be used or
reproduced in any manner whatsoever without prior written
permission from the publisher except in the case of brief
quotations embodied in critical articles or reviews.

Cover art by Maggie Rudy
Cover and book design by Ruth Gundle

Manufactured in the United States of America
This book is printed on acid-free paper.
First edition 1994
10 9 8 7 6 5 4 3 2 1

LIBRARY OF CONGRESS CATALOGING-IN-PUBLICATION DATA

Zepatos, Thalia, 1955-
    Adventures in good company: the complete guide to women's tours and
    outdoor trips / Thalia Zepatos.
        p.   cm.
    Includes index.
    ISBN 0-933377-28-2: $24.95.—ISBN 0-933377-27-4 (pbk.): $16.95.
    1. Outdoor recreation for women. 2. Women travelers. I. Title. GV191.64.Z47
1994
    796.5′082—dc20   94-8440

THE EIGHTH MOUNTAIN PRESS
624 Southeast Twenty-ninth Avenue
Portland, Oregon 97214
(503) 233-3936

For my godmother,
Constance Dadas Procopiou,
who taught me to savor adventure.

TABLE OF CONTENTS

Part II ➤ Look Before You Leap

Part III ➤ Directory of Tours and Trips for Women

ACKNOWLEDGMENTS

Each book is a journey whose destination is unknown at the outset.

I wish to thank Rebecca Shine, who joined me as editorial assistant when the road got rough and performed miracles until the cows came home. My friend, I could not have done it without you.

For her vision in creating this book and her high standards in producing it, I am grateful to my publisher and editor, Ruth Gundle. For naming this book, I thank Judith Barrington.

My heartfelt thanks to the women interviewed on these pages, who shared truths about their travels and their lives. Much appreciation to Alliah Kahn, Elizabeth Pollock, Carolyn Shine, and Joy Turner, for their research assistance. I am especially indebted to Janet Brown and Women Outdoors for the sharing of resources.

Many thanks to Els Shine for translation; to Sandy Polishuk, Peter Thacker, and Lynn Taylor for equipment loaned and encouragement given; to Cynthia Cumfer for legal advice; and to Tony Lafrenz and Catchword for cheerful computer help.

Loving thanks to my incredible community of friends, who nourished me in spirit, especially Karen Harding and the Cup and Saucer Cafe, Andrea Carlisle, Julie Davis, Maura Doherty, Eleanor Haas, Tom Norton, Kathleen Saadat, Moses Walker, and Dania Wheeler, who also cooked and left food on the doorstep.

I thank Elizabeth Kaufman for allowing me to commandeer the office; Esther Lev for helping shape this book; Linda Besant, Cris Miller,

Sandy Braun, and Ken Walker for reading and commenting on the manuscript. Thanks to Andrea Carlisle, Karen Brummel-Smith, Lana Fox, Eleanor Haas, Beth Kaye, Reva Leeman, Mary Jane McLeod, Kate Peterson, Karen Scott, Colleen Sullivan, Judith Wild and Nichola Zaklan—the Tuesday Night Writers—whose solidarity extends to every day of every week. My appreciation to everyone at Cottages at Hedgebrook for a delightful return to Oz.

And, for your steadfast love and encouragement, I thank my beloved parents, Spero and Sophia, and the members of my family—Jerry, Sherry, Jacqueline, Justin, John, Christine, Jason, Alexis, Chris, Sarah, and Nicholas.

INTRODUCTION

In 1921, two women, Clarissa and Seraphine, discussed the idea of taking a canoe trip on a New Jersey canal. "'Clarissa, my dear,' said Seraphine, spilling a little more bacon grease on last year's khaki skirt, to make the spots symmetrical, 'it will be a lesson to us. You see, up to now, all our camping trips have been taken under the wing of virile young American manhood and our duties have been to squat around the campfire while men yelled to us to bring things. But the time has come for women to have some adventures alone.'"[1]

Thousands of women have taken Seraphine's advice, and each year more and more discover the fun of sharing adventures with other women.

So, how about you?

Don't accept the idea that your days of exploration and discovery are over, especially if they've never begun. You've focused on work, on family, on taking care of others. Now it's time to challenge yourself, visit the places that inhabit your dreams, discover strengths you never knew you had or are ready to rediscover.

Women—of all ages, backgrounds, and skill levels—have opened the door to new adventures by choosing to travel in the company of other women. To them, it seems as natural as the cozy atmosphere around a kitchen table. If you've never taken one of these trips and you're wondering, "What's the appeal?" the answer can be found in the stories on these pages of women just like you—old, young, or in between; married, single, divorced, or widowed; straight or lesbian; athletic or not—who shook off their doubts and signed up for adventure. Over and over they told me:

All-women groups create a safe and supportive environment to learn new skills and venture to new places. Women who have developed expertise in many areas of life may still be novices at traveling or pursuing outdoor activities. Most of us simply feel more comfortable taking risks with other women. Ski-school instructor Patti Sherman, of Vail, Colorado, notes that 85 percent of women ski students prefer all-women's classes. "The absence of intimidation makes all the difference—learning is much faster and more fun!" Women are more enthusiastic and confident in an all-women's environment. Even after the trip is over, that confidence and enthusiasm blend into other aspects of our lives, inspiring us to tackle new challenges or make difficult personal changes that might have previously seemed impossible.

There are no "assigned roles" on women's trips. Often, without realizing it, we defer to men in outdoor situations and unfamiliar surroundings. By traveling with other women, we break that dynamic and can operate as equals more easily. There is no longer a "natural choice" about who should make the fire, set up the tent, or steer the boat. Someone's got to do it; it could just as well be you.

You don't have to talk anyone else into going along. Quit trying to drag your unwilling best friend, partner, or spouse along. Leave them cultivating their own gardens, while you spend time with others who share your interests and sense of adventure.

You don't have to plan or coordinate the trip. Let someone else worry about all the details. Even if you like to plan your own trips, consider making it easy on yourself by letting an expert do it for you. Or give yourself the gift of traveling on shorter notice than you could if you had to figure it all out yourself.

It's great fun to travel with other women. Join the easy camaraderie of a group that can be serious or silly. Broaden your outlook by traveling with women of different ages, experiences, and backgrounds. Forge new friendships in the context of discovery.

In the last fifteen years, women guides and veteran travelers have formed scores of companies and organizations to help every kind of woman meet every type of adventure. Because most of these companies don't have large advertising budgets, it can be difficult for the average person to find out what's available. But I have done the hard work for you—I have spent months gathering information on the most interesting trips and companies worldwide. Now all you have to do is settle in a cozy chair by the fire (or a comfortable hammock in the shade) and pore through these pages to find the group that beckons you to join them for an adventure in good company.

Thalia Zepatos

TO THE READER

This is a book about organized travel for women. Every company I could locate that regularly offers women-only trips was invited to be included. No one paid to be listed.

Since this is a compilation of resources, the fact that a company is included does not mean that I am recommending it. My intention is to provide enough information about all the options available so that you can find the company and trip that is right for you.

When you contact companies for additional information, please mention that you read about them in *Adventures in Good Company*.

How to Use This Book

The first section, **"Next Stop: Adventure,"** describes over thirty kinds of outdoor trips and activities, along with a list of the companies that offer trips in that category. Start with this section if you want to find out about activities that are new to you or if you want to get a sense of the full range of what's available in the world of international and outdoor programs for women.

The second section, **"Look Before You Leap,"** gives you guidance in choosing a company and trip that's right for you. There are also chapters on what to expect during your trip, how to prepare, and what to take along. Read this section when you're ready to make plans.

The third section, **"Directory of Tours and Outdoor Trips for Women,"** is an alphabetical listing of ninety-eight companies worldwide. Each company's history, philosophy, and basic information is provided along with sample trip offerings and prices. Use the directory to find full information about companies as you come across them in the text. Some readers will want to start with the directory and read the listings from beginning to end, then go back and read the rest of the book.

Only companies which offer organized trips for women on a regular basis are listed in the directory. Other companies of interest mentioned in the first two sections, along with membership organizations, products, and events, are accompanied by complete contact information in the text.

Indexes at the end of the book provide quick reference to trips and companies by geographic area. Addresses are in the United States unless otherwise specified; toll-free numbers are good only in the country of origin unless otherwise specified.

Send Us Your Feedback and Suggestions

Adventures in Good Company will be revised and updated on a regular basis. Please send information, feedback, and ideas for new listings to Thalia Zepatos, c/o The Eighth Mountain Press, 624 Southeast 29th Avenue, Portland, OR 97214.

I

Next Stop: Adventure

What Will It Be?

Admit it. Just to yourself, just this once. You'd like to have a real adventure. Do something you've never done before. Could you really climb a mountain? Canoe down a quiet river? Or travel overseas to join a camel caravan? There's a voice in your head that says, "Go ahead, you can do it." And another that follows right after, whispering, "Maybe you can't."

Meet your challenges beside a cheering section that will teach, guide, and reassure you—a chorus to convince you that you *can* do it, and drown out the little voice that says no. It's time to think about the kind of adventures you would like to have. When you dream of a trip, what images come to mind? What will you see around you, what will you do during the day, where will you eat and sleep? Do you long to interact with other cultures? learn new skills in the outdoors? rest and be taken care of? or push yourself to new heights?

Would you like to travel with women your own age? Spend time with your mother or daughter? Do you hope to get in better shape or build your self-esteem?

Focus on what you would enjoy doing rather than what you think you 'could' or 'should' do. The right trip for you matches your sense of adventure, physical comfort needs, fitness level, and budget. Consider each of these factors as you start to shape your plans.

What Is Your Ideal Adventure?

- What have you always fantasized doing?
- What makes you perk up your ears when you hear about someone else's adventures?
- Are you wanting to challenge yourself physically, culturally, spiritually, or just get away from your life and have a good time?

What Is Your Ideal Adventure Level?

• How much change, uncertainty, and surprise do you feel comfortable with?
• How much confidence do you have in facing new challenges?

What Is Your Physical Comfort Level?

• Are you willing to sleep on the ground or do you prefer a cot or a bed? A five-star hotel?
• Will you pee in the woods or do you prefer a toilet?
• Do you want to have meals served or are you willing to help cook them?
• In short, what's your idea of roughing it?

Assess Your Fitness Level

Make a realistic assessment of your current fitness level. Don't fool yourself or the company you are going with. Can you walk for three hours on hilly terrain? Carry your own bag or backpack? It's fine to make a goal of getting in better condition for an upcoming trip, but don't set yourself up for frustration by choosing a trip too far above your current fitness level. (But don't underestimate your abilities, either.)

Be sure to read the literature a company provides to clarify what level of fitness or skill is required for each trip. For example, Skadi Women's Walking Holidays defines their walks as follows:

"*Gentle* walks should suit women who haven't done much walking before, are doubtful of their fitness, or simply prefer more leisurely days. We walk six to ten miles a day, with less than 1,000 feet uphill.

Energetic walks are more physically demanding—they may be longer and/or include some hill-walking. We walk approximately seven to twelve miles a day, with up to 2,000 feet uphill.

Strenuous walks are designed for fit women with some hill-walking experience. We walk approximately eight to fifteen miles a day, with up to 3,000 feet uphill."

If you are unsure about your fitness level or feel you are on the border between two categories, use these tips from The Nantahala Outdoor Center to determine which way to go:

"Take a lower level course if you are a bit wary or tentative, if you exercise twice a week or less, if you are rusty, or if you have had little formal instruction.

Take a higher level course if you are engaged in a regular fitness program or exercise more than twice a week, if you are confident and aggressive and willing to jump into new situations, or if you have had more than three days of formal instruction."

Determine Your Budget

How much will the trip cost? Pay close attention to what is not included in the price of the trip and remember to add in the cost of getting to where the trip begins. How much money do you have to spend? If money is a concern, consider these options:

Some companies offer work-exchange, barter, scholarships, or flexible payment plans to clients. Look for the notation " Scholarships available" in the listings in Part III. Forty are listed in the index.

Use the geographic index to determine which companies are closest to home. Cut your travel expenses to a minimum and still have an adventure.

Tell your friends and family how important this is to you and ask them to pitch in. Let your loved ones know that you want help taking a trip for your graduation, your fortieth birthday, or another significant milestone.

Do something special to raise funds for your trip! A friend whose hobby was astrology did a series of special astrology readings to raise money for her sailing trip to Greece. Organize a fundraising spaghetti dinner or gourmet brunch.

Read the chapter "Organize Your Own Group" in Part II to find out how you can travel free of charge or at a significantly reduced cost.

Keep an Open Mind

Don't disqualify yourself too quickly from any adventure. Read the chapters that describe things you think you'll never try. Take inspiration, as I did, from *Women's Sports and Fitness.*[2] Started in 1974 by Billie Jean King (and then called *WomenSports*), it covers a wide range of women's involvement in sports and outdoor activities. Don't rule out any of the options in this book. Almost everyone who's mentioned on these pages is doing something now they never imagined they would be doing.

Bicycling

Bicycles have been transforming women's lives since the turn of the century. Bicycling was exported from England in the early 1870s, and by 1900 was considered a "craze" in the U.S., Canada, Australia, and New Zealand. Thousands of women joined bicycling clubs or formed their own. Because their long skirts got caught in the gears and wheels, many women adopted the controversial pantaloons designed by Amelia Bloomer. Bloomers caused a social uproar, partly because they helped free women from the constraints of Victorian society. Bicycling and other sports helped women become more active, independent, and mobile. Sunday rides turned into competitive races and organized week-long tours of the countryside.

Bicycles and Gear

All you really need to start cycling is a bicycle and a helmet. If you can't afford a fancy new bike, buy a used one. Do yourself a favor and make sure it fits. To test the fit of a standard frame bicycle, stand flat on the ground and straddle the top bar—you should have three-quarters of an inch to an inch of clearance between your body and the tube. If you do, then get on the bike and take a test ride.

Mechanical engineer Georgena Terry, manufacturer of Terry Precision Bicycles for Women, points out how to examine the fit as you lean over to reach the handlebars. "You should be able to ride with your hands on the brake levers, your elbows slightly bent and your arms relaxed. You shouldn't feel like you are stretching."

Terry builds bicycles to fit women from 4'10" to 5'11". Differences in the lengths of our limbs, the amount of muscle as well as distribution of women's body mass call for bicycles with a shorter top tube. Terry's bicycles are shorter from the seat to the handlebars, with slightly narrower handlebars and the brake levers set closer together. Terry is one of a small group of bike builders who have finally addressed the need for fitting bikes specifically to women's proportions. Terry Precision Bicycles for Women offers a catalog full of bicycles, gear and lots of helpful information at 1704 Waynesport Road, Macedon, NY 14502 (800/289-8379). Ask about the annual Terry Tour of Vermont!

Mountain Bike World Champion Jacquie Phelan describes the problem of fitting bicycles like this: "Bikes are set up for a certain proportionality between torso and legs. Our torsos are shorter compared to a man's, while our legs are generally longer. So when we sit on a bike built for the average fellow, our arms can't reach the bars without overstretching. Women often don't realize that a shorter stem can lead to much greater comfort. Instead they take a ride, find they've got an aching back, and say, 'Oh, I'm terrible at this, I think I'll give it up,' fours hours after they've gotten into it."

Jacquie Phelan goes on to point out that, "Before you start paying attention to brands, find a bike shop that makes you feel welcome. You want to find a shop that doesn't laugh you out of the store if you don't know exactly what you want. They sometimes have the attitude 'when you figure out what you want, come on back.' But they won't spend time teaching you what you need to know. If the shop doesn't have a woman salesperson, or if you feel like you're being talked down to by an eighteen year old, then go back out the door. Try two or three shops, until you find someone willing to work with you to figure out what you want and need."

Because men's bike saddles are not designed for our "sit" bones, which are set wider apart, they can be instruments of torture. Women's saddles are built wider and shorter. Buying one revolutionized my cycling comfort. A bicycle helmet should be a mandatory part of every ride; purchase one that has been safety approved by ANSI.

Toe clips, which secure your feet to the pedals, will improve your efficiency dramatically. With toe clips, you're not just pushing down with one foot at a time, you're pulling up with the other foot simultaneously. Toe clips can seem intimidating if you imagine your foot getting stuck in the cage and causing you to fall. I got accustomed to toe clips by using them one at a time at first, starting with the straps very loose and then gradually tightening them. It's amazing how quickly you can get your foot out of the clip when necessary—my clips have never caused me to fall.

Cycling clothes and gloves add comfort and efficiency, and just a bit of glamour. When buying cycling shorts with a padded crotch, make sure the crotch has no center seam, which is irritating to most women. Look for cycling clothes and accessories designed by women. Aerotech is a woman-owned company that manufactures bicycle clothing for women. Call or write for a catalog at 1128 Fourth Avenue, Coraopolis, PA 15108 (412/262-0993). The Woman Outfitter offers a catalog of products designed and tested by women for cycling as well as hiking, walking, swimming, mountaineering and running. P.O. Box 2820, Orleans, MA 02653 (800/795-7433).

A Woman's Guide to Cycling[3] by Susan Weaver is an excellent resource for new and experienced riders, with many tips specifically for women. The WOMBATS—Women's Mountain Bike and Tea Society—newsletter is full of helpful hints, such as "used mascara brushes are perfect for cleaning bicycle chains." P.O. Box 757, Fairfax, CA 94978 (415/459-0980).

Bicycle Touring

My first major bicycle tour was a ten-day trip through Holland. Before that, I'd only done overnighters, but I thought I could survive the flat Dutch countryside without too much trouble. The week before the trip, I nonchalantly slipped out of my friends' house in the town of Nijmegen each day, pedaling madly into the countryside, on levees, past dikes, and low farmhouses with thatched roofs, pushing myself to go farther and faster to build my stamina.

On our day of departure, my two friends and I arose before dawn and were out the door at 6 A.M. I was sure I'd drop by noon, and we still had many towns to pass until our first night's resting place. Then the rains came, and I learned the secret of the Dutch wind: no matter which way you're traveling, it's always in your face. The downside of riding in flat country manifested gradually over the next two days— saddle sores. No variation in the terrain meant no relief from the seat of the pants hitting the seat of the bike.

Sound terrible? Actually, it was great fun. After a pre-dawn start each day, we'd cycle until about 10 A.M., when we made a ritual of stopping for coffee and huge plates of Dutch pancakes piled with fresh fruit and whipped cream. We passed windmills and crossed drawbridges, hailing wooden-shoed farmers as they pedaled their clunky, two-wheeled roadsters. On our third day we broke 100 kilometers—a mileage record for me at the time. My friends cheered and flourished bouquets of flowers as I crossed the "finish line."

Each day served as training for the next; each day we broke a new distance record. We took turns drafting—riding closely behind each other to take advantage of decreased wind resistance. The Dutch have two sets of road signs to point the way from town to town: the automobile route and the bicycle route. The bicycle routes had little traffic and were endlessly scenic, like a collage of jigsaw puzzle pictures from the dime store. The wind and rain never let up, but after the first day or two it didn't bother us. We had kilometers to cover.

Most organized bicycle tours are not grueling endurance tests, and many do not require previous touring experience. Roads with little automobile traffic are chosen; daily mileage averages twenty-five to fifty miles for three to five hours of cycling, with refreshment stops in between. The wonderful thing about bicycle tours is that you can stop frequently along the way, to sample local food or just talk to the cows. It's a mode of transport that invites conversation from other riders and the people you pass. International cycling tours often create commonality with local people, as bicycling is a major form of transportation in many parts of the world.

When signing up for a tour, check to be sure the average daily mileage is something you can handle, day after day. Get specific information about bicycles, if they are provided by the operator. Consider bringing your own bike along, or just bring your saddle to help ensure your riding comfort.

Narrow-tired bikes, called road or touring bikes, are aerodynamically efficient (they offer less road resistance) and the top choice for bicycle touring and road racing. Drop handle bars allow you to change your posture periodically, as they provide four different positions for your hands. This is helpful during long rides, but takes a bit of adjustment if you're not used to them.

Many bicycle tours include "sag wagons," vehicles that transport luggage (and occasionally tired riders) to each day's destination. Tours without a support vehicle require a higher level of fitness; the added weight of your clothes and tent, packed in saddle bags (called panniers), can make the bike more difficult to handle and take some getting used to.

You should feel quite comfortable on a bike before setting out on a tour. Organize your own conditioning program to get ready—ride daily and build up to weekend rides of thirty or forty miles. When you can cover that mileage in two or more consecutive days, as you will have to do on tour, you will be ready to go. Many riders do their conditioning by riding their bicycles to work and to do errands around town. If you will be carrying your own gear on tour, build up the amount of weight you can carry in your panniers. Also, practice climbing hills with your panniers packed—the added weight really affects braking and stopping time, not to mention the uphill climb.

Novice cyclists frequently make the mistake of using higher gears than are necessary; low gears reduce the strain on knees and muscles and allow you to pedal longer and farther. This is especially important to those with knee or ankle problems. When climbing hills, always shift to a lower gear before you think you will need it in order to maintain momentum.

Bike Trips

Tours available to women include daytrips in upper New York State, a week cycling through California wine country, and a two-week bicycle tour of Ireland or New Zealand. Some trips involve camping out, while others include stays at small inns.

Backroads
Outdoor Vacations for Women over 40
Pack, Paddle, Ski
Women of the Wilderness Australia
Women's Outdoor Adventure Cooperative
Woodswomen

Mountain Biking

Jacquie Phelan, the first woman inducted into the Mountain Bike Hall of Fame, says, "Mountain biking is the ideal sport for women, whether they're gnarly or nervous!" Mountain bikes are the off-road vehicles of the bicycling world. They have fat (also called knobby) tires, straight handlebars, and enough gears to climb a tree. They are fun to ride, since you can jump curbs and rocks and travel through many kinds of terrain. They are less efficient for street use or long tours because the wide tires slow you down with increased road resistance. As the name implies, mountain bike riding involves climbing mountains. It offers a great workout with a view much better than the one at the gym. Trails are marked and are sometimes shared with hikers.

Don't wait until you get a mountain bike to start training—just get on any bicycle and start climbing hills. Then find more challenging terrain and start going up and down mountain trails as soon as you get a mountain bike. Experienced mountain bike riders recommend that you not sit during rough descents; stand on the pedals, use your knees as shock absorbers, and keep your body centered over the bicycle.

Cross or hybrid bicycles are also gaining popularity. They combine the narrow tires of a road bike with the upright seating position and low gears of a mountain bike.

Mountain Bike Trips

Get acquainted with the sport of mountain biking or improve your skills in California, Alaska, or the Blue Mountains of Australia. Daylong clinics, weekend bike hikes, or a full week of instruction get you on your way. Companies offering mountain bike trips include:

Alaska Women of the Wilderness
Wildwise
WOMBATS

I'm a sculptor, and I also teach art. I took my first trip with Woodswomen when I had a sabbatical leave from my teaching position, and I wanted to do something very special, something that I would otherwise never do. So I took a trip to Nepal.

Then last summer, I went on a cycling tour of Ireland with Woodswomen. There were five of us in the group, ranging in age from our early thirties to late fifties. Three staff accompanied us: our leader was Val and there were two apprentice leaders-in-training, one of whom drove the support vehicle that carried our luggage.

I'd never been on a bike trip before. Woodswomen sent me guidelines explaining the level of physical fitness I needed to achieve ahead of time. It included questions like, "Can you sit on a bicycle for three hours? Can you cycle thirty miles in three hours?" I trained by riding my bicycle the fourteen miles from my home to my studio twice a day. Once I was able to do that easily, I felt confident that I could handle the trip. And I was well-acquainted with my bicycle by then.

After the very challenging trek in Nepal, Ireland seemed like a piece of cake. We would get up early and load up on carbohydrates for breakfast—we ate a lot of cereal and bread, and fruit. Then we would ride at our own pace. You didn't have to stay with the group. Before we set off, we always discussed where we were going and how to get there. Someone rode in the lead, and another person brought up the rear, so no one could get lost or left behind.

We would ride in the morning for three to four hours, take a break for lunch, and then ride in the afternoons for another three hours or so. Some days were longer than others, depending on our itinerary. The support vehicle cruised back and forth to see if anyone needed a ride or had an equipment breakdown. One woman opted to ride in the support vehicle twice, but there was no stigma attached to it.

We stayed in bed and breakfasts that ranged from private homes to more formal hotels. They were all nice, clean, and wonderfully different. We had breakfast there, and sometimes dinner too, or we went out for dinner together. We usually had lunch along the way—we would buy whatever we wanted from a market or, if it was raining, we would stop and eat indoors in a pub.

The Irish people were cordial and gracious. They seemed genuinely glad that we were there. We never encountered anything negative about the fact that we were all women traveling together—it didn't concern anyone.

Some days were harder than others; a lot of it had to do with the weather. When the wind and rain were in our faces, that made it difficult. Rarely did we have the wind at our backs. The terrain was varied but mostly hilly, which I quickly learned to love because it was much more interesting than riding flat stretches.

Over time the bicycling got easier; one's body does get stronger. I felt a real difference by the end of the trip—I was physically much stronger and had thighs of steel! That was one of the ironies—by the end of the trip is when you're really in shape to go! We could have ridden like the wind for another week or two.

Aside from biking, the other emphasis of the trip was looking at the remains of the ancient goddess religions and the role of women in Ireland in ancient times. We stopped at stone circles and other sites, and our leader, Val, gave us a lot of information. It was very empowering to be near the remains of a culture that honored women for their wisdom, strength, and sensitivity.

Val is a homeopathic physician. She had all kinds of wonderfully arcane knowledge to share with us at dinner, and it was fun to ride along beside her and carry on long conversations about a broad range of subjects. She was easy going and a good leader—she led without being overbearing. She knew where we were going—the trip was thoroughly planned—but we always had the option of taking a side-trip for an extra hour or so, if we wanted to see something special. If we arrived at our destination early enough in the afternoon, it was certainly all right to go off and explore some more.

One of the assistant leaders had lots of mechanical skills and plenty of tools, but we didn't have many breakdowns. I took my own bicycle on the trip. By then I really knew that piece of machinery and what it could do. I wore long cycling pants (because it was a little bit cool and I felt more comfortable in them) and a lightweight jacket that was wind and rain resistant. Style was not an issue in the group; you could wear street or cycling clothes. What I've found is that cycling clothes are not so much a matter of fashion as they are a matter of comfort. The clothes fit in a way that allows you maximum freedom of movement without chafing or undue flapping. They're very sleek, so there's no wind resistance, and they keep you warm and dry. Other than the pants and jacket, I had no other official bicycling clothes. I just wore sneakers and whatever shirts I had.

The bicycle is not just a recreational vehicle in Ireland, it is a major means of transportation. We met many Irish people cycling; they knew instantly that we were Americans because we wore helmets. The roads are narrow, and so you have to be aware of where you are on the road in order to allow ample room to pass. Both the other cyclists and the cars were considerate, so we had no difficulty sharing those small roads. I never felt in any kind of danger.

One of the wonderful things about the trip was that a good friend went with me. We don't see each other very often—she lives in Washington, D.C. and I live in Boston. It was a great way to have a reunion. We spent time together, but we were able to create new friendships as well.

There's a special chemistry that happens when you travel with a group of women. There's less emphasis on competition and more concern that everyone do the best that she can possibly do. My friend had a real challenge because she was overweight and had not ridden her bike much before. She met that challenge, and we all triumphed with her. By the end of the trip she was really getting strong. Another woman, probably our strongest and our youngest member, had a hearing impairment that made it difficult for her to hear what people said. We all learned to speak so that she could read our lips. She taught us what it meant to really listen and added a wonderful dimension to the trip. When you travel like that, you come back a changed person, with a larger vision of the world and a greater appreciation of your own abilities and others' strengths as well.

I have a lot of faith in Woodswomen—they are excellent in the way that they plan and organize things. I'm already planning my next adventure with them.

The name of the game is *traction*. And the fun thing about mountain bikes is that traction isn't a given. You've got to earn it, fight for it, and win it. In the meantime, you forget about your shitty job, your pathetic relationship with your parents, the state of the world and how it's going down the tubes. You just pay attention to moving forward.

Mountain biking is not as dangerous as it's been represented to be. The image of the sport is of a glamourized, testosterone-driven exercise of highly accentuated danger. People see the advertisements created to sell the bikes and they are frightened. In reality, most riders are timid and polite. Mountain bikes have big fat tires, which serve as an insurance policy, so new riders often choose a mountain bike as their first bike. If you are afraid of traffic and want to get away from cars, you can push your bike up the hill until you are strong enough to ride part way up. Ultimately, you will get strong enough to ride all the way up. And you can inch your way down until you can coast down. Eventually, you will be able to pedal down. I think it's the road bikes that appeal to a tougher, more fitness-oriented person.

I started to ride a bike in 1970, when my parents refused to drive me to high school. After I graduated from college, I moved to San Francisco and found that a bicycle—while not the most obvious means of transportation around town—was the cheapest. I got into good shape riding a girl's five-speed bike up the hills. Then someone told me I should race, so I did. I won my first road race and never looked back.

By 1981, people were starting to race with fat tires on the dirt. From 1981 to 1986, I never lost a mountain bike race. I never had a flat tire. I only broke one crank. I had an impeccable record. At the time, there were hardly any women racing, so my impetus was to start a women's mountain bike riding club. It was obvious to me that there needed to be women-only hideouts in these male bastions, where women could practice in private with other women.

I've also been motivated by an incident in 1984, when I tried to interview a big-name road racer for a magazine article. She was training for the Olympics, and she wouldn't give me the time of day. Was she ever cold! People develop a different kind of personality when they become champions; the whole world comes chasing after them with gym outfits and free dinners and whatever. They get this sort of weary entitlement attitude. So I took some mental notes and marched in a different direction. I would be a champion, but I would also be approachable.

As the first big-time mountain bike racing champ, I wanted to start off by hitting a certain friendly note and then make everybody else try to match it. So I started to pass out cards on the trail, inviting women on bikes to "Tea and Gab" at my house on Sundays. When I mentioned riding together, they'd say, 'Oh you're too fast,' and I said, 'No, I'll go your speed.' So I learned to lead from the rear, and let others set the pace.

The name WOMBATS came in '87. I'd heard of a climbing group called the Women's Sewing Circle and Terrorist Society, and I loved the dissonance between sewing and terrorist. I wanted a group with a meaningful acronym, so that's how Women's Mountain Bike and Tea Society, WOMBATS, was inspired.

A cadre has built up over ten years—I'd say there are about twenty women that have actually stuck around since the beginning. Usually the club appeals to beginners. Once they get better and meet women they want to ride with, they feel they don't need the club anymore. That's fine, I don't mind nurturing the chicks until they fledge.

For those who do stay around, the organization can provide networking insurance to keep you from ever having to ride totally by yourself, even when you're on a business trip. There are informal chapters in Los Angeles, Connecticut, Boston, and Idaho. To form a local group, I ask people to join and be on the data base, wear T-shirts, take new riders out, and serve tea. Otherwise, the name just gets appropriated and starts to mean Women Who Love Mud Too Much.

The camps are really fun. The Fat Tire Finishing School is the week-long camp, and Camp Winnawombat is the weekend version. A typical day at Camp Winnawombat starts out with me serving tea and scones while we wait for the stragglers. Then we'll all cruise off to the site of the camp and have maybe an hour of "Let's look at our helmets," because no one's helmet is adjusted right. It's usually being worn like a bonnet or yarmulke, depending on your cultural heritage, and it should really be worn snug and down low over the brow.

Then I explain a handful of crucial things about camp. Most women are really in touch with their "Help, this is scary!" reflex. I want them to listen to that, and know that they can hop off and walk their bikes if they feel intimidated for any reason. Women have to listen to their inner voices and get away from their boyfriends, or their gnarly girl-friends, or even me as the substitute gnarly boyfriend. If I am urging them to do something that sounds like *too much*, then they're going to be pretty tense.

There's always quite a range of riding ability. There are a handful who just got a bike and their husbands bought them the weekend. But they do great, and they have a good time. With twenty people, we split into several groups with names like Heavy Sweaters, the Wombadeers, the Gnarly Chicas, or the Hammer Chicks. They get to name their own squadron.

Women never think they're good at anything. Only one out of four hundred women has told me, "You know, I was a little worried that maybe camp would be too easy." The other 399 said, "Oh god, I just hope I'm good enough."

We get into groups and we ride on the fire road. Then we stop and talk. And the joke is, "How many women does it take to ride around the corner on a fire road? One, and ten to discuss the implications."

Part of camp is getting women to realize that there are a lot of different bikes out there. We swap often, and it's a great chance to try a bike that's already built and slightly dinged up; nobody's going to frown if you tip it over.

The first fear of women who come to camp is, what am I going to do with all these strangers? The second fear, although everyone may not own up to it, is the fear of looking like an idiot. By heaping on the humor and the whimsy, we make it a little easier to look like an idiot. And, when the idiot talking to them (me) is the boss, it's de rigueur to cut a caper now and then.

Some women are afraid of getting hurt, especially if they're used to riding on asphalt. But we can allay their fears pretty quickly by explaining that they can walk down every darn hill.

Until this year, we've used a camp facility in Marin County, just across the bay from San Francisco. We get graduates of the local culinary academy to cook, and they spoil us. Now, we're having camps in Maine on Sugarloaf Mountain and in Durango, Colorado. Who knows where we'll be next?

Melanie is one of our WOMBATS success stories. She came on a lot of day rides, for about a season. It was not possible to go faster than her downhill. I saw that she had potential, so I urged her to race. She started at the second level (sport level), and then instantly got into expert. She's become a world-class downhiller, and she's one of the camp counselors now.

Mamoura ran away from home at fourteen and has supported herself since then. I met her when she was thirty-three and had just bought a bike. She attended a women's symposium and joined right then and there, and it changed her life. She told me that when she bought her bike, she took it to her room and couldn't go to sleep because she kept opening her eyes and saying, "I have a bicycle, oh my God!" She couldn't wait, every day, until she went out and rode it. Then she got into the WOMBATS, and she is definitely a great bat troupe member.

For many women, the bicycle indicates a turning point in their lives. It is the symbol of liberation now, as it was a hundred years ago. It started with bloomers, and didn't stop until women got the vote, threw away their heavy corsets, and banded together against intemperance, creating the biggest women's union in the world at that time.

Canoeing, Kayaking, and Rafting

Whether it's paddling a canoe or kayak or riding a raft into the rapids, there's an unmistakable allure to powering a small craft across water. Exit the concrete highway and follow the sounds of rushing water to the intersection of leaf, rock, and sky. As Mary Wickham Bond said in "The Passionate Paddler" in *Rivers Running Free*: "There's something about canoe and kayak that creates for the paddlers a profound intimacy with tides and changing winds, with remote coves and endless hours of quiet happiness."[4] Whether you consider yourself cautious or a daredevil, prefer a kayak, canoe, or raft, there's a paddling trip to fit your level of comfort, fitness, and quest for adventure.

Canoeing

I recommend reading *Rivers Running Free: Canoeing Stories by Adventurous Women*[5] edited by Judith Niemi and Barbara Wieser. You will gain the perspective that women have been canoeing forever and have gone everywhere. You'll learn that native women not only sewed canoes from bark, they paddled them long distances across great expanses of wilderness. You'll give thanks to "Canoeing Ladies" at the turn of the century who abandoned their long skirts for knickers and quit their sedentary positions admiring the paddler in the stern of the boat to turn around, pick up a paddle, and steer their own course. And you can marvel at Valerie Fons who canoed twenty-one thousand miles from the Arctic to Cape Horn, was the first woman to canoe around the Baja Peninsula, and held the speed record for paddling the length of the Mississippi River—2,348 miles in twenty-three days. Helen Broomell describes herself as a "typical suburban housewife who wore high heels and smoked for forty years." At age sixty-five, she canoed alone for six hundred miles along the Yukon River. Two years later, she returned to the truck stop where she had left her canoe and put it back into the Yukon to paddle the remaining seven hundred miles to the Bering Sea. She plans to go back to the Yukon when she's eighty and canoe the whole river in one season.

In *Down the Wild River North*,[6] another excellent Seal Press book in their series on women outdoors, Constance Helmericks tells the story of taking her two teenaged daughters canoeing down two thousand miles of Arctic rivers in 1965. Years later, her daughter Jean Helmericks Aspen returned to homestead in the Brooks Range and wrote *Arctic Daughter*[7] about her experiences.

Canoes are strong and stable craft, symmetrical until the seats are put in. Thereafter the front of the canoe becomes the bow, and the back the stern. Basic paddling techniques are easy to learn, and steering is not difficult. There's plenty of room for waterproof bags to carry camping gear and food.

Most recreational canoe trips travel downstream along rivers and across lakes. If the canoe approaches a big rapid, the guides pull ashore to study the situation and decide whether to paddle through or portage (carry the canoe overland) to avoid the rapid. A portage requires walking back and forth a couple of times as you ferry the canoe (carried above the head and shoulders by you and your paddling partners) and then return for your gear. Canoes have to be loaded each morning and unloaded every night that camp is changed; you may want to check with the outfitter if you have a concern about carrying heavy bags.

If you can get in and out of a bathtub, you should be able to get into and out of a canoe. No special strength is needed to paddle, although those with weak upper bodies may find the motion tiring. Paddling with a partner helps share the burden, and novices are often matched up with stronger and more experienced paddlers. Exercises that build the upper body, such as lifting weights, are good preparation for canoe trips. Larger women may find a canoe more comfortable than a kayak, and generally more stable. (Blackhawk Canoes makes the Shadow, a solo canoe sized for women—contact Women in the Wilderness for information.)

Canoe Trips

Dozens of canoe trips and courses are available throughout the U.S., Canada, Australia, and New Zealand. Try a multigenerational trip or combine yoga with canoeing in the Brooks Range. Many different levels of challenge, varied locations, and a range of trip lengths are available from companies such as:

Adirondack Mountain Club
Adventure Associates
Adventures for Women
Alaska Women of the Wilderness
Artemis Wilderness Tours
Bushwise Women
Canadian Outward Bound Wilderness School
Earthwise
Equinox Wilderness Expeditions
Et-Then
Hawk, I'm Your Sister
Her Wild Song
Hurricane Island Outward Bound School
Inside Outside Adventures
Lois Lane Expeditions
Mahoosuc Guide Service
Nantahala Outdoor Center
Outdoor Vacations for Women over 40
Pacific Crest Outward Bound School
Pack, Paddle, Ski
Rainbow Adventures
Voyageur Outward Bound School
Widjiwagan YMCA Camp
Wild Women Expeditions
Wildwise
Women in the Wilderness
Women of the Wilderness Australia
Women's Outdoor Adventure Cooperative
Woodswomen

Kayaking

As you skim over azure water in the stillness of early morning, you keep the other members of your group in sight, their kayaks up ahead and off to one side. You traverse an envelope of quiet broken only by the sound of your two-bladed paddle as it dips into the shining surface of the sea. A trio of pelicans fly in formation alongside you and seem to surf a cushion of air above the water. Up ahead your guide yells, "Gray whale at three o'clock," and you whirl to the right in time to see a spray from the blow spout as it fades to mist in the air.

Kayaks, like canoes, are ancient craft. They were designed and perfected by native peoples for transportation and carrying goods. Modern kayaks are generally divided into two types: ocean and river kayaks. River kayaks are smaller and tip more easily; they are well suited for maneuvering through river rapids. Ocean kayaks are broader, more stable, and have room for camping gear, food, and other supplies. The center of gravity is close to the water, which gives the paddler more control and requires smaller movements to adjust the boat. Most ocean kayak trips take place on protected waters (between islands or on inland waterways) instead of on the open sea.

Although previous kayaking experience is not necessary for most trips, participants should know how to swim and feel comfortable in the water. Large women should check to ensure that they will feel comfortable in the craft that will be assigned to them. The first day of any beginner's trip is spent on instruction. Participants will have a chance to practice paddling techniques in shallow water before setting out. Most sea kayak itineraries include two to four hours of paddling each day, often starting early in the morning. The rest of the day can be devoted to snorkeling, hiking, and setting up camp.

An advantage of kayak travel is that you are seated only a few inches above the water (although that can at times create problems for short paddlers.) Some ocean kayaks seat two paddlers; guides often team novices up with more experienced paddlers. A kayak moves swiftly and quietly across the water, facilitating bird and wildlife watching. Most outfitters provide kayaks, paddles, tents, and waterproof bags for your clothing and sleeping bag.

Still another in the wonderful Seal Press series is *Water's Edge:*

Women Who Push the Limits in Rowing, Kayaking & Canoeing[8] by Linda Lewis, which tells the stories of women who paddle in national and international competitions.

Kayak Trips

Develop your kayaking skills, or combine other activities such as whale watching or photography with a paddle trip. From the San Juan Islands to the rivers of North Carolina, from Mexico to Maine, the following companies can get you started or provide new challenges:

Adventure Associates
Adventure Spirit Hawaii
Alaska Women of the Wilderness
Blue Moon Explorations
Bushwise Women
Canadian Outward Bound Wilderness School
Eco-Explorations
Elakah! Expeditions
Equinox Wilderness Expeditions
Her Wild Song
Nantahala Outdoor Center
National Outdoor Leadership School
OceanWomyn Kayaking
Pack, Paddle, Ski
Paddling South
PeerSpirit
Wildwise
Women of the Wilderness Australia
Women's Outdoor Adventure Cooperative
Woodswomen

Rafting

You're paddling slowly down a calm river, watching the scenery and enjoying the sun. The sound of birds calling in the trees is suddenly drowned out by the roar of the river up ahead. You round the bend and focus on the churning, foamy water dotted with rocks before you. Everyone in the boat reflexively leans forward, gripping their paddles. It's time to run the next rapid!

If you think of a canoe as a comfortable sedan on the water, and the kayak as a low-slung sports car, then the whitewater raft is a roller coaster ride. Each moment of calm is spent in anticipation of the next thrill of riding the rapids.

Whitewater Rafting in Western North America[9] attributes the birth of modern commercial river rafting to Georgie de Ross-Clark, a woman from Chicago. In the mid-1950s, Georgie, unwilling to believe that river running was for men only, successfully lashed surplus World War II Army bridge pontoons together, creating the first oar-guided rubber raft. Since those days, the industry has exploded to hundreds of outfitters operating in western U.S. rivers alone.

Commercial river rafting trips are appropriate for most beginners because the outfitter supplies the boats, paddles, and safety equipment along with a guide who knows the river and has experience navigating it. For those who seek the scenery of the river without the adrenaline rush of the rapids, less intimidating float trips are also available on many rivers. Float trips take you down the calm sections of rivers where rapids and other obstacles are very small or nonexistent. A one-day float or easy whitewater trip would be a good introduction to rafting for anyone considering a longer or more challenging trip.

Oar-Guided Versus Paddle Rafts

Most river rafts are made of inflatable nylon or polyester, so they can bounce off rocks and bend slightly to absorb shock. The two major types of rafts in use today are known as "oar-guided rafts" and "paddle rafts."

Paddle rafts require the effort of everyone on the boat for navigation. Each person is issued a paddle, and a pre-trip briefing by the guide instructs the group on paddling technique. On the river, you sit on the inflated tubes that make up the edges of the raft and follow the instructions yelled out by the guide sitting at the rear as she or he chooses the strategy to navigate each rapid. "Forward paddle! Stop! Right side back paddle, left side forward paddle!" Paddle rafts are fun and exciting, and build team spirit because everyone is involved in the success of each run. Everyone gets wet, and occasionally someone falls out of the boat.

Oar-guided rafts are propelled by a single guide using two long oars that hook into a frame attached to the boat. The guide sits up high at the back of the raft. Your job as a passenger is to hang on and enjoy the ride. Oar-guided rafts have made rafting safer and more accessible to children, to adults who physically cannot paddle, and to those in wheelchairs. Oar-guided rafts are the burros of rafting expeditions; they are stable and carry loads well and will be piled with food and camping equipment on multiday trips.

Veteran river guide Sheri Griffith responds to her customers' three most common misconceptions about rafting as follows: "Rafting is hard work." *We do the work.* "You have to have experience." *We teach you as much or as little as you want to know.* "You have to be able to swim." *No, but you must wear a life jacket.*

Classification of Rapids

Whitewater rapids worldwide are rated for their level of difficulty, with Class I being the smallest and Class VI the most difficult. As the water level on a river changes with the seasons, so can the difficulty of its rapids. Because everyone on rafting trips is required to wear flotation life preservers, non-swimmers are allowed to go rafting on Class I through Class III rapids. For Class IV and higher whitewater rivers, all participants should have good swimming skills.

Be sure to check the weather and water temperature when planning a raft trip. Many rivers are fed by mountain streams or glacier runoff and can be cold even when air temperatures are warm.

Raft Trips

From a mild float to a whitewater adventure, join women guides from these companies:

Artemis Wilderness Tours
Call of the Wild
Earthwise
Equinox Wilderness Expeditions
Lois Lane Expeditions
Mariah Wilderness Expeditions
Outdoor Vacations for Women over 40
Rainbow Adventures
Sheri Griffith Expeditions
Women in the Wilderness
Women of the Wilderness Australia

I went on an eight-day all-women's canoe trip with Et-Then. "Et-Then" is a native word for caribou and the company is based out of the Hoarfrost River Homestead in the Northwest Territories, Canada. Kristen Gilbertson Olesen was the leader of our trip. She and her husband, Dave, built the homestead. A lot of people homestead to get away and to drop out. But their philosophy is to get people out in the country, educate them about walking in balance with nature, and show them it's a great place to be.

We went up in the "barrens," along the Hoarfrost river, down a few lakes and almost to Great Slave Lake. I'd done some single overnights in a two-person canoe but never anything this extensive. I was excited and a little nervous about the trip. Kristen had sent reassuring letters saying we didn't have to have any experience. She included a list of everything we would need, explained what the trip would be about, and what the weather would be like.

Knowing that it was an all-women's trip took the edge off of a lot. When you do things in mixed company, it's very easy to fall into role-playing. On this trip everyone took a turn, everyone took the initiative. All the other women were Canadian. One other woman besides myself was in her twenties, but most of the others were between thirty and forty. Some had canoeing experience.

The wind was cold and fierce, but it was always at our backs. We had some sails for the canoes—handmade sails—and after we were out for about five minutes on the first, day I turned around and said, "The wind's at our backs, let's put up the sails." And from that point on, we sailed almost the whole way. So that put us ahead of schedule, and made it really casual—we could sleep as late as we wanted. We were in charge of how we wanted the trip to go. If we had wanted to spend more time hiking, we could have done that, and then just paddled a little farther each day to make up the distance.

We only had a set wake-up time one morning. On the other seven days, I usually slept in. Some of the "morning people" relished getting up early while everybody else was sleeping to enjoy the quiet alone. Breakfast was already made by the time I got up. It was coffee or tea, with granola or toasted oats on some days, eggs, or pancakes with blueberries we had gathered on other days.

After breakfast we'd casually pack stuff up and load the canoes. Kristen supplied most of the equipment. We had a *wanagan* to carry all the kitchen stuff. A *wanagan* is a cabinet, a wooden box that you strap on to a pack to portage (carry) it. It's got a spice rack on the door, and you can put your plates and utensils inside, so it's like a portable kitchen.

Before setting off, we'd look at the maps to see where we were going and discuss potential camping spots and other stops down the line. We'd get on the river between ten and eleven. We had two twenty-four-foot cedar strip canoes, with four women in each canoe. (They were beautiful, long canoes, lighter and more maneuverable than plastic or aluminum canoes but also more fragile.) All four paddled. Everyone maintained a nice steady stroke, but we never felt pressured to keep going. If we saw a caribou, we'd stop, pull over, take some pictures, and watch.

We all took turns at the stern so we could practice steering and maneuvering the sails when we had them up. On a more difficult route, we would put one of the more experienced paddlers in the stern for control.

We'd paddle until maybe two or three, then break for lunch for an hour or so. Lunch was usually sandwiches, bread and cheese, crackers, granola, and fruit, with tea or something hot to drink. Then we'd get on the river again. Sometimes we'd stop and pick berries—cloudberries, blueberries, and cranberries. Our course followed the wild geese migration, so geese were flying overhead all the time. We saw a herd of musk ox, and lots of caribou, otters, and we caught fish.

We'd stay on the water a couple of more hours until we found a nice sandy beach to camp on. Then we'd unload the boats, turn them over, and put the paddles and life jackets underneath. One woman would start gathering wood and stones to set up the fire, another would get the fire going, and someone else unpacked the dinner and decided what to cook. Others were putting up the tents. We always put up the wind tarps so we'd have a warm place to sit. Then maybe we'd hang out or some women would go for a hike.

We took turns cooking, without a schedule. The food was excellent. Kristen had prebaked bread—rye, rosemary, and sourdough. And she had prepackaged most of the meals. For example, she packaged all the ingredients for soup in a bag and put the recipe in. If you were cooking that night, you just followed the instructions.

We really ate well. There's something Virginia Woolf once said about good food and good conversation, and we sure had it on that trip. We even made blueberry shortcake in a Dutch oven one night, and it was great.

Once we stayed two nights at one campsite. We had found a good spot, and we were ahead of schedule and wanted to take some hikes. Most nights, we camped in three small tents. But that night we put up the wall tent, a larger canvas tent that can fit the whole group. It was like a little cabin—you could fit all the kitchen stuff in there, the stove, the cooking gear, plus all the people. We could cook inside by putting the stove in the corner and opening the chimney flap.

In the evenings, we'd pull out the songbook and sing—we also sang rounds while we were paddling, "My paddle's keen and bright, flashing like silver…." I learned some Canadian folk songs. We were willing to be silly or sing a little off key. Kristen told us that in six years of mixed gender trips, they had never been able to get people to sing.

I learned to live in a low-impact way. Most people, when they catch a fish, filet it and throw the rest out. We'd filet it, and eat the cheeks. Then we'd make chowder. The next morning we would fry up the eggs and have them for breakfast. We'd do everything we could with it so there would be very little waste. Half the adventure comes from learning how to do new things. At night, we'd make a little teepee out of three tall poles and put it over the campfire to dry our clothes.

We had rain, hail, snow, wind, and it was really cold the whole time—by normal standards, what you would call awful weather. But no one ever complained about it. It started our first day—we had only been out maybe twenty minutes, when we looked up and there was a herd of musk ox on the shore. We got really quiet, moved in closer, and just as everyone was priming their cameras, it began to hail.

On clear nights we could watch the northern lights—we had incredible lights a couple of nights. Usually the lights are green, but I saw red twice on this trip—just dancing out there, doing a jig. We would stay up and watch and not be able to drag ourselves to bed. Our last night, the lights were better than a movie. We made popcorn, hung out on the side of the esker (a long, sandy mound), leaned back, talked, and just watched.

At the beginning, when we talked about what we wanted from the trip, a lot of women said, "I'd like to spend some time by myself and get away from things." On the last day we realized that no one had spent much time alone because we enjoyed each other's company so much! I think we enjoyed the friendships as much as we enjoyed exploring the countryside.

I was the youngest, the only American, and one of the least experienced on the trip. And something I learned from being with these women was that I didn't have to prove myself. If I didn't know something, great, I could learn it. I could ask, Hey, tell me how to build a fire. No one ever said, "You're doing that wrong." It would be, "I do it differently, maybe you'll like this way better, maybe not."

One of our big discussions on the trip was about fear and how it is the main obstacle to everything. If you boil down insecurity or jealously or anger, in its raw form it will be fear. Kristen has a great saying, "Take care, take risks, take time." One night by the campfire, we agreed that taking risks was necessary for us all to grow. Everyone on this trip was taking a risk of one kind or another. It's just so much easier to do with a group of women.

RAFTING IN ALASKA: Connie Griffith

Prior to going on a fourteen-day river raft trip in Alaska, I had a lot of anxiety about the trip. I couldn't visualize what it would be like in the Arctic so I asked questons like, Won't it be cozy at night when we build fires? And I was told, "We probably won't be able to have fires because there are no trees in the tundra." Then I thought, Oh my God, where am I going, what am I doing?

I had some concerns about my physical abilities as well. I've been biking for years, and I used to be a runner, but I don't have a lot of upper-body strength. The information from Equinox, who sponsored the trip, said that if we were in good physical condition we would be okay. But I wanted to be sure that I had a few muscles strengthened before I went, so I worked out with free weights. My partner and I did some daypacking with heavy packs on our backs, and I ran up and down stairs a lot.

The leaders were secure and enthusiastic, which was contagious. The other eight women on the trip ranged from twenty-seven to about fifty and they represented a variety of walks of life, including a park ranger, psychologist, psychiatrist, a medical doctor, an environmentalist, and a writer. They were a very interesting group.

We traveled in two rafts and a kayak; four of us were in a large raft, three in a medium-sized raft, and two in a small inflatable kayak. We rotated among them; at least some of us did. Some were too intimidated by the kayak and never went in it, and I think at least one woman never or rarely left the large raft. I went into the kayak on about the third or fourth day; it was fabulous. I'm the kind of person who wouldn't immediately volunteer to kayak. But after getting my river legs, I hopped in and was raring to go. I really enjoyed the workout, the exercise, and the excitement of it. The only problem was that I was cold the whole time because it held a lot of water in.

Some women pushed themselves much harder than I did—they would hike for a full afternoon, while I would prefer to take a short hike and come back and read a book. And that was okay. I liked a balance between group time and alone time, and I was able to have that.

We had two kinds of days. On some days, we would get up in the morning and have breakfast around 7:30 and then hike out into the tundra for about three hours, fording icy streams. We'd see arctic fox and arctic swans through binoculars, and once we watched bears across the river all afternoon, nibbling on berries and chasing ground squirrels. We found arrows and little flints. Because there are so few people in the tundra, many things are left there undisturbed. We left everything just where we found it. We had to be careful not to step on nests, because the birds all nest in the tundra.

Sometimes we would spread out as a group, and I'd get the sense of being in an incredibly vast, open space. It didn't take a lot, sometimes just having some people a hundred feet ahead and others thirty feet behind, so that I wasn't interacting. Then I felt the hugeness, the awesomeness, of being there. I was never totally in solitude; I always needed to feel that someone could hear me. There were a couple of women who walked on alone after others had turned back.

One day one of the women said she wanted to rest on a ridge, so we left her there for about an hour and picked her up on the way back from our hike. She said she felt relaxed and was just taking things in until we were out of sight, then she became super alert. She constantly looked around her, to keep the panorama in view. She said she felt very much a part of things, but also that she couldn't depend on other people's senses or on the group to protect her. And she was actually relieved when she saw our little bodies in the distance. It's very, very powerful out there.

When we were out on our hikes, we'd be gone for four or five hours, just taking our time, going along ridges. We usually took lunch with us. Sometimes we'd see beautiful wildflowers on the tundra. We would come back to camp in the afternoon and rest, maybe nap a little bit, or read. For dinner, our guide cooked really wonderful, well seasoned, wholesome meals, with a lot of fresh food that we brought in a big cooler.

We were there right after the summer solstice, and the sun doesn't set in the arctic in the summer. So we would go to bed knowing the next morning was going to come very early, but frequently we'd read for several hours before sleep. Usually I would wake in the middle of the night when the sun hit the river in the canyon and it got very bright. Then it would go back behind the next ridge and get dimmer. You get a real sense of the earth rotating around the sun, since you are perched on top of the world there.

Every second or third day, we broke camp. On those days, we'd load everything onto the big raft, bundle up into rain and rafting gear, get into the boats and head out. We would usually raft for about three hours, stopping somewhere to have lunch. We'd also stop if we saw wildlife—one day we saw a musk ox feeding at the riverbed, so we pulled in and watched this incredible creature with our binoculars, just drinking water and scratching its head and swinging its long woolen skirts that hang down to the ground. Usually by mid-afternoon we were pretty tired, and we would start looking for a campsite. We'd try to find dry tundra—a couple of us would get out of the rafts and check out the area, and either wave the others on or wave them in. On one or two occasions we settled for a fairly soggy patch because we were just too exhausted and the winds were too high to go on.

The first five days were sunny and warm, and we were even in shorts some of the time. When we were on the water we would layer up, because there was a lot of *aufice*, or overflow ice, along the edge of the river, and the temperature would drop rather dramatically as you passed these glacierlike things. The closer we got to the Arctic Sea and the more we came out of the Brooks Range onto the open coastal plain, the colder and windier it got. By the time we were looking for a final camp (where we would be picked up by a bush pilot), we were wearing all of the clothing that the guide had told us to bring and my fingers were still numb. The temperature was probably in the low thirties by the end, although it had been in the upper seventies in the beginning.

I bought some special gear, but you could get away without it, too. I borrowed rubber boots and bought some Gore-tex gear and polypropylene long underwear, which was my best investment. I had glove liners, waterproof gloves, a fleece hat, and one of those little headbands that wrap around and cover your ears, which kept the wind out nicely.

I was a little afraid of heading off into "noncivilization"—I was afraid that I might be attacked by some kind of wild animal, or that there might be an accident of some sort. I was very afraid of bears. What I learned on the trip was that once I left the violence of urban living and of "civilization," I began to relax in ways I never had before. My fear of violence and specifically male violence is something that I carry in my psyche and in my body all the time. While we were in the arctic there were thirty people there, three different groups with about ten on average. We never encountered other people until our bush pilot flew over to check on us once.

I found utter release. At some point I realized it was okay if I were to be attacked by a wild animal, because somehow that made sense: I was in their territory. And I was able to set aside that fear and just relax and open my whole being to the experience. I can rarely do that at campsites, in places where there are a lot of other people, and I can't do that in the city. That was a big revelation for me—that there was a way of being that I had never known and that I had to leave behind when I returned home.

We go gliding over the land on our paved highways and sit in our little box buildings. We can go through a day in the city without remembering to look at the moon or take a moment to gaze at the stars. But in the arctic I found a sense of harmony and grace. I came back with a greater sense of being able to be centered in that.

I remember one night looking around me and turning in circles and thinking, I know there's no way I will remember this beauty, but I will try. I looked to my left, and ahead of me, and to my right, and everything was so beautiful and so majestic and so large. I actually took three photographs, one after the other, although I knew what a futile act it was to make that little triptych. I knew there was no way I could capture it. I just needed to sit there and take it in: the snow off in the distance on the mountains and the sun shining down and the little wildflowers all glowing with bursts of color. I realized then that the only sound besides our voices that I had heard for those two weeks was the distant rushing of the river.

Fishing

For some, fishing is just an excuse to spend some quiet time outdoors on a sunny day. For others, it is a passion that drags them lurching out of bed at 3 A.M. to stand for long hours in the dark. Over twenty-two million women fish recreationally in the United States alone. Some prefer to fish in streams, others in lakes, reservoirs, or the ocean. They fish from boats, the river bank or beach, or from a pier. They put on wading boots and venture into the current to fly fish.

Fisher Jeri Hise describes her passion for the sport: "I have my fishing buddies, and I love to camp out in the country. For me, fishing is both the camaraderie of the friends I go with and the solitude of wandering off and fishing alone. We once went to Fishbone Flats—acres of beautiful flat meadow with a meandering, wide river running through. We'd cast for seven or eight hours, slowly moving through the water. Twilight would come and go and we'd still be there. We were lost in it all and only called it quits when it was too dark."

I don't own any fishing gear but always enjoy fishing when invited along with someone who has an extra pole. And I love the lore—explanations of how the moon or tidal action, the seasons and temperature, affects whether fish will bite, how particular bait or fishing techniques will work. Fishers are almost superstitious about their lures and flies.

The basic types of fishing are identified by what you tie to the end of your fishing line: *Bait fishing* refers to fishing with live bait. "Lures" are fake bait—things like plastic worms that have names like jigs or plugs or spoons. *Fly fishing* requires the use of a "fly," a collection of strings and feathers tied together in a way that resembles bugs that naturally inhabit the area. Fly fishing is mostly done on streams and rivers; a fly rod is usually longer than other fishing rods.

"Tackle" is all the gear you use for fishing, like hooks, leaders, weights, or swivels. There are many kinds of poles and reels, which are put together in a myriad of combinations. "Casting" is the art of getting the end of your fishing line from the pole out to where the fish are. "Spinning" or "spin casting" refers to the use of a spinning reel. (A closed reel allows the fisher to push a button and cast and is often used by beginners.) Fly casting is acknowledged to be the most difficult, as the fishing fly is very light and requires the most skill to cast. The fishing line is "stripped out," or pulled off the reel, before you cast a fly rod.

Landing a fish is the goal; once it strikes at your bait or fly or lure, you will use all your skill to reel it in. The time between when the fish bites and when you land it is called "playing the fish" and is the subject of countless fishing tales. Many anglers now practice "catch and release" methods, fishing for the thrill of the catch and then gently unhooking the fish and releasing it back into the water.

Early morning and late evening just before dark are fish-feeding and also fish-catching times. Fish swim deeper as sunlight increases on the surface of the water. That's why trout fishers favor the shady side of the stream. Fish usually face upstream, so you want to be fishing downstream and cast up above them, or to the side, so the fly or bait can drift down over their noses.

Uncommon Waters: Women Write about Fishing edited by Holly Morris, proves that women have been fishing as long as the sport has existed. The earliest known essay on sport fishing was written in 1421 by Dame Juliana Berners. Dame Juliana, a noblewoman and a nun as well as a sportswoman, explains how to "cut, between Michaelmas and Candlemas, a fair staff, a fathom and a half long, and as thick as your arm, of hazel, willow or aspen" for your fishing rod and instructs readers to "take, from the tail of a white horse, the longest and best hair you can find"[10] to make fishing line. The twelve fly patterns she described are still in use today.

In *Uncommon Waters* you'll also be treated to stories about how women have learned to fish beside their mothers and fathers, sisters and friends, and how special relationships develop between neophyte and mentor.

Some women fish with partners for years, depending on them to tie their knots and put bait on the hook. If you are ready to learn to fish, or take the next step toward independence, try attending a fishing school or camp, or hire a guide for a day of personalized instruction.

Bass 'n Gal, formed in 1976 as a fishing organization for women, has over thirty-two thousand members and over one hundred affiliate clubs throughout the U.S. Members compete in local and national tournaments; affiliate groups may also participate in local conservation and children's projects. For membership information write: P.O. Box 13925, Arlington, TX 76013 (817/265-6214). The National Headquarters of Bass 'n Gal Affiliate Clubs is located at 2625 Wicker Road, Indianapolis, IN 46217 (317/889-6549).

Fishing Gear

Dirt Roads and Damsels makes a special fishing vest for women. It has seventeen pockets, a collar that turns up against the wind, and a ribbed waist band to keep the vest in place when you bend over to land a fish. It's functional and designed to fit. Request information from P.O. Box 989, Gresham, OR 97030 (503/667-6602). You might also check out the Orvis catalog, which carries fishing flies, rods, reels, and wading gear for both women and men. P.O. Box 798, Manchester, VT 05254 (800/548-9548).

Fishing Camps, Trips, and Guides

Take a fishing class, or hire a female guide to personally accompany you to the best spots on the river. Unravel the secrets of fishing with:

Alaska Women of the Wilderness
Dirt Roads and Damsels
Earthwise
Jennifer Smith Fly Fishing Guide Service
Maggie Merriman Fly Fishing Schools
Orvis
Outdoor Vacations for Women over 40
Reel Women Fly Fishing Adventures
RVing Women
Woodswomen

Horse, Mule and Llama Packing, and Ranch Vacations

The trail dead-ended at the base of the mountain, where giant boulders were piled on one another up into the sky. The old rancher turned in his saddle to face us. "Now," he said in Spanish, clutching the jet-black mane of the horse as he crouched forward and placed his face alongside the animal's sweaty neck, "you must hold on like this when we climb up."

"Up where? How?" we asked, swiveling our heads in search of a path.

"Up," he said, pointing to the summit. He chucked his heels and the horse leaped onto the first boulder. The others scrambled behind, sure-footed as mountain goats and jostling for position. I hung on desperately, not believing it possible even as we were doing it.

"Only horses born in the Sierra learn to climb like goats," he told us.

That was my introduction to the elegant ways in which four-footed company can ease the difficulty of primitive backcountry travel. A wilderness camping trip with pack animals allows you to extend your reach farther than you could go on your own and provides a glimpse into life lived long ago and far away. Pack stock should never be used in fragile backcountry settings, but many parks and wilderness areas have trails appropriate for stock use. If you don't have much riding experience, take a one-day familiarization ride before signing up. Then consider which type of pack trip appeals to you:

On a *dunnage pack trip*, you hire a wrangler (animal handler) and animals to carry your backpack and base camp gear into a prearranged campsite in the wilderness. They drop the gear off while you hike in separately. Handy for families or packers with back trouble, you can either prearrange to get packed out at the end of your stay, or carry your backpack on the return (which by then is much lighter because you've consumed virtually all the provisions).

On *walking pack trips,* the animals carry the gear and food as you hike and lead them along the trail. Llama pack trips are always walking trips, and a wrangler usually accompanies the group.

A *pack safari* is the full service trip; you ride the stock (usually horses or mules) alongside a guide or wrangler who provides food and assistance for the full length of the trip. You'll be responsible for bringing only your clothes, sleeping bag, and personal items such as a camera, binoculars for birding, etc.

Why Llamas?

Llamas are becoming increasingly popular as pack animals in the northern hemisphere for a number of reasons. Gentle by nature and easy to maintain, they leave less of an impact on wilderness environments than other pack animals.

Two comprehensive guides to llama packing are *Packing with Llamas*[11] by Stanlynn Daugherty, owner of Hurricane Creek Llama Treks, and *Llamas on the Trail: A Packer's Guide*[12] by David Harmon and Amy S. Rubin. Harmon and Rubin describe the long-necked, wooly animal of the Andes as an "agile and companionable pack animal which fills the niche between backpacker and horsepacker."

These highly social creatures prefer to travel in pairs, or to follow their friends while tied in a pack string (several animals tied front to back so they travel in a line). They do less damage at campsites than tied pack stock because they roam freely and munch a la carte; they simply aren't interested in wandering away. Mature llamas can carry eighty pounds of food and gear, enough to supply one to two people for three to five days.

You can rent llamas for a weekend or longer from Hurricane Creek Llama Treks. There is a two-llama minimum and a training session is required before you and the animals are transported to the trail head.

How to Best Enjoy a Riding Trip

Ask for riding tips if you are inexperienced; proper form can keep you from getting overtired. Take the time to make sure that stirrups are adjusted properly; your legs should be slightly bent. Pushing against the stirrups offers a bit of resistance and keeps your weight balanced on the saddle. Lean slightly forward in the saddle and relax. Riding with tensed muscles can quickly make you tired.

A variety of hilly and flat terrain can help you avoid the soreness that comes from using only one position on the saddle. If you are concerned about saddle sores, get down periodically and walk for a bit, especially in the first few days. When in doubt, lead animals across steep, wet, icy, or other difficult areas. Don't ride in questionable terrain unless a wrangler assures you that the animal can handle it.

Riding and Pack Gear

As in all kinds of travel, only wear shoes that are properly broken in. If you are tempted by a new pair of cowgirl boots, put a few miles on them first and see how they feel. Light hiking or running shoes work really well with stirrups. Heavy-soled shoes (like heavyweight hiking boots) can be problematic. An extra pair of camp shoes to switch off to at night is a good idea.

Ask for help to ensure that you are packing the animal correctly. Saddle bags are for small items only; don't overload saddle bags as they rest on the animals' kidneys and can cause pain if overloaded.

Horse and Llama Pack Trips

Trek with llamas, ride in a covered wagon or astride horses or mules in terrain as diverse as the Canadian Rockies, the beaches and forests of Holland, or the backcountry of New Zealand. Companies offering horse and llama pack trips include:

Adventure Associates
Alaska Women of the Wilderness
Cloud Canyon Wilderness Experience
Dare You!
Firma Hagi
The Heart of Adventure
Hurricane Creek Llama Treks
Lois Lane Expeditions
Paddling South

Rainbow Adventures
Sacred Sedona
Women of the Wilderness Australia
Woodswomen

Ranch Riding

Stay in a bunk house or loft, or just hang out and experience life on a ranch in the Teton Valley, the Flint Hills of Texas, or the high pastures of Colorado. Or, for the daring, herd cattle a hundred miles across Montana.

Bar H Ranch
McNamara Ranch
Prairie Women Adventures and Retreat
Skylink

MULE PACKING IN BAJA: *Thalia Zepatos*

I drained the coffee from my cup while the others drowned the smoking embers of the campfire. We checked our saddle bags one last time, got onto our mules and headed down the arroyo. It was our first morning in the Sierra Gigante; the central portion of the mountainous spine that bisects the length of the Baja Peninsula in Mexico. We were headed for Los Pilares, a ranch that could only be reached on foot, mule, or horseback, and I was starting to feel like a cowgirl.

I'd been making an annual winter migration to a coastal town in Baja for several years. Like most returning pilgrims, I had my annual rites. There was the ceremonial tasting of the fish tacos, to determine which plywood and palm-frond *tacqueria* along Calle Hidalgo offered the choicest condiments, which had the freshest fish and which chef harbored the fry pan flair required to deliver the quivering white meat in a crisp, nongreasy, brown overcoat. (El Rey de Tacos remains first prize winner three years in a row.)

Each year I made a pilgrimage to the nearby mountains, snatching only small glimpses of life at rural ranchos that clung to the dry and dusty landscape of the *monte*. I knew that many ranch families raised cattle and a few crops if the weather was kind, and that they often went to market on foot, or by burro or mule. I was intrigued by the mountain-ranch life, and its modes of travel that seemed to fit the terrain. When my friend and *compañera* Esther called and invited me to join a mule-packing trip through that arid high country, I said yes quicker than you can flip a tortilla.

The trip was organized by Trudi Angell, who has lived in Baja since 1975. There's not a gringa who knows Baja better than Trudi. For years she's led kayak trips along the Sea of Cortez for her company, Paddling South. But her love of the people and the landscape of the peninsula has brought her into the mountains, too. Trudi shares this lesser-known aspect of Baja on organized mule pack trips, under the name Saddling South.

Our small group gathered at midday in Loreto. Aside from Trudi and her young daughter, Olivia, the group included Esther and me,

Esther's friend Ann—a Baja resident in her seventies—and Leslie and Rachel, instructors from the nearby National Outdoor Leadership School on holiday.

We loaded our gear into a couple of trucks, drove a few miles down the paved highway and then turned onto a rough track that pointed like an arrow toward the Sierra Gigante. We negotiated the ruts in the road for over an hour until we pulled up to the mesquite fence at Rancho Viejo. We were welcomed by Teesta, short for Juan Bautista, a longtime friend of Trudi's who had gathered the mules from nearby ranches for our ride. We shook hands formally in the Mexican style, then sat and drank a cup of coffee. We were then ushered inside the *casita* where we changed out of shorts and T-shirts and into our riding clothes—long pants and long-sleeved shirts that would protect us from the scratchy brush and hot sun of the high *desierto*.

Then Trudi and Teesta paired us up with our mules. It was a delicate process of matchmaking in which both humans and animals were sized up by temperament and bulk. Teesta placed a pair of reins in my hand and introduced me to Cuervo, a tall, dark mule that immediately belied my image of a little burro. Trudi would ride Pimienta, with three-and-a-half-year-old Olivia sitting before her; she wrapped a sweatshirt around both their waists to secure the child. The others were introduced to their mounts, who had names like Alacran and Enrique. A Mexican rancher, Raoul de los Santos, would assist Trudi, riding a burro called Tequila while leading Barquito (Little Boat), so named because she rocked from side to side as she walked, piled high with our sleeping bags and foam pads.

We packed our gear, adjusted the stirrups, waved good-bye and finally rode off. It was mid-afternoon, comfortably beyond the hottest part of the day. We passed through an ever-changing dry landscape. A line of bright green vegetation ahead marked the location of a desert river or spring, with date palms and fan palms outlining its course.

As we ambled along the arroyo, I picked fears and concerns off my shoulders and dropped them like a trail of crumbs behind me. I'd been a bit unsure about mule packing—what exactly would I have to do, and could I handle it? I'd harbored a nightmare vision of myself inching along on a stubborn little burro, my long legs dragging the ground on each side. Instead, I was sauntering high above the desert floor on an energetic and responsive animal. I had managed to get up on the mule without falling off and everyone in the group seemed pleasant and easy-going. We ranged from well-experienced riders to those, like me, who had only ridden a handful of times before. The pace was comfortable, and we formed and re-formed into conversational pairs and trios as we rode.

I rode up alongside Trudi and asked why she chose mules instead of horses. "Mules are much more sure-footed and less temperamental in the desert," she told me. "Everyone up here prefers mules for both work and riding stock." The one horse we had along on the trip, Trudi's own, confirmed her comments by acting touchy and skittish from the start.

After two hours, we came to El Palmarito, an abandoned rancho in a clearing surrounded by plane trees, where we made camp for the night. The corral served to hold our animals, and Raoul gathered food and made them comfortable after Barquito ran off and was fetched in a comic chase. We gathered scrap wood for our campfire and feasted on roast chicken and potato salad. It was a night that called for sleeping out, and we laid our beds under a star-encrusted sky.

We rose before dawn to the smell of hot coffee, ate a quick breakfast, and saddled up to make time before the heat of the day. Arroyo Santa Isabel, a dry riverbed, was a mule highway through scrub-covered desert. Esther pointed out the cholla, barrel cactus, and pitayas as we passed. Then we entered a forest of *cardón* cactus. Some of the giants were fifteen feet high, their massive heads and stocky arms festooned with delicate white flowers. Hawks and peregrine falcons played the updraft along the cliffs as we approached, then dove closer to investigate our group.

We continued at a comfortable pace, stopping in the shade of an occasional grove of palo verde trees to wander off for a quick pit stop, eat an orange, or share dried fruit and nuts. We carried bottles of water and small treats in our saddle bags, hand-tooled by local saddlemakers into a perfect combination of utility and beauty.

Midday was announced by the pungent *olor* of yerba buena as it toasted under the hot sun. We continued on through palm groves and oases, where the mules bent their heads for a quick drink in the green rivers. Soon after we reached Las Pilares, a ranch named for the pillars of columnar basalt striating the giant wall that points like a road sign to its gateway. We tied the animals under the shady trees near the river and walked up to the *casita* to greet Doña Ester and her sons. "You'll love Doña Ester," Trudi had said that morning. "She's eighty-seven, more or less, but no one really knows for sure. She lives with her bachelor sons—they're in their sixties."

Traveling with Trudi is like going with one friend to visit others. Fluent in Spanish, she conveys a deep respect for Mexican tradition and an appreciation for the crafts of the ranchers. In a circumspect fashion, she has found ways to share the income of her work with the local community: she hires mules locally rather than buying her own and pays the ranchers to come along as mule rustlers. She encourages artisans in remote places by bringing foreigners to admire and buy their work and has trained young people from the area as local guides. She had proven herself a friend in these parts the only way it can be proved—over time.

Doña Ester welcomed us with a report on the mountain lion that had killed a pig on their ranch a few nights before. The Doña's wiry body glided between the wood fire she kept tending inside the cookhouse and the outdoor sitting area under a *palapa* roof where we gathered. The oldest son, Silvestre, brought out some of his fresh farmer's cheese to sprinkle on our tostada lunches. We returned to the flowing river to set up our camp, and then Trudi pointed the way to a swimming hole that swallowed up the rest of our afternoon.

The next day was Mother's Day in Mexico. Doña Ester's second son, Salvador, walked the fourteen miles from Comondu early that morning to observe the tradition by singing "Las Mañanitas" to his *mamá*. Silvestre took us into his shadowy workshop to see the saddles he made and the ropes and lariats he braided in complex patterns. One style was made by weaving eight different lines together; Rachel asked intent questions and then tried her hand at the weaving. Silvestre's shy smile indicated his approval.

Early the next morning we packed up and rode to Rancho Monte Alto. I tightened the chin strap on my borrowed straw hat, nudged Cuervo past the others and galloped full speed down a long straightaway. I'd never ridden so far, so fast, and I loved it! Then I turned and raced back to the others, just for the joy of flying along. Once I had questioned whether three days of mule packing would be too much; now I was ready to sign up for the two-week journey to the cave paintings and far-flung ranchos.

The only consolation in heading for home was the news that we were stopping for the midday meal at Chari's (short for María del Rosario de los Santos de Romero). She is a famous cook in the *monte*, and we consumed the feast with gusto while sitting on the ranch's wide *palapa*-roofed terrace surrounded by potted plants and flowers. Little Olivia switched into Spanish upon sight of Chari's son Juanito, and they galloped around after each other on horses fashioned from sticks with strings for reins. We could only convince ourselves to leave by tucking more of Chari's sweet bean burritos into our saddle bags.

Two by two we returned the mules to their ranches, then took our seats in Trudi's pickup truck. After only a few days, the sight of the truck was rude, its ride bumpy and unelegant. For more than a hundred years, the only way to travel these mountains had been on foot or by saddle. In a way, it still is.

Rock Climbing and Mountaineering

The sport of rock climbing began as mountaineers developed techniques to overcome sheer rock walls on alpine climbs and practiced those techniques on boulders, low cliffs, and craggy rocks. The practice sessions inspired sport climbers who enjoy the challenge of climbing, whether or not they ever apply those skills to mountaineering.

Nonclimbers have the perception that only the super-fit can scale rocks. Women climbers report that those interested in the sport need only good balance and a moderate level of physical fitness to start. Dancers and gymnasts would make good rock climbers. Hand and finger strength are important to climbers but can be developed over time.

Climbs are graded in a classification system as follows:

Class 1: hiking on trails

Class 2: hiking and bushwhacking

Class 3: scrambling in which rope may or may not be used;

Class 4: climbing where some protection (anchor or piton) is occasionally used

Class 5: the most severe free climbs that require the use of protection;

Class 6: direct-aid climbs in which devices must be used to assist in the climb

The term *technical climbing* refers to climbs on ice, snow, or rock that are rated Class 5 or above. These classes are further subdivided, so you will hear climbs referred to as 5.6 (called "five-six"), or 5.8 or even 5.10. Climbs rated 5.13 and above are considered world-class climbs. Ten or fifteen years ago, 5.9 was thought to be the ceiling for women climbers; women now routinely surpass that level. Since climbing is a young sport with constantly developing techniques and equipment, the rating system gets revised and augmented as new levels of difficulty are attained. Specific climbs are named and rated; guidebooks list the ratings, or you can ask someone who's familiar with the climb.

Basic climbing moves involve a combination of handholds and footholds on rock, including jamming hands and feet into cracks in the stone. Nuts, pegs, and other devices are also wedged into cracks to hold ropes that are tied to a climber's harness as a safety device. Climbers often work in pairs—to "belay" is to hold the end of the rope and arrest the fall of a partner if necessary. The climber runs the rope through a belay device, and the "second" keeps taking in the rope so that it's tight. That way any fall will only allow a drop of a couple of feet. The first person ascending the rock, who chooses the route, is the "lead climber," or leader. After learning basic skills, a good way to study technique is to serve as "second" to a lead climber.

Women's Rock Day, held annually in June, draws almost four hundred participants each year to the International Mountain Climbing School, which can be reached at Box 1666, North Conway, NH 03860 (603/356-7064).

Rock Gyms and Walls

Rock gyms are indoor sites for learning and practicing rock climbing skills. They simulate many different rock climbing terrains, from the most accessible to the most difficult. There are about fifty rock gyms in the United States, and another fifty or so outdoor climbing walls (most of which are located at colleges, universities, and health clubs). Rock gyms provide a great introduction to the sport, access to climbing clubs and networks, and places to practice when the weather is cold or rainy. Listings of rock gyms can be found in *Rock and Ice Magazine*.

Gear

While climbers eventually need specialized gear, you should be able to try it out for a day or two with running shoes and your own clothes. A climbing harness wraps around your legs and waist for roped climbs; until recently, during a long climb, women climbers had to choose between dehydration and the danger of removing their harnesses to urinate. Black Diamond now markets the "XX Harness," designed specifically for women; a Velcro tab lets you unhook the leg loops without undoing the waistbelt. Order from Black Diamond, 2084 East 3900 South, Salt Lake City, UT 84124 (801/278-5533).

Climbing Trips and Clinics

Many opportunities exist for women to get basic instruction in rock climbing, from two-hour introductory clinics to week-long seminars. Moderate and advanced level climbers will find challenges too, such as a twenty-eight-day trek and climb in the Himalayas. Climbing trips and clinics are offered by:

Adirondack Mountain Club
Adventure Associates
Alaska Women of the Wilderness
Appalachian Mountain Club
Boulder Rock Club
Canadian Outward Bound Wilderness School
Colorado Outward Bound School
Equinox Wilderness Expeditions
Lois Lane Expeditions
Mahoosuc Guide Service
National Outdoor Leadership School
Pacific Crest Outward Bound School
Sylvan Rocks
Vertical Ventures
Voyageur Outward Bound School
Wildwise
Women of the Wilderness Australia
Women's Outdoor Adventure Cooperative
Woodswomen

Mountaineering

Mountaineering is the sport of getting to the top of difficult peaks. The first known mountain climbers (aside from indigenous tribespeople whose feats were not recorded) were the men and women who climbed peaks in the Alps in the late 1700s.

Julia Archibald Holmes, an early feminist, was the first woman on record to have climbed a mountain in Colorado. As described in *The Magnificent Mountain Women* by Janet Robertson, Julia wore bloomers, the official costume of the suffragists in the 1850s, as she walked across the prairie with a group from Kansas.

"I commenced the journey," Julia wrote, "with a firm determination to learn to walk. At first I could not walk over three or four miles without feeling quite weary, but by persevering and walking as far as I could every day, my capacity increased gradually, and in the course of a few weeks I could walk ten miles in the most sultry weather without being exhausted."[13]

The group camped at the base of Pikes Peak for more than a month, and staring at the peak day after day must have inspired Julia to attempt the climb. She wore her bloomers all the way to the top, an ascent of over fourteen thousand feet. Later, she wrote to her mother:

"I have accomplished the task which I marked out for myself and now I feel amply repaid for all my toil and fatigue. Nearly every one tried to discourage me from attempting it, but I believed that I should succeed; and now, I feel that I would not have missed this glorious sight for anything at all. In all probability I am the first woman who has ever stood upon the summit of this mountain and gazed upon this wondrous scene, which my eyes now behold."[14]

Clothing presented special logistical problems to nineteenth-century women with high aspirations. Some devised hiking skirts that could be hitched up or pinned to make walking easier, others changed to trousers or bloomers as they approached steep ascents. But long after the dress code changed, twentieth-century women climbers were still being told that they didn't have the "right stuff" in terms of physical strength or emotional endurance. In the introduction to her book *Annapurna: A Women's Place*[15], Arlene Blum recalls a 1970 announcement inviting her to participate on a climb of Mt. McKinley: Women climbers would only be permitted to go as far as the base camp, where they were to help with the cooking.

Instead of ironing her hostess apron, Arlene joined a women's team to plan their own ascent. Despite being told that they lacked the physical strength to carry loads and the leadership experience and emotional stability to complete the expedition, all six women reached the summit.

The first woman to climb Mt. Everest, the highest point on earth, was Junko Tabei, a self-described "housewife" from a suburb of Tokyo, and member of a 1975 Japanese team. The second woman on top was Phantog, a Tibetan climber who asserted, "We really hold up half the sky."

In 1978, the first American ascent of Annapurna (at 26,500 feet, the tenth highest mountain in the world) was achieved by Arlene Blum and a team of thirteen women. *Annapurna: A Woman's Place* tells the story of that history-making climb.

I probably won't make it to the top of Everest or Annapurna, but every time I see pictures of those craggy peaks I revel in the knowledge that women have been there. If you'd like to read a variety of women's inspiring accounts of the sport, read *Leading Out: Women Climbers Reaching for the Top*,[16] edited by Rachel da Silva. For a historical overview, read *Women Climbing: 200 Years of Achievement*[17] by Bill Birkett and Bill Peascod.

Mountaineering Trips

Climb Mt. Olympus, learn technical ice climbing skills and traverse glaciers under the guidance and support of one of these groups:

Adventure Associates
Alaska Women of the Wilderness
Appalachian Mountain Club
Call of the Wild
Colorado Outward Bound School
Pacific Crest Outward Bound School
Women's Outdoor Adventure Cooperative
Woodswomen

CLIMBING WITH CONFIDENCE: *Cathie Hoofard*

My sister Cindy had been rock climbing for years, but I had always thought it was something I could never do. Then one day Cindy took me to a rock gym, an indoor structure that has synthetic holds attached to the wall so that you can simulate climbing different kinds of rocks. We started out on something very simple called the traversing wall, which doesn't go up very high and has ropes bolted up along the top that you can connect your rope to. Your climbing partner can be on belay on the other end of the rope, which means they can hold the rope in case you fall, so you will never fall very far.

I was sure that I would be a failure at it, but my sister was very supportive and encouraging. We spent an afternoon playing around, and I got to thinking, Well, maybe I could do this, this is fun! I was definitely intrigued.

A couple of months later, Cindy invited me to Smith Rock, a mecca for rock climbers in the central Oregon desert. I was sure that I wouldn't do very well at this, I really lacked self-confidence. The first route we went up was scary. After I got a little ways up I wanted to quit. But I pushed on up the rock and made it to the top. It was a 5.5 or 5.6 climb (a beginner's climb). It was about forty feet to the top, but to me it felt like I had just climbed to the top of the world. Since then I've been hooked.

I realized, that first time, that the strength it took was more mental and psychological than physical, and climbing continues to be an empowering experience. Each climb is a matter of will, of wanting to go up. If you're not wanting to go up, not psyched to do it, if you mind isn't focused, then it can be too hard.

Climbing provides an inward focus, which my life lacked before. I manage a lot of little things in the course of my everyday life—with my job as well as my family—and it can be pretty stressful to keep all the details in order. But when I get out on the rock I can't think about the next project deadline at work, or what anybody else is doing. I'm not thinking of a hundred things, I'm just thinking about my body in relationship to the rock, the conquering of my fear, the will to go up, and my balance and foot and hand placement. Being able to focus is a key to success and also a key to relaxation.

I was a couch potato throughout my twenties. Now I climb two days a week, I walk my dog, got certified as a lifeguard, and last summer I ran an outdoor wilderness program. I'm more health conscious and fitness conscious. I don't think I've lost much weight, but I have redeveloped and reshaped my body's muscles since taking up climbing.

Ten or fifteen years ago, 5.9 was considered the ceiling for women climbers. These days, I am climbing 5.10s and finding them challenging. The best I've led is a 5.10 once, and a 5.9 several times. I'm also working on how to do an overhang, which is where the rock forms a roof or ceiling above you. You're horizontal instead of vertical, and gravity is pulling you down, so you have to hang on and also be able to move at the same time. It not only takes sheer strength, but also things like knowing how to place your feet, how to push and pull, and what position your body needs to be in so that you can move.

In rock climbing, you have to rely on yourself, and you have to learn to trust the equipment and the belayer. I think that the experience of trust—trusting myself and someone else—had a profound impact on me. And the self-confidence I've gained from climbing has spilled over into other parts of my life. It's changed my habits, my routines, what I think about myself, my body image—it's changed my feeling of inner strength.

I had been needing to end an unhappy marriage. Thinking about the separation was like looking up at that forty-foot rock and wondering if I could climb it. Climbing gave me the knowledge that I could do what I set my mind to do and rely on myself to accomplish it.

I attended Vertical Ventures's Women's Climbing Clinic, and I thought it was wonderful. I was particularly inspired by two women in our group of about twenty. One, who was forty-seven, had incredible strength. She didn't look like Superwoman, but she could hang onto that rock like nobody I've ever seen. She did it rather nonchalantly. When I'm forty-seven, I want to climb like her.

The other woman, whom I was paired with in the beginning, was fifty and began climbing after a double mastectomy. Her two grown sons had told her, "Mom, when you can raise your arms again, we're gonna teach you how to climb." Climbing has been part of her recovery from cancer. She wears long sleeves, long pants and a straw hat in the sun because she is very concerned about skin cancer. But she climbs like it was second nature.

Recently, I developed an outdoor wilderness program for kids on probation through the county court, where I work. I watch kids who are gang involved and otherwise act like they are the most powerful creatures on earth battle their fear. One young woman kept crying and wouldn't come down until she had made it to the top. When she finally came down, she stood by the rock and pointed up and told everyone who walked past, "Do you know, I just climbed that rock?" Another one said, "This is better than drugs." I've seen climbing become a motivator for kids who are not motivated by very much in their environment—they know that appropriate behavior can get them more climbing time. I've also had kids ask, "Do I have to commit another crime to continue to do this?"

We split the boys and the girls into separate groups. The girls climb much better when separated because they're afraid they'll be made fun of if they fail in front of the guys. Girls are much more apt to disqualify themselves and more tentative about beginning. They are much more focused on their body image: "I'm too fat" or "I'm out of shape, so I can't do it" are common mental blocks. Yet the girls are more supportive and encouraging of each other than the guys are.

I have two sons, who are ten and four. Christopher, the ten-year-old, is climbing and he thinks it's great. The four-year-old is wondering when he can start. I don't have a harness for him yet, but I will probably get him climbing pretty quickly. These days I read climbing magazines and have pin-up pictures of rocks. I can't get enough of it.

Sailing and Cruising

You don't need to be athletic or physically strong to sail. Whether sailing a small sunfish or a large schooner, what's required is to know how to combine wind and sails in the most efficient manner.

Women have skippered sailing ships as long as history has been keeping footnotes. *Seafaring Women*[18] by Linda Grant De Pauw charts the maritime history of women from the twelfth-century pirate, Princess Alvilda of Sweden, to women crew members of Greenpeace vessels in the 1970s.

Women have worked on crews of whaling ships and trading vessels. In the mid-1850s, nineteen-year-old Mary Patten commanded her husband's ship for fifty-two days. She sailed around Cape Horn, quelling a mutiny attempt along the way, while four months pregnant. Women have captained steamboats on the Mississippi River and cargo ships on the Great Lakes.

Women have served on warships since ancient times; women commanders were recorded at the Battle of Salamis in 480 B.C. and the battle of Actium in 31 B.C. In the nineteenth century, women of European and African heritage who wanted to see the world served in disguise, revealing their true identities only while collecting their pensions. Sparse lighting below-ships and water rationing, which prohibited bathing, conspired to keep their secrets. *Seafaring Women* describes "William Brown, a black woman who for many years held the rank of Captain of the Maintop in a British warship, an assignment given only to the most skilled and agile sailors."[19] In 1980, Lt. Junior Grade Beverly Kelly was the first American woman ever to be put in command of an American warship, a Coast Guard cutter.

Women at the Helm[20] by Jeannine Talley lists other modern women's firsts in sailing: Ann Davidson, who, in 1952, became the first woman to sail alone across the Atlantic; Sharon Sites Adams, who, in 1969, was the first woman to cross the Pacific alone; Krystyna Chojnowska-Liskiewicz from Poland, who, in 1978, became the first woman to circle the globe singlehandedly. *Women at the Helm* recounts Talley's four years of sailing adventures across the South Pacific with Joy Smith:

"I never sailed a boat until in my thirties, yet for all those years I knew I would. I could taste the salt on my lips and feel the surge of the deck; I could see the sails full, their whiteness gleaming in the sun. I could hear the wooden blocks creaking rhythmically as the wind fingered the rigging. The oceans of the world called to me in a series of images, smells, physical sensations. The ocean—serene, grandiose, frightening—was an entity mirroring my own soul."[21]

Tania Aebi was the youngest person to ever circumnavigate the world alone. An eighteen-year-old heading for trouble, she accepted her father's challenge: he would buy her a small sailboat if she would sail it around the world. Her twenty-seven-thousand-mile voyage lasted two and a half years and finally brought her home to herself. The story is told in her book *Maiden Voyage.*[22]

Despite the accomplishments of their sisters, most women's experience of sailing is that of being relegated to an auxiliary position while following the commands of male captains. Many women report being yelled at or otherwise intimidated to the point of questioning whether they can handle a boat alone. A great proportion of women who go to sailing schools are there to find out the answer.

Sailing Schools, Cruises, and Boat Trips

There are many options for learning sailing hands-on. In classroom sessions and on board, you will learn the special vocabulary of sailing, starting with which side is port and which is starboard. You can learn how to rig (attach) and raise the sails, how to trim (adjust) the sails, and the laws governing right of way on the sea. For beginning to advanced-level sailing instruction, contact:

Adventure Spirit Hawaii
Artemis Sailing Charters
At the Helm
Earthwise
Herizen: New Age Sailing for Women

Hurricane Island Outward Bound School
Onn the Water
Poseidon Services/Izarra Cruises
Sea Safari Sailing
Sea Sense
Vaarschool Grietje
Womanship
Women of the Wilderness Australia
Women's Outdoor Adventure Cooperative
Women's Sailing Adventures

Trips offered by the companies below allow you to try out your "sea legs" while focusing more on fun than instruction. Itineraries take you sailing, houseboating, cruising, and canal boating in Greece, the South Pacific, the coastal waters of the Atlantic, the Gulf of Mexico, and along the coast of Australia :

Adventure Associates
Earthwise
Onn the Water
Outdoor Vacations for Women over 40
Portuguese Princess Whale Watch
Poseidon Services/Izarra Cruises
Rainbow Adventures
Sea Safari Sailing
Wander Women
Women in the Wilderness
Women on the Water

I had always wanted to learn to sail. I've always been a very outdoor, athletic person. So I went with the Sea Safari Sailing School on the five-day course aboard the *Ileana,* and then I wrote an article for *Coastal Cruising* magazine about learning to sail when I was seventy-two.

There were just two of us on that course, myself and Sharon, a forty-year-old gal from Maryland. She and her husband were sending the last kid off to college and were thinking about living aboard a sailboat, and she wanted to learn how to handle the boat and know what she was doing.

We would have about two hours of lecture with the handbook and then we would practice what we learned. We anchored out, we read charts and charted our courses—we did everything. Laurel is an extremely knowledgeable and experienced sailor and captain. She'd done chartering and cargo delivery and all that sort of thing, and she is a fabulous experiential teacher.

We slept and ate on the boat the whole five days. We anchored out every night but one, when we tied up (because you need to learn to do that too) and went ashore and had a nice dinner out. I'm an old camper, so I wasn't a bit put off by the primitiveness of sponge-bathing and that kind of jazz.

Sharon and I worked well together as students. We learned to do the compass drills—she was a little sharper at mathematics; I stuck to first grade arithmetic. But when the seas got high she got queasy, and fortunately for me, I've never been bothered by bad weather. It was my turn to do KP, and I was downstairs trying to make a tossed salad. We were really into heavy weather, and I said it gave a whole new dimension to a tossed salad: just put the stuff in the bowl, and it got tossed. Have you ever tried to use the head (toilet) when the boat was rocking like crazy? Life is at bare minimum on board; you don't worry about cosmetics, you concern yourself with the basics. You can't worry about lack of privacy.

If you really want to learn to sail, you have to love the outdoor life. You have to love the water, you can't be afraid of it. "A hand for the boat and a hand for yourself," Laurel always said, which means you must always make sure that you hold on to the boat with one hand, or station yourself properly so that you won't fall overboard if you need both hands to do something.

Lowering the mainsail in a driving rain is the outstanding memory of my week at sailing school. The waves were choppy, four to five on the scale, and Sharon was too scared to do it, so I was up lowering it in blowing high seas, soaking wet. I broke into song, "If my kids could see me now...." After I did it, I felt really proud; it's wonderful to know I can do that and enjoy doing it!

I've always been a swimmer, but I also recently went snorkeling for the first time. I just went as deep as the snorkel; it was like swimming around in a tropical aquarium. It was beautiful. My other love is theater—last year I played Mamita in *Gigi*. I've gotten so many women of my age into theater, all phases of it. They may only be the prop mistress, but they love it! Let's face it, there are so many widows in my age bracket, and we were raised to believe that you can't do anything without a man. Forget it! You can! And you don't have to travel with a gaggle of widows, either. Go for it on your own! Our culture is changing. Our society is finally beginning to respect women for our intelligence. We're no longer type-cast.

Recently I met a man with a sailboat and now go sailing quite a lot. Yesterday we had a fabulous sail, with winds to 7.9 knots. It was my sail—I did everything, put up the jib, put up the mainsail, did the whole thing. When the jib got jammed up, I had to crawl on my hands and knees up to the bow and lock my legs around the pulpit in order to release the hasp that was stuck. It was challenging and fun. Jack had to take over the helm when my arms got a bit tired—I'm going to be seventy-five in February. We also race; we've raced five times together and won every time.

I'd say this for every woman: don't negate your interests, follow your heart. Dare to do it, for god's sake! My kids say, "Mom, please don't tell us if you've gotten a motorcycle." But no, I won't get a motorcycle.

TAKING THE BOAT OUT OURSELVES: *Donna Nilson*

I first went with a friend to a three-day sailing school. I'd never sailed before. I went because she was interested and it sounded like a good idea. She and her husband have a sailboat and whenever we went on the boat together, our two husbands did everything. We wanted to learn how to do things on our own, so we left our husbands at home to play golf.

The following year we went on a women's trip. Being with other women appealed to us. I organized a group of six women, who came from all parts of the country, for a one-week sailing school in the gulf. I'm a singer, a Sweet Adeline, and they were from other singing groups (we did a bit of singing on the boat, of course).

By now we've gone three years in a row. This year there were just three of us and the captain, which was great because we got a lot more sailing in. I'm getting to the point where I can do a few knots now. I can sail, but I still feel more comfortable with the captain aboard. I'm not quite ready to bareboat out in the Atlantic yet, but I'm working my way up to it.

My favorite is being at the helm—it is a special feeling. A couple of the women were better at navigating. Although the boat has instruments, we're taught the basics—if your Loran (radar) and compass were broken, how would you function? One of the main things you have to know at all times is the position of your boat. If something goes wrong and you radio in for help, you must know where you are.

I don't know if I would have learned as much from a man. I think you're more receptive to someone that you respect, and whom you feel respects you too.

Often you must work as a team—when you're out on the ocean and needing to get the sail down and the wind is howling and pushing you around. One woman was too frightened to stand up and work on the sails, so I just asked her to put her body beside mine and hold me onto the boat, otherwise I would have fallen off.

On the last day of the trip, a school of about thirty dolphins came right up to the boat. We got real close so we could see their sleek little bodies as they played and frolicked for about forty-five minutes. They looked us over, as much as we were looking them over. That was a delightful experience.

There is a camaraderie among women that doesn't exist in a mixed group. There is also a high level of comfort. If you're all female on the boat and your shorts get wet, you can walk by in your underwear to the shower—it's no problem. I went to the store and bought one of those rub-on tattoos that lasts for about a week. It was the ugliest one I could find: a skull and crossbones. I put it on my arm and it was a kick.

A couple of times we sailed into port at night. When you come into a cove full of gleaming lights, you see the city in a different way than you would if you had driven a car. Of course then you have to dock the boat, with all the problems that you might encounter. When we'd finished doing the job correctly, we went to a restaurant, ordered a big pitcher of beer, a Greek salad, and some fresh shrimp right off the ocean to celebrate.

Learning to sail gave me the courage to face other things in my life. About ten years ago I had breast cancer. I'm fine now, but I'm a lot more aware of the importance of life—the fragile balance we maintain—and how that can change at any time. I know that life is for living; I want to do good things and help other people and enjoy all the opportunities that I can.

This is turning into an annual thing, although we didn't mean to leave the men behind all of the time. They might be starting to feel a little left out now. It happens that my friend's husband and my husband are avid golfers, and they do their thing in a different direction. We're waiting for next summer, when we can get back on the boat. Hopefully, if the fellas want to go to the golf course, we'll just take the boat out ourselves. By then we'll feel confident enough to do that. And I can't wait.

Skiing, Snowshoeing, and Dog Sledding

A blanket of snow creates the world anew, inviting you to make fresh tracks. Instead of hibernating this winter, check out the many ways you can come out and play. Advances in technology have created warmer clothing, and gear is more versatile and user friendly than ever before. There are lots of classes, clinics, and trips where women can have fun in the snow.

Downhill Skiing

"Alpine skiing is like flying. To stand at the top of the world. To launch into space and plunge down fast or slow, in time with the music in your own mind, isolated by wind and cold, stimulated by the visual beauty, a little bit afraid, aware always of the risks but always in control."[23] That's how Elissa Slanger felt about downhill skiing, and she wanted to share her knowledge with women who felt frustrated about learning to ski. She wrote *Ski Woman's Way* along with Dinah Witchel, because an aggressive, fast ski style is not necessarily the ideal of every skier. She proposed that some skiers, including many women, may choose to "caress" the mountain instead of "attack" it.

Aside from differing attitudes, Slanger describes how anatomical differences affect the way women ski. A wider pelvis changes movement and turns, and may call for a slightly wider stance. Since a woman's body mass is concentrated lower than a man's, women have a slightly lower center of gravity. That means women must make an extra effort to move their body weight forward on their skis.

The fact that women ski differently and prefer to learn from women pros has inspired most major ski resort areas in the United States to offer clinics for women. All the programs listed here feature women instructors, use of video feedback for improving skills, small classes based on student ability (to help women of all levels, including first-time skiers), and technical information on ski equipment and selection. Be sure to ask if prices include lift tickets and accommodations on multiday trips.

•Alpine Meadows, Women's Ski Weeks: P.O. Box 5279, Tahoe City, CA 96145 (800/441-4423, ext. 210) or (916/581-8225, ext. 210). Week-long clinics.

•Breckenridge Ski Resort, Women's Skiing Seminars: P.O. Box 1058, Breckenridge, CO 80424, (800/789-SNOW, ext. 7201) or (303/453-3250, ext. 7201). Three- and four-day clinics.

•Copper Mountain Resort, Women's Skiing Seminars: P.O. Box 3001, Copper Mountain, CO 80443 (800/458-8386, ext. 7). Two- and three-day seminars.

•Crested Butte Mt. Resort in the Rockies, Women's Ski Adventures with Kim Reichhelm: 237 Post Road West, Westport, CT 06880 (800/992-7700) or (203/454-0090). Four days with accommodations at the Grand Butte Hotel.

•Killington Ski Area, Women's Ski Escape: Killington, VT 05751 (802/422-3333). Three-day programs.

•Park City Ski Area, Holly Flanders' Ladies' Ski Adventure: P.O. Box 39, Park City, UT 84060 (801/649-8111). Three-day seminars.

•Patti Sherman's Vail Freestyle Program: P.O. Box 1862, Edwards, CO 81632 (303/479-4441). Three- and four-day workshops for women.

•Ski Cooper, Powder Ski Seminar: Christy Sports Centre Reservations, P.O. Box I, Dillon, CO 80435 (800/223-6248). Two days.

•Snowbird Ski and Summer Resort, Snowbird Ski School: P.O. Box 92900, Snowbird, UT 84092 (801/742-2222, ext. 5170). Three-day seminars.

•Squaw Valley, Just for Women: P.O. Box 2007, Olympic Valley, CA 96146 (916/583-0119). Three- and five-day clinics.

•Steamboat Ski Resort, Women's Ski Seminars: Steamboat Ski School Ticket Office, 2305 Mt. Werner Circle, Steamboat Springs, CO 80487 (303/879-6111, ext. 531). Three-day seminars.

•Sugarloaf Sports and Fitness Club: PO Box 5000, Kingfield, ME 04947 (800/843-5623) or (207/237-2000). Women's weekend program in January and week-long course in February.

•**Sunday River Ski Resort, Women's Ski Experience**: P.O. Box 450, Bethel, ME 04217 (207/824-3000). One- or six-day programs.

•**Winter Park Resort, Women's Ski and Snowboard Seminars**: P.O. Box 36, Winter Park, CO 80482 (303/726-5514, ext. 337). One-day clinics or one-day each of three successive weeks.

Snowboarding

"Where the hill got a little steeper, I began to pick up speed; crouching, I found my center of balance. I leaned slightly into a wide, arcing turn and instantly my board took off. Rocketing down the hill, I was somehow levitated off the surface of the earth. The black board at my feet seemed to be hovering above the ground like a magic carpet, sweeping me over and down the mountain."[24] So Susannah Levin describes the experience of snowboarding in her article "Shredding Inhibitions."

Snowboarding is like surfing on snow. Those with skiing experience should be able to pick up snowboarding techniques after a week of practice that may include a few bumps and falls.

Because snowboarding is such a new sport (only about ten years old), equipment designs change faster than you can carve a turn. Symmetrical boards (each half is shaped identically) are stable, more predictable, and good for beginners. Asymmetrical designs allow for a quicker ride and better turns.

While initially considered the exclusive domain of teenage boys who adapted skateboard maneuvers to the snow, many others are now getting hooked on the sport. The Wild Women Snowboard Camp at Jackson Hole Ski Resort, the first for women, has inspired several more:

•**Alyeska Ski Resort**: P.O. Box 249, Girdwood, AK 99587 (907/783-2222). Two-day clinics on alpine-style snowboarding for all abilities as well as a backcountry snowboarding clinic.

•**Homewood Ski Resort, Homewood Women's Clinics**: P.O. Box 165, Homewood, CA 96141 (916/525-2992). Two-day clinics as well as day lessons in alpine snowboarding.

•Jackson Hole Ski Resort, **Wild Woman Snowboard Camp**: P.O. Box 290, Teton Village, WY 83025 (307/733-2292). Three days.

•Winter Park Resort, **Women's Ski and Snowboard Seminars**: P.O. Box 36, Winter Park, CO 80482 (303/726-5514, ext. 337). One-day clinics or one-day each of three successive weeks.

Telemark Skiing

Telemark is the name of a specific downhill turning technique that employs a deep knee bend to create long, arcing turns. The repeated deep knee lunges provide a good workout and take some training to build up to. Telemarking has become a popular aspect of Nordic skiing. While cross country skis can be used for telemarking, special telemark skis that are slightly wider provide more of a base for turning.

Telemark skiers may use ski lifts to gain access to downhill runs or ski up the mountain using mohair or synthetic "skins," which attach to the bottom of the skis. The skins have a one-way nap that helps keep the skier from sliding backward while climbing uphill. Use of skins allow telemark skiers access to remote downhill runs. Telemark lessons may be available where either cross country or downhill lessons are taught.

Hut-to-hut ski trips are backcountry multiday pack trips on skis. Skiers may stay in huts or in yurts (large, round, portable yet sturdy dwellings based on nomadic Mongolian tribal homes). On some trips, you carry your own gear; on others a dog sled transports it for you.

Cross Country Skiing

Take a picnic lunch and leave the crowds behind as you establish your own peaceful rhythm along trails that meander through snow-covered forests and meadows. Think of cross country skiing as hiking or skating across the snow—in fact, the sport originally developed as a means of backcountry transportation in winter.

Nordic skiing is the broad term for any type of skiing that uses free-heel equipment (as opposed to alpine skiing in which both toe and heel are attached to the ski by bindings). Nordic ski activities include cross country skiing, telemark skiing, ski touring, and ski jumping.

Cross country skiing involves climbing uphill and down over varied terrain with lightweight ski equipment. Classic track skiing creates a rhythmic kick and glide flow in a forward motion, in which one skier follows in the tracks of another. Technological changes in equipment and a desire for greater speed has led to "skating," a technique where the skier pushes out hard to one side first with one ski, then the other. Many skiers now combine the two techniques, skating where wider tracks allow.

The sport involves all the major muscle groups, making it a highly efficient, yet low-impact form of exercise. Cross country skiers say that if you can walk, you can learn to ski in a day. Women, with a greater proportion of long-fiber muscles (providing endurance rather than explosive power) often feel better suited to cross country than to downhill skiing.

Some cross country ski areas have narrow-track trails for family outings that include children; special sleds for kids too small to ski are called "pulks," which you can pull along behind you.

Programs for women are available at at least five Canadian and thirty-five U.S. cross country ski touring areas, listed in *The Best of Cross Country Skiing*, a how-to and where-to guide published by the Cross Country Ski Areas Association. It is available for $3 from CCSAA, 259 Bolton Road, Winchester, NH 03470.

Cross Country Ski Trips

Learn and practice ski touring, telemark, and track skiing in any one of many locations. Stay in yurts or cabins, stop at hot springs or view a herd of elk passing by. Combine skiing with animal tracking or dog sledding. Choose from many companies, including:

Eastern U.S.

Adventures for Women
Appalachian Mountain Club
Earthwise

Her Wild Song
Mahoosuc Guide Service
Outdoor Vacations for Women over 40
Women's Outdoor Adventure Cooperative

Midwestern U.S.

Inside Outside Adventures
Voyageur Outward Bound School
Women in the Wilderness
Woodswomen

Western U.S.

Adventure Associates
Blue Moon Explorations
Call of the Wild
Lois Lane Expeditions
Outdoor Vacations for Women over 40
Rainbow Adventures
Woodswomen

Alaska

Alaska Women of the Wilderness
Equinox

Canada

Canadian Outward Bound Wilderness School
Et-Then

Australia/New Zealand

Bushwise Women
Wildwise
Women of the Wilderness Australia

Ski Equipment

To get started you will need skis with bindings, boots that fit the bindings, and ski poles. One of the differences between downhill and cross country skis relates to length. The average downhill ski measures head-high against the skier with considerable adjustments based on skill level. By contrast, cross country skis reach the crook of your wrist when your arm is raised, with little variation due to ability. Skating skis are lightweight, shorter, and narrow. Waxless skis require less maintenance and are recommended for beginners. Try renting equipment and taking lessons to get started. Basic rental packages usually consist of skis, boots, and poles. Some ski stores rent new skis and will apply rental fees to the purchase of new skis. Once you know that you want to continue the sport, you can consider purchasing your own skis and other equipment.

Snowshoeing

Native Americans crafted snowshoes from bent branches and rawhide strips. Early designs were patterned after a bear's paw, and the entire shoe was lifted with each step. The addition of a toe hole in the design allowed the heel to rise and the shoe to be dragged across the snow rather than lifted, a great energy conserver.

The classic tear-shape of the snowshoe requires a somewhat bow-legged walk to prevent tripping, caused by the rubbing of the shoes against each other. Newer-style oblong shoes, like the lightweight designs by Redfeather, are easier for beginners to use. Large, long shoes give support when backpacking or carrying other heavy loads; smaller, lighter shoes are easier to maneuver.

Snowshoeing Trips

Many snowshoe trips combine with cross country skiing or dog sledding to give you a choice of options to traverse the silent backcountry. Whether you prefer to camp out or stay in a cozy cabin, there's a trip for you:

Appalachian Mountain Club
Earthwise
Et-Then
Her Wild Song
Inside Outside Adventures
Women in the Wilderness
Women's Outdoor Adventure Cooperative

Dog Sledding

Asian and North American peoples who live at the top of the world have relied for thousands of years on dogs to help them survive. Dog sledding involves harnessing a team of six to twenty-four dogs to a special sled for travel over snow-covered terrain. While dog sled racing has been somewhat more visible, recreational mushing is quickly gaining in popularity.

Alaskan Malamute, Siberian Husky, Samoyed, and Alaskan Husky (a crossbreed) are thick-coated breeds that live and thrive in cold weather conditions. They pull sleds of many sizes and designs; the driver stands at the rear, holding the reins, giving verbal commands, steering, and setting the brake when necessary.

Dog sled racing is a specialized sport involving years of training and preparation. The most famous dog sled race, the Iditarod, is a twelve-hundred-mile marathon from Anchorage to Nome. In 1985, Libby Riddles became the first woman to win the Iditarod; she also won the humanitarian award, given to the driver who took best care of the dogs during competition. You can read about her epic journey in *Race Across Alaska*.[25]

While a person of average condition can enjoy dog sledding, the more flexible and better conditioned you are, the easier it will be. Walking, running, skiing, and stretching all help prepare you for dog sledding.

Long distance dog sled trips involve many hours of cold weather travel, so proper gear is essential for your comfort. Dog sled trips are available in Alaska, the northwoods of Canada and the U.S., including Minnesota and Maine.

Dog Sledding Trips

Learn the art of dog mushing, or choose to ski or snowshoe without the burden of a heavy pack. Contact these groups to find out more:

Alaska Women of the Wilderness
Appalachian Mountain Club

Call of the Wild
Canadian Outward Bound Wilderness School
Et-Then
Her Wild Song
Mahoosuc Guide Service
PeerSpirit
Voyageur Outward Bound School
Wintermoon
Women in the Wilderness
Women's Outdoor Adventure Cooperative
Woodswomen

Other Winter Sports

Babson Women's Ice Hockey Camp offers two week-long summer sessions for women ages twelve and up. All levels of experience are welcome. Participants need to know how to skate, be in good shape, and bring their own equipment. Over a hundred girls and women attend each session and are split into three groups according to age and ability. Coaches from a variety of eastern colleges lead players through on-ice practice, chalk talks, power skating, scrimmages, and more. The cost of $450 per session is all-inclusive, with accommodations at Babson College. Babson Women's Ice Hockey Camp, Program Office, Babson Recreation Center, 150 Great Plain Avenue, Wellesley, MA 02181 (617/239-6020).

AT SKI SCHOOL IN COLORADO: *Marty Dougherty*

I have been taking women's skiing seminars in Breckenridge, Colorado, and I think they are wonderful. I skied a tremendous amount as a youngster in Massachusetts. Then I married and moved to New Jersey. I had six crazy children flying around me. Skiing was so expensive, and we were a young family starting out, so it got left by the wayside. We just didn't have that kind of money.

Now that I'm in my sixties, my kids are grown and I'm foot loose and fancy free. Last year two of my girls and my sister-in-law came with me to Colorado. We all did the seminar together. You rate yourself as to what group you should be in based on your level of expertise. You can start out at any level. There were five students in my group. Our instructor was in her late twenties and she was an expert skier. She made herself available to any of us whenever we wished to talk with her or had questions about skiing. It's very nice to be in the company of a woman who knows her business.

I find it absolutely fascinating to be taught by women and to be learning with other women. When a woman instructor says you can do something, you believe her. I think men have a tendency to put us down, and we don't trust their judgment, because they do ski differently than we do. They are hell bent to compete and be the first one down. Women are much more tuned in to their technique.

After three days I lost my fear, which, of course, a lot of women have regarding skiing. On Saturday night, it snowed like crazy, and when we got to the slopes on Sunday morning, some of the slopes weren't even packed down. So we skied the powder and it was lovely. We were delighted that every one of us made it down. I think the challenges draw you closer. We're living in a marvelous world, with all these opportunities opening up; women just have to know that they can do it.

It was very nice to take the seminar with my daughters. In some respects, they're better skiers than I am. So they were off in their own groups, and my sister-in-law was in another group, and then we would meet and talk in the evenings. We experienced something together, and we sure had a good time. I don't know if they're going to come with me this March, but I'm going to go again. I don't have too many close friends who do these things with me—their lives are not as athletically inclined as mine. My friends still have husbands, so I'm the odd woman out, but I don't feel that way with them. They've got their husbands to take care of, I've got mountains to ski! I think I got the better deal.

I went to Brimson, Minnesota, about fifty miles north of Duluth, to a place called Wintermoon. Kathleen Anderson runs the homestead there. The dog mushing trip was offered in conjunction with PeerSpirit. Ann Linnea and Christina Baldwin facilitated the more spiritual part of the experience, while Kathleen was in charge of the dog mushing, the adventure part.

This is a remote place, out in the middle of nowhere, without electricity or running water. There were eight women on the trip, and we all stayed in the "Bunk-her" together. It was a cozy, comfortable, wooden cabin, with a wood stove and beds. Right down the path from where we stayed was a sauna. We'd wrap ourselves in towels and put our big boots on and walk from the bunkhouse to the sauna. Inside was a wood stove where we boiled hot water, so we could bathe there too.

We all took saunas together. We'd sit in there for a long time, and then we'd go out and play in the snow, and then come back into the sauna and sit and talk and drink lots of water and wait for the next batch of water to boil. It was great being in a community of women. I found myself really listening and having others really listen to me. We all opened up. It felt so different from everyday life, where we're so busy that we only give each other forty-five minutes to do lunch. Now I continually remind myself, *Don't lose that.*

The coldest it got while we were there was fifteen degrees during the day. I had been worried about being cold, but we never felt too cold because we had the right gear. They sent us a complete list of what to bring, and in fact, I brought too much stuff.

Most of the women were from Minnesota or the Pacific Northwest. I had thought maybe some pairs of friends would show up together, but none of us knew each other beforehand. I was the youngest, at twenty-eight, another woman was twenty-nine, all the rest were in their thirties and forties, with varying degrees of fitness. I had recently had reconstructive knee surgery and was very conscious of my physical limitations.

There were single women, married women, straight and lesbian women, it didn't seem to matter. One was a management consultant for a big company, another was a graphic designer, another had an outdoor equipment company with her husband. On the first day we all talked about why we were there, and where we had come from, and one woman said, "I don't really know why I'm here—I don't like the cold weather, I'm not very athletic, and I'm not particularly fond of dogs." We all laughed, and periodically teased her about it. By the end of the trip, she said, "I'm a dog musher! All right!"

Dog mushing was great fun. First Kathleen took us around to introduce us to each one of the twenty-six huskies and five puppies. They all have names, all have histories, and she's raised every one of them herself. So you learn who is the grandmother of who, and which is the puppy from which litter. At first there were so many that I was overwhelmed, then I started to learn their names and see their personalities—this is Wolfie Girl, and that's Denali, and they're very distinctive. Kathleen starts the puppies getting used to people at a very young age, and they're very friendly. Each dog has its own warm house with dry hay inside and its name carved in wood above the door.

Then we learned about the sleds and the harnesses. Ace was my favorite dog—he would pick up his paw and put it right into the harness. It's kind of chaotic when you're harnessing up—all the dogs are howling and excited to go. And the dogs that don't go on that run howl because they don't get to go. On the way back, the dogs left behind would hear us coming before we could see them, and they would howl to welcome us, or maybe because they wanted to go next.

Kathleen had two women assisting her as dog handlers, and we'd take out two or three sleds at a time. One basic principle is that you have to be sure to hang on to the sled. If you let go, the dogs are so excited that they will just take off without you.

Each sled had five to six dogs hitched to it, and we'd go for one-hour runs. The first time out we rode on the sled, with the drivers standing behind. The driver stands on the sled runners that stick out the back of the sled; there's a foot brake between the runners as well as a snow hook brake.

The lead dogs follow commands: "gee and haw" mean right and

left, and "hike, hike, hike," means go, go go. When you say that, the dogs go nuts. The next day we got to steer the sleds ourselves, although the handler always came with us. There were a few places where it was too difficult; if we had to cross a road or stream, we'd get off and they would drive.

When you're out on the sled, you have to be really focused on the dogs. If they don't feel your attention, they'll stray. You have to be very conscious of what you're doing. If there's a trail, they stay on it pretty well, but when the trail splits off, you have to tell them which way to go. As soon as they do the right thing, you praise them. If you're going up a hill, you say "hike, hike, hike," to encourage them. Sometimes you run alongside the sled to help the dogs out, which creates a feeling of teamwork between the dogs and the musher.

I was afraid that I wouldn't be able to drive because of my knee. I was worried that I'd fall. I kept saying No, I'm not going to drive, and Kathleen would say, "Yes you will, just wait." Finally when we got to a place that was straight and flat, I drove and it was such a thrill!

We had chores each day that we did in pairs, and that was always really fun. I pumped water and chopped wood, things I've never done before. Preparing the dog food was another chore—chopping the meat, chicken, and whitefish. Being a dog lover, I particularly liked helping to take care of the dogs.

We took our time at dinner and we ate well. It always ended with chocolate—that was our bonding thing—chocolate cheesecake, chocolate fudge, cookies, whatever. It was nice to see women really eating. We were hungry, we'd worked hard and been outside, and there wasn't a feeling of "I shouldn't eat any more." It was more like, "Give me some more food!"

We weren't always all together. We usually separated into little groups; some would go dog mushing, others would do journal writing, and others would go off into the wilderness for an hour. You could cross country ski, or walk around, or sit by a tree by yourself. Surrounded by the snowy peacefulness of eighty acres of wilderness you realize there is a sound to the silence. When it's quiet enough, you can hear it. Afterward we would talk about what we saw and felt and thought about.

Journal writing was hard for me because my critical voice kept interfering. I would sit down to write and nothing would come. But once I let down my defenses, the words started to flow. Christina suggested that instead of writing, "today I did this and that..." we come up with questions to ask ourselves in our journal. We also wrote a short piece and then pulled the words out of it that we liked, which resulted in a poem of sorts. We practiced meditation and did a lot of circle work.

An important aspect of the trip for me was celebrating the winter solstice, which I had never done before. The winter solstice marks the shortest day and the longest night of the year. After the solstice, the days get longer. Out there, where there's no electricity, that really means something. Here we flick on a switch to compensate for the lack of light. But in the natural world, you need to be quieter in winter, to sort of hibernate in the dark. Once the days get longer, you start coming out of that.

We celebrated the winter solstice on our last night. Christina and Ann made luminaries—paper bags with candles in them—and we lined the quarter-mile walkway to Petrell Hall, where we had our celebration. Another woman and I provided the music (we played the Indigo Girls, and some African drumming music), and we danced all night. We started out with taped music and played along with it, and then we just continued to play our own music with drums and maracas and bells, and we really had some good energy going there.

Later, we had a bonfire. We each wrote on a piece of paper what it was we wanted to let go of with the coming of the light. We sang a song, and then we all stood around the fire and watched the papers burn. One woman's piece took so long to burn, it made us all laugh. It kept skirting the flames. It would singe a bit, the wind would blow it around, and then finally it just torched up and we all cheered. We said, "Whew, that's a hard one to get rid of." We each received little earth gifts to bring home and keep with us, to remind us of that time.

The trip was only four days, which was much too short. But it made me realize that even though I'm busy, I can always take some time out. To have an adventure doesn't require a month-long excursion— even four days can really make a difference.

Snorkeling and Scuba Diving

A mask and fins grant you passage to a blue-green universe below the surface of the sea. Follow a sea horse as it explores among fan coral, or hang suspended in warm water while a school of angelfish swim past. Whether snorkeling or scuba diving, every dip below the surface begins of a new adventure.

Snorkeling

Snorkeling is a low-cost, easy introduction to the magic of the marine world. Snorkeling allows you to swim near the surface of the water, while relying on your own breath with the aid of the snorkel (a tube that extends from your mouth past the surface of the water to the air above). By wearing a face mask and snorkel, you can swim for an extended period of time and get a panoramic view of underwater life. Dennis K. Graver, in his well-illustrated book, *Scuba Diving*,[26] points out that the human head weighs nearly the same as a bowling ball. Lifting your head continuously in and out of the water is much more tiring than simply floating while wearing a mask and breathing through your snorkel.

Adding fins multiplies the effort of your leg movements, frees your hands from swimming motions, and greatly increases the distance you can travel. The only other equipment you may need is a diving vest to keep you warm in cold water (and for extended stays in moderately warm water) or a T-shirt, which helps you avoid serious sunburn caused by the magnifying effect of sunlight through water.

Snorkeling Trips

Combine snorkeling with sailing in Florida or Puerto Rico, scuba diving in the Caribbean, or backpacking in Hawaii:

Skin Diving

Skin diving, breath-hold diving, and free diving are all names for diving under the surface with the air that you can hold in your lungs. In many parts of the world, divers train to hold their breath for lengthy periods while they spearfish or gather shellfish or sponges. Some skin divers wear snorkels and masks and add weight belts to their equipment. Skin diving requires excellent physical condition. With practice, you can learn to stay under the surface for two or three minutes. Accomplished divers say that relaxation is a key to long skin dives; an agitated frame of mind burns up oxygen much more quickly.

I snorkeled for several years on the surface of the water before building up the confidence to dive down. My friend Ken taught me two ways to clear the snorkel after diving. Although it's tempting to take the mouthpiece out of your mouth to empty it once you regain the surface, these methods are safer and quicker. While practicing any method of clearing your snorkel, don't wait until you are desperate for air; clear the snorkel while you can still easily hold your breath. The obvious way is simply to blow hard into the snorkel once you complete your dive and get above water; a single blast will usually clear the water out. The next breath you take should be a shallow one, to verify that the tube is clear before taking a deep breath.

The alternate method requires a bit more practice but is elegant in its use of air pressure. While you are swimming underwater, tip your head back and look up at the surface and exhale a small amount of air into the snorkel tube. As you rise to the surface, that air bubble will rise through the tube and push water out. When you tip your head forward as you break the surface of the water, exhale again to get the last bit of water out of the tube. This works well and doesn't require as strong a blast as the first method.

If you feel comfortable with skin diving and find you want to linger under the surface, you may want to explore scuba diving.

Scuba Diving

The self-contained underwater breathing apparatus, or SCUBA, was invented about fifty years ago, but the term *scuba* has since become popularized as a word in itself. Scuba divers add weights, a scuba air cylinder with valve and regulator, and a dive knife to the mask and fins that snorkelers employ. With all their gear on, divers are clumsy-footed, heavy beings; crossing the surface of the water transforms them into weightless, lithe dancers of the deep.

Divemaster Mickey Foster gave me this description of a special encounter while scuba diving: "We descended right into a school of jellyfish, a type called lion's mane jellyfish. There must have been thirty or forty of them, and they looked so fragile as we passed among them. We were in exposure suits and were very careful to stay untangled from their streamers, which were thirty feet long, colored in shades of auburn, tan and milky translucent white. We made the descent back to back, circling and pointing out the streamers to each other. As we got below them, we looked up at the sun shining down through the opalescence of these creatures and they were simply glowing in the water. It was a moment I will never forget."

Diving Certification

Because diving can be a dangerous sport, the industry is extremely concerned with safety. You cannot rent diving equipment or have air tanks filled without showing a certification card (called a "C-card") to prove that you have completed a specified course of training.

Diving is a strenuous activity. If climbing a full flight of stairs leaves you winded, you need to improve your fitness level before diving. Anyone (over the age of twelve) who is comfortable in the water and can swim two hundred yards nonstop can learn how to dive. Those with special medical conditions should check with a doctor before taking a dive course.

There are certain physical laws that you must learn and abide by in order to dive. When you snorkel and dive down your ears pop and feel clogged—that's pressure, which increases in proportion to your descent. The deeper you go, the more compressed any air or gas you are carrying in your body or tissues will become. What gets compressed on the way down must expand on the way up, so the closer to the surface you get, the more rapidly any air you have in your body expands. Descending and ascending safely is a major part of scuba training.

Most training programs require a minimum of four classroom sessions, followed by four sessions in a swimming pool or other area of confined water, and finally, four supervised dives in open water—a total of thirty to forty hours of instruction. You should always dive with a partner and stay within the hundred-and-thirty-foot limit for recreational diving; greater depths are restricted to professional divers only. Many divers spend the majority of their time somewhere between sixty and a hundred feet, where the light is still good and the big fish play.

Aside from maintaining a high level of fitness, divers must honestly assess their health and well-being before every dive. Even minor sniffles can create serious problems in the marine environment.

Divemaster Mickey Foster points out that getting certified is only the beginning of a long learning process. "Your basic scuba course gives you permission to go out there and learn. You get a little card that lets you go in and buy air for your tanks and get your own scuba gear, because you've read the manual and know where the brakes are. Now you are ready to learn how to dive."

Resort Schools

"Resort schools" are vacation diving schools in resort environments that get novices into the water in a highly condensed period of time. Resort courses are set up so that a student is under the watchful supervision of an instructor at all times. Think of it as a guided tour of diving—it gives you a taste of what diving is like. Just be sure that all your activities are properly supervised and never dive unescorted or without proper instruction.

Resort schools do not replace scuba diving certification courses. You cannot learn to dive safely in one week, and a resort scuba course does not entitle you to dive elsewhere.

Considerations for Women Divers

Dr. Karen Signelle points out that, as women, "we have an advantage because we have more lung power. We don't use as much air as men. During many trips, I was the last one out of the water because I was diving entirely with men."

Some women divers prefer to use a smaller air tank, both to lessen weight and increase comfort. Shorter women may find that the backs of their legs hit against a large tank while swimming. It's wise to rent equipment for your first several dives, both to ensure that you want to continue with the sport and to fine-tune what your equipment needs will be.

Many women find the supportive help of a female dive instructor worth the trouble of looking. She may have special tips on handling the tanks and other equipment (which can weigh half as much as your body). Check out instructors and dive shops very carefully. Mickey Foster advises, "If you go into a shop, and you're brushed off or feel uncomfortable, politely leave and go somewhere else. Ask for a private instructor if you have to. More than anything else, trust your feelings, because your instincts are giving you the correct information for yourself." She recommends women instructors, "especially for mature women, simply because we're past the boy-girl games. We're learning a sport for our own enhancement and it's got nothing to do with sexuality games."

Because most equipment, dive training, vacations, and diving groups are geared toward male divers, the Women's SCUBA Association was formed in 1992 to represent the needs of women divers. A Women's Equipment Test Team is providing feedback to manufacturers about developing equipment for women divers, and Women's Dive Seminars are being scheduled in several locations. The bicoastal association can be reached at 6029 South Atlantic Avenue, New Smyrna Beach, FL 32169 (904/426-5757) or P.O. Box 627, Blue Jay, CA 92317 (714/337-4695). The National Women's Scuba Society is a membership organization of female divers from across the U.S. and offers trips and travel advice for members. Their address is P.O. Box 451, Pittsford, NY 14534.

Scuba Trips

Go scuba diving in Mexico or the Caribbean or swim with dolphins on the island of Roatan off the coast of Honduras. Take the plunge with:

Adventure Spirit Hawaii
Club Le Bon
Eco-Explorations
Women of the Wilderness Australia
Woodswomen

SNORKELING IN THE LAST WILDERNESS: *Karen Signelle*

Snorkeling is delightful and easy. Of course, scuba is a tremendous thrill too, I have to admit. I've done both scuba and snorkeling, but I mainly do snorkeling now because it seems to me you get so much more, and it costs nothing. The ocean is the last wilderness.

Snorkeling is easy and peaceful: you simply float and the fish come right up to your nose—angelfish, all sorts of amazing fish. It's wonderful exercise—slow motion movement for hours—and you feel so good afterward. You might see a turtle swimming by, or stingrays near the bottom, big rays, beautiful and graceful, grazing like cows. It's a quiet, safe world.

You can learn how to do it in half an hour. Snorkeling is as safe as scuba is potentially dangerous. Another difference is that with scuba you dive for a short period—twenty minutes, maybe thirty. With snorkeling, I'll go for hour after hour, from one bay to the next. Of course, you need to go with a partner. My partner and I have a little plastic bag that we carry with us in the water. We'll come out, eat our lunch, drink some water, and then swim back the way we came through all the bays. You get whole days of snorkeling, not just one quick trip of twenty minutes under water.

Snorkeling has virtually no coverage in the media because it's essentially free. Once you buy a bit of equipment (for less than $50) you're set. I like to snorkel from shore, rather than from a boat, so I can go out and come back when I feel like it. You can also go along on scuba trips and do snorkeling instead. If you're attracted to scuba but don't want to take that giant step and incur that huge expense, then go as a snorkeler. You can bargain to pay less. You can see almost as much at twenty or thirty feet (where you can come up as much as you want to) as you can at forty or a hundred or whatever. Find out if the dive boat is going to a coral reef that is near the surface, which they often do. Sometimes they go somewhere and you have to dive way down to find the reef—so far down that you can only see it by scuba. But many times the reef is near the surface where you can see it by snorkeling.

At some of the resorts that scuba groups go to, you can just go out from shore yourself. In fact, I bargained for that in a place near Cozumel, Mexico. They had a tour, and I said, "I'd like to go, but I only want to scuba every other day—give me a cut on the price," and they did. Sometimes they need one or two more people to fill out the trip. You're not taking the place of someone who'd pay the higher fee.

I grew up in the water. My father was in the Navy, and I was around water all the time. I dove at a young age, and the memory stayed with me. When I got away from diving, I promised myself that I would go back. So twenty years later, when my youngest was seven or eight, I told my husband, "I'm going to dive again." It was something I had to do for myself. It was pretty intense—I was working sixty to seventy hours a week, and I came home to all the housework. But I really wanted to dive. I tried to change things around in the family so that I wouldn't be too exhausted. That in itself took a bit of doing.

I was smoking two and a half packs of cigarettes a day at the time. And I was not averse to a brandy and water at the end of the night. Both of those are real diving no-no's. I was underweight, I was sick, and I was exhausted—and here I was showing up for this dive class.

The class started out with eight men and women, and one by one, all the other women dropped out. Of the four of us who finished, I was the only female. Those guys were all a lot bigger than I was, and it became very stressful for me. I have never been in an all-female class. I have always ended up with these Arnold Schwarzenegger types, and that's where my poor opinion of my skill level comes from. I can't seem to shake it. Women keep giving me feedback that I'm very powerful in the water, but I don't often feel that way.

After a while I got bronchial pneumonia. I had worked myself into a state of exhaustion. Our family physician said to me, "You're going to have to make a choice. You can either continue diving, or you can continue smoking. You can't do both, because you won't last long."

I had already been thinking that I wanted to explore further training in diving—formalized training—to see where it would take me. And I really didn't want those cigarettes. So I threw out the cigarettes, quit my job, and signed up for the advanced class.

I was the only woman. I was also the only woman in my search-and-rescue class. But by Divemaster level, I was no longer willing to be "sweet little submissive Mickey." I was becoming assertive, and I was very, very confused and stressed over what was happening to me in all of my personal relationships. My husband and I were quarreling for the first time in a fifteen-year marriage, and I started fighting with my diving partner and longtime friend, Tim.

We had a spectacular fight at South Monastery. I climbed up on a bed of kelp, and he chewed me out, up one side and down the other. I was so angry, I was crying. I was lying on this kelp, in forty feet of water, just screaming at him. He couldn't figure out what the hell happened. I had been raised to always anticipate what my partner wanted, not what I wanted. I was no longer willing to accept that in my life.

When you dive, the bottom line is that you're personally responsible for yourself. You can point the finger all you want at someone else, but no one else is responsible for your gear and the only one that's gonna get hurt if you don't take care of yourself is you. To be willing to accept that kind of personal responsibility, you have to grow up. For me, that meant looking very long and hard at areas that, being a housewife and mother, I was conditioned not to deal with.

I had to change my relationship to my husband and to many other people. It was the beginning of a major turnaround. My family is still in shock over this, with a lot of high emotions and some very unsettled reactions. Between the two of us, we have twelve children with seven of them still at home. The youngest has just turned twelve. And the mom who always did for everyone—who was on call twenty-four hours a day for fifteen years—well, she isn't there anymore.

I discovered that there were a lot of people I had put up with for years, simply because it was expected of me, whom I really didn't like. So I started branching out and meeting new people, meeting new divers.

I've really had to struggle to find women to dive with. The expectation at the shop where I certified out is that a woman is always attached to a male. On our own, we are considered second class. And I wasn't willing to settle for that. I absolutely refused.

I have nothing against men. I have a select group of male divers that I am genuinely honored to dive with. It's the power differences between men and women that I can't abide. It seems to be changing in diving now. I've heard horrendous stories from some female instructors—these women have lost jobs, been snubbed, and ostracized. My own worst incident was when an instructor told me, "You're not going to be on my boat because you don't drink beer, you're married, and you won't spread." This was said in front of a roomful of guys, and it was presented as a joke. That kind of attitude is going out the door because we're refusing to accept it.

I started connecting with a lot of very strong, very powerful women when I came across the Northern California Rainbow Divers.[27] They in turn have introduced me to other women. It's been fascinating to network. The Rainbow Divers are out of San Francisco and are the gay and lesbian scuba club. Those people are wonderful to dive with; there are no games with the men or the women. I have a good time with all of them.

I think all-women's groups are absolute heaven. As an instructor, I love to teach them. Women are much more receptive to listening to what you have to say. Women tend not to play the "I am better than you" game, and they prefer to approach things slowly. They want to get a good look-see before they go sticking their bodies out there, which is an admirable trait in diving. In women's classes, there's a lot more laughter. There's more of a willingness to function as a unified whole.

Men are more aggressive and maybe more spontaneous in the water. They also seem to pick up the physics part of diving more easily, but they also forget it more quickly. A woman generally doesn't forget it. When a little blinker goes off in her head that says, "130 feet: *no*," she may not remember why, but she's got that number and she's going to stop and not approach it. She's going to remember that fifteen-foot safety stop, and she's going to remember to ascend and descend slowly. Whereas lots of guys will say, "Hey, what's this book stuff? Nothing happened to me, let's do it again."

Every dive is different. I remember one that was magic. I had a harbor seal dance with me. Harbor seals, with their huge eyes and speckled coats, are so graceful under water it is heartbreaking to watch them. This one would nudge me and then make a spiral or a turn and glide to rest beside me and look at me. Then I would mimic it, and it would dance back. It showed me where all of the rockfish were, pointing just like a little Labrador.

I was guiding a novice diver. This guy was in heaven. It was as if the kelp parted for us. I looked down, and there were two little leopard sharks gliding around. I turned in the water to be sure that he had seen them, and over his shoulder, in the distance, this intense blue patch moved toward me. It was like part of the liquid blue water solidified and came gliding toward us. It was a blue shark. I had never seen one before. I sank down near the rocks and watched this awesome creature leisurely swim toward us. Then it turned broadside and just glided off into the distance.

We saw monkey face eels and otters, and when we made our exit this guy looked at me and shook his head. He said, "I have never, ever, seen anything like that in my life." Well, neither had I.

I'm very happy in the water, and I never want to get out. I really wish I had gills. There's a timelessness and a peacefulness, a serenity that I haven't found anywhere else. And it's hauntingly beautiful. The ocean is never still, there's always movement, always something happening. There's a rhythm that gets in your blood, or maybe it's always been there and you just learn to respond to it. It's a ballet, a duet between you and the ocean. Once you become aware of it, you are not willingly going to give it up.

Surfing and Windsurfing

Combine your energy with that of waves and wind, and you'll learn to harness nature, rather than struggle against it. Surfers and windsurfers promise that once you connect with that awesome power, you'll keep going back for more.

Surfing

Surfing began as the sport of royalty in Hawaii. The famous kings and queens, princes and princesses, some of whom were originally from Tahiti, rode long planks of koa wood on rolling waves. It was considered a gift of the gods, and the royal family members were the only ones allowed to do it.

Hawaii and Australia are the surfing meccas of the world. The great majority of competitive women surfers are from Australia, and that country promotes surfing more than any other. Surf teams start in junior high school and go through college level, with numerous competitions (including a women's league).

The United States has comparatively little promotion of women's surfing, with the exception of Southern California. Women are actively involved in surfing in Ireland, England, South Africa, France, Spain, Tahiti, Fiji, Indonesia, and the Polynesian Islands.

Surfing is still predominantly a male sport, and many women are introduced to surfing by boyfriends or husbands who surf. Surfing etiquette can be harsh—women are not always welcome when they paddle out to the lineup, although that is changing in some places.

Prospective women surfers may feel intimidated by the men, the ocean elements, and even the weather in nontropical surf spots. Women in search of camaraderie like to surf with other women, and quickly learn which men are supportive of their presence.

Women who want to surf should be strong swimmers who can

swim one or two hundred yards against a steady current. In emergency situations, if you get separated from your surfboard, you will have to rely on your own abilities to swim back to shore. You should only swim in conditions in which you feel confident about your skills. Don't count on nearby surfers to be aware of your need for help.

Look for a companion who is more experienced than you to act as your surf buddy or mentor. She or he should be willing to take you out several times to show you the basics. You need to learn about waves, how the riptide and the undertow work, and how to tell the direction of the swell. You will need to practice getting in and out of the water and learn how to turn around and catch the wave. A "right" wave breaks to the right, a "left" breaks left when you're out on the surfboard looking toward shore.

Surf shop manager Lexie Hallahan recommends that women interested in surfing begin by riding boogie boards. "They can get you immediately in touch with the thrill of surfing, which is riding a wave." A *boogie board* is about four and a half feet long; you lie down on it like a sled, hold on to the nose of the board with your hands, and use swim fins on your feet to propel it through the water.

A *surfboard* is light yet durable and is made from a piece of foam that has been shaped and sanded. Sheets of fiberglass cloth are laid over the foam blank, and a liquid fiberglass resin is poured on top.

The length of the surfboard you ride is determined by personal preference, the size of the waves, and your size and ability as a surfer. Just as skiers may like slightly shorter or longer skis, surfers have their preferences about board length and shape; most serious surfers own several surfboards in their "quiver."

You will hear surfers talk about shortboards, longboards, and even eggboards. A shortboard is 6'6" and under, and generally has a pointed nose and tail. Longboards can get as long as 9'6" and are more rounded. An "egg," also called a mini-longboard, is recommended for beginners. It is a hybrid board that is rounded at the ends and wide in the middle, thus providing more stability.

A urethane leash connects your foot to the board for easy retrieval after you get knocked off by a wave. Leashes came into use in the mid-seventies, when surfers started using them to retrieve boards quickly, and to avoid getting their boards damaged by rocks.

Prior to that, surfers had to swim after their boards each time they floated away; surfers had to be exceptionally strong swimmers. Now all surfers rely on leashes, which save time and energy but can lead beginners to feel overconfident. Surfers should always be prepared to swim if their leash breaks and they lose their board.

Surfing and Boogie Boarding Schools and Trips

Wildwise offers a women's surf camp in New South Wales, Australia. Learn to boogie board or surf from women who know how to catch waves.

Mary Lou Drummy, a veteran twenty-year competition surfer and surf teacher, operates the coed **Endless Summer Surf Camp** for adults and young people in Southern California. If you can organize a group of at least four women, Mary Lou will schedule a special all-women's week-long surf camp. Beginners are welcome, and all participants must be strong swimmers. You can reach them at P.O. Box 512, San Juan Capistrano, CA 92693 (714/493-2591).

Windsurfing

Windsurfing combines the wind-play techniques of sailing with the exhilaration of surfing. Women who are strong swimmers can learn to windsurf and can perform and compete equally with men. *Women's Sports and Fitness* writer Lisa Chase reports that during a windsurfing course in the Bahamas, the instructor announced that "women learn windsurfing faster, and go faster, than men."[28] One reason is that women tend to rely more on technique rather than strength to handle the sail.

Windsurfing is best learned with some introductory instruction; in this sport, trial and error can be a frustrating experience. Since a windsurfing student may initially spend more time in the water than on the sailboard, many would-be wind jockeys attend clinics or classes in tropical locations.

Five-time world windsurfing champion Rhonda Smith says the key to learning is "balance, not strength. If you develop your balance, the strength will build accordingly." Those with sailing experience have the advantage of being familiar with how sails respond to the wind.

Most classes make use of a simulator—a windsurfing rig on wheels that allows the student to get the feel of handling the sail on land before putting it all together on the water. The next level of training uses a "flotation trainer"—a sailboard with floats attached that make it virtually impossible to flip over. Although the first several weeks of windsurfing may be very wet ones, most students make rapid progress.

Windsurfing Gear

A sailboard has two basic parts: the board and the rig. The board is similar to a surfboard, except that most boards have footstraps to help keep your feet in place. Boards come in varying lengths: short boards are for wave and speed sailing in high-wind conditions, medium length are slalom boards, and long boards, which are best for beginners, can be used for freestyle surfing.

The sail, mast, and boom configuration that attaches to the board is called the rig. The mast stands upright and the boom rides perpendicular to it at shoulder height. The sail is attached to both. Holding and moving the boom allows you to adjust the position of the sail, allowing you to control both speed and direction. Once you can sail comfortably, you may want to make use of a harness, which hooks your body to the boom. A harness provides good back support and can be unhooked quickly when necessary.

Training programs require a life vest to be worn at all times. Cold weather windsurfers use wetsuits or drysuits, gloves, hats, and boots.

Windsurfing Trips

Rhonda Smith Windsurfing Center offers day classes and weekend clinics at the Columbia Gorge in Oregon as well as a one-week windsurfing camp at a tropical location.

I used to sit out on the rocks all day long on the Oregon coast, watching my husband surf. After two or three years of that he finally said, "You've got to get out here with me."

The north coast of the Pacific has some pretty cold water, and I didn't want to be cold. But I tried going out with a wetsuit and a boogie board; Tom gave me a few lessons out in the cove. I realized that I could be very warm in a wetsuit, and I felt more protected inside the cove, away from the big breakers. It took a few months to feel confident on the boogie board.

The first wave I caught when I was boogie boarding was one of the best waves of my life. I caught this wave and was rising all the way through it, and I felt like a pro. I was in a pocket in the speed zone of the wave just flying at warp six; I couldn't believe the speed! I kicked out with my board and thought to myself, Yes, this sensation is pretty close to orgasmic. It has to be the closest thing to sex that I've ever known. I've done a lot of things in my life—snowboarding, skiing, waterskiing, hiking, and parachuting from airplanes, trying to find things that are the most exciting to do.

I feel in touch with the ocean. Every day before I enter her, I ask her to give me waves and let me experience her and be safe. I go out feeling that she's going to give me what I am expecting. I paddle out with complete confidence and strength into big wave conditions and think to myself, I'm coming out here to line up and I'm going to find the magic spot. When I find it, I'm going to turn around and ride the wave I'm given, and I'm gonna give that wave the best ride I can. And then I'm going to kick out and come out of the wave safely, paddle back out and catch about ten more like that. That's how I visualize what I'm going to do.

You have to be able to judge your skill level. You can easily drown or get thrown up on the rocks and hurt yourself. You have to look out at the waves and ask yourself, are these waves too big for me? Are they too gnarly? Are they something I can't cope with? I never surf unless I feel close to a hundred percent confident that I can make it out there, can catch waves, and make it in safely. Gradually, over the years, I've built up my confidence, always knowing when I can ride bigger waves. Now, eight or nine years later, I feel that I can charge just about anything that comes through the cove. Now I can surf waves with twelve-foot faces, even fifteen- to twenty-foot on a perfect day.

Last year, I caught one of the most phenomenal waves of my life. I went down to the cove with two girlfriends, and we were going to catch the "lefts," but once I got suited up at the water's edge, I looked over and saw the most perfect "right" happening just down the beach. It was about six feet high, barreling perfection, and nobody was on it. I told my girlfriends, You go on to where you're going, I'm heading out to that "right."

I happen to be "regular foot" on a surfboard, which puts me frontside on that right-breaking wave. I'm facing the wave when I'm surfing it, which is the most advantageous position to be in. If I'd gone to the other break, I would have been backside, which is less advantageous and not nearly as fun. So I looked down the beach and thought, That wave has my name all over it.

It was a hell paddle to get out there; there wasn't much of a channel and I was breaking through a lot of waves. I finally got out, waited through about three waves, and then this peak comes through, and I thought, This is the perfection peak, this is a perfect right, and I'm frontside on it. This wave was made for me. I turned around and started paddling, and I knew it was going to be the biggest wave I'd ever caught. I started paddling into it on my 8'5" board, which is real hot-dogged out, and caught it.

I dropped in on it, hit the bottom, then came pulling up. The amount of speed I was getting was unbelievable. I came up and hit the top part of the section, I hit the turn back down to the bottom, came off the bottom turn, back up again into the lip, and slashed down into the pit. The whole time I was in the green water—not the whitewater—right in the green water, which is the speed section of the wave.

I must have ridden it a hundred and twenty yards, up and down all parts of the wave, until I was just in ankle-deep water. I had the sensation that it had been the wave of my life—it was the euphoria of the century. When I kicked out of the wave, I was so overwhelmed my eyes were tearing up. Then I said, I'm back out there! and immediately started paddling back out for another one, or ten more.

It reminded me of my boogie board wave, but this time I had just surfed a surfboard through the same kind of wave—I had a board under my feet and was pumping it all the way through. It's an amazing feeling—you're harnessing the energy of the wave, and its got so much power. People think I'm half-looney for talking like this, and maybe they can't understand it, but it's like you've got the whole power of the ocean harnessed into the pit of a wave.

I've been involved with feminism for years, and there is nothing that has ever gotten me closer to nature than surfing. You're out there and you have to deal with the ocean, the fear, the survival, the achievements and challenges, and the feeling of ecstasy. All that makes you feel that you've got to stay with it.

My surf buddies are a dozen other women. The men are competitive and cut each other off to get waves, but the women get along well and we all encourage each other. If we're lucky we'll have four women out in the lineup on one day.

I'm the manager of a surf shop, and I tell people who want to get involved with surfing that something will happen out there that you've never had happen before, and you won't understand it until it happens to you.

When you're in the ocean and experiencing its strength, you feel like a magician who just got hold of something that you never thought you would be allowed to have. Something the planet gave you like a gift. It's better than dancing, it's better than sex—you feel that nature just touched you on the nose and said, "That was for you." For a few seconds you are one with that wave. I've never had that sensation before with anything else.

Walking, Hiking, Backpacking, and Trekking

Walking, hiking, backpacking, trekking—what's the difference between all these terms, anyway? One woman's walk is another woman's hike. What might be called a backpacking trip in Canada is known as a trek in Tibet. The terms tend to overlap at times, but they represent a continuum of challenge and a demand for increasing levels of fitness.

Walking

Walking is our original form of transport. Regular walks around your neighborhood improve the strength and efficiency of the heart, boost the metabolism, build strength, and retard the effects of osteoporosis. Those who walk regularly report a noticeable increase in stamina.

Walking is also a delightful way to travel; the pace you set is your own, and there's always time to stop and admire the flowers. Women have walked across continents and around the world.

All you need for a walking holiday is a pair of shoes with good support. A water bottle is helpful, as you should try to drink at least two quarts per day.

Walking Trips

Take a walking holiday in the U.S., or explore England, Switzerland, Italy, Australia, or New Zealand on foot. Walk inn-to-inn or stay at a base lodge and take day strolls. Learn map and compass skills, sharpen your photography skills, or write in your journal each day.

Adventures for Women
Bushwise Women
Outdoor Vacations for Women over 40

Rainbow Adventures
Skadi
Wildwise
Women of the Wilderness Australia
Women's Outdoor Adventure Cooperative
Woodswomen

Hiking

Although there is some overlap with walking, hiking generally refers to more vigorous walking in the outdoors—up and down mountains or hills, across deserts, or through forests. Hiking produces stronger muscles and improved breathing capacity over time, but most people hike for the sheer enjoyment of spending time away from an urban environment, their work, or other responsibilities.

You don't have to have a lot of expensive gear to go hiking. Layers of old clothes from your closet, a daypack for water and snacks (along with a flashlight, extra jacket and a few items of emergency gear) and a pair of comfortable running shoes, sneakers, or work boots are enough to get you started.

To build up for a hike, start walking three times a week for at least a half hour each time. Work in some inclines, stair-climbing, bicycle riding, or sit-ups to prepare you for the challenge of hiking uphill.

Always consult a guidebook or map to be sure of your route. Look for hiking trails and maps that are marked for level of difficulty. Start out with easy hikes of three to four miles. If you haven't been getting much exercise, don't overdo it on your first hike—and don't wear a new pair of shoes. You're not likely to continue if you come home sore and miserable.

Always hike with a friend; two are better than one in case of a turned ankle or if you get lost. It's easy to spread out far enough along the trail to get some time walking alone, if that is what you want.

Before signing up a for a long hiking trip, try an outing with a local organization. Many branches of the YWCA, your city parks department, hiking or walking clubs, the Sierra Club, or Audubon Society offer day hikes. Also, look for signs posted at outdoor outfitters.

Hiking Trips

Start with day-long joy hikes in the northeastern U.S., sign up for an eight-day hike with gourmet meals cooked by a chef in the Pacific Northwest, or challenge yourself with a hike to the summit of a volcano in Kuaui, Hawaii.

Adirondack Mountain Club
Adventure Associates
Adventure Spirit Hawaii
Adventures for Women
Alaska Women of the Wilderness
Ancient Forest Adventures
Appalachian Mountain Club
Bushwise Women
Call of the Wild
Canadian Outward Bound Wilderness School
CenterPoint in Aspen
Earthwise
Inside Outside Adventures
Outdoor Vacations for Women over 40
Paddling South
Rainbow Adventures
Sacred Sedona
Wildwise
Women in the Wilderness
Women's Outdoor Adventure Cooperative
Woodswomen

Backpacking

Backpacking is hiking while carrying a pack on your back containing the food and equipment you'll need for a stay of one or more nights. If you feel comfortable hiking and want more time in the woods, try an overnight or weekend backpacking trip. Backpacking may seem intimidating, but by choosing easy routes and going with a group to help share the load, you can get an introduction to living in the wilderness that will inspire you to keep going back for more.

Backpacking with a group of women provides an ideal way to learn the skills and techniques for self-sufficiency that you can later practice on your own. Don't invest in expensive gear unless you are sure you will be using it.

There's great pleasure in setting up camp by a river or lake, making a fire just so, erecting the tent in a perfect spot, then sitting back and experiencing a pleasurable tiredness. Taking yourself far away from pressures and modern conveniences brings a sense of calm. The sights, sounds, and smells of your surroundings are more vivid when you remove the "comforts" that keep it at a distance. The stars are brighter, the sound the wind makes is more eloquent, the colors of the wildflowers more intense. After a day's climb, meals taste like heaven, even if made from reconstituted potato flakes. The feeling of being self-reliant in the wild stays with you beyond the trip.

Backpacking Tips

Set an easy pace if you want to go far—the energy expended in walking doubles with each mile-per-hour increase in speed. Don't overestimate the miles you can cover. Time yourself on a one-mile walk with a fully loaded pack to estimate what you can do in the woods. Figure on about one mile per hour in wooded terrain, less if it is very steep. Stay within the ability level of everyone in the group; remember that the slowest person is working at least as hard as you are.

Fasten your pack securely around your waist, and pack it so it is not top-heavy. This is particularly important for women, since it will transfer the load from your back to your hips and legs.

Walk erect, not bent over, to reduce pressure on your back and keep it from getting sore. Use a walking stick for added stability and support. When hiking up hills, shorten your strides for better balance.

Backpacking Trips

Welcome springtime with a backpack trip in the desert of the southwestern U.S., celebrate summer in Alaska or Maine, follow fall foliage as you backpack the Sierra Nevada, or bundle up for winter in the Appalachian Mountains. These companies offer a wide range of backpacking trips:

Adirondack Mountain Club
Adventure Associates
Alaska Women of the Wilderness
Appalachian Mountain Club
Call of the Wild
Canadian Outward Bound Wilderness School
Cloud Canyon Wilderness Experience
Colorado Outward Bound School
Earthlodge and Womenspeak Journeys
Earthwise
Equinox Wilderness Expeditions
The Heart of Adventure
Her Wild Song
Inside Outside Adventures
Outdoor Leadership Training Seminars
Pacific Crest Outward Bound School
PeerSpirit
Voyageur Outward Bound School
Widjiwagan YMCA Camp
Wilderness Hawaii
Woodswomen

Trekking

Trekking is travel on foot—walking long distances over a number of days or weeks. You may or may not be carrying your own pack; many organized international treks in countries like Nepal include hired porters to carry the load for you. Some treks use horses or mules to transport gear. You may or may not be camping out; some treks include staying in small guest houses along the way.

My own trek in the Himalayas was strictly a do-it-yourself version. I hooked up with two other Americans, a doctor and a nurse (it couldn't hurt to travel with my own medical team), and we chose a route that we knew would guarantee food and places to stay. Without the burden of carrying tents, food, and cooking equipment, we were able to carry enough for our personal needs in our backpacks. We rented down sleeping bags and jackets in Kathmandu, and off we went. We used Stephen Bezruchka's book, *A Guide to Trekking in Nepal*,[29] which was invaluable.

I didn't completely comprehend until I got there that trekking is just traveling the way the Nepalese do. Outside of Kathmandu and Pokhara, there are very few roads suitable for motor vehicles in that mountainous country. Instead, wide paths, sometimes paved with stone, wind their way up and down mountainsides. They serve as pedestrian highways.

When it's time to climb a mountain, the track doesn't switch back and forth to keep the climb as gentle as possible; it just turns into stairs. I spent hours each day climbing up and down stairs. (The first time I saw a stair-climbing machine in a gym, I thought it was training equipment for trekking in Nepal.) Luckily, at the top of almost every steep stair climb is a teahouse that provides the perfect place to stop and rest.

All manner of freight is transported along those routes—you may pass mule trains of thirty mules, with the lead mule sporting a bell and lots of red tassels. You will undoubtedly be passed by Nepalese carrying heavy loads. I'll never forget one morning when I was climbing a long set of stone stairs cut into the mountainside, maintaining a deliberate pace, when I heard a noise beside me and turned to see a barefoot Nepalese man passing me on his way up at a running pace, six wooden crates of Coca Cola bottles strapped to his back. Another man we passed had a wooden chair tied to his back; an old woman was tied to the chair. He had been trekking for several days and was still two days away from the hospital where he was taking her for treatment.

Mountain treks are measured in elevation gained as much as miles covered. The Annapurna circuit is a well-known circle trek around that magnificent peak. The distance is forty-five miles, and usually takes about three weeks to complete. The total climbs and descents amount to thirty thousand feet, and the highest pass you will cross is at seventeen thousand feet. Other treks are not nearly as vigorous, but conditioning is required for any mountain trek. High-altitude trekking can cause altitude sickness, although slow ascents and planned overnights at lower altitudes can somewhat lessen the effects.

Trekking Trips

Visit the Himalayas, Pakistan, or Africa in the company of local guides. You can spend eight days trekking with the caribou in Alaska or twenty-five days exploring regions of India and Nepal. Find out more from:

Adventure Trekking
Alaska Women of the Wilderness
Equinox Wilderness Expeditions
Himalayan High Treks
Lois Lane Expeditions
Skylink
Travel Walji's
Wildwise
Woodswomen

Walking, Hiking, Trekking, and Backpacking Gear

Backpacks

There are two basic kinds of backpacks: internal and external frame packs. Your choice should be guided by the type of trails you will be hiking on and the fit of the pack to your body. Buy a pack from a store with knowledgeable staff; an improper fit can hamper your ability to carry loads, making you tire more quickly.

Internal frame packs fit close to your back. They have no exposed aluminum frame parts to catch on rocks and branches, making them easier to control in rugged terrain. Aluminum stays that slide into the pack should be bent to help adjust the pack to the shape of your body. This makes it more difficult to borrow an internal frame pack and have a correct fit.

External frame packs are appropriate for developed trails. The frame is curved to match the curve of your back; the weight is distributed to the hip belt. You can strap your sleeping bag and pad easily to the outside frame, which allows you to carry lots of gear.

Women can suffer real discomfort when forced to use packs and other outdoor equipment designed for men. Smaller packs are not the answer. Besides, there are large women who need backpacks too. Proportions must be redesigned to fit a woman's body. When buying a backpack, Lynn Thomas, author of *The Backpacking Woman*[30] suggests you watch out for:

•Too-tall frames that force the head forward, producing stiff necks and cramped upper-back muscles;

•Frames that are too broad, which can bruise upper arms on narrow-shouldered women;

•Broad, untapered shoulder straps, which cut painfully into breasts;

•Sternum straps placed too low, which constrict breasts and breathing;

•Inadequately padded hip belts, which produce blisters and bruises (because women's pelvic bones are shaped differently than men's).

Several pack manufacturers have responded to women's needs by designing packs with narrow torsos, special straps, and a lower center of gravity. Look for women's packs designed by North Face, Kelty, Mountainsmith, Lowe, and Mountain Systems.

Boots

Boots are the most important piece of gear you'll buy. Purchase them long in advance of any major hiking trip. Use them during training hikes to break them in. All-leather boots last longer, especially on rough trails, but leather/fabric combinations are lighter and much easier to break in. Ask for boots designed on a women's last (form). Vasque and Hi-Tec are brands that offer multiple insoles for proper width. Women's heels tend to be narrower than men's, so watch for slippage at the heel, which can cause blisters on the trail. Waterproof your boots, if necessary.

Sleeping Bags

Sleeping bags are filled with natural down or synthetic fill like Quallofil or Polarguard for warmth. Down compresses better, but synthetic fills retain their insulating qualities when wet. Sleeping bags are rated by the temperature to which they will keep you warm; most campers will find a 20° or 5° bag sufficient.

Many average-size women find standard sleeping bags too long and extra wide. North Face sells a bag for petite women (up to 5'2") called the "Littlefoot." Kelty's "Hot Foot" sleeping bag is proportioned for women, with added insulation at the bottom to keep your feet warm.

Clothing

One way to greatly add to your comfort is to wear two pairs of socks when hiking. A thin inner sock of cotton/nylon blend, polypropylene, or other synthetic is best. The outer sock should be thick; wool is preferable except in high heat. The socks rub against each other and absorb friction that would otherwise be transferred to your feet. Bring a light pair of shoes to wear around camp; I prefer slip-ons, which save time during nighttime toilet breaks. Teva sandals can be used for this purpose and can also be worn for swimming and light hiking.

The secret to dressing for hiking and backpacking trips is to wear several layers that you can put on and take off during the day. When hiking uphill makes you warm, peel off your sweater and just wear your long-sleeved shirt. At the summit, when you stop to take in the view and enjoy a drink of water, and the breeze on your sweaty body creates a chill—put the sweater back on and add your windbreaker after a few minutes. Clothes and gear will be determined largely by the weather; be prepared for weather changes—even summer hikes require more than just shorts and a T-shirt.

Think in terms of three basic layers of clothing. Cool to cold weather hikes require an inner layer of long underwear. I'm a big fan of cotton clothing, but even I have to admit that cotton thermals are just no good when wet. Polypropylene and other synthetics "wick" the perspiration from your skin, moving moisture away to keep your body dry and warm. Zanika Long Jaynes let you pee without taking your pants down (see Section II, "How to Pee in the Woods" for details).

Next, wear a long-sleeved shirt of wool or synthetic fiber; you can get away with a cotton blend here. A wool sweater, pile vest, or jacket makes the top layer; wool retains heat when wet, making it preferable to cotton. Pants should be of wool, pile, or polypropylene—bring two pairs, so you can switch off on multiday trips (substitute shorts in hot weather). Special hiking pants have zip-off legs that let you switch quickly from pants to shorts.

If there's even the slightest chance of rain, pack a waterproof outer layer—a rain jacket and pants or a poncho. Get rain gear large enough to fit over all the other layers so that you won't feel like a stuffed sausage while wearing it. Always pack a wool hat—a soft cap that pulls on over your head packs well and can be worn while sleeping if the nights are cold.

If you're worried about spending a lot of money on clothing, here's a budget shopping plan: *Dig in your closet for:* shirts and pants. *Borrow:* wool hat, rain gear. *Buy new:* polypropylene long underwear, inner (liner) socks. *Buy used or army surplus:* wool socks, wool pants, wool sweater, poncho, or rain gear.

The future of the remaining old-growth trees in our national forests has become the subject of Oregon's own family feud. Like a distant relative, I knew the arguments on both sides but really hadn't jumped into the fray. Oh, I had an opinion; I just didn't feel equipped to argue it very well. That's why I joined Ancient Forest Adventures on a hiking trip into the old-growth forest. I already believed we should save the trees; I wanted Mary Vogel to tell me *why*.

Mary Vogel started Ancient Forest Adventures in 1990 to help more Americans learn about their endangered natural heritage—the ancient forests of the Pacific Northwest. "They are every bit as magnificent as the Grand Canyon or Yellowstone National Park," Mary says, "and I want to help people experience this place in the most relaxed, safe, and knowledgeable way possible."

The six-day trip consisted of daily hikes along trails near the Oregon Coast Range. Mary prepared vegetarian meals for us at Oregon House, a comfortable lodge overlooking the Pacific Ocean in Yachats that served as our base camp. Each morning we laced up our hiking boots, packed lunch and snacks into our daypacks, and set off. Our group numbered a half-dozen; the others had traveled from Texas, Florida, and Alabama just to get a look at our trees.

Only a few paces onto the Cape Perpetua trail that first day, Mary conducted our first impromptu lesson—how to differentiate between sword and deer ferns (the secret is in the spores).

A half-hour later we entered the cathedral of the old-growth forest. Our joking banter fell away as we reverently took in the majestic bark columns, leaning our heads back to survey the vaulted ceiling of the verdant canopy above. Chittering sounds dispersed the silence. Squirrels, the forest sentinels who announce the presence of predators, warned their neighbors to beware of humankind.

In that lofty grove we learned to identify the bark of the spruce trees, and the lacy foliage of the hemlock. I was amazed when Mary explained that the bark of the Douglas fir can grow to ten feet in thickness by the time the tree is seven hundred and fifty years old. That thick exterior offers protection from forest fires, leaving the tree viable even when as much as half the bark has burned away.

The forest could survive and compensate for almost everything but the saw.

We followed the Hobbit Trail another day; it was a scene that could make you believe in druids. Passing a stand of second-growth trees decorated with fluorescent-green lichen, we entered a grove of rhododendrons twenty feet high. Mushrooms of great variety lined both sides of the trail; the new arrivals sported moss and pine needle hats where they'd pushed up through the ground. We exclaimed over fiery red russulas and coral mushrooms, collected prized chanterelles for dinner and dutifully ran our fingers along the slimy top of another type before learning its unofficial name—cowboy's handkerchief!

Even the rain was benign, drizzling lightly while we were under tree cover and abating when we emerged to hike a section of beach. I felt embraced by the forest's fertility; I was sure that if a button dropped onto the trail, it would grow into another jacket.

Codependence is a fact of life in the deep woods. Fallen trees incubate spruce and hemlock saplings, and one hundred and fifty years later, the adult trees display buttressed root formations as a permanent memorial to the nurse logs that nourished their adolescence. Dead standing trees, called snags, play their part too. Even a century after the tree dies, the snag remains an apartment house for spotted owls, pileated woodpeckers, and small mammals.

Free samples of edible plants and berries along the trail rivaled a supermarket grand opening: the wood sorrel's lemony tang; miners' lettuce, with enough vitamin C to prevent scurvy among gold miners; and the sweet-sour taste of the elderberry. We called a warning over our shoulders not to step on the orange-bellied Pacific newts that crossed our trail; later we studied a giant salamander that froze in its tracks when we approached.

Our easy pace was determined by the abilities of the group and all you had to do for a rest stop was ask a question. We didn't need to conquer mountains, we were having too much fun.

Our wanderings took us past a pond where great blue herons lorded over dark-eyed juncos, and beavers constructed lodges below.

Mary pointed out the cattails in the marshy wetland, explaining how native tribes roasted the brown tops and ate them like corn on the cob. They cooked the root and stalk, and used the fluffy seed to stuff pillows and bedding, and make baby diapers and menstrual pads.

I kept a mental list of the myriad uses indigenous tribes had for plants they gleaned from the woods: the waterproof spores of the club moss made a natural baby powder. Some lichens were edible; others used as dyes. The smoke from burning a plant called pearly everlasting treated paralysis. A paste from the sword fern effectively salved wounds.

Before this experience, I'd found it difficult to remember the names of trees and birds and plants. I consoled myself by thinking that I could enjoy the natural world without having to label it. This time was different; traveling through the woods with Mary, a former park ranger, let me solidify each day's knowledge by building on it the next. I understood and could explain some basic aspects of ancient forest ecology.

Mary Vogel's clients come from across the U.S., Canada , Australia, Japan, and Europe, and she is not shy about encouraging them to go forth as advocates for the ancient forest. "Once they have experienced the forest personally, my clients are well equipped to talk to legislators and to public policymakers," Mary says. Since decisions on old-growth issues are made in Washington, D.C., by officials who may never have experienced the ancient forest themselves, constituent contacts can be persuasive. "I bring literature for each group with the latest on the forest issue and tell my clients specifically what they can do about it," she said. "One of my all-women's groups drafted and sent a letter to their congresspeople and the newspaper while still on the trip."

Describing other eco-tourism practices of her company, Mary said, "Without talking a whole lot about it, I try to model less consumptive ways of relating to the earth, like using cloth instead of paper napkins, and resealable boxes to carry our sandwiches rather than a new plastic bag every day. There's even a message in the food I serve. I try to use organically grown food, which is much less polluting to the earth, and I serve vegetarian meals.

In the evenings, we watched video documentaries relating to the forest issue that Mary had brought along. One night, Mary joined us in the sitting room dressed in turn-of-the-century costume. Portraying Dr. Bethenia Owens-Adair, a historical figure from Oregon's pioneer days, Mary took us back in time to what life—and the state—had once been like. She vividly described what we now see as forest as a sparsely tufted patch on a region that has been stripped bald.

After her talk, Bethenia turned and asked us some very pointed questions. "For years when I had a rural medical practice in Warrenton, Oregon, I made many a house call by foot because the trails were so overhung with vegetation, not even a rider on horseback could get through. Now if you go up in one of the Wright Brothers' contraptions, those aeroplanes, nowadays, you'll see that the trees are just a little stripe along the road, hiding the fact that almost all the rest have been stripped away. So where has all the forest gone?"

We looked at one another, silent.

Our stammering attempts to answer brought one point perfectly clear: saving the earth is not someone else's job. It's mine and yours and ours.

Empowerment, Leadership, and Wilderness Skills

Almost all the outdoor adventure programs listed in this book teach basic outdoor skills; whether you sign up for it or not, on any camping trip you'll learn how to set up camp, live, cook, and sleep in the outdoors. However, there are courses that focus specifically on skill-building for those who want to be more self-sufficient in the outdoors. These courses use the term "wilderness skills."

Another type of course (which may include some instruction on wilderness skills) presents physical challenges to help you build confidence and overcome fears. These are usually described as "empowerment" courses.

A related kind of trip focuses on the intellectual and emotional challenges of leadership. They use the out-of-doors as a classroom and may incorporate "ropes courses" and "team building" to help you gain leadership skills that you can apply in your life at home or at work. Even if you don't plan to spend much time in the outdoors, these courses can be invaluable if you want to expand your leadership skills. These are often described as "leadership development" courses.

A specialized type of leadership training called "outdoor leadership" builds skills for those who want to lead outdoor and wilderness trips, either as a professional or as a volunteer.

Team Building

Meeting natural physical challenges (a rock wall to climb, a river to cross) as part of a team gives you an opportunity to think about group decision making and learn how to become a more effective team member at home or in the workplace.

If you participate as an individual, you will be assigned to a team and learn communication methods that you can apply to other teams you work with in the future. If you bring your own group (family, support group, or work team) you will learn valuable lessons about team dynamics that will help you operate more smoothly in the future. Many corporate, governmental, and nonprofit work teams report great benefits from outdoor retreats. Team building is often incorporated as part of other trips.

Challenge Course

Sometimes called a "ropes course," this is a set of physical obstacles in the outdoors. Individuals or teams surmount challenges using walls, cables, climbing ropes, trapezes, perches, ladders, beams, and platforms.

Our lives are organized to eliminate the unexpected, the dangerous, and the unknown. An empowerment course gives you the opportunity to test yourself, to draw from personal reserves not frequently called upon. Although you may go alone, you will find there is a group energy that develops; everyone in the group helps one another succeed. Everyone encourages one another to go for the extra challenge that each individual might not take on by herself. Safety and emotional support are paramount; this is not boot camp, where humiliation and failure are thought to build character.

Wilderness Skills Programs

Classes that teach basic outdoor skills cover techniques in map and compass reading, first aid, and survival in outdoor situations. These courses will help you feel more comfortable and independent in the wilderness. Check out the programs these groups offer:

Adirondack Mountain Club
Adventures for Women
Alaska Women of the Wilderness
Appalachian Mountain Club
Colorado Outward Bound School
Hurricane Island Outward Bound School
Skadi

Wilderness Hawaii
Wildwise
Women of the Wilderness Australia
Woodswomen

Empowerment Programs

Empowerment programs are designed to help you get in touch with and develop your personal power. These programs are for those who want to feel more self-confident, who want to test and expand their limits. Facilitators may use a challenge course, discussions, meditation—any number of methods to help you achieve your goals. Groups offering empowerment programs are:

Adventure Associates
Alaska Women of the Wilderness
Canadian Outward Bound Wilderness School
Colorado Outward Bound School
Hurricane Island Outward Bound School
Inside Outside Adventures
Mahoosuc Guide Service
PeerSpirit
Wilderness Hawaii
Women of the Wilderness Australia
Women's Outdoor Adventure Cooperative

Leadership Development Programs

These programs help you acquire and practice leadership and decision-making skills that you can apply to your life when you return home. Even if you've spent relatively little time outdoors in the past, or don't plan to spend much more in the future, you may benefit by removing yourself from your customary environment and challenging your abilities outdoors.

Inside Outside Adventures
North Carolina Outward Bound School
Pacific Crest Outward Bound School

Wildwise
Woodswomen

Outdoor Leadership Skills Development

These are courses for those who want to be leaders in outdoor programs; if you want to explore working outside, leading groups pro-
fessionally or as a volunteer, these trainings provide advanced-level
skills as well as group management theory and practice.

Some of your learning will come by examining how you deal with
difficult situations that arise during the course. By taking a turn as
group leader, you will learn about your personal leadership style and
how differences in styles affect group management. You will find
opportunities to explore your values and acknowledge your personal
strengths. Find out more from:

Adventures for Women
Alaska Women of the Wilderness
Colorado Outward Bound School
National Outdoor Leadership School
Women in the Wilderness
Women of the Wilderness Australia
Women's Outdoor Adventure Cooperative

What About Outward Bound?

If you think Outward Bound only works with troubled youth, or
that they force people into an outdoor "survival school," you're
wrong. The organization helps people of all ages discover and act
upon their own strengths; seasoned instructors encourage participants to do their best. Empowerment, wilderness skills, and leadership development are part of every trip. No coercion is involved.

Outward Bound was founded in Wales in 1941 by the progressive
educators Kurt Hahn and Sir Lawrence Holt. They saw that younger
seamen were often unable to survive the ordeal of floundering in
harsh conditions, while older seamen fared better. Hahn and Holt felt
the problem was a lack of confidence rather than any shortage of skill

or equipment. Thus, they proposed a training program that would challenge the young seamen to recognize the depth of their abilities and strengths. The name refers to the moment a ship leaves its moorings, committing itself to the open sea. Today there are forty-four Outward Bound schools in twenty-two countries.

Over the years, various Outward Bound schools have scheduled five-day empowerment courses to help women survivors of breast cancer and other cancers renew their self-confidence and self-esteem. You can sign-up your own local cancer support group or join other cancer survivors. Although no longer regularly scheduled in their program, Colorado Outward Bound School contracts with hospitals and local support groups and will try to accommodate your interest in attending one of these sessions. They currently offer a three-day, co-ed session called "Challenging the Course of Cancer." Contact COBS Health Services program and ask about future open enrollment programs.

Hurricane Island Outward Bound School has a week-long canoe program for survivors of sexual abuse and assault, as well as a five-day program for women who have or have had breast or ovarian cancer.

Colorado Outward Bound School regularly schedules three-day "Survivor of Violence" courses for victims of sexual assault, incest, and domestic violence. Coed courses also include a fourteen-day mountaineering course with an emphasis on recovery from addiction; four-day courses that deal with recovery from alcoholism, drug dependence, or eating disorders; and a three-day course for male and female Vietnam veterans.

There are Outward Bound schools in Australia, Belgium, Bermuda, Canada, Czech Republic, France, Germany, Hong Kong, Indonesia, Japan, Kenya, Malaysia, Netherlands, New Zealand, Singapore, South Africa, Sri Lanka, Tanzania, United Kingdom, United States, Zambia, and Zimbabwe. For more information, contact the International Secretariat, Outward Bound Trust Ltd., Chestnut Field, Regent Place, Rugby CV21 2RJ, Great Britain (44/788-560423 or fax: 44/788 541069).

I was a vice president of an insurance company in Maryland. The company that owned ours was in Zurich, Switzerland, so I had an opportunity to travel abroad. I also traveled all over the United States on business for about two years. I got the bug and started traveling more and more for personal reasons.

In the beginning, I started out doing fitness trips—aerobic workouts in Big Sur, retreats in other parts of California. Each time, I got a little bit more adventurous. Then I decided to see major cities in the U.S. Once a month I would go on a trip to a major city and spend four or five days there. No one ever hassled me as an African-American woman traveling alone.

Then I went on package tours of European countries—the motorcoach route—but when I came home I felt like I'd never been anywhere because I stayed in hotels that were just like at home.

I started experimenting with traveling on my own. I went to a spa in Mexico and did some more traveling in Europe. When I came back, I felt that I needed to take the next step so I started looking at the adventure travel companies. I took an adventure trip to Thailand with a group of twelve people.

Soon I learned about women's travel companies and signed up for Adventure Associates' "Empowerment and Challenge Personal Discovery Retreat." On the first day, we did exercises on the ground to build trust and confidence among the members of the team. There were about fifteen of us. We did a lot of sharing and I thought the stuff was pretty easy. So I started volunteering to do things—we had to climb six feet up a tree and then turn around and jump off backward and let the group catch you. Other people seemed afraid, but I trusted that the group would catch me.

When we got to the site Saturday morning and I saw the ropes course set way up in the trees, I was terrified and so was everyone else. Beforehand, I had thought, How bad can it be? Even if you knew what to expect, there was something about actually seeing our instructor up in the trees, with the ropes and stuff, that was scary.

Before we started that day, we sat in a circle and shared how we felt. There was a woman there who worked for Nike, and I remember saying, "I hate to use your phrase, but I'm just gonna do it—whatever the exercises are, I'm not going to think about it." So during the whole day, I didn't think about how difficult something was going to be. When it came to my turn, I just did it.

There was a combination of exercises on the ground and aerial things. The thing I got the most bruises from was the wall. It was a wooden wall, made of planks, about seventeen feet high. They told us we had a certain amount of time to get everyone over the top, from one side to the other, and that each person could only assist three times. They gave us crash helmets, and then we had to figure out how we could get everyone over the wall.

At the top of the wall was a ledge— you could stand on the ledge and assist from the top as well as the bottom, and we soon realized that somebody had to stand on the top to help pull people over. We got the first one or two up by building a human pyramid. We picked the smallest and most athletic to walk up the backs and shoulders of the rest. That's how I got the bruises.

When I was at the top, it was difficult because I have a fear of heights. I felt like I had someone's life in my hands, since I was holding their hands as they walked up the wall. I knew that if I leaned over too far, they would fall, and I would fall with them.

Another thing I did was to walk from one end of a log and back, between two trees. Sort of like walking a tightrope except it was a log. When I first went up there, I couldn't breathe. It seems like a hundred feet up, but it was probably only twenty. So I got up there, and walked the log, and was finally feeling okay. On my way back, Cris, the leader, said, "Stop where you are." I did, and then she said, "Now, take a step backward." I thought, If you think I'm walking backward on this log, you are crazy. And she said, "I know you can do it. All I'm asking is for you to take one step." So I thought about it, and then I took one step. Then she said, "I know you can take just one more." And that's the way I did it—not thinking about the end, just taking it one step at a time—and I walked all the way backward.

Then they put you on a tightrope, and you have to walk that. That really scared me, because when I got nervous and started shaking, it shook the wire too. I got three-fourths of the way across, and the wire was shaking really bad.

After you get across the tightrope, they tell you you're not going back down the ladder, you have to rappel down (lower yourself down with a rope). When you let the rope out, you drop, and when you pull it in, you stop. It takes a coordinated effort between letting out some rope and using your feet to bounce yourself off the tree so you don't hit it. It was pretty frightening.

I didn't tell them of my fear of heights; I had come so far and I felt it was too late to back out. Everyone was afraid of the course in some way.

The most difficult challenge I saved for last. There was a bare tree standing upright with all its branches off. You had to climb a steel ladder to get near the top, but the ladder didn't go all the way up and it would swing around while we were climbing. So first you had to figure out how to get from the ladder to a standing position on the top. Some people would get on to the log but not be standing up, and it would take them twenty minutes to get from a stooped position to a standing position.

Then once you're standing on top of this tree, which is the width of a medium-sized pizza, you have to jump and grab a trapeze swing about five feet away. That was the hardest thing—people would stand up there for twenty or thirty minutes without moving. Everyone else on the ground would give them ideas on what to do and encourage them.

I made up my mind that I had to stand up immediately because of my fear of heights. I didn't want to sit on top for twenty minutes with everyone trying to convince me to stand up. I was determined that when I got off that ladder, I would come up standing up, and I did. I jumped for the trapeze after about two minutes, and I missed it. I wound up swinging in the air, because my team had me on a rope belay. All the time you are climbing up, you don't think about being on a rope, because you're just terrified. I swung around for a while, grabbed the log and climbed up again. I jumped a second time and missed it again. Then I said, I've given it my best; I jumped twice.

All the members of my team really encouraged and supported me. My tent mate, Pia, was from Denmark. She saved that log thing for last too. And she walked up to me and said, "I think I've done enough, I don't need to prove anything else." And I talked her into doing it—she climbed up, and she made it.

Cris and Sandy, the leaders, were right there with us. One stayed on the ground and gave us instructions on what to do to get up; the other was up on the platform to handle all the ropes. They just seemed to know how far to go and when to stop.

Sandy took pictures. She sent me the picture of when I jumped to the trapeze, and it showed that my hand had actually touched the bar. I took pictures of other people making the jump—some were crying when they did it. One woman climbed all the way up there, didn't do it, then waited twenty minutes and climbed back up. She missed it, but it took a lot of guts to go back up.

When I was standing on the ground, I thought the things we were going to try could not humanly be done. Once I did it, it was a lot easier than it looked. I thought, Wow, that was tough, but not impossible. We really faced our fears out there.

As my trips became more bold and adventurous, I got more and more bold at work. I wonder sometimes how much of an effect that empowerment experience had on my getting up the courage to quit my job. Even though I can't put my finger on it, I really think it had a lot to do with it. I look at fear differently now.

Quitting my job was like jumping off that platform—taking a big leap into the unknown. After that trip, I'm not really afraid anymore. I'm sometimes a bit nervous, but I'm not *afraid*, afraid.

It's hard to explain to other people. My mom still can't believe that I made six figures a year and that I would just quit. She can't believe that I'm selling my house and all my stuff. I have a Mercedes, all I ever wanted, and it's too much. There was nothing left for me to buy.

I'm going to get my affairs in order and then spend a year in Europe. Every step I've taken has led me to the next step. Each time I come back from a trip, I'm different; I have more confidence in myself.

Retreats and Spiritual Journeys

There are needs within us, truths that need quiet space to emerge. Most of us feel the need to periodically get away and reflect on the lives we have created for ourselves. Although not advertised as such, many of the trips in this book become mini-retreats, where time spent traveling with a group of women allows you to reflect on your life. If you don't want to leave that aspect to chance, if you crave a special atmosphere of quiet and meditation, if you want to practice yoga, or travel with a group leader concerned as much with inner reflection as with physical adventure, then explore the options listed below.

At the Mountains

Hike along rugged trails and broad valleys from your base camp or canoe, swim, and sun yourself from a mountainside chalet. Enjoy journal writing, discussions, and relaxation. Renew yourself with daily stretches and hikes. Take time to develop a quiet inner world, using guided meditation and other Eastern practices.

Adventure Associates
CenterPoint in Aspen
Earthwise

In the Water

Combine kayaking and yoga practice or scuba diving and journal writing. Unobtrusive dolphin swims with a licensed psychotherapist encourage you to use the sea as a source of symbols and a metaphor for the inner space of your life. An island retreat might take you to Hawaii, Mexico, or the Caribbean and range from an intensive personal discovery workshop to a relaxing resort vacation.

Adventure Associates
Adventure Spirit Hawaii

Adventure Women
Eco-Explorations
Elakah! Expeditions
Equinox Wilderness Expeditions
Hawk, I'm Your Sister
The Heart of Adventure

Writing Retreats

The Flight of the Mind Writing Workshops for Women offers two one-week sessions each summer at a retreat center on the McKenzie River in the foothills of Oregon's Cascade Mountains. For brochure, send a first-class stamp to Flight of the Mind, 622 Southeast 29th Avenue, Portland, OR 97214 (503/236-9862). Canoe down the Penobscot River in Maine each morning and develop your writing skills in the afternoon. Explore your inner and outer landscapes in Northern England with morning workshops and gentle afternoon walks or practice journal writing at a New Zealand lodge.

Bushwise Women
Hawk, I'm Your Sister
Her Wild Song
Skadi

Dream Quests and Vision Quests

Explore the powerful messages of dreams by sharing them, drawing them, and acting them out. Visit ancient goddess sites in Europe or venture out on your own spiritual journey in the high chaparral of Los Padres National Forest in Southern California or the Rocky Mountains in Colorado. Programs may emphasize music, storytelling, or mask making.

Alaska Women of the Wilderness
Earthlodge and Womenspeak Journeys
The Heart of Adventure
Her Wild Song
Journeywell

Outdoor Leadership Training Seminars
PeerSpirit
Tours of Interest to Women
Venus Adventures
Women of the Wilderness Australia

Getaways

If you just want quiet time, with no program or leader, consider a getaway. Talk, walk, read, or simply rest. If you want to alternate adventure and renewal, you may be able to hike, canoe, or swim. Whether staying at an island retreat, log cabin, or working ranch, refresh yourself in the natural world. Special lesbian getaways feature cruises, island vacations, and resorts.

Club Le Bon
Earthwise
Inside Outside Adventures
New Dawn
Olivia Cruises and Resorts
Prairie Women Adventures and Retreat
Skylink
Wild Women Expeditions

Yoga

The **Kripalu Center for Yoga and Health** offers several week-long women-only workshops, including "Women and Yoga," "Women at Midlife," and "A Woman's Journey Out-of-Doors." You can reach them at P.O. Box 793 Lennox, MA 01240 (800/967-3577). Companies that offer yoga as part of an outdoor trip include:

Adventure Spirit Hawaii
Equinox Wilderness Expeditions
The Heart of Adventure

I went on the "Women's Wilderness Experience and Vision Quest" with Mahoosuc Guide Service. The leader, Polly Mahoney, was gentle and encouraged us to try things, but no one felt pushed. She challenged each of us in the way that we needed to be challenged. The whole group didn't have to do an activity in the same way. (Everyone doesn't have to climb to the top of a cliff. For one person, the challenge might be just in tying in.) She respected where we were and the process we were going through. Polly taught us campcraft. I learned new things that I hadn't known about sanitation in the woods and about being kind to the environment.

Polly's co-leader on this trip was a psychotherapist named Paula Gates, who helped lead the spiritual side of the trip. We meditated and did yoga. We sat in a circle and talked and shared ideas, and just relaxed to the point where it was easy to get into guided visualizations. There were six or seven other women from all around the U.S., and I felt comfortable and not at all self-conscious with the group. There was a nice age mixture in the group—we ranged in age from women in their twenties to those in their fifties.

It was wonderful to be doing these spiritual practices out of doors—it added a special element that I had not experienced when I'd tried doing them inside. We did some body work, and one evening after a hike, we all gave one another a foot massage. I never would have thought of doing that, but it was wonderful to be able to relax and lie back and accept that.

We camped beside Caribou Mountain, and on the second day we set out to climb the mountain. One young woman in her early twenties was out of shape—she had not done a lot of outdoor activities and felt she would not be physically able to make it up the mountain. Polly had brought one of her sled dogs on the trip, and the dog actually helped the young woman get all the way to the top. The dog encouraged her over the steep parts, and since she was holding on to the leash, the dog actually pulled her at some points. One of the most exciting moments of the trip was when she reached the summit.

This was the first women's trip I'd been on. I found that little things, like setting up my own tent and not negotiating my space meant a lot to me. My husband is really supportive of my doing things, but it was so easy to fall into role-playing when we went camping together. Being alone in my tent was a new experience for me—I picked a great spot, and I slept well all night. I liked the idea of not being with anyone who already knew me—no one could anticipate what I might or might not be able to do. That freed me up to try out new parts of myself. I'm sorry that Polly isn't currently offering this trip.

I've done several other women's trips with Mahoosuc—the women's dog sled weekend really got me interested in dog sledding. I also took a women's whitewater canoe instructional trip. Recently, I was very fortunate to join Polly and a group of women to go out west on a month-long canoe trip on the San Juan river. On all of these trips I've felt able to challenge myself in a safe way.

After that first trip I made a lot of changes in my life. I had been in business with my sister, and we decided to get out of it and go on to other things. I was tired of working inside—I wanted to work in the outdoors. So I bought a dog sled and then bought two puppies from Polly and her partner, Kevin; Kevin later gave me a couple of dogs from his team. I'm doing things now that I wouldn't have ever thought a forty-year-old woman would do, like mushing dogs across the back woods of Maine, and working part-time for Outward Bound. It all started out with the vision quest weekend.

I talk a lot with my husband about all the changes I'm going through. We're both enjoying the fact that now I'm the one bringing new adventures and activities into the relationship.

I discovered through these trips that I am most who I am when I'm outdoors, and that my spiritual connection is with the outdoors. If I could live in a house built of windows, I would do that. The outdoors is my church.

Spa Vacations

What comes to mind when you imagine a spa vacation? For Europeans, spa retreats meant healing thermal waters, mud packs, and evenings of dancing in grand old ballrooms in formal attire. Americans imagine spas as either private enclaves where the rich and famous get beauty makeovers, or "fat farms" with boot camp images of pain and suffering. All of those pictures have drifted out of focus.

As health and fitness habits of Americans have changed, spas have evolved and expanded, incorporating new age practices, feminist principles, and alternative health and outdoor adventures to address the needs of the body, mind, and spirit. At the same time, they have increased in number from about forty American spas in 1980 to over two hundred today.

Spas are emerging as places where adults can go to camp—where you can choose from many daily activities, meet others in an easy way, be yourself, and be good to yourself. The term *spa* is defined very broadly, covers a wide category of services, and includes everything from cruises or resorts with a "spa package" of whirlpools, water aerobics, and massage, to highly structured residential programs that provide personal trainers and a broad range of workshops. There are vegetarian spas, spas that specialize in stress reduction and spas that can help you stop smoking.

Choosing a Spa

About 75 percent of all spa clients are women. While a handful of spas are for women only, most spas rotate women's, men's, and coed sessions. Prices range from $700 per week at the Women's Mountain Tune-Up Mini Spa to $4,000 per week at the award-winning Golden Door (modeled on Japanese Honjin Inns with a ratio of three staff members per guest). Some of the more interesting options include:

•**Skylonda Retreat** in the redwood forests on the San Francisco Peninsula regularly schedules women's weeks. They have a unique post-natal program for nursing mothers and their babies, a parent/child week, and a special week of seminars for menopausal women. The cost is $2400 per week. Skylonda Retreat, 16350 Skyline Boulevard, Woodside, CA 94062 (800/851-2222 worldwide).

•Founded in 1940, **Rancho La Puerta,** three hours south of Los Angeles at Tecate, Mexico, inspired many imitators to offer a mind and body tune-up. They featured spa cuisine before the term was invented, yoga and tai chi before they became hip. With separate facilities for men and women, this retreat honors the landscape and architecture of Mexico. The cost range is $1300-$2100 per week. Rancho La Puerta, P.O. Box 463057, Escondido, CA 92046 (800/443-7565).

•Stay in a restored stagecoach inn high in the Colorado Rockies and hike, cycle, and ride mountain bikes with former Olympic athletes at the **Women's Mountain Tune-Up Mini Spa**. The cost is $700 for six days, summers only. Women's Mountain Tune-Up Mini Spa, Keystone Activities & Dining Center, Box 38, Keystone, CO 80435 (800/451-5930).

For More Information

Spa Finders, organized in 1986, is a travel agency that specializes in matching each person to the proper spa vacation. They will consult with you on your desired activities and budget, send you brochures, and help you book your trip at no charge to you. Their catalog lists over two hundred spas worldwide, organized by categories such as stress reduction, weight loss and nutrition, supportive retreat environments, outdoor adventure programs, and new age and spiritual quests. Their quarterly newsletter offers special discounts. For more information, call or write to 91 Fifth Avenue, Suite 301, New York, NY 10003 (800/255-7727).

International Travel

"I'll never forget waking up early one morning in Lamu, on an Arab-style ornately carved bed covered with mosquito netting. From outside I could hear the Islamic morning prayers and the stirring of the neighborhood at four or five in the morning, people getting up and starting their charcoal fires—I could smell the smoke and the donkeys walking down the alleys. I sat up and looked out the window past the bougainvillea and saw the sunrise over pastel architecture and thatched roofs, and knew I was in a foreign land." That's how Gail Winterman describes her trip to Africa with Adventure Associates. As director of a women's health education program in the U.S., she decided to collect surplus medical equipment and supplies to bring over with her. She convinced an army surplus store to donate duffle bags to carry three hundred pounds of adhesive tape, gauze, syringes, and medication she had assembled over four months. A meeting was set up with the Kenyan Women's Medical Association in Nairobi. "The women physicians prepared tea and little sandwiches for us and were extremely gracious. Although it was late in the afternoon—time for them to go home to their families and make dinner—we sat and talked about everything from health care in Kenya to feminism and their parliament. It was a wonderful way to connect with people, and it really affected me."

Making connections. That's the key to international travel with women. Women connecting with women, laughing at the similarities, puzzling over differences, reaching out to one another.

Expand your horizons. Travel in a style completely unlike anything you've ever done before. Take a canal boat through Holland to France, bicycle the back roads of Ireland or the dirt roads of Mexico, kayak the tropical waters of Costa Rica or sail along the coast of Turkey.

Focus on women's history or current issues. Feel safe and secure as you join other women and expand horizons together.

International Tours and Trips

Over fifty companies in this book take travelers to destinations outside the United States. You can go trekking in Nepal, Pakistan, or Uganda, visit goddess sites in Greece and western Europe, or relax at resorts in Mexico and the Ivory Coast. Companies offer everything from safaris in East Africa to spiritual journeys in Switzerland. There are horsepacking trips in Holland, paddling expeditions in Peru, windsurfing vacations in Aruba, and sailing excursions to Turkey. Fly fish in British Columbia or the Bahamas, or snorkel and scuba dive in the Caribbean or Central America. Guides will take you on a walking tour in Italy, canal boating in Wales, or bicycling through Ireland. The index lists companies according to their trip destinations.

Women's Cultural Exchange Programs

Meet women in Tanzania, Kenya, Tibet, Nepal, Australia, Bolivia, and Costa Rica. Join them in their daily activities and stay with them in their homes. Discussion through interpreters allows the sharing of experiences and ideas. Some also include an active component, such as trekking, or an additional excursion, such as a wildlife safari.

Adventure Trekking
Wildwise
Womanpower Enterprises
Women to Women Cross-Cultural Adventures

Join a Group from outside Your Native Country

Join a group organized outside your home country and multiply the adventure! Consider traveling with a group made up of women from another country or culture and share new experiences through each other's eyes. It's a bit more expensive to call and takes longer to communicate by mail, but the benefits are great. British, Australian, and Canadian readers of this book have a myriad of opportunities to join the American groups featured here. U.S. readers are urged to contact the following groups:

Adventure Trekking
Bushwise Women
Canadian Outward Bound Wilderness School
Et-Then
Firma Hagi
Herizen: New Age Sailing for Women
New Dawn
Skadi
Vaarschool Grietje
Wild Women Expeditions
Wildwise
Women of the Wilderness Australia

The first river I canoed extensively with Women in the Wilderness was the Noatak in Alaska in 1984. It was on that trip that I made the resolve to do one river, or part of one river, every year. I've paddled the Missinabi in Ontario, and I'm signed up for an exciting one next August, the Nahanni, which is in the Northwest Territories and a really beautiful river.

In between, I have gone on rivers with my husband and son, and rafted down the Colorado, which was a nice way to cheat. There have been big rivers and little rivers and it's a wonderful thing to have on my docket. Everybody knows I'm doing this, so the question is "Where are you going this year?" instead of "Are you going anywhere?"

I like adventuring on my own, but some things are too much for me to do alone, so then I go with Judith Niemi and Women in the Wilderness.

I did not have a lifelong fantasy to go to the Amazon, but I had spent very little time south of the border, and I was interested to see more. I didn't have apprehensions—I didn't really know what to expect. When I went for my shots, a computer printout said by no means should I go to Peru, because of the political upheaval caused by the Shining Path. But since we would be on the other side of the mountains, there really wasn't any danger.

In the Amazon, we weren't exactly canoeing or kayaking, but we spent lots of days paddling around in little dugout canoes, which were really fun. The forest was totally flooded, so you had to paddle everywhere—that was our basic form of transportation.

At base camp, they would lay out a little menu of things you could do each day. For example, you could go on a bird-watching expedition and try to find some bizarre bird. On one of my favorite days, they took us on motorboats (dragging the dugout canoes behind us) up to a lake. We looked around to see what was there and then paddled back to base camp ourselves.

One of the reasons I chose to go on the trip is because I'm a real water person, and the brochure said that you could swim with pink dolphins. They took us up to Lake Cumaceba to see the dolphins— it's a place where they almost always appear. As soon as we got there, I just flipped overboard and swam out by myself. Within ten minutes, the dolphins were circling me. One came up almost right underneath me, and that was a little startling. I was with them for about an hour and a half, and they were totally curious about me. I really felt that I was communing with them. It was a fantastic experience.

Our group totaled about thirteen, but then some other women were at the base camp too. I had taken my favorite tent, thinking I might want privacy, and it turned out that they really needed me to use that extra tent. So I slept out back behind the rest, which was quite an adventure because at night all the little critters came out. They've got serious snakes down there—pit vipers called fer-de-lances that aren't big but are very deadly. That's why all the people sleep on platforms on stilts.

It gives you a lot to think about; fortunately it's so hot you don't have to pee often at night. One night my tent-mate did have to go out; and we prepared ourselves and went out—not far. We jumped back into the tent, and she was already stretched out as I was taking off my boots, when something came skittering over my shoulder. I flipped it off of me and then picked up the first thing that was handy, which was her leg, and squashed it. All she said was, "Did we get it?" It was a spider.

At first you feel like you're on a big adventure. But when you're actually with the local people, and you have been told to keep the ants and little critters out by being fully covered, while they're running around in their little shorts, you look like a lady from civilization and feel kind of wimpy.

Something special happened to four of us. We took a hike through the jungle to get to a tributary of the Amazon, where we were supposed to meet a boat to go exploring in that region. But when we got there, the boat's motor wasn't working. The four of us ended up camping at the edge of a primitive village—one we had heard about because a shaman from the Achuara tribe lived there who visited our base camp sometimes. Since we couldn't use the boat, and we had provisions for several days, we just holed up there beside his village.

The people there weren't exactly high on tourists. So we just did our own quiet little things and were very respectful. During the day we would go out in dugout canoes with the shaman, and our guide, who was named Moses. On one day they shot a bunch of wild peccary (animals related to hogs), and we saw them dress those in the village.

Another day we watched Moses and the shaman cut a yellow parrot tree down and make paddles from the wood, using only an axe and a machete. We sat around and looked at butterflies and wonderful birds while they made the paddles.

One day the shaman asked if we wanted to have a healing ceremony. We went out and gathered herbs, and he had us over to his place that night. We sat around, and of course, I couldn't understand what he was doing. He blessed the herbs that we gathered by singing and chanting and shaking the rattle for a long time, and he put the herbs into something they called firewater, which was some kind of bad gin. Then he had us all drink about a half glass of the stuff. We had already been fasting for a long time. Judith kept saying, "Do you think we're buzzed?" I didn't know; it was all outside of my reality.

We were supposed to remember our dreams that night for the shaman to interpret in the morning—it was part of the ceremony. Either under the influence of the drink or the whole situation, I just dreamt my brains out. The dreams were all about snakes. In the morning I told the shaman about this big, pink snake, and he told me something about a garlic plant that would guard over me forever. It was a good report. I've wondered about it since then. Sometimes I say, "Where are you now, pink snake?"

I decided at some point that I was so hot that I was going to swim. In this group, I probably swam more than anyone. When I was in the shaman's village, in the early afternoon siesta time, I would go out and float and attach myself to a tree or something because of the current. I could sleep floating, just like a cork, and I think it endeared me to him. I'd look up and here was this shaman with his funny smile full of mottled teeth, laughing and pointing me out to his friends. He quickly learned my name and called me "Treesh." The villagers all swam, and I realized that nothing nibbled at me while I was in there.

I'm always so totally happy on those women's trips. Sure, I will admit to being hot and steamy and wet the whole time we were down there. It rained on us one of the first days we were out walking, and I didn't have my rain gear with me. I started wondering why they didn't take us back to get dry clothes—I just have this Minnesota mentality that I'm going to get hypothermia if I'm wet. Well, of course, that was not a problem down there, although rotting might be.

I love doing things with women, especially with a leader like Judith Niemi. She creates a group with no hierarchy and a feeling of enjoying what's there. It's a pure appreciation of nature. I bailed out of male things long ago—you know my husband used to have estimated times of arrival for every portage!

Once I started going with women, I've never stopped. I've been taking groups of women up to canoe country for twenty-two years. During the last five years, I have run women's retreats called "Celebrate Your Woman Spirit" in a cabin up in northern Minnesota. I much prefer traveling with women, anywhere.

I'm a psychologist and a gerontologist, and I deal with hospice and a lot of people at the end of their lives. From them I've learned that life is about figuring out how to live as fully as possible, and adventures like this create wonderful opportunities to do something memorable.

For Younger Women, Older Women, and across Generations

In addition to the unique kind of support and inspiration we get from being in an environment of all women, at times we feel the need to huddle with our own age group or join hands across generations. Women's travel programs have a direct line into the current issues and needs of women. Trip leaders hear talk around campfires about ways in which women want to connect with each other, and create innovative programs to meet those needs.

Trips for Girls

I love the idea of special programs for girls (aged ten to seventeen) and plan to send my nieces to one as soon as they are old enough! Campers can learn to set up a tent, build a fire, cook outdoors, read a map, and use a compass. Organizations that offer programs for girls are:

Alaska Women of the Wilderness
Canadian Outward Bound Wilderness School
Equinox Wilderness Expeditions
Hawk, I'm Your Sister
Widjiwagan YMCA Camp
Women of the Wilderness Australia
Women's Outdoor Adventure Cooperative

Age-Specific Trips for Women

Widjiwagan YMCA Camp has a trip for women aged nineteen and above. All of **Pacific Crest Outward Bound School's** programs are for women twenty-one and older. **North Carolina Outward Bound School** brings together women twenty-one and older, and thirty and older. **Hurricane Island Outward Bound School** has courses for women eighteen and older, thirty and older, and forty and older. **Rainbow Adventures** defines itself as serving women aged thirty and older. Women forty years and older can take advantage of trips from several groups: **Journeywell, Outdoor Vacations for Women over 40, Paddling South, Rhonda Smith Windsurfing Center, Sylvan Rocks Climbing School and Guide Service,** and **Wander Women.** While not always specifically defining what they mean by the term, the following organizations offer trips for "older women":

Alaska Women of the Wilderness
Bushwise Women
Equinox Wilderness Expeditions
The Heart of Adventure
Sacred Sedona

Cross-Generational Trips

Some of the most exciting developments in women's travel are the many trips being offered across generations. Mothers and daughters, grandmothers, aunts and nieces, or any two women with a special intergenerational bond may want to try hiking, bicycling, climbing, paddling, swimming, cruising, sailing, fishing, or just hanging out together. Groups offering trips in this area include:

Adventure Spirit Hawaii
Alaska Women of the Wilderness
Blue Moon Explorations
Cloud Canyon Wilderness Experience
Elakah! Expeditions
Equinox Wilderness Expeditions
Firma Hagi
The Heart of Adventure
Lois Lane Expeditions
Mariah Wilderness Expeditions
Outdoor Vacations for Women over 40
Wildwise
Womanship
WOMBATS
Women in the Wilderness

Women of the Wilderness Australia
Women's Outdoor Adventure Cooperative
Woodswomen

At Camp Widjiwagan, we plan our own routes. We can say we want a "push" trip or a relaxed trip—where we do some fishing, get into camp early and lie around. There are requirements for nutrition for each day. With those guidelines in mind, we plan the kind of food we want to eat and pack it ourselves before we go.

I can't believe I came back after my first year. We had a bad experience with some wind on a lake—we were only twelve years old and weren't strong enough to paddle in it. But I liked the woods and learning new things, and knew I needed to give it another try.

The second year I went "on trail" for ten days. I was familiar with the area so it wasn't scary anymore. We saw some really cool waterfalls and did a mile-long portage that I hated. I thought it was the longest thing in the world. There were a lot of physical challenges, but the hardest thing for me was getting to know people. I used to be a lot more shy than I am now. Now I love to go up and say, "Hi, how are you. What's your name? My name's Genny." I like getting to know what other people are like.

My third year I went for three weeks. We canoed a hundred and seventy-five miles that year. We were on trail for fifteen days, and it was sunny and hot, like being in the Bahamas. We brought a hammock. It was cheap, light, and took up about two cubic inches of space. We swung back and forth on that thing, having a great time, for hours. We camped on an island that was all trees and white sand. You could go out to the middle of the lake and see down to the bottom. One morning we canoed down the lake and met up with a guys' group that had a campsite where we could cliff-jump from a big rock face that dropped straight off into the water.

That same year we were on our way to a portage when we saw smoke. We figured it was a forest fire because there was a fire ban, but we wanted to make sure it wasn't on the portage. My counselor and I and one other girl started walking the portage. We came around a corner and smelled it. There was a wall of flames, and we saw a huge tree engulfed in flames fall toward us. We turned around and ran. We had to backtrack that night to get to where we needed to be. I was scared, but it was such an adrenaline rush. I'd seen pictures of fires that big in *Life* magazine, but to actually see it within twenty yards of us was something else.

Another time, we were sitting out on the point of our campsite, just after dinner. We hadn't washed the dishes yet and when we turned around, there was a black bear with its nose in a cooking pot. We started singing "Zippity Doo Da" really loud and the bear just ran away. I used to be terrified of the idea of seeing a bear, but there I was in hysterics, I was laughing so hard. We were serenading a bear!

Last year we went up by the Atikokan in Canada and paddled down through a huge series of lakes. I think we covered two hundred and twenty miles in twenty days. It was the strongest group I've ever been in. In other years, only the counselor and one or two other girls could lift and carry a canoe across the portage. But this year, we were having contests to see who could carry it across the longest portage. Last year, when everyone talked about the Grand Portage, I thought, There's no way I'm going to be able to carry a canoe for nine miles, are you kidding me? We had two wooden canoes and those things are heavy!

There were two girls' and two guys' groups. We finished the Grand Portage and set a record for girls with four and half hours and beat all the guys' groups that year. While we were waiting for the vans to pick us up, a lot of people came up to ask us if we had actually done the Grand Portage. They were amazed that teenage girls had carried one-hundred-and-twenty-pound canoes for nine miles.

I have a map on my wall that has all my trips outlined and I think, Look at all these places I've been to! And I love being able to say, I was just in really remote Canada for twenty-five days with five of the coolest women I've ever met.

I know about map reading, taking care of equipment, how to set up a tent on a point so that it won't get blown over if it's really windy, how to cook different foods so you don't gag at dinner. And I'm not into appearances. If I'm on trail for twenty days and I don't take a shower and my hair's so greasy it looks wet—it doesn't matter. It doesn't matter even if I'm around guys, because the guys up at Widji are cool too. When we finished that Grand Portage, they said, "You just rocked that." I know a lot of other places where the guys'll take one trip and the girls'll take an easier one.

At Widji I learned respect for things, for people, for the equipment, the environment. The bottom of the canoe is only supposed to touch air, water, and bread dough, (we put our bread dough on the canoe when we make bread). You don't want to drag a canoe made of wood up on rocks. We wear boots and get out before the canoe gets close to shore. Instead of taking things for granted, slamming them around, and not caring about what's happening to them, Widji teaches you to be careful with things so they'll last longer.

This summer I'm thinking of taking some of my friends up to the Boundary Waters for four or five days. I'm signed up for Advanced Explorer. We'll be on trail for twenty-five days and do whitewater. After my senior year, we'll be on trail for forty-five days in the Arctic. I can't wait to do that.

It is expensive, and the first couple of years we couldn't afford the full fee. I got a "campership," and I'm really grateful for that. Now I pay $25 a month, my mom pays $50 a month, and we get a partial campership. When my youngest sister was in kindergarten, my mom started to put herself through college, going to night school and working two full-time jobs. Two years ago, she got her law degree. So I've had a good role model on how to make things happen for myself.

Widji has changed my life. I know that if I can be happy in the middle of a lake, soaking wet, freezing in the rain, paddling a canoe, happy just to be there, that things like getting up early to get the school bus can't faze me. I'm more confident with myself. When things get hard, I think, I can do this, I know I can do this. If I can carry a canoe for nine miles, I can do this.

I've lived on a cattle ranch in southwestern Montana for forty-three years. When we bought the place, it was just a small, older house with no electricity or running water. It was in the backcountry—our children rode their horses to a rural one-room school. My husband and I kept busy raising our family and trying to make a living, so we took very few vacations. It wasn't just financial difficulties; it was very hard to go away and leave the cattle. I hardly traveled for a long, long time.

After my husband died, I saw an ad in the county newspaper for a group of Montana people to go to Alaska. We toured the state in a bus, and then we ended the last three days on a cruise ship. I enjoyed that first big trip so much that I wanted to keep traveling.

In 1987, a neighbor lady who was listening to the radio heard about Outdoor Vacations for Women over 40 and thought, I bet that is something Betsy would like. So I wrote to the company and just fell in love with what they offered. First they send a brochure with all the trips planned for the year. And if you are interested in one trip, they send you an itinerary of the day-to-day activities. I took two trips with them that year, and from then on I have taken an Outdoor Vacations trip nearly every year.

We went rafting on the Salmon River in Arizona, and we took a trip to Yellowstone Park, which I loved. Even though I live very near the park, I did things on the trip that I had never dreamed of doing—like camping out all night, staying in beautiful inns, and hiking in the park. Those were new experiences for me. The average group is about fourteen women, which is a lot less than the thirty people you get on a typical tour bus. It's very comfortable to travel with them.

One nice trip was up the Northwest coast, from Seattle to Victoria. Another time, I went to Mexico, way down into the interior, away from where the tourists go. I liked that so well, I went twice. And now I am looking forward to going to New Zealand in February.

At first I was terribly afraid of going into airports. I come from a part of the country that's extremely low in population, and seeing so many people crowding together at the airport kind of bothered me. But I got used to crowds and learned that people are very helpful.

With that group, even where you stay is sort of an adventure. The small hotels and inns they choose are rather unique. There was one in Sedona, Arizona that was a French inn. The menus in the dining room were in French, and there were several courses to the meal. Of course, the waiters could translate the things from the menu, and it was all delightful because it was a little taste of being in France. They never take you to regular old motels.

When you're camping out, you feel much more comfortable and at ease with all women. One woman on last summer's trip had never gone to the bathroom outside. She was from England, and she was about forty. I told her, "There's nothing to it. Let me take you over here and we'll get behind some bushes and I'll watch out for you." When she came out she said, "I did it!" We both laughed.

The pace is comfortable. If it's a more strenuous hike, those who want to go fast just walk on ahead. I'm not a swift walker, but I can keep up pretty well. We rest often, and nobody is ever made to feel like a weenie, a weakling, or a slowpoke. They do urge people to be in fairly good shape, but you don't have to be a superwoman to enjoy these things. My fitness program is to walk two miles every day that I can and to take my vitamins every morning.

Even though they send a suggested list of clothing, most people take too much stuff. I find that I don't take enough. But you can always borrow from the people who take too much, so eventually it evens out.

Throughout all the trips, there have been wonderful, spontaneous moments—maybe a woman will tell about how she's conquered a certain fear, or how the ladies have encouraged her to a new and better life, or how her travels have opened up a new future for her. There've been times that have been very heartwarming.

My daughter went with me to Mexico the first time I went to Copper Canyon. She had always said, "Mom, I can't wait until I'm forty so I can go on some of those trips." So when she turned forty she came along, and that was her present to herself. We traveled by train from Chihuahua city to a small town called Creel. On the train, a man started to play the guitar, and it wasn't very long before all the Mexican passengers were singing the most beautiful songs. Later we took an old school bus a hundred miles farther down into the interior of the canyon, from mountainous country on down into the tropical country, so we had a taste of two worlds.

This past summer, my daughter-in-law and I spent a weekend on a sailing ship in Long Island Sound. It was an eighty-seven-foot schooner with two tall sails—a beautiful boat. She, too, is a ranch person, and we were thrilled to share the experience of being on the water, something we had never done in our lives. I had never spent that much time with my daughter-in-law before, and we were so glad to share that trip together. All the other women had their daughters or daughters-in-law with them too.

The most challenging thing I ever did was during the whitewater rafting trip on the Salmon River. They bring inflatable kayaks along for people, generally the younger people, who want to do something daring. I got in the little rubber kayak and rode through the big rapids alone. I'm usually pretty daring, but that was *really* daring! I was absolutely, totally petrified. After I lived through it, I was extremely proud of myself. Of course, the trips are very safe, and no one has to take challenges like that.

Another time I bodysurfed through one of the rapids—the guide said there were no rocks and it would be safe to do. Of course I had my life jacket on, but that was almost too much—I scared myself so bad that I decided I had to set limits for what I could do.

I think most of the women go because they want an adventure. And I'm sure that those who feel a bit timid get reassurance from all the others. You meet so many nice people because they're all ordinary people like you. Many of them are widows, some are teachers; they come from every walk of life. But they all want to have an adventure with other women.

Once I went to New Zealand with a senior citizen group. It was wonderful, but it was not an Outdoor Vacations for Women kind of trip. The group was very large, more than thirty people, and we were always on the bus. We had no chance to take hikes, or to stay very long in one spot. I don't mean to put the poor senior citizens down, but the women that I have met on the women's trips have been much more stimulating. First you visit with one, and then you visit with another one, and pretty soon you find out that you like them all!

I met a woman named Rhoda on my very first trip. We've corresponded, and she and I have been on four of the same trips. She lives in Boston, and though I've never been to see here there, she came out to Montana and we went camping together. She's sixty-nine, I think, and is a wonderful person who loves to travel. She holds the record for taking the most Outdoor Vacations for Women over 40 trips.

I have never been on an Outdoor Vacations for Women over 40 trip that I didn't totally enjoy. Each one has enriched my life. I would encourage other women of my age, if they are in good health, not to waste another day. Anybody who feels they need something new in their life should reach out and contact one of these companies. Just pick out a trip that you think you'll love and *do it!!*

After you travel around and have all these adventures, you have so much to think about. You look at your pictures and remember all the wonderful people you've met, and then you're planning the next trip. It makes you stay on the ball.

For Lesbians

For lesbians, it can be important to be able to get away to a place that feels safe and supportive, in the company of others who have similar experiences and struggles. Let someone else do the research and make the arrangements for you, identifying locations and people who want your patronage.

After being confronted daily with homophobia and heterosexism, you may find nothing more pleasing than the idea of a trip in which you do not have to hide, explain, or deny who you are. If you feel isolated in your community, gain support by spending time with other lesbians.

Resort, cruise, and getaway vacations offer opportunities to relax in a private environment. International trips may include networking with lesbians across cultures. Tracy Michaels of Skylinks Travel describes such a trip: "We took a group of forty American women to Australia. We had arranged a reception with a lesbian political group over there. At one point, I looked around and thought, Despite our different cultures, we have more in common with each other than we do with many of our own countrypeople."

Although it is not always easy to recognize lesbians across cultures, some cues are unmistakable worldwide. Zenzi Poindexter tells of a time in Greece when her partner ate something that gave her hives. The doctor sent Zenzi to the pharmacist to buy some cream, and she got lost on her way there. "I was just sitting there confused, and a Greek woman came up to me and said, 'You're not from here,' which was pretty obvious because I'm black. I told her that I was from the United States. Then she started laughing and said, 'You've got this T-shirt.' I had forgotten that I was wearing a T-shirt with a big pink triangle. Of course, she and her friend knew exactly where I wanted to go and took me there, even though it was way out of their way. Then they made sure that I got back on the right bus and told the bus driver to tell me when to get off. If they hadn't recognized me as a lesbian they might have just thought, Oh, look, there's another crazy American.

If it is important to you to know that you will not be the only lesbian on an organized trip, choose one of the companies that offer lesbian-only trips or check out travel options advertised "for gays and lesbians." Chances are good that on any of the women-only trips listed in this book there will be both lesbian and heterosexual women, but you may prefer to go with one of the companies that identifies itself as lesbian-friendly. Look for travel agencies that specialize in serving lesbian—or gay and lesbian—clientele, and let them know if you'd like to see a broader range of trip offerings for lesbians.

Lesbian Trips

Some companies book entire resorts (such as Club Med) in the Caribbean or Mexico that offer a full range of sports, outdoor activities, and live entertainment as well as sightseeing and social opportunities. Most cruises set sail from U.S. ports to Canada, Mexico, or the Caribbean.

Enjoy a spa vacation in Northern California or join an all-women's cattle drive in Montana. Spend one or two weeks sea kayaking in Baja, the San Juan Islands, or Canada, or take a day or sunset sail in Key West, Florida.

Club Le Bon
Equinox Wilderness Expeditions
Mariah Wilderness Expeditions
OceanWomyn Kayaking
Olivia Cruises and Resorts
Skylink
Women on the Water

Resources for Lesbian Travel

Women Going Places: The Complete Guide to International Travel[31] has over seven hundred pages of places where women can find and spend time with other women. *Ferrari's Places for Women*[32] is a comprehensive listing of bars, bookstores, and organizations, with sections on women's tours, festivals and special events.

While not exclusively for women, the following resources provide information on events, festivals, and travel options—including group trips—of interest to lesbians: *Out & About*[33], a gay travel magazine, is helpful not only for its articles but the many ads for gay travel opportunities throughout the magazine. *Our World: International Gay & Lesbian Travel*[34] is a glossy magazine that covers gay resorts, with a column called "Women's Travel Hotline," which includes descriptions of women's tours. *Ferrari's Places of Interest*[35] is a guide to lesbian and gay life worldwide, with informational listings supplemented by seventy-three articles covering lesbian and gay life in places like Finland and Ireland. *Inn Places*[36], also published by Ferrari, is the guide to gay-friendly accommodations that lists inns, B&Bs, hotels, and campgrounds worldwide. It has a women's index to help you find women's accommodations if you plan to stay extra days after a group trip. *Are You Two…Together?*[37] by Pamela Robin Brandt and Lindsy Van Gelder is a guide to European travel that gives you excellent historical background and listings of gay-friendly accommodations.

I went on a Skylink trip to Provincetown, Massachusetts, last October. There were about a hundred lesbians on the trip—I'd never traveled with a group quite that large before. About two-thirds of us flew on a single flight, so the plane was pretty lively. The flights there and back were a highlight since we took over the plane; there were so many people walking around that they didn't even ask us to sit down after a while.

The trip coincided with Women's Week in Provincetown, and the package included travel, accommodations, and some entertainment. My lover, Martina, and I went together. We have similar interests when it comes to travel, but one of the great things about going with a large group was that if we wanted to do different things, we could always find someone to do them with. Martina likes to play pool, and she never wanted for a pool companion.

Most of the women came from the Los Angeles area. They ranged in age from about twenty-two to seventy-two. They seemed to cross the entire socioeconomic spectrum, which made the trip really fun. Everybody fit in and we got to know women we wouldn't otherwise have had the chance to spend time with. Since so many were from Los Angeles, I met many women from my area who like to travel and with whom I can easily keep in touch.

Most of us stayed at the Provincetown Inn, a large hotel by Provincetown standards, and we constantly saw women from our group on our way to breakfast or to one of the ballrooms. Women's Week is pretty dynamic; women kept arriving, and by Thursday there were large numbers of women everywhere. By Saturday we could barely walk down the street—in every direction there were masses of women. I went to two concerts and several different comedy shows. A high point for me was the Provincetown scene—art galleries, jewelers, and bookstores.

Most of my traveling has been alone or with one other person, and I found it empowering to be with a group of lesbians. It's a great feeling to be in the majority, even if just for a week, when you live your life amid a daily onslaught of messages that declare you "abnormal." It must have been even more empowering for those who came from smaller communities. I met several women who were isolated in smaller, rural towns, whose experience was that they'd never walk down the street holding hands with their lover.

The lesbian travel agents and companies who put together trips seem willing to give back to the community. I was a board member of United Lesbians of African Heritage, and this past year Skylink donated a free trip for our fundraising event. Also, every woman who signs up with Skylink for the Gay Games trip and mentions ULOAH earns a $50 donation for our organization.

I know some think of travel as a luxury, but I see it as a necessity. I could make a lot more money, but then I wouldn't have the time to travel. The experiences I've had from traveling far surpass anything money can buy. Lesbian travel groups often offer payment plans without a finance fee. I've told several friends who think they can't afford a vacation that they can go anywhere if they plan far enough in advance—the payments are smaller than their phone bill.

Travel doesn't have to be expensive, and you don't have to go far; you just have to break out of your everyday life and experience something new, even if you just camp out in the living room of a friend's house who lives a hundred miles away.

For Disabled Women

Women of disability, like all other women, have enjoyed expanding their skills through international travel and outdoor-based trips. A variety of disabilities are covered under this very generalized category; your specific needs and situation will determine which trips can accommodate you.

In cooperation with Mobility International U.S.A. I have been contacting groups that offer travel to disabled people to inquire if any of them currently offer, or would consider, group trips for disabled women. At this point, few all-women's trips are being offered because the companies believe there is no interest in such trips. If you are interested in a women-only trip, be sure to contact disabled travel organizations to demonstrate that there truly is a demand.

For the most part, disabled women now have to choose between women's trips that can accommodate their needs or trips for disabled that are coed. The Nantahala Outdoor Center often offers a coed canoe and kayak instruction course for people with mobility impairment. Instructors include a rehabilitation therapist and paddlers with mobility impairments themselves. The best resource for coed trips is *A World of Options for the 90s: A Guide to International Educational Exchange, Community Service, and Travel for Persons of Disabilities*[38] by Cindy Lewis and Susan Sygall. This excellent reference is filled with opportunities, encouragement, and ideas. Another publication of Mobility International U.S.A., *Including Women with Disabilities in Development Projects*, promotes integration of women with disabilities into international community development efforts in order to expand networks of women with disabilities worldwide.[39]

A catalog of aids for camping, fishing, hunting, and boating is Products to Assist the DisAbled Sportsman, 13 Via di Nola, Laguna Niguel, CA 92677 (714/363-9831). The *Guide to America's National Parks* has information on disabled access. National Park Foundation, 1101 17th Street N.W., Washington, DC 20036 (202/785-4500).

Trips for Disabled Women

JOS Sailing in Holland owns a hundred-and-ten-foot double-masted clipper ship built in 1897 and completely refitted in 1979 as an accessible teaching sailboat. *The Lutgerdina* cruises Holland's historic waterways and offers a unique opportunity for people with a variety of disabilities to learn how to sail. People with limited arm or hand functions can steer the boat with a hydraulic device, and an interactive electronic device speaks (with a British accent) to instruct blind helmspersons. Navigation charts are also available in Braille. JOS Sailing offers active fourteen-day holidays to Amsterdam, North Holland, and Robinson Crusoe Island. The crew and passengers together design a custom itinerary that can include visiting cafes, museums, boutiques and parks, canal tours, water sports, and visits to traditional villages. Although JOS Sailing doesn't schedule all-women's trips, they are willing to do so if fifteen to eighteen women contact them. The crew may be coed; the skipper is male. Their U.S. contact is Nick J. Russo, 411 Carondelet Street, New Orleans, LA 70130 (800/345-8159 or 504/561-8922; fax: 504/522-8814). Outside North America, contact: Jan Olijve, Boerewagen 20, 1625 HA Hoorn, The Netherlands (phone and fax: 2290-45305).

Similarly, **HORSES** (Horseback Outdoor Recreation Specialized Equipment), while not regularly scheduling all-women's trips, will do so upon request. HORSES is a wilderness horseback-riding program for people with disabilities that specializes in outdoor recreational riding. They offer summer trail and scenic rides, camping and pack trips, winter trips, and specialized training. Ride on the beach, in the forest, or in Oregon's central desert during a one- to two-hour trail ride or a three-day camping trip. You can stay at the bunkhouse of a central Oregon ranch and help round up the cattle or take a five-day pack trip into the Mt. Jefferson or Three Sisters Wilderness areas. Group size depends on levels of disability; support personnel may include men. You may contact them at P.O. Box 5, Scotts Mills, OR 97375 (503/873-3890).

Canada's Canoe Adventures, operated by the Canadian Recreational Canoeing Association, a nonprofit organization dedicated to preserving and protecting wilderness waterways, can custom design "integrated trips for the physically challenged" for a group consisting of three to fifteen. Over thirty canoe and sea kayak destinations in Canada are available. Trips focus on canoe or kayak instruction, enjoying campsites, natural hot springs, and nature interpretation. They may be reached at 1029 Hyde Park Road, Hyde Park, Ontario N0M 1Z0 Canada. (519/473-2109 or 541-1261; fax: 519/473-6560).

Women's Trips That Welcome Disabled Participants

When a disabled woman joins a trip of "abled" travelers, everyone's experience is expanded and enriched. Several outfitters hire staff who have worked extensively with disabled travelers. Some trips are accessible to travelers in wheelchairs, while other trips are accessible to the hearing and sight impaired. Contact each group for details. These twenty-five companies have indicated that their trips are in some way accessible to disabled women:

Adventure Trekking
Adventures for Women
Adventure Women
Ancient Forest Adventures
Artemis Wilderness Tours
Blue Moon Explorations
Canadian Outward Bound Wilderness School
Cloud Canyon Wilderness Experience
Eco-Explorations
Et-Then
Her Wild Song
Inside Outside Adventures
Mariah Wilderness Expeditions
Nantahala Outdoor Center
National Outdoor Leadership School
Olivia Cruises and Resorts
Pacific Crest Outward Bound School
Portuguese Princess Whale Watch
Reel Women Fly Fishing Adventures
RVing Women
Skylink

Widjiwagan YMCA Camp
Wildwise
Womanship
WOMBATS
Women on the Water

II

Look Before You Leap

Choosing a Company and a Trip

Once you've determined the kinds of adventures you want to pursue, your next step is to find a company and a trip that meets your needs.

The third section of this book, "Directory of Tours and Trips for Women," supplies all the basic facts that I would want to know about a company. Who are the people behind the brochures? What are their stories? Their motivations? Every group has a particular flavor: some are more spiritually oriented, some offer physical challenges, some focus on having fun. Many offer a mix of these experiences. Make these listings the *starting* place of your investigation. Continue your research by requesting brochures. Study them, and then consider: what information is not included or not entirely clear to you? Use the list below to help outline your own concerns, and call, write, or fax the company directly if you need additional information or clarification.

Questions to Ask about the Company

- What is the company's philosophy of travel?
- Does the company itself run the trip or do they subcontract with another company? (Will a representative of the company always accompany the group?)
- Who are the guides for the trip? What qualifies them as guides? Do they have training in first aid and CPR?
- How long has the company been operating tours in the area?
- What exactly is included in the price of the trip? What specifically is not? What about transfers, tips, taxes, and admission fees?
- How large a group will you be traveling with? (What is the minimum size for the trip to take place? What is the maximum number that will be allowed?)
- What is the average age and age range of those who have signed up?
- What do their clients have to say about them? (Ask for references.)

Questions to Ask about the Trip

- Where and when does the trip begin and end? Is it possible to arrive early or stay longer at the end? Will the tour company assist you in planning for the time you will be on your own?
- How flexible is the itinerary? Can it be adjusted for unexpected opportunities?
- Is there a contingency plan for bad weather, health problems, and emergencies?
- Who pays transportation costs to the starting point?
- What type of accommodations are arranged? Are they shared?
- How many meals are included? What type of meals?
- What's the typical daily pace or schedule?
- Does the itinerary include daily moves to a new location or will you have several days in one spot?
- Will you have any alone time?
- Will you be able to explore on your own as well as with the group?
- What is the weather likely to be at that time of year?
- Do clients have responsibility for preparing food or performing other chores?
- Are appropriate environmental practices employed while traveling? (How does the company handle garbage, human waste, noise pollution, disturbance of wildlife, etc.?)

Questions to Ask about the Equipment

- What is needed? Who provides what equipment?
- How much gear are clients expected to carry?

Questions to Ask for International Trips

- Does the tour company validate local culture by supporting their economic efforts? Do they use locally owned guest houses, hotels, restaurants, etc.?

- How often and in what ways will you have the opportunity to meet the local people? Does the tour company employ local guides?
- Will local guides or interpreters be hired to assist with language translation?
- Who is responsible for obtaining visas? Paying for them?
- What immunizations or medications are required?
- Is any special gear or equipment needed for the trip?

Avoid a Mismatch in Skill Level

The Nantahala Outdoor Center reports, "Our guests often underestimate or overestimate their own skill level." While most trips easily absorb participants of varying skill levels, a drastic mismatch can lead to problems and frustration.

A beginning-level trip does not require any previous experience or current facility with the activity. However, while you can learn to kayak on your first day of a week's trip, you probably don't want to learn how to ride a bicycle just before setting off on a seven-day tour. If labels such as "moderate" or "challenging" are confusing to you, call the company and describe your experience and abilities in detail. Ask specific questions: What will I have to carry? How many hours of walking each day? What level of proficiency is required of me? Don't worry, you won't be the only one with those fears or concerns. Be aware, however, that it is much more common for women to *under*estimate abilities. We tend to imagine that the activity is more difficult than it really is, or that we won't be strong enough. Usually, we are.

Be Aware of Trip Cancellation Policies

After you look at the pictures and read the glowing descriptions on the travel brochures, go to the bottom of the back page and look for the "conditions," which are often written in small print. These conditions state the policies of the company regarding trip cancellation— the kind of details many of us do not read until problems arise.

What Happens If You Have to Cancel?

Each company has its own deposit and cancellation policies. Here are two examples:

For a domestic trip: A $100 deposit will reserve a space on the trip. The balance is due sixty days prior to the trip. The deposit is nonrefundable; the balance is refundable only if cancellation is made more than thirty days prior to the trip. If made less than thirty days, credit will be given for a future trip.

For an international trip: Full payment is due ninety days before departure. Up to ninety days prior to departure, all monies will be refunded less a $200 nonrefundable deposit. In addition, for cancellation between eighty-nine and thirty-five days before the trip, 50 percent is nonrefundable; for cancellation between thirty-four and fourteen days before the trip, 75 percent is nonrefundable; for cancellation between thirteen days and the day of departure, 100 percent of land costs are nonrefundable.

As you can see, penalties are linked to how long in advance you attempt to cancel your commitment. Most companies will charge you a minimal cancellation fee once you have signed up for a trip, no matter how far ahead of time you cancel. After all, you have engaged their time and energy, and they are relying on your place being filled.

What Happens If the Company Has to Cancel?

Sometimes a company will have to cancel a trip due to lack of enrollment. Most companies retain the right to cancel a trip at any time, for any reason, with a full refund made to those who have enrolled.

Be Informed of Insurance Issues

There are two kinds of insurance considerations to keep in mind when selecting a company, and later, when preparing for a trip. One is the liability coverage the company carries to cover claims of negligence. The other is insurance that you can purchase to supplement the company's coverage and to cover contingencies that it doesn't cover.

Liability Insurance Coverage for Companies

Most outdoor outfitters are covered directly through carriers or through membership organizations such as the Worldwide Outfitters Guides Association, for as much as one million dollars. Companies operating within national park boundaries are required to carry insurance.

Some companies however, especially those that are new or very small, feel they cannot afford to carry liability insurance coverage. What does that mean for you, the client? It means that should you be injured as a result of their negligence, you could only obtain compensation from *their* assets (and not from an insurer), which could very well be negligible. You shouldn't necessarily eliminate a trip from consideration just because the outfitter is not insured, but you should be aware of what risks you are assuming and be sure to obtain adequate private insurance coverage for the trip.

Travel Insurance You Can Purchase on Your Own

Travel insurance can be purchased from private companies to cover illness, baggage loss, accidental death or dismemberment, and trip cancellation. Before you buy trip insurance check your homeowner or renter policy to determine if baggage is covered, and check your health insurance policy to determine if you are covered outside your state, province, or country of origin. Examine exclusions to make sure there are none that apply to your proposed adventure trip.

For organized trips of the kind described in this book, where most expenses are paid up front, trip cancellation insurance is a good idea. Trip cancellation insurance (which can be combined with an overall travel policy) provides a refund if you have to cancel the trip after making payment. If illness prevents you from traveling, or if you have a car accident on the way to the airport, the policy will cover all non-refundable deposits.

Waivers and Negligence

A waiver, sometimes called a "participant agreement," or "release and acknowledgment of risk," is a written form presented to participants of most outdoor trips. By signing the form, clients acknowledge the inherent danger of the activity and agree that if they are hurt or killed they (or their heirs) will not hold the company liable. Many companies will not allow you to participate on a trip without a signed release or waiver form. (Outfitters working within the jurisdiction of U.S. National Parks are prohibited from requiring waivers. Instead, some outfitters videotape their safety lectures to prove that clients were adequately warned of risks.)

What are the purposes of these forms? One goal is simply to assure that clients read cautionary statements about the dangers of outdoor and adventure trips, such as, "I acknowledge that certain risks and dangers may exist or occur, including but not limited to, the hazards of traveling in mountainous terrain."

Danger contributes to the appeal of adventure and is an inherent part of many activities. Outfitters want their clients to know they cannot control everything that may happen. Whitewater rafting outfitters, among others, hope the waiver will motivate clients to pay close attention to safety lectures because, if a client falls or is dumped out of a boat, the client is responsible for taking care of herself until a guide can rescue her.

Another purpose of the waiver is to release the outfitter from liability if something goes wrong. Language such as, "I hereby agree to pay for all and any expenses..." or "I have and do assume all the above risks and waive all claims against..." seems to indicate that the outfitter cannot be held liable for accidents due to negligence, no matter what happens.

In fact, courts in several jurisdictions have disregarded waivers where negligence has been proven. In other words, if equipment is sound and the guide well trained, and you get hurt because you were careless or not paying attention, or just had some bad luck, you will probably have no recourse. But if you can prove faulty equipment or inadequately trained guides, a signed waiver may not prevent you from getting compensation.

What You Can Expect from Your Guide

They can mush dogs in the Iditarod race across Alaska, ascend mountain summits, run rapids with aplomb, create culinary masterpieces over a campfire, and transform city slickers into competent cowhands. When you join these amazon women (and maybe a few men) in overseas adventure and wilderness experiences, you put your hopes, your faith, and maybe even your life into their hands.

Most guides are skilled leaders with a passion for their work. Although some are part-time seasonal workers, Margaret Griffith, of Sheri Griffith Expeditions, points out that, "many guides have chosen this as a career, not a summer job. We have geologists, engineers, and a former high-powered Washington, D.C. attorney leading trips."

Kate Geary, a participant in several Women in the Wilderness trips, describes guide Judith Niemi as a consummate group leader. "I love the way she subtly helped the group come together. Before very long—some of the women were fairly experienced and some were almost complete novices like myself—we were doing consensus leading without realizing it. If a problem developed, she spotted it right away and was able to get it resolved smoothly. It takes a certain kind of person, after having so many women come through on her trips, to actually focus on each one. That's one of Judith's exquisite skills."

It's easy to romanticize the life of the woman leading the pack toward thrilling adventure. Women on the Water's Kathy Kirkland reminds us, "There is a misconception that guides live one long vacation, and that they make a lot of money."

The truth is that guides work extra-long hours to provide your cushion of leisure—each day on the trip is backed up by many long days spent preparing equipment and checking logistics. While on duty, guides work virtually twenty-four hours a day, keeping an eye open for problems (or weather changes) even while everyone is sleeping. Then they're up at 5 a.m. to ensure that your coffee is ready at 6.

"The task for the guide," says Esther Lev, who leads ocean kayak trips, natural history and international expeditions, "is to find a balance point for the whole group. The guide has to choreograph the trip based on the strengths and weaknesses, interests and expectations of everyone involved. If one person is unhappy or out of synch, the guide has to attend to that person and must arbitrate differences or disagreements if they arise."

At times, the guide must help clients grapple with the complex personal and emotional issues that arise when people challenge their fears or examine their lives.

Guides tend to be underpaid for their level of responsibility and training. Many of the companies listed in this book were founded by guides who worked for larger organizations and then struck out on their own. Some, such as Nantahala Outdoor Center, are organized as employee-owned companies.

A Guide Should Be Knowledgeable and Familiar with the Territory

Your guides should know the terrain—both the natural environment and the cultural landscape—and be able to interpret geography, marine and animal life, as well as foreign languages and customs. Whether called upon to negotiate for better hotel rooms at midnight in Ankara, Turkey, or negotiate the Little Niagara Rapids of the Colorado River, the guide should be well versed in the skills needed to carry out the trip. Guides on international trips may hire locally based counterparts to fill in any gaps they may have regarding local dialects or customs.

A Guide Should Facilitate, Not Dominate a Trip

"The guests make the trip. We are here to guide and lead; but the trips are for the participants," says Gail Burchard of New Dawn Caribbean Retreat.

The guide's job is to provide a positive and memorable experience for each participant. Aside from preparing for the physical, food, safety, and entertainment needs of everyone on the trip, the guide should teach and encourage those who want to take on new skills.

Guides should try to get to know each participant without showing favoritism. Romantic involvements with clients are routinely discouraged or disallowed, as is drinking, drug-taking, or any other activity that would impair the guide's ability to do her job.

A Guide Should Be Ready and Able to Handle Emergencies

Risk is an inherent part of wilderness and outdoor travel; your safety should be paramount in planning every activity. Besides their particular area of expertise, most wilderness guides are trained in first aid, CPR (cardiopulmonary resuscitation), mountain or river rescue, and evacuation. They know what to do when there's no phone to dial 911. International guides should know how to locate English-speaking doctors, if needed.

What Your Guide Will Expect of You

I asked guides from close to a hundred organizations for their thoughts on what makes for the best trips. They told me that they hope to encounter clients who are willing to do the following:

Participate Fully in the Experience

"Bring a willingness for new experiences, even if you're uncomfortable (physically or emotionally)," says Alison Reitz of Cloud Canyon Wilderness Experience. "The trip works best when everyone shares and participates."

Julia Renfro of YMCA Camp Widjiwagan summed up the feelings of many guides when she said, "The wilderness can be a place of growth, but the amount of growth depends on what you put into the experience."

Cris Miller and Sandy Braun of Adventure Associates put it this way, "Part of the experience on our trips flows from the fact that the women are fully participatory. Each group creates its own 'center'— everyone contributes to the success of the trip."

Be Culturally Aware and Environmentally Responsible

June Campbell of Adventure Trekking encourages her clients to "respect local customs and other peoples' lifestyles." Edie Harrop of Bar H Ranch points out the need to "appreciate wildlife and the wilderness and learn how to enjoy it in a low-impact way."

We have a "personal responsibility to tread lightly, to protect the natural and cultural resources we encounter," says Eco-Explorations director Lori Katz. Margaret Griffith of Sheri Griffith Expeditions adds, "Our guides run rivers all over the world—the river canyons are their backyard; they want you to help preserve them."

Give Feedback

Your guides want to hear from you! Judith Niemi, of Women in the Wilderness, explains why: "The more a client knows her own abilities—and her own wishes—and lets the guide know, the better time she'll have on a trip."

"You should express what you are uneasy about, says Alison Reitz of Cloud Canyon Wilderness Experience. "We've all been there and can help."

"If you feel under the weather, you should let the guides know," advises Esther Lev. "And if you have a personal goal for the trip, something you want to see or do, let someone know so she can help you get what you want or need."

Be Flexible and Maintain a Positive Attitude

Living with a group of people, even for a short time, requires cooperation and flexibility. Donna Hunter of Mariah Wilderness Expeditions wants clients to be aware that, "variants arise in an adventure that cannot always be anticipated; you must sometimes deal with spontaneous solutions."

Guides get yelled at and blamed for the wind, the rain, bugs, and unpredictable transportation glitches. One wilderness staffperson urges you to, "Speak out about your real needs or fears, but don't whine. All good trips have their hard parts."

The fewer expectations you wake up with each morning, the more you'll be open to and thrilled by what you experience. Try to maintain the attitude that everything that happens is part of the adventure.

And now, a few last words from your guides:

"We're leaders, not servants."

"We're human, also."

Oh, and by the way, tips are permitted. Read your pre-trip information or make a discreet inquiry to find out how to appreciate the staff that do so much to create a memorable trip for you.

Just What Can Go Wrong?

We seek adventure travel because we want the challenge of the unknown, the thrill of the unanticipated. So why should we be upset when everything doesn't happen exactly as planned? When raccoons eat all the bread that was supposed to supply the sandwiches for a week, it's time to get creative and realize that it will one day make a terrific story.

Usually very little goes awry on international tours and adventure trips. But it's important to be realistic and have the right attitude. The following are some of the typical problems that can arise.

Changes in Weather

Sailing and cruising, paddling and many other types of travel are dependent on wind and water conditions. Safety considerations may dictate an unanticipated wind, or rain, day when you'll stay huddled in camp rather than go out on the water. Outfitters know the weather patterns of each season and usually build enough flexibility into the schedule to handle one or two days of bad weather.

Ever-hopeful travelers all too easily ignore warnings in the pre-trip packet about the need to be ready for rain, cold, and other weather extremes. One guide observed, "People don't dress for the weather, as described in the literature; they dress for their idea of what the weather will be like."

A Hitch in Transportation

Airline strikes, train delays, and car or jeep breakdowns are especially nerve-wracking if they come at the beginning or end of your trip. These problems are more common in, but not limited to, international travel. Even the most carefully planned arrangements can fall through—the shuttle bus pickup doesn't happen, or a reservation in a hotel is not honored.

Try not to schedule your return so tightly that your future happiness depends on getting out of the jungle on Monday, off the river at noon, onto the train by sunset, or down from the mountain in five hours. Check with your travel company for the likelihood of transportation problems, and plan an extra day or two for possible delays if they seem at all likely.

Off-Cycle Menstruation

Get around a group of women and those pheromones make things happen! Be prepared for an early or late menstrual period. In groups of women spending a lot of time together, it is not unusual for some members of the group to get thrown off their regular schedules.

Sickness and Accidents

Most health mishaps on trips of this type are terribly mundane—flu, cough, cold, diarrhea. Food reactions, bee stings, jellyfish stings, poison ivy and oak, rashes, and burns from campfires are a bit more exotic and make better postcard copy. Your guides should be able to treat all these occurrences and more (although you should bring the bee sting antidote if you are allergic). Wilderness trip preparation includes emergency evacuation planning, in case it is needed.

Missing Luggage

The airlines could lose your bag, or it could fall off the side of the boat. One effective strategy is to travel light (avoiding the need to check baggage on airlines). Keep to the bare essentials and handle your luggage yourself as much as possible.

If you do lose your gear, you'll have to ask your travel companions to pitch in and share theirs. This requires some diplomacy but does allow those who have overpacked to off–load some of their excess baggage.

En route to an epic raft trip in Borneo, Tracy Johnston's duffel bag, carefully stocked with all her river gear, was lost. Read her tale of the adventure, *Shooting the Boh: A Woman's Voyage Down the Wildest River in Borneo*[40] to learn how she managed to survive the trip with little more than the contents of her carry-on bag—two sun dresses, a pair of white sandals, some makeup and thirteen books.

Equipment Problems

Try not to let time spent patching rafts, changing bicycle tires, or repairing equipment trigger major disappointments. In the spirit of making everything that happens part of the adventure, you can decide that you've always wanted an opportunity to learn how to make seamless patches.

Group Dynamics

Room, tent, or canoe sharing provides plenty of time to observe the character flaws of other people. If someone else's behavior gets in the way of your positive participation in the trip, share your concern confidentially with the guide, who may have a solution. It's better to seek a diplomatic way to create a change than to drag your resentment around like a wet sleeping bag.

I joined an Adventure Spirit Hawaii trip to the remote Kalalau Valley on the island of Kauai, which was only accessible by kayak or an eleven-mile hike. It has hundred-foot waterfalls and caves full of water—it's the perfect image of the Hawaiian or tropical paradise. Even though I live in Hawaii myself, I thought it was fabulous.

We camped there about five days, during which time we talked about testing our edges and confronting our fears. The four of us did some kayaking and snorkeling off the coast; we swam over to caves full of water and tried to swim as far back as we could into the dark. But that was nothing compared to the hurricane.

It was perfectly calm the evening before it hit, almost too still. The sun was just going down when I had a vision—I looked up and saw billowing clouds rushing across the sky. I said to the group, "Wouldn't this be a great place to ride out a storm?" And they all said, "Ohhh, no." They were sure the storm wasn't going to come.

The next day, helicopters landed on the beach to evacuate us to the airport. The helicopter was vibrating, due to the fierce winds. I was sitting next to the pilot, and I could see that he was very nervous. They couldn't take us to the airport so they had to drop us on a beach.

Our first shelter was a bed and breakfast, and we started helping to prepare for the storm. I was taping a stained glass window in the front door when I had a flash that the whole place was going to be completely destroyed except for that one window that was in my hands. Coincidentally, on the first plane out of Kauai after the hurricane, I met the woman who owned the bed and breakfast. She told me the whole place was gone except for this special stained glass window, which she was so glad to recover.

I kept seeing these two-second pictures of what was going to happen, and somehow I convinced the other three women of what I was seeing. We went to three or four shelters in the next five hours, and I saw them all levelled; we kept moving until I was satisfied. Every place we had been was destroyed except for the place where we finally rode out the storm, the Princeville Hotel. Until that time, I'd always been the one who went along with the program—whatever other people wanted to do was usually fine with me. This experience marked an intensely personal change for me.

This was Hurricane Iniki, with two-hundred-and-thirty-mile-per-hour winds. They say that you can survive getting caught in winds of over a hundred m.p.h.; it's the debris flying through the air that can kill you. We saw the thin strips of copper flashing that had been on the side of the hotel, three or four miles away, wrapped around trees and cars like they were flying guillotines. The roof blew off the Princeville Hotel and there were waterfalls coming in from everywhere. The skylights in the lobby shattered. Ten-foot couches were pushed across the room; water was pouring out of people's rooms from underneath their doors. Although the destruction was terrible, I was spellbound watching the forces of nature at work.

The four of us changed rooms in the Princeville about five times. Finally we were sleeping on the floor of the hall, in a safe place, sort of camping outside a door. The couple, whose door it was, were there on their honeymoon, but they invited us in.

Two of the women had grabbed a stove and a water filter from our campsite, and after the storm we were able to get drinking water when there was nothing available. We went to a stream near the hotel for water (It was strange to go from camping in a remote valley to camping in a five-star hotel.) We were the only ones who could supply hot coffee and hot tea!

The next day everything was shut down. Even the helicopters that had rescued us had been destroyed. I was worried about my five-year-old, back on the Big Island. There wasn't anything flying except one small plane that brought the mayor in, and they announced that the plane was going back to Oahu and would take five passengers for medical or emergency reasons.

There were about twenty-five of us standing by, and the thing that shocked me about myself is that I went straight up to the front desk and said, This is my name, I've been separated from my child, and I'm going on that plane. The clerk put my name down.

Every action I took after that was like a person who knew where she was going and what she was doing. They told me I could have the seat if I could get to the airport in three minutes. I didn't have a vehicle and so I just went outside and got myself a ride. I made it all happen. When I got to the airport, they said I needed $79.95 to get on. I didn't have any cash, checks, credit card, nothing—I had been airlifted off the beach in a bathing suit and sunglasses leaving everything else behind. I told them, "I don't have the money, but I'm going anyway."

Even after I landed in Honolulu, I still had to get another plane to my home on the Big Island. I talked my way there. I got home without a nickel in my pocket. Usually you hear about people facing their fears by rappelling off a cliff, or taking a kayak trip, but I camp out a lot and have always done a lot of things in the outdoors. My fears were focused on other things in life—making a phone call, going to a job interview. I don't know if it's the result of the prejudice I've experienced as an American Indian, or for being a woman, or because I was knocked down every time I tried to have an opinion on anything. During the hurricane I had a real awakening. I had always thought of myself as timid, even weak, and it turned out that I was very strong.

I know I can handle anything now. I'm not operating from a place of fear anymore. Before, I would give in rather than stand up for myself, and now I stand up for myself. My relationships with a lot of people have really changed. My friends notice the difference—some think it's about time, and others say how could you do this? We liked you the way you were before....

I appreciate myself more, and I'm no longer easily controlled or manipulated. I can make phone calls and not get intimidated by people and their show of power. I started a new direction with my artwork. I used to be afraid of mechanical things, but now I can fix the swimming pool pump or chainsaw a tree.

The moment I go back to over and over again is the one when I walked up to that desk and asked for a seat on that plane so I could be reunited with my child. The old Teri would have stayed at the end of the line and waited her turn to explain her little story. She would have said, "Oh, no more seats, that's okay."

The lessons for me came not by physically challenging myself in nature but through my interactions with people during an emergency. Why be upset when your plans get changed? Be open to the idea that it's the unexpected that will help you grow.

Fifteen Most-Likely-To-Forget Items

Most adventure travel companies provide detailed and thorough packing lists. Yet even their specific advice is sometimes ignored. Here are the fifteen items that participants most often forget on adventure travel and group trips, as told to me by guides and tour organizers. The list is in the order of frequency mentioned by guides. (Please note that you should only pack items that appear on the packing list for *your* trip.)

- Adequate water bottles for personal day use (this could be one to two liters)
- *Good* rain gear
- Warm clothes (wool socks, wool hats, and long underwear)
- Sunscreen, sunglasses, and sun hats
- Enough film and spare batteries for your camera
- Flashlight
- Earplugs (great for long flights, rattling trains, restless tent partners, early morning crows, and howling winds)
- Boots
- Personal medications
- Itineraries
- Bug spray
- Sleeping pad
- Water purifiers
- A variety of small necessities taken for granted in everyday life, such as aspirin, lip balm, etc.
- Sanitary supplies for menstruating women

Getting in Shape

How fit do you have to be to sign up for an international or outdoor adventure trip? Each trip is different, and some do require more physical exertion than others. The truth is, many trips are available for women of average fitness. Listings in this book generally describe three categories of trips (easy, moderate, and difficult), and sponsors of trips are always willing to provide detailed descriptions of the specific physical skills necessary to participate.

Before you dismiss your own level of ability, consider that organizers and guides of outdoor, adventure, and international trips for women report a consistent theme from contacts with their clients:

Everyone Thinks She Is More out of Shape Than Everyone Else

Rather than evaluating ourselves among the true spectrum of real women, we compare ourselves to superfit or superthin models that television and magazines parade before us. Here's what Marion Stoddart of Outdoor Vacations for Women over 40 says: "Everyone thinks everyone else will be in better shape than they are, and that they won't be able to keep up. Whatever shape our customers are in—fat, skinny, slow, fast, old, or young—they're just fine the way they are. They won't be left behind, and we're not in competition with each other."

One of the delights of traveling with groups of women is that the pace is determined by the abilities of the group, not by externally imposed schedules. "Each person often fears that she will hold up the group," says Betsy Thomason of Adventures for Women. "However, when everyone listens to her body and walks accordingly, the pace is usually agreeable to all!"

"You don't need to be in great physical shape to come," says Beth Mairs of Wild Woman Expeditions. "Consider a canoe trip as a way to get in shape, not something to get in shape for. Our trips are relaxed and cooperative, so we as a group travel at a pace comfortable for whoever signs up for a particular trip."

Cris Miller and Sandy Braun of Adventure Associates sum it up this way: "Adventure is not only for the young, hardy, and athletic!"

Don't disqualify yourself from a trip before you know the true facts about what may be required of you. Send away for detailed trip information, and if it's not specific enough, call up and ask questions.

Replace needless worries about your current level of fitness with a positive effort to boost your abilities up a notch or two. Outdoor guides and trip organizers report a second truth:

The Fitter You Are, the More You'll Enjoy Your Trip

Adventure travel vacations are more active and challenging than standard tours. You may be expected to do more physical work than you usually perform, transporting yourself—on foot, by boat, or bicycle—as well as your gear.

Many women are motivated by the prospect of an upcoming trip to begin a training program or boost their current program. The best guidelines for training come in the form of pre-trip information packets from adventure and travel companies. They describe what will be expected of you and outline fitness activities to help you prepare for the trip. Here's what Cloud Canyon Wilderness tells clients to expect on their backpacking trips:

"On most days, we hike three to four miles—some days less, some days more. Our routes will be on rolling terrain, with lots of ups and downs, and a few steep ascents and descents. Packs will weigh approximately thirty-five to sixty pounds, depending on the length of the trip."

Paddling South sends their kayaking clients a suggested strengthening and stretching exercise routine, and explains: "No previous kayaking experience is necessary. With an early morning start, most days we kayak five to ten miles to one of many beautiful beaches. After setting up camp, we spend the rest of the day snorkeling and exploring our new environment."

Getting in Shape

Start your conditioning program right away, no matter how far in the future your trip may be. Consult a doctor, if necessary, and schedule time to exercise regularly, at least three times a week. If you are already in good shape, maintain or expand your fitness program.

The more rigorous outdoor trips require stamina, flexibility, and strength. Training in all three areas helps reduce accidents and injuries, and increases your enjoyment of the trip.

Build your *stamina* through activities that get your heart beating at a fast rate—walk at a brisk pace, run, take aerobics classes, swim, ride a bicycle—your best choice is the activity you most enjoy. Set a goal of three to five sessions a week, at thirty to forty-five minutes each.

You don't need to spend money on equipment or health club memberships; remember that your goals can be achieved by taking a daily walk outdoors. As your endurance improves, increase your walking distance or speed and seek out more challenging terrain.

Build your *strength* by focusing some special effort on muscles or muscle groups that will be called upon to perform during your trip. For example, for paddling trips, you can lift weights to build upper body strength. If you are preparing for a backpacking trip, you can load books into your pack and take it along on your daily walk, increasing the weight of the pack over time. Sit-ups, push-ups, pull-ups, and weight lifting all build strength.

Stretching exercises and yoga promote *flexibility* and help you transition from one activity to another. Make it a practice to stretch and warm up before beginning your exercise activities.

Your upcoming trip should help you get inspired, not intimidated. If you feel that you are out of shape and have trouble finding a regular exercise program that meets your needs and feels comfortable, you might want to consider going to a fitness spa. Adventure spas offer a wide range of outdoor activities, and you can come away with a personal fitness program by the end of your stay.

How to Pee in the Woods (and Other Adventures in Feminine Hygiene)

Not long ago, I found myself on a hike with a woman who seemed to truly enjoy the woods. As we ambled along, she told me that she doesn't plan hikes longer than three hours because she's never peed in the woods in her life.

I found myself ruminating on the misfortune of being tethered to a toilet. It seems that many people who want to travel to remote parts of the world, or just go camping in the woods, are held back by a common phobia—fear of squatting.

People of many cultures spend a good portion of their lives squatting near to the ground—while waiting for buses, talking and visiting with neighbors, or attending to their toilet practices. Yet Western ways have made most of us dependent on chairs and other devices for sitting. When confronted with the need to squat in the woods or anywhere else, many of the unpracticed tumble right over. When presented with a "squat toilet," they aim from on high and create a regrettable splash.

The best place to learn how to squat is at home, where a fall during practice won't hurt your pride or your posterior. Rest your elbows on the insides of your knees for balance, and lower your butt as far as you can. Now stay that way as long as possible. Keep practicing until you can comfortably squat with both feet flat on the ground. Try watching TV while squatting on the rug.

Peeing in the Woods

The first step to peeing in the woods is finding the right spot. Most people seek out a private location, which is not difficult in deep woods. The spot should be relatively clear so that you are not in danger of touching poison ivy or poison oak. Do be careful when stepping off trails in steep terrain, where a loss of balance could cause a serious fall. Beware of hanging onto a plant or root—it may come loose if the ground is wet. Desert conditions present special difficulties, because trees and bushes are small and low. Don't squat near or behind a large cactus unless you have good balance and great confidence.

A plastic funnel called the FUD—Feminine Urine Director—provides a convenient alternative to squatting down. The funnel is the size of your hand and fits against your body while standing up. A short tube slides out from the funnel to direct urine away from your body. Longer tubes are available for use on boats or from inside a tent! They are priced at $15.50 each for the reusable plastic, or $4.50 for a package of six disposable paper FUDs. Order from FUD, Inc., 13628 Everton Ave., Apple Valley, MN 55124 (612/432-2129). Another brand is Freshette, produced by Sani-Fem and is available for $15.00 from an excellent catalog, WorkAbles for Women, Oak Valley, Clinton, PA 15026 (800/862-9317).

When traveling with a guide, always follow their instructions for toilet procedures appropriate to local conditions. Outfitters on some heavily traveled rivers are required to pack porta-potties for clients' use. Urinating on wet sand alongside river banks may be environmentally responsible in some areas and discouraged in others.

Toilet paper should never be left behind. In wooded areas, large leaves make a splendid natural replacement but be sure you can identify and avoid poison oak and poison ivy leaves.

When taking care of more serious business, environmentally conscious campers carry a small plastic bag with a partial roll of toilet paper and a box of matches. Use a small trowel or your boot heel to dig a small hole, and cover it back up when you're done. This kind of instant latrine is important to avoid spreading germs by keeping human waste from washing into rivers and streams—a major concern now that more people than ever are spending time outdoors. Hike above the high-water line in canyons and gorges. Burn used paper thoroughly after use, or stash it in a plastic bag until you can toss it in the campfire later that night.

For lots of funny stories and great tips, including a chapter for women, "How Not to Pee in Your Boots," read *How to Shit in the Woods*[41], by river runner and outdoorswoman Kathleen Meyer. For those who find squatting difficult, Kathleen recommends sitting on a log or smooth rock and hanging your rear over one end.

Menstruation

Menstruating women should be prepared for an early onset of their periods when traveling with other women. It's not uncommon for women to cycle in with each other when spending lots of time together. Pack a supply of sanitary napkins and/or tampons in several small plastic zipper bags; bring extra bags along for disposal of these products after use. Women who generally use tampons without applicators should consider using tampons with biodegradable applicators while camping as you may not always have clean hands when you need them.

In "Female Hygiene in the Backwoods," distributed by Women Outdoors, author Sandra Neilly says that "used sanitary napkins should be burned to eliminate odors, especially in bear country, and then packed out in double ziplock bags. Burn items in a fire or scorch over a stove before placing in bags. Mothballs in baggies will also help kill odors.

"Burying refuse will only attract animals, habituate them to our body odors and alert them to our trail. If you must bury, burn items first and bury them deeply, away from water or ravines that will be filled with water during rains."

Information about bears being attracted by the blood of menstruating women is inconclusive. What is known is that bears are attracted to odors. Used sanitary products should be double-bagged in bear country and never stored in your tent.

Menstrual Cramps

Moderate exercise has been known to alleviate cramps. Don't overdo it, however. Let your guide or trip leader know if you need an easy day.

For those who find a heating pad helpful for cramps, a portable, nonelectric option is now available for use in the outdoors. A Little Comfort heating pads are made by Medi-HEAT and, once activated, produce ten hours of steady warmth at 120 degrees. The thin pad has adhesive strips so you can stick it onto your T-shirt or underwear. Our testing team is uniformly enthusiastic about its results. A Little Comfort is made of natural, nontoxic ingredients and can be used to relieve other kinds of muscle pain. The product is available at some drugstore chains and you can order it directly from Innovative Dependable Products, Inc., P.O. Box 54930, Atlanta, GA 30308 (800/533-7349).

Vaginal Hygiene

Practicing good vaginal hygiene while camping eliminates odors and helps reduce vaginal and urinary tract infections. Maintain good air circulation by wearing cotton underpants or polypropylene long underwear. Avoid tight pants and try to change out of wet clothing as soon as possible.

While a full bath and shampoo are usually not feasible in the woods (and in fact can pollute natural water sources), a sponge bath of the vaginal area is a good daily habit while camping. Use biodegradable soap and dispose of soapy water away from natural water sources. Bring along a packet of moist towelettes, if you find those easier to handle, or take advantage of snow in season.

Clothing Options

Skirts and sarongs are useful to wear when local conditions inhibit privacy while squatting. Another fantastic development for those of us who are tired of getting caught with our pants down is a line of clothing called Zanika. Designer Veronica Morgan has developed hiking shorts, briefs, and Long Jaynes that allow you to answer the call of nature without the inconvenience of disrobing.

Zanika shorts and pants have an invisible zipper hidden in the center seam that zips all the way to the back. Briefs and Long Jaynes have overlapped, double layers that simply pull apart at the crotch.

These terrific products not only make women feel more comfortable—like those stuck in open boats for hours during fishing tournaments—but they help women win races too. Ultra marathon runner Lynn O'Malley reports that she no longer has to be slowed down in races when making pit stops. Write Zanika at P.O. Box 11943, Minneapolis, MN 55411 (612/529-1785). Large and tall sizes are available.

Joining a Club or Organization of
Like-Minded Travelers

To build ongoing relationships with others who share your interests, consider joining a club or organization that focuses on an activity you enjoy. The examples described below are just a few illustrations of the wonderfully creative ways women have found to set up networks across geographic and cultural boundaries. Some of these groups are listed in Part III of this book (if they also offer trips led by guides). They are included here because they provide ongoing connections and support to the women who get involved.

To locate clubs that might interest you, check with local community colleges and universities, stores that sell sporting goods, bulletin boards at women's centers, and travel bookstores. If you don't find the perfect club, consider starting one yourself!

Adventures for Women
P.O. Box 515
Montvale, NJ 07645
201/930-0557
Contact: Betsy Thomason

Marty Dougherty describes herself as one of the "golden girls" who's been involved with Adventures for Women since it began: "Betsy Thomason started this group back in 1980. Since then I've mainly done hiking and cross country skiing. When asthma caught up with me about four or five years ago, I was determined not to let it take over my life. So I joined a trip where we hiked in with backpacks for three miles. I hadn't had a backpack on my back in years—and I made it almost to the top of Mount Marcy. That was a wonderful experience, and I reflect back on that period thinking, Wow, I made it there and out!

"I think men do have a tendency to take over. They feel that they are the better campers, the better fire makers, the better tent putter-uppers. Women are much more courageous on a hike when they know there are only women along. Many women can't get over how much they really can do. It gives them a marvelous way to recognize their own strengths, their own abilities.

"Betsy appeals to a tremendous spectrum of women, from very young to even older than I. It's like a big club—some of the same women are involved for a long period of time. There's always someone around that I've met on previous trips with whom I enjoy spending time."

International Organization of Outdoor Women
P.O. Box 559
Cumming, GA 30130
800/781-6669 or 404/781-8386
Carol Wiseman, Founder and Executive Director

The International Organization of Outdoor Women was formed in 1992 in order to "increase the accessibility of outdoor activities for women, children, and the disabled." It is a membership organization with over six thousand members in the U.S. and Canada. Annual membership dues are $25 and will entitle you to a logo patch, the quarterly magazine, *Outdoor Women,* and information about (and discounts on) outdoor education programs, events, and products developed specifically for women. IOOW offers "a chance to share your experiences with other women with similar interests or learn from and ask questions of women experts." Members can, if they wish, field-test newly introduced outdoor products for women. The organization seeks to impact decisions concerning the environment and natural resources, on state and national levels.

IOOW, through state and local representatives, offers hands-on seminars for women in all woods and water activities. An unusual program teams up members who wish to have a low-cost adventure by teaching outdoor skills to each other. Two members, for example, could exchange a canoe trip for a mountain biking trip. IOOW maintains an "equipment loan bank of refurbished and donated equipment," which is made available to women with limited financial resources.

Merry Widows
P.O. Box 31087
Tampa, FL 33631
800/374-2689
Contact: Phyllis Zeno

Phyllis Zeno, creative director for AAA Auto Club South in Tampa, Florida, went on a cruise in 1976 and noticed the shortage of dance partners for older women. She created the concept of dance cruises, where male dance hosts are hired to dance with single, widowed, or divorced women. Since then, more than sixty-five dance cruises have traveled to destinations worldwide.

For those who prefer to do their dancing on terra firma, Merry Widows organizes land tours, such as one that combines Big Band dancing with a trip to the Georgia Sea Islands, one that offers a week of daytime spa treatments and nighttime dancing at a Sanibel Island Spa, and one that features dancing in the evenings in Sedona, Arizona, with days filled touring the Grand Canyon and the surrounding area.

There is no fee to join the club, and it is not limited to AAA members. Age is not restricted, but most participants are women from their late fifties and into their nineties. Phyllis Zeno shares the secret of Merry Widows' success: "We do Latin and ballroom dancing, and issue dance cards to assure that everyone gets an equal number of dances. (The ladies take their dancing very seriously, and we don't want any hard feelings at the end of a trip.) Either my assistant or I accompany each cruise, and we work very hard to make sure everything is handled correctly.

"The men are selected for their dancing ability and must have references. There are over two hundred men on the waiting list, hoping to get a free cruise as a dance host.

"About five hundred women have been on the trips and cruises to date—once they start, they never want to stop. On each cruise we crown a queen, who has been on the most trips—any number of women have been on more than twenty cruises. One ninety-three-year-old comes all the time and she never misses her turn on the dance floor."

RVing Women
201 East Southern
Apache Junction, AZ 85219
602/983-4678
Contact: Lovern King

Founders Zoe Swanagon and Lovern King had been full-time RV travelers for several years when they decided to try and connect with other women in RVs. They started a newsletter in 1991, and the organization has quickly grown to over three thousand members. They sponsor more than fifty rallies each year (where women in RVs, campers, and vans meet at a central point for several days), which include seminars on safety, maintenance, and repairs.

Lovern shares some of RVing Women's philosophy: "We make a specific point of saying that all women are welcome, and that the organization is not a forum for personal issues—we don't discuss politics, religion, or sexual preference. We've created a very accepting arena; we focus on our similarities and don't push people on their differences.

"When women come to rallies and events, they find such a loving, accepting atmosphere that they immediately grow to like the women there. As they get to know someone new they may realize, Gee she's not really like me, and she doesn't have the same philosophy that I do, but I like her and enjoy her company. One of the exciting things for us has been to see that, as women get to know each other, they are not so threatened by each other's differences.

"Every state is represented, all the provinces of Canada, even Germany, Italy, and Japan. We have a lot of retirees on fixed incomes who have to watch their pennies, and we also have physicians and lawyers and all kinds of businesspeople who may be a bit more comfortable. Many members have left high-powered positions because they're tired of the rat race.

"Often women join thinking they can't do this or that. Then they see other women doing those things, and they think, Well, if she can do it, then I can do it. That's how they build their confidence. Two women who took some of our maintenance classes really wanted to do more, so now they have joined an RV technician course that's eight months long. When they graduate, they will be qualified to work in an RV repair shop.

"Some women come who don't have RVs—they drive their cars to a rally. It's a good way to check out the different kinds of RVs and get information from women who own them, before investing in one."

Membership costs $39 per year and includes a subscription to the RVing Women newsletter and a listing in the membership directory, if you wish to be included.

> Wander Women Travel and Adventure Club
> 136 North Grand Avenue, #237
> West Covina, CA 91791
> 818/966-8857
> Contact: Shirley Giesking

Wander Women is a membership organization for women over forty who like travel and adventure, but all women are welcome to subscribe to their newsletter, *Journal 'n Footnotes*.

Journal 'n Footnotes invites women to share travel and adventure experiences, and the newsletter is full of lively tales. The newsletter includes a bulletin board that lists readers willing to host others in their homes, women looking for travel companions, and information about women's trips and tours. Members also receive discounts on special travel and event packages. Send two first-class stamps for a free sample copy of *Journal 'n Footnotes* to the address above.

Founder Shirley Giesking explains how she got started: "I'm a teacher, and I really like my Macintosh computer and wanted to find some way to go into desktop publishing. I was out hiking with my dog one day, and it hit me—I could combine those things with my love of travel! I kept fooling around with variations on the words "wonder woman": wonder women, wander woman, wander women, and that was it!

"Since then the organization has taken a two-pronged approach: *Journal 'n Footnotes*, our newsletter, is designed to provide information about travel and adventure for all women. But because there was so much available to younger women, I decided to concentrate the

Wander Women Travel and Adventure Club on women over forty. We have about two hundred members in the travel club and many more subscribers to the newsletter. We try to serve all women—single, divorced, gay, and straight. Everyone is welcome. We all get along, and the camaraderie is great."

Women Anglers of Minnesota
P.O. Box 58063
Minneapolis, MN 55458-0653
612/339-1322
Contact: Membership Director

The annual calendar of events of Women Anglers of Minnesota includes ice fishing in January and a fishing tournament each June. Monthly meetings feature guest speakers; the newsletter covers fishing techniques, experiences, and personalities. Membership is $24 per year; $19 per year for an associate member.

WAM membership director and publicity coordinator Diane Westphal explained that the organization started in 1977 to provide support for women who like to fish, some of whom felt isolated after the loss of long-term fishing partners.

"We have about ninety members—from age eighteen to eighty—married, widowed, young, old, experienced, and beginning. Non-members are allowed to participate in the annual Women's Fishing Tournament. Last year about forty boats went out, and the host town—Park Rapids, Minnesota—rolled out the red carpet with banners and signs to welcome us.

"We try to sponsor a hands-on clinic each spring to help new women get started in fishing. We teach the basics of how to run a boat and motor, as well as different fishing techniques. For those who do quite a bit of regular hook-and-line fishing already, we try to offer a fly fishing clinic.

"The response from the men is getting a lot better than it used to be. Each year we have a mini-tournament that we cosponsor with one of the local bass clubs; we team up one woman angler and one of the bass guys. That's another way our members can learn new things.

Last year one of our new members, who said she'd never caught a fish bigger than a minnow, got to run the trolling motor and caught a lot of fish that day.

"We have trips scheduled throughout the year, and we try to help the newer members on those weekend trips."

Women Climbers Northeast
P.O. Box 440441
Somerville, MA 02144
617/666-5334
Contact: Paula Ferguson

"About a month after Women's Rock Day 1993 in North Conway, New Hampshire, a group of women met and climbed at Pawtuckaway State Park, and then held the first meeting of Women Climbers Northeast. The purpose of the organization is to provide opportunities for women to climb with other women.

"WCNE welcomes women from all walks of life, all ages, and all skill levels. We were all beginners at one time; we know that the only way to gain experience and confidence is to go out and climb. WCNE is not, however, organized, certified, or insured as a teaching group.

"The primary activity is climbing in its various forms; rock climbing, ice climbing, and mountaineering. If participants are so inclined, the focus can expand to include other activities, such as hiking and backpacking, or winter hiking and skiing.

"A bimonthly newsletter informs members about upcoming events, which can range from small group climbs at local crags to weekend jaunts at remote locations. We plan at least one "Host-a-Crag" event every month during climbing season when someone familiar with a particular crag sponsors a day of climbing. These are meant to encourage women from different regions to meet other climbers in the area.

"Members are encouraged to plan and coordinate trips. We plan to maintain a directory of women climbers. This directory will be updated and distributed twice a year with the aim of helping members identify women who share complementary interests and abilities."

Women Outdoors, Inc.
55 Talbot Avenue
Medford, MA 02155
(No phone)
Contact: Janet Brown

While sharing stories of her fourteen-day river trip to Alaska, Connie Griffith reflected on her history with Women Outdoors:

"I could never have done the river trip in Alaska if I hadn't first been involved in Women Outdoors trips. They paved the way for me by helping me develop a sense of security in the out-of-doors.

"One thing about Women Outdoors that I felt was very important was that we were a mixture of straight women and lesbian women. We supported and respected one another. There was a motto that was occasionally stated, which was, Never Assume. The real vigor behind our coming together on these trips was to support ourselves as women and to affirm one another in becoming strong, healthy, and adventuresome. There's a tremendous energy and excitement to be gained from pulling together as women."

Women Outdoors, incorporated in 1980, is a nonprofit national networking organization of women who love the outdoors. The annual membership fee of $20 includes a subscription to the quarterly *Women Outdoors Magazine,* a comprehensive first-aid pamphlet, a decal, and an opportunity for a leadership development scholarship. Members can attend the annual gathering in the Northeast at reduced rates.

National Women Outdoors supports the formation of local groups that organize trips in their regions and in conjunction with other organizations. Currently, there are groups in Connecticut, Massachusetts, New York, North Carolina, Ohio, Rhode Island, Texas, and Wisconsin. In addition, there are regional networkers in Alaska, Maryland, Michigan, Minnesota, Maine, New Jersey, New Hampshire, Oregon, and Tennessee that can provide information about women's activities in their areas. Write to the address above for information on how to make local contacts.

Resources available for a nominal cost include:

•"Women's Adventure and Skill Programs"—A list of outfitters and organizations that sponsor women's trips, women-friendly inns, and campgrounds. Twelve pages. Available for $1 prepaid.

• "Getting a Job Out There"—A list of twenty-eight publications advertising outdoor, environmental, and sport positions and twenty-one listings for volunteer opportunities. Four pages. Send 25¢ and an SASE (self addressed, stamped envelope).

• "Women Outdoors Bibliography"—An annotated list of seven hundred current and classic books by women on adventure travel, and wilderness and country living, cross-indexed by location, sport, and topic. Sixty-six pages. The cost is $4 prepaid. (A condensed version of the bibliography features a best and worst list: seven pages, 25¢, and SASE.)

The Women's Climbing Club
c/o Student Activities, Whitman College
Walla Walla, WA 99362
509/527-5367
Contact: Kim Moriyama

Kim Moriyama, a fourth-generation Japanese American, had only been rock climbing for six months when she started the Women's Climbing Club at Whitman College in Walla Walla in 1993. This informal club has no dues or membership rules—members invite women from the college and local community to use the climbing wall of Whitman College one afternoon each week. Kim started the club because, "outdoor activities have been one of the most significant parts of my life and have helped me to raise my self-esteem, gain skills and confidence, and develop my leadership. I'm interested in helping more women tap into outdoor programs and what they have to offer.

"Maybe because there's not a whole lot of diversity within outdoor programs, many people don't see themselves as the type of person who can do that sport. The posters and magazines are predominantly Anglo, and by far the majority of people participating are Anglo. So I wanted to open up the door and create a comfortable, non-intimidating environment for *all* women to get interested in climbing.

"About ten women usually show up each week, but not always the same ten. We help them work on the bouldering wall, which is an introductory wall, or on the climbing wall, which requires a harness and ropes. Someone might come and just watch for five weeks in a row; on the sixth week, she'll try it. Last week, a group of seven Hispanic girls came with their counselor from a middle school dropout-prevention program.

"They were nervous and giggling and didn't pay much attention until one of them, Lupe, tried climbing the wall. She kept stopping and telling the others she couldn't do it, but they cheered her on saying '*Ándale*, Lupe!' One member would help her find a foothold, and the girls would yell, '*Otra*,' urging her to move the other foot too. Eventually, she climbed very high. All the girls cheered, and one by one, they all climbed the wall that day.

"Carmen, a twenty-nine-year-old volunteer who works with juveniles at the court, has recently started to climb. She doesn't speak English, so one of our group has been translating for her. We've taught her the signals, so I guess some of her first English words are 'on belay.' By using sign language and a few English words, I can climb with Carmen.

"The neat thing is that no matter who we are, where we come from, or what language we speak, when we're standing in front of that climbing wall, we all have something very much in common—we have to overcome the same fears in order to go up. And we help each other do that."

Organizing Your Own Group

I've got enough wanderlust to supply the French Foreign Legion. Even if I were to win the Publishers' Clearinghouse Sweepstakes (which I enter faithfully), I'd be hard pressed to find the time to make all the trips I have tucked into the back alleys of my mind.

Any opportunity for low-cost adventure flashes like a neon sign on the Main Street of my brain. Not long ago I came across an alluring nugget of information, the kind of idle comment that somebody drops at a political fundraiser, and later on you have absolutely no memory of who said it but have retained a word-for-word playback of the dialogue: "You know, if you organize a group of people to take a trip, you get to go for free."

How does it work? I wondered. How many is enough? Does someone watch you come through customs and then give you a prize if you've got fifteen people with you?

Many of us know what it's like to arrange a weekend house for friends at the mountains or seashore. Maybe you've organized a group for a day's cross country skiing, or flung together an impromptu gang of international travelers to hire a guide for a day.

Now you can take that willingness to organize to a new level. Virtually every travel company listed in this book will gladly book a custom trip for a private group that you organize, on a date of your choosing. In return for bringing the group together, the organizer (who may be called the group leader or tour organizer) travels free, or at a large discount. The minimum group size needed to make a trip "go" can be as small as four or as large as eighteen. Specific arrangements vary with each company and must be negotiated individually.

If you have a network of friends, are a teacher or member of an organization with a particular interest, and are willing to exchange your time and energy in return for a trip, tour organizing may be for you. Don't underestimate the amount of work you will be called upon to do in exchange for the free or discounted trip. You will sign up the travelers and serve as intermediary between them and the company, you will count heads and baggage many times during the trip, and may have to take on any hotel mix-ups or transportation problems that arise.

Be aware that similar deals are sometimes offered by airlines; if you are booking airfare for the group to and from a trip starting point, ask about discounts for organizers of groups traveling with the same itinerary.

Just as I was exploring the concept of becoming a tour organizer, an opportunity arose for me to try it out. If I could get enough of my friends to sign up for a one-week chartered sailing yacht trip in the Greek Isles, I could go at no cost. I decided to go for it. After figuring out a lot of things on my own, I came across two books written about chartering boats, either with crew or without, that I wish I'd found sooner. For boat charters anywhere, look for *Deck with a View: On the Water Vacations in Greece and Turkey* (or the same title for the Caribbean).[42]

By the time eighteen of us left for Greece, I'd made some mistakes, and also many discoveries. These are my recommendations for organizing any kind of group:

➤Organize well in advance—your first gathering of those who may be interested in the trip should be eight to ten months before the date of departure. Be clear from the start that you, as organizer, will be going free or at a reduced rate in return for arranging the trip.

➤Don't count your chickens. Many friends will enthusiastically promise to sign up. The realities of life, finances, and other commitments mean that not all of them will actually come through in the end. Over-recruit and be clear that whoever pays first, goes.

➤If possible, have enough money on hand to advance deposits yourself. Then collect it back, as people sign on. This may be necessary to hold a place for your group while the latecomers decide. Of course, you have to be fairly confident of your ability to get enough people together to do this.

➤Friends or not, once you take people's money, or convince them to spend it, you're doing business. Don't rely on informality—make agreements on paper and keep detailed notes.

➤Don't ask twenty people for their preferred date of departure—set a date that makes sense to you and *then* search for people who can make it on that date. It is frustrating for everyone involved to have to juggle work and family vacations around an ever-changing schedule.

➤Don't quote a specific price until it has been verified by your written contract with the outfitter—it's much better to overestimate than to have to raise prices.

➤Be clear about your role from the start—what will and won't you take care of before the trip? During the trip? Don't underestimate the time it will take for you to fulfill your obligations.

➤Keep it simple, especially your first time around. Find a travel agent or deal directly with the outfitter to arrange for all-inclusive packages; trying to help people get individual airline tickets and hotel rooms can be difficult and complex.

➤Keep in touch with everyone who's signed up for the trip. I sent a couple of homemade newsletters with updates, packing tips, weather predictions, etc.

Custom Trips

Many companies that regularly schedule women's trips may also offer trips specially tailored to the needs and desires of your group. You can ask any company if they are interested in designing an adventure for you. Many specifically offer this service. For example:

•**The Heart of Adventure** frequently guides custom-designed trips worldwide. Debbie Koehn spent six months a year in Peru for twelve years. Trips to Macchu Picchu include trekking, river rafting, and interaction with healers, artisans, and Andean villagers. Nepali treks visit monasteries and remote villages. You can learn about Tibetan Buddhist life in Ladakh, India, by visiting monasteries perched on rocky crags high in the Himalayas.

•**Eco-Explorations** offers custom-designed packages that include air fare, accommodations, and diving in such locations as Fiji, Australia, and New Zealand.

•**Call of the Wild** will custom design any of their trips for your group. Usually seven are needed, and they offer one free trip for every eleven paid guests. They've custom-designed Mt. Whitney climbs for women celebrating fortieth and fiftieth birthdays. Yes, everyone made it to the summit!

•After eleven years of organizing pre-planned adventures, **Womantrek** now leads private groups to any destination worldwide. Special interest groups have chosen to travel to such places as Nepal, Macchu Picchu, and China. Custom itineraries are prepared based on your group's interests and needs. P.O. Box 20643, Seattle, WA 98102 (800/477-TREK or 206/325-4772).

Special Offers from Adventure Companies

Don't hesitate to ask any company if you can organize a group in exchange for free participation. Some examples of the trips available to tour organizers are:

•Earn a free two-week trip into the Amazon with **Amazonia Expeditions** by signing up six paying customers. Contact Paul Beaver, Amazonia Expeditions, 18500 Gulf Blvd., Indian Shores, FL 34635 (800/262-9669).

• **Bushwise Women** of New Zealand offers the following discounts on any of their trips to those who organize a private group—a 5 percent discount if you bring four to five people, a 10 percent discount for a group of six to seven people, and a 12.5 percent discount (i.e., one free place) for a group of eight.

•**Wildwise Adventures for Women** in Australia says you can get your trip at half price by bringing four friends along; if you get eight friends organized, you can set the date of your own trip, and you can go free!

Women's Trips by Special Request

Many companies that don't (yet) offer women-only trips would love to put one together for you and your group. Be sure to ask for women guides if that is your preference. Some of the most interesting options I've come across include:

•Organize your own yurt-to-yurt ski tour on the western slopes of the Grand Tetons. Yurts are cozy, twenty-foot-diameter dwellings with wooden floors and skylights, equipped with wood stoves, bunks, and sleeping bags. You need only carry your daypack during spectacular days of backcountry skiing, while **Rendezvous Ski Tours** provides guides, instruction, and lots of hearty and healthy food. There's a two-person minimum. Contact Carole Lowe or Glen Vitucci at Rendezvous Ski Tours, 219 Highland, Victor, ID 83455 (208/354-8489).

•Travel to Turkey with **Ana Tours** on the trail of the great goddess. The trip focuses on women's spirituality, ancient religions, and the role of women in history and society; trips are open to women and men, but you are welcome to organize a group of women. Contact Melissa Miller at Ana Tours, 480 South 12th St., San Jose, CA 95112 (408/293-0881).

•Explore the Zambezi River on river rafts from Victoria Falls through canyons and gorges or take a canoe safari on flatwater sections of the Zambezi to see wildlife and birds. **Sobek Expeditions Zambia**, P.O. Box 30263, Lusaka, Zambia (2601/224-248).

•Among many other trips, **Wilderness Journeys** organizes a bluegrass trip down the Salmon River in Idaho; watercolor painting and illustrated journal-writing seminars in Bali and Java, Indonesia; and walkabouts in Japan (hut-to-hut hiking with stays in country inns and guest houses). Wilderness Journeys, Box 807, Bolinas, CA 94924 (800/786-1830).

•Stay at one of three wilderness lodges or on a floating riverboat lodge in Papua New Guinea, owned by **Trans Niugini Tours.** Help save the rainforests of the Gulf Province by showing your support for an alternative industry: conservation tourism. Manager Judy Gordon would be happy to arrange all-women's trips upon request. Contact her at P.O. Box 371, Mount Hagen, Papua New Guinea (52-1438).

III

Directory of Tours and Outdoor Trips for Women

HOW TO USE THE DIRECTORY

The purpose of this directory is to provide access to the full range of companies that offer one or more trips for women and to give you the flavor of each organization—a feel for its values, experience, way of operating, and types of programs—so that you can decide which ones you want to explore more fully. The information has been provided by the companies themselves.

➤Companies are listed in alphabetical order.

➤Trips are categorized as *easy, moderate,* or *challenging.* If a course requires experience with a particular skill or includes instruction, it is listed as *beginning, intermediate,* or *advanced.* Some programs are open to all levels of experience and are noted accordingly.

➤All sample trips are for women only. Many companies offer coed trips as well; however, only their all-women's trips are described.

➤The "sample trips" described are just that—they are examples of what each organization offers, but because companies frequently change their programs, those particular trips may not be offered every year. The list is by no means complete; it is a sampling. The full range of a company's offerings, however, is reflected in the text listings and in the indexes at the back. Where companies are represented by less than a full page of sample trips, it is because they offer only one or two women-only trips.

➤Prices are rounded off and listed in the currency of the country in which a company is based. If you want to know the rate of exchange, look in a major daily newspaper or call a commercial bank.

➤You can assume that prices include transportation during a trip and any necessary guide service or instruction, but not airfare to and from the starting point. "Group equipment" refers to such items as canoes and snorkeling gear, as well as shared camping equipment such as cooking supplies and tents. "Personal equipment" refers to clothing, rain gear, and items such as backpacks, sleeping bags, and pads. Any exceptions are noted under "prices include" or "prices do not include."

➤Guides are women, unless otherwise noted.

➤Addresses are in the U.S., unless otherwise specified; toll-free numbers are good only in the country of origin, unless otherwise specified.

Adirondack Mountain Club

P.O. Box 867
Lake Placid, NY 12946
518/523-3441   fax: 518/523-3518

Learn Outdoor Skills and Wilderness Ethics in Upstate New York

Began operating: 1922
Number of trips offered per year: 122
Number of all-women's trips per year: 2
Usual group size: 6–8
Typical age of participants: 35–55
Range of ages of participants: 15–80

The Adirondacks include more than forty peaks over four thousand feet, extend over six million acres, and are host to an abundance of waterways and wildlife. Explore the area's wildlands and learn about its natural history, develop new outdoor skills, and practice low-impact camping. The Adirondack Mountain Club guides four-day introductory programs that teach backpacking, rock climbing, canoeing, and camping skills while emphasizing education, conservation, and responsible recreation.

IN THEIR OWN WORDS
"Because we keep our courses small, we are able to offer flexible programs that can fulfill the needs and interests of our clients. Our goal is to open the door to a greater respect and appreciation for the wilderness."
—Terry Brosseau, Education Assistant

HISTORY/BACKGROUND
Founded in 1922 as a nonprofit, membership-driven organization dedicated to protecting the Adirondack and Catskill parks, the Adirondack Mountain Club promotes public understanding, appreciation, and support for New York's forest preserves through wilderness programs and political action. It has developed a variety of Elderhostel, natural history, creative arts, outdoor skills, and wilderness programs, and operates lodges and backcountry cabins and campgrounds. There are chapters in New York, New Jersey, Pennsylvania, and Connecticut.

SAMPLE TRIPS

➤**Backpack to Indian Pass**—Emphasizing responsible stewardship of the land, this introductory course teaches basic backpacking and camping skills. Learn about campsite selection, hanging a bear bag, personal hygiene, nutrition, and baking bread in the wilderness. Discussions focus on environmental and ecological issues, natural history, and low-impact travel and camping techniques. Travel may be strenuous at times with packs weighing between thirty-five and forty-five pounds; a healthy level of fitness is recommended. Four days/$150/beginning.

➤**Women's Challenge**—An Adirondack Mountain Club invitation to first-timers as well as women who want to get back to the outdoors. Spend one day rock climbing, and two and half days canoeing and hiking in the St. Regis Canoe area. No experience is necessary. Acquire a knowledge of basic back-country first aid and practice map and compass skills. The final two days include overnight camping. Come in good physical condition. Four days/$150/beginning.

Prices include: Meals, accommodations, and group equipment.

Prices do not include: Personal equipment (backpacks may be available for loan or local rental).

Guides: Adirondack Mountain Club education staff, New York State–licensed guides, and trained volunteers.

Training for guides: Many have New York state licensing and outside training from such programs as Outward Bound and NOLS; all have experience in the Adirondacks.

Liability coverage: No.

Adventure Associates

P.O. Box 16304
Seattle, WA 98116
206/932-8352 fax: 206/938-2654

Spirited Outdoor Adventures for Responsible Travelers

Began operating: 1987
Number of trips offered per year: 25
Number of all-women's trips per year: 75%
Usual group size: 8–12
Typical age of participants: 35–50
Range of ages of participants: 22–72

Scholarships available: Flexible payment plans available.

Adventure Associates takes beginning and experienced outdoorswomen hiking, backpacking, climbing, sea kayaking, canoeing, llama trekking, skiing, and sailing. Join an empowerment or spiritual retreat to explore your kinship with the natural world through readings, journal writing, shared discussion, and quiet listening. Adventure Associates' unique wilderness camp combines wilderness hiking and gourmet meals. They offer programs throughout the Northwest U.S., Baja, Mexico, and the Greek Isles. Coed programs are available to South America, East Africa, China, and other international destinations.

IN THEIR OWN WORDS
"Our programs promote an ethic of care with respect to the natural world, one another, and ourselves, through adventure-based experiences. We seek to build quality relationships that foster a sense of personal discovery and land stewardship. Our programs are gay- and straight-friendly."
—Cris Miller and Sandy Braun, Directors

HISTORY/BACKGROUND
Adventure Associates founders, Sandy Braun and Cris Miller, both have twenty years' experience in outdoor education and leadership and both have been college professors in outdoor recreation. Adventure Associates grew out of their love of the natural world as well as their belief that travel and adventure are empowering experiences that help people understand themselves and their world better.

SAMPLE TRIPS

➤**Sailing in the Greek Isles**—Spend a week on a Greek sailing yacht with author Thalia Zepatos exploring women's travel issues, Greek culture, and the marine environment. Fourteen days/$2300/easy.

➤**Wilderness Gourmet Camp in the Northern Cascades**—Hike among valleys, peaks, and old-growth forests, returning to a gourmet meal prepared with fresh local foods by a San Francisco chef. Eight days/$750/easy.

➤**Llama Trek in the Olympic Mountains**—Llamas transport your gear as you trek into rainforests, river valleys, and onto high rugged trails for sweeping views of the Olympic range. Six days/$750/easy to moderate.

➤**Sea Kayaking in the San Juan Islands**—Cruise along rocky shorelines, quiet beaches, and hidden coves. View wildlife, hike, swim, and practice navigation and paddling skills. Six days/$700/easy to moderate.

➤**Cross Country Skiing at Yellowstone**—Daily ski instruction is combined with tours through miles of backcountry that is home to elk, bison, frozen waterfalls, and steaming geysers. Seven days/$850/easy to moderate.

➤**Backpacking in Mt. Rainier National Park**—Explore and rejuvenate among alpine meadows, fern-draped valleys, and high mountain ridges. Some off-trail travel included. Six days/$600/moderate.

➤**Climbing Mt. Olympus**—Pack llamas carry much of your gear on this eighteen-mile approach up the Hoh River valley to your Glacier Meadows base camp. For the experienced backpacker wishing to acquire technical snow and mountaineering skills. Eight days/$750/moderate to challenging.

Prices include: Transportation between Seattle and trail head on Northwest trips, meals, accommodations, group equipment, sleeping bags, pads and packs, park and permit fees.

Prices do not include: Some specialized equipment, such as crampons.

Guides: Licensed and experienced guides.

Training for guides: CPR/first aid, apprenticeship, ten to twelve years of experience; most guides have either a graduate or undergraduate degree in an outdoor or environment-related field.

Liability coverage: Yes, also require proof of medical insurance from participants. Travel insurance package available to those needing additional medical coverage.

Adventure Spirit Hawaii

P.O. Box 4764
Waikoloa, HI 96738
808/883-9123 fax: 808/883-9307

Expeditions into Spirit and Nature

Began operating: 1991
Number of trips offered per year: 8–10
Number of all-women's trips per year: 75%
Usual group size: 4–8
Typical age of participants: 18–50
Range of ages of participants: 13–65

Multigenerational programs

Adventure Spirit Hawaii emphasizes natural health, adventure, and ecological awareness. A team of outdoor instructors, marine ecologists, and holistic fitness guides lead three- to twelve-day programs that combine outdoor training, deep ecology, and dolphin awareness. Programs include backpacking the Na Pali Coast of Kauai, kayaking the dolphin seas around Hawaii, and guided swims and free diving around a coral reef.

IN THEIR OWN WORDS
"We weave together natural health (yoga, natural foods, body awareness), spiritual awareness, outdoor challenge, and adventure as a way of life in harmony and balance with the natural world."   —Jan Roberts, Co-owner

HISTORY/BACKGROUND
Co-owner Karen Chandler is a marine ecologist, divemaster, and expedition leader who studies dolphins and explores the healing qualities of the sea. She combines ecology, spirit, and human/dolphin awareness as a way of knowing nature and oneself. Co-owner Jan Roberts is a certified yoga instructor and skilled outdoorswoman. She is known for her in-depth knowledge of nutritional healing and her imaginative approach to practicing yoga outdoors with children and adults. Chris Reid is a logistics expert, experienced in assisting dolphin consciousness groups. A ceremonialist who has studied with a Native American shaman, she travels internationally to share in ritual and dolphin-awareness programs.

SAMPLE TRIPS

➤**Mother/Daughter Series**—Hiking, camping, kayaking, and yoga. Five days/$500–$650/beginning.

➤**Women and Dolphins**—Kayaking, diving, yoga, and ocean training. Three days/$350–$400/beginning and intermediate.

➤**Inter-Island Sail Training**—Sailing, camping, and free diving. Seven days/$1300–$1500/beginning and intermediate.

➤**Napali Coast, Kauai**—Hiking, kayaking, yoga, and Hawaiian herbs. Seven days/$800–$900/intermediate.

Prices include: Meals, accommodations, and group equipment.

Prices do not include: Personal equipment.

Guides: Co-owners Jan Roberts and Karen Chandler.

Training for guides: CPR/first aid, safety, ocean skills, and leadership training.

Liability coverage: Yes.

Adventure Trekking

26 Paisley Crescent
Edinburgh EH8 7JP Scotland
31-661-1959 (same for fax)

Adventurous Journeys for Women in Nepal and India

Began operating: 1986
Number of trips offered per year: 4–5
Number of all-women's trips per year: All
Usual group size: 6–15
Typical age of participants: 30–45
Range of ages of participants: 21–72

Accessible to disabled women: Limited accessibility, depending on availability of ponies.

Travel by foot and river raft on these fifteen- to twenty-five day treks through Nepal or India's Himalayas, visiting women's development projects and ancient sites, and participating in wildlife safaris. As a member of Tourism Concern, Adventure Trekking promotes responsible tourism in regards to local people, ecology, and trade. All trips are accompanied by a leader from the U.K. and guided by Sherpa and local women. Advertisement throughout Europe tends to create groups of varied ethnic and national representation. Trips are designed for participants of average or above-average fitness.

IN THEIR OWN WORDS
"We felt a need for all-women groups and knew the people, languages, and terrain very well. As a small company, we offer very personal service."
—June Campbell, Director

HISTORY/BACKGROUND
Benedetta Gaetani and June Campbell gathered nearly twenty years' experience working, traveling, and leading treks in Nepal and India before establishing Adventure Trekking in 1986. Benedetta, a keen hillwalker and runner, is also a multilingual Italian. June, a native Scot, is responsible for the organization and administration of AT's programs. June also speaks fluent Tibetan, has a specialist knowledge of the religions and culture of Nepal and Tibet, and leads at least one trek each year.

SAMPLE TRIPS

➤**Nepal Adventure**—This journey begins with a three-day visit to Kathmandu, where you stay in the three-star Hotel Vajra, situated close to Swyambunath, the ancient Buddhist stupa considered to be the sacred center of Nepal. Setting out on your Himalayan trek, you walk five to ten miles each day, gaining altitude gradually. Your gear, with the exception of a day pack, is carried by porters. At the overnight camps, a toilet tent is provided, as is a single or double tent (according to your choice) and a sleeping mattress. Meals consist of European, Nepali, Indian, or Chinese vegetarian dishes. Seventeen days/£1600/moderate.

➤**Christmas Adventure**—This combined holiday of trekking, river rafting and jungle safari highlights the varied terrain in Nepal, from the high Himalayas to its fast flowing rivers and jungle lowlands. After six days in Kathmandu, you'll set out on a leisurely four-day walk through the hills, followed by a day of river rafting and a four-day safari. Porters carry your gear. Fifteen days/£1700/moderate.

➤**Ladakh Trek**—Sightseeing in Delhi, a visit to the Taj Mahal, and accommodations in a centrally located four-star hotel begin this trekking adventure. Your city tour is followed by three days' acclimatization in Leh. Once on the eight-day trek, you'll walk five to ten miles a day with ponies carrying your gear. Ladakh, a region of snow peaks, translucent lakes, barren terrain, and mystic Buddhist culture, is located between the Himalayas and the Karakoram range. Your reward for reaching an altitude of 15,696 feet is spectacular views. Nineteen days/£1600/challenging.

Prices include: Airfare between London and trekking site; domestic flights and transfers in Nepal and India; all meals on trek and limited meals in cities (vegetarian); accommodations; group equipment; city tours; local taxes, permits, and porter insurance.

Prices do not include: Some meals in cities, personal equipment, visas, airport tax, and tips.

Guides: Registered mountain guides lead treks in Nepal and India. Adventure Trekking staff members guide and coordinate group on treks.

Training for guides: Government training in Nepal.

Liability coverage: Yes.

Adventure Women

P.O. Box 1408
Santa Cruz, CA 95061
408/479-0473

Transformational Workshops in the Florida Keys

Began operating: 1990
Number of trips offered per year: 1
Number of all-women's trips per year: All
Usual group size: 6
Typical age of participants: Varies
Range of ages of participants: 20s–60s

Accessible to disabled women: Contact for information.

Adventure Women's "Dolphin Vision Quest" combines wild dolphin swims, daily meditations, inner process work, healing, and respect for ocean ecology. Encounters with the dolphins are gentle and unobtrusive. Adventure Women believes that dolphins have an intuitive rapport with people and that associating with them helps people get in touch with their spiritual side.

IN THEIR OWN WORDS

"The workshop is an intense experience of community, personal growth, and spiritual transformation. Any level of comfort or discomfort in the water is acceptable. We will work with and respect the avid snorkeler and the water phobic and are experienced with both. Key West is very gay-friendly and is a wonderful setting in which to slow down, reflect, and 'conch out,' as the locals say."   —Betty Havey, Founder

HISTORY/BACKGROUND

Betty Havey is a licensed psychotherapist with a private practice in Santa Cruz. She earned her master's degree from Antioch University in feminist therapy and has worked with clients in the areas of life transitions, relationships, surviving abuse, and chronic pain and illness. Betty spent twelve years as campus minister at the University of California at Santa Cruz. An avid water enthusiast, scuba diver, snorkeler, and nature lover, Betty began leading workshops in order to provide women access to the ocean environment as well as to increase understanding of its beauty and our responsibility to protect it.

SAMPLE TRIPS

➤**Dolphin Vision Quest**—Sail to the outer reefs and habitat of the dolphins. Imagine yourself bathed by the warmth, beauty, and translucence of the sea. Gliding effortlessly on the ocean's surface, you watch and observe the abundance of life below. Guided by the rhythm of your breath and the dolphins around you, you can dive within your own consciousness. Meditation, journal writing, group sharing, and time alone allow you to integrate reflections. Snorkeling instruction is provided, but prior experience is recommended. Four days/$1000/all levels.

Prices include: Breakfast, accommodations (shared accommodations in Key West are provided, single rooms are available on a limited basis for an additional charge), snorkeling equipment, sails, dolphin swims.

Prices do not include: Lunch and dinner (although participants usually eat together).

Guides: Founder Betty Havey.

Training for guides: Experience as psychotherapist and dolphin swim instructor.

Liability coverage: Yes.

Adventures for Women

P.O. Box 515
Montvale, NJ 07645
201/930-0557

Outdoor Activities in New York and New Jersey

Began operating: 1981
Number of trips offered per year: 15 daytrips; 10 multiday trips
Number of all-women's trips per year: All
Usual group size: 8–15
Typical age of participants: 40–50
Range of ages of participants: 30–72

Accessible to disabled women: To those who can walk.
Scholarships available: Especially on daytrips.

Explore the lakes and peaks of New York's Adirondacks or wander along New Jersey's trails. Develop outdoor skills or simply enjoy the camaraderie of other women. Adventures for Women offers day-, weekend-, and week-long walks, hikes, canoe trips, ski trips, and wilderness skills workshops for the novice as well as the wilderness-wise woman. Become a member of AFW and receive trip discounts, AFW's *Expanding Horizons* newsletter, and a copy of the membership roster of more than a hundred women.

IN THEIR OWN WORDS
"Adventures for Women promotes personal growth through wilderness challenges. Our aim is to give women a foundation in outdoor and interpersonal skills, to foster participation in decision making with confidence. That's the joy of being part of a group in the woods; each woman can share the power and the responsibility."   —Betsy Thomason, Director

HISTORY/BACKGROUND
Convinced that the outdoors provides the best opportunities to learn about oneself, licensed New York State guide Betsy Thomason founded Adventures for Women in 1981. Initially offering a hike with map and compass instruction, AFW has since developed additional wilderness challenges at the request of its clients. Also a respiratory therapist, Betsy directs the "Total Breathing Workshop," through Health and Fitness Outdoors in Montvale, New Jersey.

SAMPLE TRIPS

➤**Joy Hikes**—Daytrips from dawn to dusk venture along such places as the Hudson River Palisades, Harriman State Park, the Appalachian Trail, and the Delaware Water Gap. One day/under $20/all levels.

➤**Walking the Adirondack Lake Country**—AFW's most popular trip provides a relaxed walking adventure. Five days/$400/easy.

➤**Hiking and Canoeing**—Explore the Adirondacks by land and water, paddling tandem and solo in the Pharaoh Lakes Wilderness Area. Six days/$350/easy.

➤**Canoe Instruction**—Four hours of intense flatwater instruction, paddling tandem and solo, in Wawayanda State Park. One day/$50/beginning.

➤**Cross Country Ski Weekends in the Adirondacks**—Enjoy moderately paced cross country tours in wilderness areas. Instruction included. Two to four days/$150–$300/beginning and intermediate.

➤**Map, Compass, and Leadership Skills**—Learn the ways of the woods in Harriman State Park. Map skills workshops include a five-mile mountain hike followed by a no-host dinner at a country restaurant. Compass courses take you on a five- or six-mile bushwacking hike while leadership workshops allow you to use your wilderness skills to unravel clues on a six-mile mystery mountain hike. One day/$50/moderate.

➤**Hiking the Adirondack High Peaks**—Based in Lake Placid, New York, this trip offers a challenge to those who enjoy exploring the heights. Five days/$400/challenging.

Prices include: Lunch and some dinners, bed and breakfast accommodations, group equipment.

Prices do not include: Some dinners.

Guides: Director Betsy Thomason.

Training for guides: New York State guide licensing.

Liability coverage: Yes.

Alaska Women of the Wilderness

P.O. Box 773556
Eagle River, AK 99577
907/688-2226

Outdoor Programs in Alaska for Girls and Women of All Ages

Began operating: 1983
Number of trips offered per year: 25–30
Number of all-women's trips per year: All
Usual group size: 8–12
Typical age of participants: 25–45
Range of ages of participants: 8–70

Multigenerational programs
Programs for older women
Programs for young women
Scholarships available: Especially for girls' camp; sliding-scale fees also available.

See Alaska with Alaskan women! Dog mush with some of Alaska's top women mushers, kayak the Kenai Fjords, or hike in Denali National Park. Wilderness programs range from mountaineering, llama packing, and fishing to challenge courses and spiritual retreats. Winter escapes include sea kayaking in Hawaii, a vision quest in Arizona, and a trek through Nepal.

IN THEIR OWN WORDS
"Alaska Women of the Wilderness is a year-round nonprofit outdoor education program designed to promote a new sense of confidence in women who want to explore the outdoors." —Alaska Women of the Wilderness brochure

HISTORY/BACKGROUND
Since offering a four-week backpacking class in 1983, AWOW has increased its wilderness opportunities to include such activities as kayaking in Kenai Fjords, and mother and daughter llama hikes. At one time AWOW operated a wilderness therapy weekend for battered women and in 1991 received a grant in cooperation with Nine Star Enterprises to offer a three-week adventure-based self-esteem program for women receiving welfare. Now offering approximately thirty trips each year, AWOW has seen over six thousand women come through its wilderness programs.

SAMPLE TRIPS

➤**Elderhostel Glacier Studies**—AWOW's most popular Elderhostel is an educational adventure for older women. This program opens with a full day of classroom instruction in glacier geology, route finding, and glacier safety. Participants then travel to glaciers to explore, identify, and in some cases hike, on the blue glacial ice and terminal moraine. Plant study and wildlife sightings contribute further to this glacial adventure. One week/$450/beginning.

➤**Young Women, Strong Women**—At AWOW's summer camp girls learn to design and set up tent platforms, build fire circles, and establish minimum impact trails. Mornings of fire building, wood chopping, knot tying, and first aid are accompanied by afternoons of canoeing, hiking, adventure-based games, and a final day of basic rock climbing. The week is designed to build confidence, develop trusting friendships, and teach communication skills by way of morning and evening talking circles, consensus methods of decision-making, journal writing, and music. One week/$300/beginning.

➤**Outdoor Leadership Course**—Gain experience in planning and logistics, minimum-impact camping, backcountry first aid, mountaineering, and boating, while focusing attention on safety and judgment, communications models for women leaders, and women's perspectives on adventure-based activities. Four days/$250/beginning.

➤**Dog Mushing**—Learn the art of dog mushing in weekly classes or a weekend course. Teachers share training and mushing techniques as well as information on how to harness, handle, and care for the dogs. Four days/$200/beginning.

➤**Mask Making Weekend**—Mask making is a process of self-exploration. Allow your inner voice to guide you in shaping and creating your own mask in a circle of trust and support. Time planned to weave story and ceremony, music and art, movement and stillness. Two days/$125/all levels.

Prices include: Meals, accommodations, group and technical equipment.

Prices do not include: Personal equipment.

Guides: Experienced local guides.

Training for guides: Women's outdoor leadership course, previous experience in given area, advanced first-aid certification, AWOW staff training.

Liability coverage: Yes.

Ancient Forest Adventures
800 Northwest Sixth Avenue, Suite 201
Portland, OR 97209
503/248-0492 fax: 503/248-9251

Walks in the Wilds: Tours of Oregon's Ancient Forests

Began operating: 1990
Number of trips offered per year: 9–12
Number of all-women's trips per year: 1–2
Usual group size: 6–12
Typical age of participants: 40s–50s
Range of ages of participants: 20s–70s

Accessible to disabled women: Planning is in process for a wheelchair-accessible forest hike.
Scholarships available: Participants may barter for part of the fee.

With only 5 percent of the ancient forests of the Pacific Northwest still standing, Ancient Forest Adventures provides the opportunity to learn about the old-growth forests, as well as how to protect them. Among AFA's programs is an all-women's six-day hike through the peaks, rivers, waterfalls, and lush forests of the Northwest's Cascade Mountains. AFA's winter programs offer the added option of snowshoeing and cross country skiing.

IN THEIR OWN WORDS
"We focus on the magic and mystery of the Northwest's ancient forests, on the Native American uses of native plants, wildlife habits and habitats, and the latest scientific findings on the ecology of the ancient forest. We let customers know what they can do to help save the forests." —Mary Vogel, Owner

HISTORY/BACKGROUND
The first paid employee of the National Organization for Women, Mary Vogel founded Ancient Forest Adventures in 1990 in order to share the heritage of Northwest forests and show that businesses dependent upon existing forests can succeed. Possessing a master's in land use planning, Mary has been active in such groups as Public Forestry Foundation, Native Forest Council, Oregon Natural Resources Council, and the local and national Audubon Society and Sierra Club.

SAMPLE TRIPS

➤**Ancient Forest Adventure**—Thrill to the call of a spotted owl. Watch deer dig for truffles and osprey positioning for a dive. Explore the secrets of the ancient forests through savoring its delicacies, bathing in lakes or hot springs, or just sitting quietly and listening. Learn about the creatures of the night during a night walk by flashlight or full moon. Your eyes and ears will become attuned to every sound and movement. (Make an owl call, listen and wait. Sometimes an owl will answer, sometimes a coyote, sometimes nothing but your own echo.) A wildlife slide show complements the wildlife you see on the trips. One day you are joined by Dr. Bethenia Owens-Adair (1840–1926), as role-played by Mary Vogel, to dialogue about Oregon's pioneer history. Other activities enhance your connection with the earth, such as storytelling, drumming circles, song circles and participating in Native American sweat lodges. Day hikes generally cover four to eight miles and accommodations in locally owned and operated mountain resorts offer convenient access to six national forests. Six days/$600/moderate.

Prices include: Transportation to and from nearby airport, bus stations, or motels; vegetarian meals; accommodations.

Prices do not include: Personal equipment.

Guides: Owner Mary Vogel.

Training for guides: Naturalist and backcountry skills, first aid.

Liability coverage: Yes.

Appalachian Mountain Club

P.O. Box 298
Gorham, NH 03581
603/466-2721   fax: 603/466-2822

Year-round Sports in the Mountains of the Northeast

Began operating: 1876
Number of trips offered per year: 300
Number of all-women's trips per year: 5
Usual group size: 12
Typical age of participants: 30s
Range of ages of participants: 18–60+

Scholarships available: On a case-by-case basis.

Founded in 1876, the Appalachian Mountain Club sponsors educational workshops, day programs, and a Volunteer Trail Conservation Corps. AMC's all-women programs include a week of winter backpacking for experienced outdoorswomen, a weekend of snowshoeing and winter camping for those new to the winter wilderness, and a weekend of backcountry skill building. Ice climbing and dog sledding weekend workshops are led by guides from companies that specialize in these sports. AMC sponsors coed Elderhostel programs as well as workshops that focus on natural history and the arts.

IN THEIR OWN WORDS
"AMC promotes the protection, enjoyment, and wise use of the mountains, rivers, and trails of the Northeast. "   —AMC mission statement

HISTORY/BACKGROUND
The Appalachian Mountain Club manages a broad range of backcountry facilities in locations throughout the Northeast. In each setting, their goal is the same: to provide members and the public with accommodations and programs that encourage the appreciation and responsible use of surrounding wild lands. With more than fifty-seven thousand members in the Northeast and beyond, AMC pursues an aggressive conservation agenda while encouraging responsible recreation, based on the philosophy that successful, long-term conservation depends upon firsthand enjoyment of the natural environment. AMC's programs are open to the public as well as to club members.

SAMPLE TRIPS

➤**Women's Ice Climbing**—Learn to ice climb under the guidance of International Mountain Climbing School's women guides. Find out more about the world of ice climbing—from moderate slopes to vertical pillars—in a supportive group atmosphere. Two and a half days/$350/beginning.

➤**Women's Dog Sledding Weekend**—An action-packed weekend of cross country skiing and dog sledding on Lake Umbagog. Take a turn mushing the dogs and ski without the burden of a heavy pack. Polly Mahoney of Mahoosuc Guide Service leads the trip with her own team of veteran sled dogs from the Yukon Territory. One evening at Pinkham Notch Visitor Center and two evenings in the field. Three days/$450/beginning.

➤**Women and Winter**—For women new to the experience of winter backpacking. Attend an indoor session Friday night, travel by snowshoe in the White Mountains, and camp out Saturday night. Lunch not included. Two and a half days/$150/moderate.

➤**Women's Backcountry**—A three-day hiking trip traversing the Southern Presidential Range of the White Mountains of New Hampshire. Experience the alpine flora in full bloom in the company of ten women hikers. Meals and lodging are provided at backcountry huts. Three days/$200/moderate.

➤**Women and the Wilderness**—Focus on outdoor skills (such as map and compass reading and low-impact camping techniques) and women's spirituality while traveling as part of a group of women. Hikes may vary from four to nine miles per day. Due to the strenuous nature of backpacking in the White Mountains, AMC strongly recommends that participants have mountain climbing and camping experience and be in good-to-excellent physical condition. Lunches and the first night's dinner are not included. Five days/$250/challenging.

Prices include: Meals unless otherwise noted, accommodations, group equipment.

Prices do not include: Personal equipment (sleeping bags are available for rental), specialized winter clothing.

Guides: AMC or other professional staff.

Training for guides: First aid, experience and expertise in given field.

Liability coverage: Yes.

Artemis Sailing Charters

P.O. Box 297
Driggs, ID 83422
208/354-2906

Winter Sailing Trips in the South Pacific and the Sea of Cortez

---

Began operating: 1993
Number of trips offered per year: 4–6
Number of all-women's trips per year: All
Usual group size: 4–6
Typical age of participants: 50
Range of ages of participants: 25–70

Board a forty-foot 1993 sloop with three double staterooms, two full heads, a fully equipped galley, and main salon for one- or two-weeks cruising in the South Pacific or Mexico. Cruise the islands of Tahiti or Tonga at a relaxed pace, anchoring often to swim, snorkel, and explore the islands. Daytime highs average eighty-four degrees in the South Pacific and are accompanied by ten- to fifteen-knot trade winds to keep you comfortable. Spend a week on the Sea of Cortez or two weeks if you want to sail farther north along the Mexican coastline. Baja offers warm and sunny days in the winter, with plenty of marine life in sight. Artemis sailing trips require no previous experience and itineraries are determined in large part by the group.

IN THEIR OWN WORDS
"These trips are for women of all ages, experience, and fitness levels. Your skipper enjoys introducing sailing to first-timers or, if you are an old salt, your knowledge is always an asset."   —Gloria Smith, Owner

HISTORY/BACKGROUND
Artemis Sailing Charters owner and skipper Gloria Smith has logged several ocean passages on the Atlantic and the South Pacific Oceans in her twenty-five years of sailing. Gloria has cruised extensively in the Caribbean, Gulf of Mexico, San Francisco Bay, and along the coast of California.

SAMPLE TRIPS

➤**The Leeward Islands of Tahiti**—Cruise Bora Bora, Tahaa, Raiatea, and Huahine, each island encircled by its own reef. After a leisurely breakfast, set sail for three to five hours. Anchor in the clear calm sea and dive overboard to enjoy the eighty-five-degree waters. Swimming, snorkeling, traveling ashore, or simply relaxing with a book are all options. Seven days/$1050/all levels. Thirteen days/$1600/all levels.

➤**The Island Kingdom of Tonga**—Just west of the International Dateline lies this Polynesian archipelago. Because this island kingdom has remained off the beaten path for centuries, Tongans have retained their ancient heritage, language, art forms, dance, music, and culture. As with the Leeward Islands trip, itineraries are flexible, with the group deciding collectively on the amount of sailing they want to do and on the activities that interest them during anchorages. Seven days/$1050/all levels. Fourteen days/$1750/all levels.

➤**Sea of Cortez**—Jagged mountain peaks, isolated beaches, and clear waters greet you in Baja, Mexico. Wildlife abounds and fishing is always an option as you sail among dolphins, bat rays, and whales. After boarding the yacht in the Mexican city of La Paz, explore the uninhabited islands along the way, including the Giant Cactus Forest on Isla San José. Seven days/$1050/all levels. Fourteen days/$1750/all levels.

Prices include: Meals, yacht accommodations, and snorkeling equipment.

Prices do not include: Personal equipment and alcoholic beverages.

Guides: Owner Gloria Smith.

Training for guides: Twenty-five years' sailing experience.

Liability coverage: Yacht insurance only.

Artemis Wilderness Tours

P.O. Box 1574
El Prado, NM 87529
505/758-2203

Rafting and Canoeing in the Southwest

Began operating: 1977
Number of trips offered per year: 30
Number of all-women's trips per year: 12
Usual group size: 8–12
Typical age of participants: 30s
Range of ages of participants: 6–80

Accessible to disabled women: On a case-by-case basis; experience with blind and deaf participants.

Paddle with the river's flow along Southwestern canyons. Day- and week-long Artemis Wilderness Tours programs teach basic paddling and outdoor skills in New Mexico, Colorado, and Texas. Most programs do not require any previous river experience. Artemis Wilderness Tours guides river trips that allow women to develop relationships with the natural environment, individually and as a group, and that emphasize recreation. In addition to their women's trips, AWT offers outdoor guide trainings and programs for kids, families, schools, and universities. They guide many custom programs that include a broader range of activities than their scheduled trips.

IN THEIR OWN WORDS
"All trips are recreational, providing learning opportunities for women who like to have fun."   —Mary Humphrey, Founder

HISTORY/BACKGROUND
Founder Mary Humphrey has substantial experience with professional outdoor recreation and education programs; she has previously worked with the University of Texas's recreation program. In the 1970s Mary saw that there was a dearth of outdoor programs that met the needs of women. She established Artemis Wilderness Tours to provide new opportunities in a friendly and supportive atmosphere. Mary is active in professional outfitting organizations as well as river environmental politics.

SAMPLE TRIPS

➤**Rio Chama Rafting**—Raft through the canyon country that inspired artist Georgia O'Keeffe (red, ocher, and yellow amalgams, ponderosa pines, and cottonwood trees). The river's gentle flow alternates with rollicking rapids. No experience is necessary. Three days/$250/easy.

➤**Rio Dolores Rafting**—Rio Dolores, whose name translates as the "river of sorrows," drops eighteen hundred feet in ninety miles with canyons of red rock lined by green trees. Look for signs of ancient cultures in the overhangs around you. Six days/$600/moderate.

➤**Rio Grande Rafting**—An introduction to wildwater paddle rafting through the lower gorge near Taos, New Mexico. Trips begin with a scenic float through a basalt canyon before you hit the rapids. One day/under $100/moderate.

➤**Big Bend National Park Canoeing**—An eighty-seven-mile canoe and raft trip into the heart of the Chihuahuan Desert near Big Bend National Park. Expect soaring raptors, warm springs, and the familiar call of the canyon wren. Seven days/$700/moderate.

Prices include: Meals, group equipment, and waterproof river bags for gear.

Prices do not include: Personal equipment (sleeping bags are available for rental).

Guides: State licensed and certified year-round professional guides.

Training for guides: Intensive training, CPR/first aid.

Liability coverage: Yes.

At the Helm / Watergate Yachting Center
1500 FM 2094
Kemah, TX 77565
713/334-4101   fax: 713/334-6017

Sailing and Rowing School on the Texas Gulf Coast

Began operating: 1987
Number of trips offered per year: 75
Number of all-women's trips per year: 60%
Usual group size: Up to 30
Typical age of participants: 38
Range of ages of participants: 26–72

Programs for lesbians

Cruise Clear Lake and the upper and lower Galveston Bay, home to the third-largest boating community in the nation. Explore Trinity Bay, the Port of Galveston, and the Intracoastal Waterway that threads through thousands of acres of undisturbed bayous, marshland, and wildlife refuges. At the Helm invites first-timers as well as those with some sailing experience for one to five days of sailing and teambuilding. ATH also sponsors sailing and rowing clubs.

IN THEIR OWN WORDS
"For me, the appeal of sailing is the sound of the water, the wind in the rigging, the restorative alpha waves. It is also learning about leadership, teamwork, interpersonal relationships, and confidence building. These skills have directly enhanced my personal and professional growth, and have helped me steer a successful course through life's passages. I invite you to join us on our journey of adventure to discover the joys of sailing."
—Rochella Cooper, President

HISTORY/BACKGROUND
At the Helm president Rochella Cooper took her first sailing lesson on a Sunfish in 1972 with the intention of teaching her three young sons to sail. She continued on to explore the waters of Florida, the Virgin Islands, and the Yugoslavian Dalmatian Islands. Originally for women only, ATH now offers programs for men, couples, and youth. ATH has led corporate teambuilding courses and a sailing program for battered and abused women.

SAMPLE TRIPS

➤**Sailing Lessons**—Individualized hands-on instruction for six hours a day on a twenty-four- to thirty-eight-foot sailing vessel. Acquire boat handling, navigation, safety, and sea skills. Learn the art of rigging, docking and undocking, points of sail, tacking and jibing, knot tying, sail trim anchoring, reefing, and safety afloat. Develop teamwork and leadership skills, taking charge of the vessel when you are ready. One to five days/$200–$600/beginning to advanced.

➤**Rowing Lessons**—One day/$50–$100/beginning to advanced.

➤**Teambuilding**—Two to five days/$200–$900/beginning to advanced.

Prices include: Some meals, some accommodations, sailing and rowing equipment.

Prices do not include: Some meals, some accommodations, personal equipment.

Guides: Licensed captains.

Training for guides: Captain's license, ATH training.

Liability coverage: Yes.

Backroads

1516 Fifth Street
Berkeley, CA 94710
800/462-2848 or 510/527-1555 fax: 510/527-1444

Bicycling Trips in Colorado, California, and Baja, Mexico

Began operating: 1979
Number of trips offered per year: 1000
Number of all-women's trips per year: 3
Usual group size: 10–26
Typical age of participants: 20s–40s
Range of ages of participants: 20s–40s

Pedal leisurely through the countryside or push yourself to your personal limit. Either way, Backroads bicycling trips can accommodate your ability level. Energetic beginners as well as intermediate and advanced bicyclists are welcome on all-women's trips. Your leaders provide daily route options so you can choose the distance and terrain you want to cover. Ride through California's Mendocino and Sonoma Counties, southwest Colorado, or the tropical peninsula of Baja, Mexico. Spend the night at local inns or camp under the stars. Coed trips travel throughout the United States, Europe, Asia, and the Pacific.

IN THEIR OWN WORDS

"Backroads is committed to providing for our guests an active vacation of exceptional quality. We select first-class lodging and cuisine that reflect the character of the areas through which we travel. Over 75 percent of the guests traveling with Backroads each year were guests on previous Backroads trips or came because of a personal recommendation."

—Megan McBurney, Public Relations

HISTORY/BACKGROUND

In 1979, Tom Hale, an avid bicyclist, hiker, and runner, founded Backroads. Since then Backroads has led worldwide bicycling, walking, running, cross country skiing, and multisport programs and developed trips specifically for singles, families, students, seniors, and tandem cyclists. Bicycling trips exclusively for women began in 1994. More than twenty-five thousand people have participated in a Backroads adventure between 1979 and 1993.

SAMPLE TRIPS

➤**California's North Coast**—Set out from Bodega Bay, pedaling along California's rugged coastline. Ride the Skunk Train to Fort Bragg, visit small wineries in the wine country, art galleries in Mendocino, and a Russian trading post dating back to the 1800s at Fort Ross State Park. Travel sixteen to sixty miles each day. The terrain is mostly rolling, with many short hills and one longer grade. Enjoy one night's accommodations at the Mendocino Hotel and four nights' camping. Canyon Campground is set in a redwood grove, Cloverdale Campground among oak and pine trees. Manchester State Beach offers a hot tub after a day's bicycling and Salt Point State Park provides coastal hiking trails. Five days/$650/energetic beginning to advanced.

➤**Colorado**—Backroads' most challenging women's trip leads you through Colorado's San Juan Mountains. A train takes you from Durango to Silverton (nine thousand feet). From there you ride over mountain passes, through alpine meadows, cattle country, and historic towns. For some variation, rent a mountain bike, horseback ride, or hike to Bridal Veil Falls. Visit the Anasazi ruins at Mesa Verde National Park, built more than a thousand years ago, returning by shuttle to Durango. Accommodations in inns and lodges along the way provide access to hot springs, oversized tubs, and dramatic views. Routes include mostly gradual grades, three mountain passes and one longer grade. Five days/$1150/energetic beginning to advanced.

➤**Baja, Mexico**—A winter vacation with beaches, breezes, and Latin hospitality. From San José del Cabo on the shore of the Sea of Cortez, ride over cactus-covered plains, along deserted beaches, past maize fields and the largest living coral reef in the eastern Pacific Ocean. Spend a day swimming, snorkeling, fishing, and hiking or take a siesta beneath the swaying palms. Explore the countryside as you travel through sleepy villages and farming communities. Seaside camping four nights with one night at the Hotel California in Todos Santos. Riding is mostly rolling with some level areas and several longer grades. Five days/$700/energetic beginning to advanced.

Prices include: Most meals and all accommodations.

Prices do not include: Occasional meals, personal equipment (bikes are available for rental).

Guides: Extensively trained Backroads trip leaders.

Training for guides: Backroads provides ongoing training in first aid, bicycle repair, interpersonal skills, culinary arts, driving, and public speaking.

Liability coverage: Yes.

Bar H Ranch

Box 297
Driggs, ID 83422
208/354-2906

Horsepacking and Ranch Riding in the Grand Tetons

Began operating: 1986
Number of trips offered per year: 4–5
Number of all-women's trips per year: 3–4
Usual group size: 5
Typical age of participants: 40
Range of ages of participants: 21–58

Experience the solitude and serenity of the Grand Tetons while enjoying ranch life, or set out on the trail for a horsepacking adventure. Bar H Ranch is located in Teton Valley, not far from Yellowstone National Park, Grand Teton National Park, and Jackson Hole. The Teton River, which flows through the valley, provides riparian habitat for more than one hundred species of migrating birds. In summer and fall, fishing, boating, hiking, and biking are easily accessible in the surrounding mountains. The area's annual events include sled dog and ski races, a hot-air balloon festival, and the High Country Cowboy Poetry Festival.

IN THEIR OWN WORDS
"We are a genuine working cattle ranch dedicated to the preservation of the wilderness. Sharing the solitude and beauty of nature and its wildlife—all in a low-impact way—is very gratifying to us."
—Edie Harrop, Owner

HISTORY/BACKGROUND
Edie Harrop is a third-generation Teton Valley cattle rancher who began to offer guided trips in 1986 as an extension of her ranch work. In order to accommodate weekly visitors, Bar H Ranch added a loft in 1988 with Blue Mountain pine interior, an old-fashioned claw-foot bathtub, Navajo rugs, and a fully equipped kitchen.

SAMPLE TRIPS

➤**Trail Riding in the Grand Tetons**—From your base camp at the mouth of the canyon, you have access to two hundred miles of trails. Day rides to the high country provide spectacular views of peaks and glacial lakes. Feel free to bring extra equipment for photography, hiking, fishing, or bird watching. Designed for the less experienced rider. Five days/$750/moderate.

➤**Ranch Riding**—Join Edie at the Bar H Ranch for a loosely structured vacation. On the days you choose ranch work, saddle your own horse, move cattle, fix fences, or trail ride in the nearby Targhee National Forest or Jedediah Smith Wilderness. Opt for free time and hike, fish, read, paint, or sightsee. Or simply relax and enjoy the privacy of the uniquely appointed and cozy loft. One week/$400 for two people (plus $75 per horse per day)/moderate.

➤**Horsepacking in the Grand Tetons**—Explore the Idaho side of the Grand Tetons, its meadows, mountain passes, glacial lakes, and towering peaks. These high-country trips take you through the wildflower-studded Jedediah Smith Wilderness, across steep mountain passes, and into remote areas of the Grand Tetons. Your secluded base camp is located in the mouth of North Leigh Canyon, affording easy access to trails. Designed for the experienced and adventurous rider. Five days/$800/challenging.

Prices include: Transportation between airport and ranch on horsepacking and trail riding trips (rental car available for ranch riding trips), meals, accommodations, group equipment, gratuities, forest service fees.

Prices do not include: Personal equipment.

Guides: Owner Edie Harrop and assistants.

Training for guides: CPR/first aid, wilderness techniques, horsemanship.

Liability coverage: Yes.

Blue Moon Explorations

P.O. Box 2568
Bellingham, WA 98227
206/966-8805

Cross Country Skiing, Kayaking, and Whale Watching

Began operating: 1988
Number of trips offered per year: 70
Number of all-women's trips per year: Half
Usual group size: 6
Typical age of participants: 35–45
Range of ages of participants: 5–75

Accessible to disabled women: Sea kayaks usually suited to lower-body disabled.
Multigenerational programs
Scholarships available: To women applying for internship program; barter
 possible.

Explore the Pacific Northwest by kayak. Watch for humpback whales in Hawaii. Take a one-day bald eagle float trip or spend up to five days cross country skiing at North Cascades Hot Springs. BME trips combine exploration, celebration, and contemplation. Some programs are timed to coincide with the solstice, equinox, or full moon. In the past, BME has led mother and daughter kayaking trips and Costa Rican and Canadian excursions.

IN THEIR OWN WORDS
"The earth, contrary to all we've been taught, is not a frightening and hostile place. We view the earth with respect, as mother, teacher, and healer. Our hearts are open to learn from the animals, our brothers and sisters and helpers." —Kathleen Grimbly, Founder

HISTORY/BACKGROUND
Kathleen Grimbly founded Blue Moon Explorations to lead joyful trips that celebrate the sacredness and integrity of the earth. She has been a professional guide and instructor since 1977, leading backpacking, rafting, sea kayaking, canoeing, and backcountry skiing trips. Kathleen's passions also include natural and cultural history, which she has explored in Alaska, Mexico, Hawaii, Costa Rica, and the southwestern United States.

SAMPLE TRIPS

➤**Lake Powell Houseboating and Kayaking**—Travel by houseboat to remote areas in Utah and Arizona. Explore hidden slot canyons by two-person kayak or on foot. Relax on the beaches, swim, snorkel, or fish. Visit ancient ruins and view petroglyphs of the Navajo and the Anasazi. Wildlife sightings are likely. Bunk in the houseboat or camp ashore. Five days/$600/all levels.

➤**Johnstone Strait Orca Kayak**—Kayak and camp in the heart of Orca (killer) whale territory in British Columbia, observe otters, seals, eagles, and porpoises and visit an abandoned Kwakiutl Indian village. Six days/$600/all levels.

➤**Long Beach Whale and Shorebird Watch**—Observe gray whales and sea lions in British Columbia. Explore the sandy beaches and ancient forests. Stay in a bed and breakfast or kayak and camp, depending on the time of year. Four days/$400–$525/all levels.

➤**Hawaii Humpbacks Kayak and Hike**—Kayak, camp, and hike on the Kahala Coast, viewing whales and dolphins, visiting archaeological sites, and snorkeling. Then go hiking and birding at Volcanoes National Park while camping at a retreat center on the Puna Coast, complete with sauna, Jacuzzi, and pool. Ten days/$900/all levels.

➤**Earth Celebrations**—Spend the winter solstice on an eagle-watch raft trip or kayak on the spring equinox, watching for wild geese. Enjoy the wildflowers of May Day or whale watch during the summer solstice. A Halloween celebration includes kayaking and lodge accommodations. One to three days/ $50–$150/all levels.

Prices include: Breakfast and dinner, group equipment (discount if you bring your own kayak), fees.

Prices do not include: Lunch, first night's accommodations, personal equipment, gratuities.

Guides: Founder Kathleen Grimbly and her partner, Randy Olson.

Training for guides: One-year internship, CPR/first aid, leadership training and demonstrated flexibility of leadership styles, knowledge of local natural history and culture.

Liability coverage: Yes.

Boulder Rock Club

2952 Baseline Road
Boulder, CO 80303
303/447-2804

Rock Climbing in Colorado

Began operating: 1991
Number of programs offered per year: Varies
Number of all-women's programs per year: Two weekly programs
Usual group size: 1–40
Typical age of participants: 20–35
Range of ages of participants: 5–70

Scholarships available

At the Boulder Rock Club you can attend a two-hour introductory rock climbing course as well as weekly meetings of women climbers. Over five thousand square feet of indoor climbing and training facilities allow instructors to conduct weekly classes in a controlled environment, regardless of foul weather, hours, or any other restrictions associated with outdoor climbing. The Boulder Rock Club offers a variety of coed climbing classes (both indoor and outdoor), seminars, and guided trips.

IN THEIR OWN WORDS
"Climbing can be a physically and emotionally uplifting experience, a great workout, self-esteem building, and a fun experience for a wide variety of people."   —Casey Newman, Climbing School Director

HISTORY/BACKGROUND
Established during a time of growth for the indoor climbing industry, the Boulder Rock Club has been going strong since its start in 1991. BRC goals are to provide state-of-the-art rock climbing instruction to a broad spectrum of fitness enthusiasts, aid in the evolution of climbing in the U.S., safely introduce people to a rapidly growing sport that is both physically and mentally challenging, and raise the standard of professionalism in the guiding community.

SAMPLE TRIPS

➤**Introduction to Sport Climbing**—These sessions are for women with no climbing experience or those who want a refresher course on basic safety skills. The curriculum is designed to address the abilities and interests of women climbers. Learn basic climbing skills in a supportive environment. Two hours/ under $50/beginning.

➤**Women at the Rock**—These informal sessions welcome climbers of all abilities. Meetings are an opportunity to share insights and form new friendships. No advanced sign up is necessary. One day per week/$10/all levels.

Prices include: Equipment and usage fees.

Prices do not include: Meals.

Guides: Experienced climbing instructors who are AMGA accredited.

Training for guides: Previous experience, BRC's rescue-and-safety training, first-aid certification.

Liability coverage: Yes.

Bushwise Women

P.O. Box 12054
Christchurch, New Zealand
064-03-3324952

Retreat or Explore in the New Zealand Bush

Began operating: 1992
Number of trips offered per year: 22
Number of all-women's trips per year: All
Usual group size: 8
Typical age of participants: 30–50
Range of ages of participants: 23–81

Programs for older women

Bushwise Women's programs are based out of Bushline Lodge on the west coast near Moana and lead you on weekend- to week-long adventures in New Zealand. Each trip is designed around a theme, such as journal writing, painting, gold panning, or kayaking. Among their unique offerings are bush regeneration projects and "open-home" holidays. In the past, Bushwise has offered programs specifically for mothers and daughters and lesbians, though these are now organized primarily by request. If lack of cash is holding you back, become a "friend" to get standby privileges or participate in a work party.

IN THEIR OWN WORDS
"We provide a supportive women's environment where all shapes, sizes, ages and expertise are celebrated. The pace is set by the group, not imposed by the need to get to a certain point by a certain time. We value an appreciation of the land, being in harmony with the environment, empowering women to learn new skills and become self-reliant and confident in the outdoors."
—Roz Heinz, Co-founder

HISTORY/BACKGROUND
With more than twenty-five years of experience each, Roz Heinz and Cynthia Roberts left their jobs as educational administrators to become Bushwise's founders, guides, and chefs. In 1988, Roz and Cynthia bought seven hectares of land in New Zealand's bush to build Bushline Lodge, which now serves as a base for each program.

SAMPLE TRIPS

➤**Wilderness Lovers Photography Weekend**—Bring your camera (large or small) and capture images of New Zealand's west coast. Special guests share their insights and knowledge of photographic techniques; discuss gear, equipment, and materials; and look at the work of various women photographers. Two and a half days/NZ $350/easy.

➤**Pack 'n Paddle**—Using Bushwise canoes, experience the magic of bush-fringed, tranquil rivers and lakes. Bushline Lodge provides easy access to wilderness waterways. Five days/NZ $700/beginning.

➤**Spring Work Party**—Join Cynthia, Roz, and companions in their bush regeneration and other current projects. Tasks are matched to your skill and fitness level. This program will also include a special day's expedition. Five days/NZ $150/moderate.

➤**Caverns, Caves, and Sparkling Cascades**—Explore waterworn wonders of New Zealand's west coast. Raft through a stalactite and glowworm cave or plunge into aquamarine pools. You can canoe, pan for gold in the wilderness, or simply appreciate the native flora and bird life. Return on the Trans Alpine Express. Seven days/NZ $1000/moderate.

➤**Exploring and Reconnaissance**—Explore off the beaten track with Cynthia and Roz, along the wilder and lesser-known areas around Waianiwhaniwha, Alexander Range, and Te Kinga, all the while scouting for potential canoeing rivers and lakes. Six days/NZ $700/challenging.

Prices include: Transportation between Christchurch (over the Southern Alps) and Bushline Lodge, vegetarian meals, accommodations, group equipment; side trips with other operators; permit fees.

Prices do not include: Personal equipment (some camping gear is available for lending).

Guides: Founders Cynthia Roberts and Roz Heinz.

Training for guides: Risk-management training (New Zealand mountain safety); first-aid certification; experience in New Zealand mountain and bush; knowledge of flora and fauna, training in group skills.

Liability coverage: Yes.

Call of the Wild

2519 Cedar Street
Berkeley, CA 94708
800/742-9494 or 510/849-9292 fax: 510/644-3811

Wilderness Trips with Gourmet Meals

Began operating: 1978
Number of trips offered per year: 21
Number of all-women's trips per year: All
Usual group size: 8–15
Typical age of participants: 30s–40s
Range of ages of participants: 14–68

Call of the Wild offers a wide range of wilderness trips for women from easy camping on tropical beaches to challenging backpacking at high altitudes. While concentrating on hiking and backpacking, Call of the Wild also offers trips that include river rafting, mountaineering, visiting the Athabascan Indians in Alaska, and learning about ancient Anasazi ruins in the Southwest. They also offer "Fit Trips"—outdoor trips with a focus on health. Good food is an important part of Call of the Wild trips. Out on the trail you'll dine on fresh-baked cornbread, eggplant parmesan, pesto fettucini, and other delectable dishes from Carol Latimer's cookbook, *Wilderness Cuisine*.

IN THEIR OWN WORDS
"Our aim is to have fun and to spark the experience of self-discovery. We hope that each of you will connect with the peace and harmony of Mother Earth and return home from the wilderness with a deep concern for the future of our planet."   —Carol Latimer, Founder

HISTORY/BACKGROUND
Carol Latimer is from an old pioneer family in the California gold country. Raised in the Sierra foothills, she grew up backpacking, fishing, and camping. She graduated with a rhetoric degree from U.C. Berkeley and went on to law school, but soon after, she fled for the Oregon woods and a job as a fire lookout for the Forest Service. She's also worked as a radio reporter, a newspaper photographer, a ski instructor, and a cocktail waitress in Nevada gambling casinos. Carol is assisted on some trips by her fearless dog, Beowulf, who carries his own provisions as well as some group equipment.

SAMPLE TRIPS

➤**Hiking Big Sur: Molera Beach Fit Trip**—On this weekend of exercise and relaxation, you'll camp on the beach at Andrew Molera State Park. On day hikes you'll explore trails along the bluffs and through the redwoods. The Big Sur area abounds in wildlife, and you'll have a good chance to see seals, otters, sea lions, many sea birds, and a variety of wildflowers. Exercise physiologist Tacy Weeks Hahn leads morning and evening yoga/stretch sessions and meditations. Heart monitors are available to monitor your aerobic exercise level. Delicious, low-fat, high-carbohydrate meals. Three days/$200/all levels.

➤**Arctic Village: Life among the Gwich'in**—From Fairbanks, fly in a bush plane to the home of the Gwich'in Athabascan Indians. Arctic Village is tucked into the Chandalar River Valley on the edge of the Brooks Range within the 8.9 million acre Arctic National Wildlife Refuge. Spend four days among the Gwich'in sharing the local lifestyle and culture, and travel with Indian guides by motorized fishing boats fifty miles up the Chandalar River, where you will stay in their summer fishing camps, take day hikes, and see the migrating caribou. No backpacking. Seven days/$1250/easy to moderate.

➤**Anasazi Odyssey**—Learn about the myths, history, and crafts of the ancient Anasazi culture. With a Native American guide, you'll hike to and explore seldom-visited cliff dwellings. Prehistoric-ceramics expert Jean Akens will show you Anasazi crafts, and you'll make pots and open-fire them on the ground, just as the Anasazi did. The grand finale is two days of rafting on the San Juan River (Class II rapids) where you'll take in the quiet grandeur of the Southwest and visit remote Anasazi sites. All hikes are day hikes from campground. Seven days/$700/easy to moderate.

➤**High Sierra Backpacking Adventure**—You'll walk through some of the most dramatically beautiful scenery in the High Sierra (the route goes through Sequoia National Park and John Muir Wilderness) along the Pacific Crest Trail and Muir Trail. The climax of the trip is the summit of Mt. Whitney. Elevation change: 9,000–14,500 feet. Seven days/$650/challenging.

Prices include: Most meals, all accommodations, group equipment.

Prices do not include: Some meals and personal equipment.

Guides: Founder Carol Latimer leads most trips, assisted by other guides.

Training for guides: CPR/advanced first aid, apprenticeship with Carol Latimer.

Liability coverage: Yes.

Canadian Outward Bound Wilderness School

150 Laird Drive, Suite 302
Toronto, Ontario M4G 3V7 Canada
800/268-7329 (in Canada) 416/421-8111   fax: 416/421-9062

Explore Your Perceived Limits and Expand Your Capabilities

Began operating: 1976
Number of trips offered per year: 75+
Number of all-women's trips per year: 11
Usual group size: 8–10
Typical age of participants: 28–45
Range of ages of participants: 23–63

Accessible to disabled women
Programs for young women: Adventure Girls (ages 15–16); Youth Challenge
Girls (youth at risk ages, 15-17)
Scholarships available

Adventure and challenge, trust and support, the self-confidence gained by learning you can do much more than you ever imagined, risk taking and triumph over fear, exhaustion, laughter, compassion, and a sense of community—are all part of COBWS's women's programs. Courses take place in the canoe country of northern Ontario and may involve canoeing, portaging, sea kayaking, rock climbing, hiking, and whitewater kayaking in the summer, and skiing and dog sledding in the winter.

IN THEIR OWN WORDS
"At Outward Bound, we understand women know how to support and nurture each other in unique and powerful ways."
> —Canadian Outward Bound Wilderness School brochure

HISTORY/BACKGROUND
The Canadian Outward Bound Wilderness School is a nonprofit educational organization built on a philosophy of experiential education—of "learning by doing." Part of a network of over forty Outward Bound Schools worldwide, the Wilderness School has offered special programs for women since 1985. A fully funded "Women of Courage" program, designed for women who have experienced violence in their lives, is offered on a contract basis to agencies in Canada.

SAMPLE TRIPS

➤**Women's Empowerment Program**—This course is designed for women seeking to regain self-confidence and self-esteem in a supportive, wilderness environment. It is a time to explore your perceived limits and expand your capabilities, to experience your physical self as strong and competent. Together with your nine companions and two female Outward Bound staff, you will travel through the lake country of Ontario. The course includes canoeing, camping, portaging, rock climbing, and a special solo day for reflection and journal writing. All activities are tailored to meet each woman's personal goals and emotional capabilities. An emphasis is placed on transferring new skills back to the home environment. Women who have found this to be a powerful experience include those in transition between jobs, career or relationships; homemakers; women getting back on their feet after a personal crisis; women who are survivors of violence; and those seeking personal growth and development in the power of a women's group. Minimum age is twenty-three. Seven days/CDN $995/all levels.

➤**Canoe and Kayak Courses**—Join nine other women for a special opportunity to experience the adventure and challenge of a wilderness journey in the company of women. You can choose to journey through the pristine Canadian Shield wilderness by canoes or explore the rugged shoreline of Georgian Bay in a sea kayak. A solo day is a part of every course—a time for reflection and journal writing. Nine days/CDN $1200 for canoe courses, $1400 for kayak courses/all levels.

➤**Adventure Girls Program**—Wilderness expeditions in northern Ontario for fifteen- to sixteen-year-olds to address the needs of young women in a challenging adventure environment. The trip includes extensive canoeing, rock climbing, whitewater kayaking, a two-day solo and a ropes-course activity. It is designed to build self-confidence and self-esteem, and deal with body image, hygiene, and sexuality issues. Twenty-one days/CDN $2000/all levels.

Prices include: Meals, accommodations, group equipment, sleeping bags, packs, raincoats, and special clothing.

Prices do not include: Personal equipment.

Guides: Outward Bound instructors.

Training for guides: Outward Bound training includes first aid, lifesaving, group facilitation, and communication skills.

Liability coverage: Yes.

CenterPoint in Aspen

278 Oak Ridge Drive
Aspen, CO 81611
303/920-2393 fax: 303/920-1150

Retreat, Relax and Renew in the Rocky Mountains

Began operating: 1989
Number of trips offered per year: 6–8
Number of all-women's trips per year: All
Usual group size: Up to 10
Typical age of participants: Over 40
Range of ages of participants: 25–65

CenterPoint in Aspen offers four-day retreats to help women maintain a sense of purpose and balance while juggling multiple demands. CenterPoint combines gentle day hikes, unstructured time for solitude, facilitated discussions, prepared meals, and massage in order to help women regain focus, energy, and clarity.

IN THEIR OWN WORDS
"We believe that the most valuable gift a woman can give herself is time out for renewal in a soothing environment with other women who share similar challenges and visions."   —Jackie Farley, Founder

HISTORY/BACKGROUND
As a former executive from Chicago and a trained facilitator leading programs on women and balance, Jackie Farley decided to turn her avocation into a vocation by creating a mountain retreat for women in varying stages of overwhelm and fragmentation. Jackie is a member of the California School of Professional Psychology, a past member of the Illinois Governor's Council on Fitness and Sports, and now hosts a weekly television talk show featuring conversations with female role models.

SAMPLE TRIPS

►**Hiking Retreats**—A typical day at CenterPoint might begin with an optional morning stretch and meditation followed by breakfast and an exhilarating guided hike on a choice of trails suitable for all levels of fitness. Savor the fresh air and surrounding views while you walk at your own pace and enjoy conversation or silent time alone. Your mid-afternoon return to the lodge allows free time for reading, massage, napping, or an Aspen cultural event. In the evening you gather for a dinner prepared by the retreat's chef and an evening discussion on topics ranging from personal vision statements, mentoring, leadership, risk, and change. Four days/$1000/moderate.

Prices include: Transportation to and from the airport, meals, accommodations, one massage, and seminar materials.

Prices do not include: Personal equipment.

Guides: Subcontracted licensed wilderness trail guides.

Training for guides: Emergency medicine, alpine and sub-alpine outdoor skills.

Liability coverage: Yes.

Cloud Canyon Wilderness Experience

411 Lemon Grove Lane
Santa Barbara, CA 93108
805/969-0982

Wilderness Backpacking in the U.S.

Began operating: 1992
Number of trips offered per year: 8
Number of all-women's trips per year: All
Usual group size: 5
Typical age of participants: 30s–40s
Range of ages of participants: 13–53

Multigenerational programs
Scholarships available: Work exchange possible.

All levels of experience are welcome on these wilderness backpacking adventures in California and Utah, where participants can explore forests, mountains, canyons, and deserts. Cloud Canyon Wilderness Experience trips vary in length and difficulty, but all require good basic physical condition, as you will hike an average of three to four miles each day. Llamas carry gear on some trips. All programs begin with short introductory classes on the use of equipment, route-finding, environmental ethics, safety, and judgement.

IN THEIR OWN WORDS
"Spending time in the wilderness is healing and empowering. It is a spiritual experience, on some level, for each woman, and increases her confidence and sense of freedom. We encourage each woman to meet her own challenges and to have a lot of fun. Guides are willing and able to help participants meet personal challenges. All women who can backpack are welcome. Lesbians are always welcome; we have some lesbian staff."   —Alison Reitz, Director

HISTORY/BACKGROUND
Alison Reitz founded Cloud Canyon Wilderness Experience to share the personal and spiritual growth that happens in the wilderness in small, noncompetitive groups. A graduate of the National Outdoor Leadership School's Outdoor Educator's Course, Alison holds a master's degree in geology and has been organizing and leading backpacking trips since 1968.

SAMPLE TRIPS

➤**California Coast Ranges in the Springtime**—Explore the swimming holes, pine covered mountains, wildflowers, and rivers of Los Padres National Forest wilderness areas. Four to five days/$200–$300/easy to moderate.

➤**Mothers and Daughters Backcountry Trips**—Travel among the swimming holes, mountains, wildflowers, and rivers of Santa Barbara's Los Padres National Forest. Hike, camp, cook, swim, laugh, play, and watch the stars with special times for talking, listening, and learning from each other. See and appreciate each other in new ways and in new roles. For daughters eleven and older. Four days/$250 per pair/easy to moderate.

➤**Southern Utah Trips**—Wild slickrock country, narrow redwalled canyons, still pools, rushing streams, and the silence of the desert. The power of the land helps you discover the nature of wildness in the land and in yourself. Seven days/$450/easy to moderate.

➤**Sierra Nevada Trips**—Explore the "Range of Light," the lakes, mountain passes, plateaus, and high alpine scenery of the Sierra Nevada. Emphasizes the connection between creative vision and the wilderness experience. Eight days/$500/moderate to challenging.

Prices include: Meals and group equipment.

Prices do not include: Personal equipment (CCWE will help participants get outfitted for the least possible cost).

Guides: Women trained in wilderness skills and first aid with easy-going leadership styles.

Training for guides: First aid, extensive wilderness background, ability to lead and teach in a responsible but nonauthoritarian way.

Liability coverage: Yes, participants are also required to carry personal health insurance for the duration of the trip.

Club Le Bon

P.O. Box 444
Woodbridge, NJ 07095
800/836-8687 or 908/636-1120   fax: 908/636-1363

Lesbian Vacations in Mexico, the Caribbean, and Indonesia

Began operating: 1978
Number of trips offered per year: 7
Number of all-women's trips per year: 5
Usual group size: 30–60
Typical age of participants: 30–40
Range of ages of participants: 22–65

Programs for lesbians

Club Le Bon offers upscale vacations at island resorts. By contracting an entire resort for a week, Club Le Bon creates an all-inclusive lesbian retreat. Enjoy day sails, visits to Mayan ruins, private beach barbecues, and entertainers from the women's community. Swim, snorkel, scuba dive, boogie board, or play volleyball along white sandy beaches and turquoise water. In addition to their all-women's programs, Club Le Bon also offers vacations for gay and lesbian parents and their kids.

IN THEIR OWN WORDS
"Small, personal, and discreet luxury vacations set in the most beautiful areas of the world, untouched by tourism developments. We create space that is romantic, safe, and fun for lesbians."   —Geri Luongo, Owner

HISTORY/BACKGROUND
Club Le Bon owner Geri Luongo has organized lesbian vacations through her full-service travel agency for seventeen years. With over twenty years of travel industry and tour development experience, Geri is able to offer special group airfares and customized packages for organizations and groups.

SAMPLE TRIPS

➤**Barbados**—Wake to views of the sea from your suite at the Ginger Bay Beach Club. A natural rock grotto opens onto a secluded cove. Let the breeze carry away stress as you relax on the beach. Snorkel and sail for a day on a fifty-foot catamaran. Enjoy dinners at a local women-owned restaurant and a private beach barbecue. Take a mini-moke safari among lush green valleys and white beaches, or an island tour. Eight days/$1100/easy.

➤**Yucatan, Mexico**—Sail to Isla Mujeres, "The Island of Women," for a beach barbecue. Visit Tulum/Xel-ha, the "Mayan Temple by the Sea," and Xcaret, "Nature's Sacred Paradise," where Mayans came to purify their bodies and souls in sacred baths before sailing to Cozumel to worship Ixchel, Goddess of Fertility. Opportunities to snorkel, scuba dive, windsurf, horseback ride, and swim with dolphins. Restaurant menu includes Mexican and Caribbean dishes. Eight days/$1050/easy.

➤**Bali, Indonesia**—This is a place of towering volcanoes and endless beaches, where the people still make temple offerings to the goddesses. Learn about the Bukittings, one of the last remaining matrilineal societies in the world. Twelve days/$2200/easy.

Prices include: Meals, snacks and beverages, accommodations (single shares available upon request), transfers, baggage handling, sightseeing, catamaran cruise, tips, taxes, sporting events and activities, entertainment.

Prices do not include: Personal equipment and departure tax.

Guides: Owner Geri Luongo.

Training for guides: Twenty years of experience as travel agent and tour organizer.

Liability coverage: No, comprehensive Chubb Travel Insurance is available for $49.

Colorado Outward Bound School

945 Pennsylvania Street
Denver, CO 80203
800/477-2627 or 303/837-0880 fax: 303/831-6987

Develop Leadership and Confidence in Colorado's Wilderness

Began operating: 1961
Number of trips offered per year: 140
Number of all-women's trips per year: 24
Usual group size: 8–12
Typical age of participants: 18–32
Range of ages of participants: 18–32

Scholarships available

Courses are designed to offer experiences that demand an increase in initiative, self-confidence, personal responsibility, leadership, fitness, teamwork, and commitment to others and to the environment. Whether participating in a three-day program for survivors of violence or a twenty-three-day leadership mountaineering expedition, you have the chance for adventure and reflection. COBS works to attract students and instructors from a wide range of social, cultural, economic, religious, and racial backgrounds, and instructors receive ongoing training to better understand the needs and perspective of each student.

IN THEIR OWN WORDS
"Outward Bound programs are about empowerment and choice making. No one is forced to do anything. Instructors are not guides but facilitate learning through the experiential learning process. Participants learn by doing and making mistakes. Instructors do not lead groups but rather teach participants to lead themselves." —Meg Ryan, Community Development Program

HISTORY/BACKGROUND
Founded in 1961, courses were initially offered only to young men. Now there are courses for young women, adults, coed groups, families, couples, educators, youths at risk, parents and children, people in recovery, cancer survivors, Vietnam veterans, survivors of violence, and perpetrators of violence. COBS serves three thousand students annually.

SAMPLE TRIPS

➤**Women's Empowerment**—Progressively difficult yet manageable challenges include rock climbing, backpacking, peak ascent, orienteering, a ropes course, and a solo spent in reflection. An emphasis is placed on the transference of new insights back to the home environment. Join women of all ages and walks of life on a course tailored to the group's goals and abilities. Five days/$600/moderate.

➤**Survivors of Violence**—This recovery course is designed specifically to assist survivors of sexual assault, incest, and domestic violence and is conducted in conjunction with service providers throughout Colorado. Scholarships are available to Colorado residents through the Federal Victims of Crime Act and local Victims Assistance and Law Enforcement Boards. Three days/$400/moderate.

➤**Leadership Alpine Mountaineering**—Journey over some of the highest, most breathtaking terrain in the continental United States on the original Outward Bound course. Experience jagged snow-capped mountains with endless vistas, valleys of wildflowers and clear running streams that ribbon the fragile alpine tundra. Leadership skills and teamwork receive particular emphasis as you learn navigation, rope handling, rappelling, and low-impact camping skills. Twenty-three days/$1900/challenging.

➤**Alpine Mountaineering**—A shorter mountaineering course that begins on a Friday and ends nine days later on Sunday, this course packs instruction in low-impact camping, navigation, natural history, and backcountry safety into an itinerary that includes rock climbing, soloing, peaks ascents, and an endurance run. Ten days/$1300/challenging.

➤**Canyonlands Expedition**—An in-depth canyon exploration of the Slickrock Wilderness. Includes technical travel and low-impact camping techniques, rock climbing, navigation, and a short solo. Ten days/$1300/challenging.

Prices include: Meals, group equipment, sleeping bags, backpacks, and raincoats.

Prices do not include: Personal equipment and application fee.

Guides: Diverse, experienced, and highly qualified mountaineers.

Training for guides: Extensive rock climbing and mountaineering experience; CPR/ advanced first aid; training in facilitation, conflict resolution, and skills processing.

Liability coverage: Yes.

Dare You!

P.O. Box 1018
Middleburg, VA 22117
703/364-1622 fax: 703/364-2040

Horseriding Adventures in the New Zealand Wilderness

Began operating: 1984
Number of trips offered per year: 2–3
Number of all-women's trips per year: 90–95%
Usual group size: 10
Typical age of participants: 40–50
Range of ages of participants: 21–74

Ride big-boned crossbred horses with Australian-style saddles as you explore New Zealand's ranges, native beech forests, and river valleys. Revel in spectacular ridgetop views. These ten-day trips are "aimed at the fitness level of a desk-bound woman" rather than the "abilities of the macho male," though some riding experience is necessary. Dare You! may offer two domestic rides in Virginia's mountains as a warm-up to the New Zealand trip and as an opportunity to estimate riders' experience. Outreach to native New Zealanders contributes to group diversity.

IN THEIR OWN WORDS
"Women working together and roughing it in the wilderness develop a self-confidence and bond that lasts well beyond the adventure. We take small groups into remote areas of New Zealand where we have never seen another tourist en route!"   —Sharon Saari, Founder

HISTORY/BACKGROUND
Sharon Saari was working as an environmental consultant when she founded Dare You! Sharon and a group of adventurous friends led worldwide adventure trips that included horseback riding, cattle roundups, safaris, and scuba dive trips. As word of programs spread, more women wanted to participate. In 1984, Dare You! surveyed two hundred women about their preferred trips and discovered a large demand among professional women for outdoor adventure programs that are not overly strenuous. Horseback riding was one of the most popular programs requested. Dare You! began specializing in New Zealand horseback trips in 1987.

SAMPLE TRIPS

➤**New Zealand High Country**—Enjoy ridgetop views and visit a native Kiwi forest. Climb over the native Alpine tussock grass of the Dampier Range and descend to Deep Creek. Swim in the lake country, soak in natural hot springs at Hanmer Springs Alpine Spa, and bungee jump off a bridge if you're game! During your last two days in Christchurch visit the city's gardens, museums, a craft fair, and international food bazaar. Midway into your trip a vehicle meets you to provide clean clothes, home cooking, and a hut with beds. Camp out and spend nights in cabins, lodges, hotels, and sheep stations. If you want to continue exploring New Zealand on your own once the trip ends, Dare You! provides an additional eight-day itinerary. Recommended sites, hikes, tours, dining locations and accommodations are included. Ten days/$1000/intermediate to advanced.

Prices include: Transportation to and from the airport, meals, accommodations, and group equipment.

Prices do not include: Personal equipment.

Guides: Local New Zealand male guides accompanied by Dare You! founder Sharon Saari.

Training for guides: Local guides have over ten years of guiding experience; Sharon Saari has CPR/first-aid training.

Liability coverage: No.

Dirt Roads and Damsels

P.O. Box 989
Gresham, OR 97030
503/667-6602   fax: 503/667-2917

Fly Fishing from the Bahamas to British Columbia

Began operating: 1991
Number of trips offered per year: 4
Number of all-women's trips per year: All
Usual group size: 12–15
Typical age of participants: 35
Range of ages of participants: 19–60

Dirt Roads and Damsels provides fly fishing instruction on casting, entomology, reading water, knots, rigging, and equipment. Travel to the southwestern or northwestern U.S., Alaska, the Bahamas, or Canada to hone your skills. Most trips include classroom or outdoor instruction for beginners, with tips on advanced techniques for more experienced fishers.

IN THEIR OWN WORDS
"We promote women in fly fishing. We are licensed guides, outdoor photographers, and writers. Women share a special camaraderie through our fly fishing classes."   —Donna Teeny, Co-founder

HISTORY/BACKGROUND
Pioneers in the world of women's fly fishing, Donna Rae Teeny and Rhonda Dee Sapp established a fly fishing guide, instruction, destination, and equipment service. Among their unique gear is a women's fly fishing vest. A fleece body suit, waders, hats, rod, and reels are under development. Donna and Rhonda have twenty-two and thirteen years of experience, respectively, in the fly fishing industry. In the future, they plan to develop fishing gear for children and promote activities to help them get started in fishing. They concocted the company's name from their initials: DRT and RDS.

SAMPLE TRIPS

➤**The Bighorn, Montana**—Spend five days in this famous fishing area of Montana, based in a fishing lodge with a stream in front and a small lake out back. Get daily instruction and practice reading the water, casting the stream, and fishing from a float tube in the lake. Five days/$1300/beginning to advanced.

➤**Barnes Butte Lake, Oregon**—Attend a four-day fly fishing school, learn how to cast, tie knots, and fish from a float tube on this Central Oregon lake near Prineville. Four days/$800/beginning to advanced.

➤**Andros Island, Bahamas**—Stay at the BoneFish Club, a family-owned fishing lodge with a homey atmosphere and air-conditioned rooms. Fish the turquoise water for the powerful bonefish, which average five to seven pounds and can weigh as much as fourteen pounds. Five days/$1700/beginning to advanced.

➤**Alaska**—Spend seven days at the Katmai Lodge on the Alagnak River, where you can catch all the five species of salmon as well as rainbow trout. Instruction for beginners and lots of fishing time for advanced fishers. Seven days/$3300/beginning to advanced.

➤**British Columbia Steelhead and Salmon**—Stay at Douglas Lake Ranch, the largest working cattle ranch in British Columbia, in a comfortable room in the ranch house. Enjoy country farm cooking, and observe cowhands and cattle. Classroom sessions in the morning hone your skills for afternoon fishing in float tubes for rainbow trout up to ten pounds. Six days/$1800/beginning to advanced.

Prices include: Meals and accommodations.

Prices do not include: Equipment and fishing license.

Guides: Co-founders Donna Teeny and Rhonda Sapp.

Training for guides: Licensed guides trained in CPR/first aid.

Liability coverage: No, covered by lodges.

Earthlodge and Womenspeak Journeys
2462 Matilija Canyon
Ojai, CA 93023
805/646-9721

Wilderness Rituals and Rites of Passage

Began operating: 1983
Number of trips offered per year: 8
Number of all-women's trips per year: 6
Usual group size: 14
Typical age of participants: 30s–50s
Range of ages of participants: 18–65

Scholarships available

Earthlodge and Womenspeak Journeys is dedicated to discovery and renewal. Their programs combine community ceremonies that merge ancient and modern ways and teachings with wilderness instruction in backcountry skills and ecological ethics. Aiming to transform our relationships with ourselves, our communities and the natural world, EWJ fosters a reverence for the interdependence of all living beings and a recognition of the individual's and community's movement through life by initiation, celebration, and rites of passage. EWJ leads programs for women, men, and teenagers in the U.S., Ireland, and Switzerland, and has previously guided trips to Nepal and Mexico. Mother and child programs are offered by special arrangement.

IN THEIR OWN WORDS
"Learning together in a setting that inspires respect and wonder, we reconnect with the earth, awakening essential parts of ourselves that have been suppressed and silenced by the demands of modern living."
                    —Earthlodge and Womenspeak Journeys brochure

HISTORY/BACKGROUND
Earthlodge and Womenspeak Journeys co-founder Nancy Goddard, M.A., is a wilderness therapist trained in the Hakomi method of psychotherapy. Also leading EWJ's all-women's adventures are: Colleen Kelley, an artist with a black belt in aikido and environmental educator; and Leslie Lembo, singer, performer, and songwriter who has led trips with the Yosemite Institute.

SAMPLE TRIPS

►**Womenspeak Rites of Passage**—Whether in California's Los Padres National Forest, New Mexico's Rocky Mountains, Ireland, or Switzerland, these spring, summer, and fall journeys strive to renew the vitality of body, mind, and spirit through backpacking, campwork, music making, ceremony, and eclectic wisdom teaching. Eight days/$550 (for trips in U.S.)/moderate. Eight days/$700 (for Ireland or Switzerland)/moderate.

►**Voice of the Wild**—Leslie Lembo and Nancy Goddard lead a journey to create music in the wild. Backpack to a river and waterfall, cook over a campfire, and learn wilderness skills as you birth a spirit song. Enjoy fun vocal exercises that help to relax you. Join in song circles throughout the day. Singing in a group will give you permission to sing freely. When you let yourself sing you can learn to sing. Four to seven days/$500/moderate.

Prices include: Vegetarian meals and group equipment.

Prices do not include: Personal equipment.

Guides: Professional wilderness guides, primarily Nancy Goddard and Colleen Kelley.

Training for guides: Apprenticeship with Nancy Goddard and Colleen Kelley, advanced first-aid medical training, and training in group dynamics.

Liability coverage: No.

Earthwise

23 Mount Nebo Road
Newtown, CT 06470
203/426-6092

Active Adventures and "Get-Away" Weekends

Began operating: 1986
Number of trips offered per year: 30
Number of all-women's trips per year: 98%
Usual group size: Up to 10
Typical age of participants: 30–50
Range of ages of participants: 16–75

Multigenerational programs
Scholarships available

Try a snowshoeing and meditation sampler in Vermont, combine canoeing and island camping in the Adirondacks, or raft the Green River in Utah. Earthwise leads weekend- to week-long adventures, including personal awareness retreats and fly fishing in spring, backpacking, canoeing, and sailing in summer, and skiing in winter. A multigenerational hiking and canoeing trip is dedicated to mothers/daughters/grandmothers/granddaughters/aunts/nieces. The newest addition to Earthwise's varied list of excursions is a trip to Hungary that includes sightseeing and outdoor activities.

IN THEIR OWN WORDS
"We believe that women learn well when they choose their own goals. Intentional stress is not built into our programs. We work with women individually on skill building, according to their own interests and experience."
—Lesley M. Nagot, Director

HISTORY/BACKGROUND
After fifteen years as an office manager in the corporate world, Lesley Nagot became director of Earthwise when founder Marcia Bourne-Barber retired. With over thirty years' experience in the outdoors, Lesley is an Adirondack-licensed New York State guide, award-winning nature photographer, published poet, and was nominated "Woman of the Year –1991" in Danbury, Connecticut.

SAMPLE TRIPS

➤**"I Need to Get Away" Weekends**—Whether you like the idea of curling up with a good book beside a roaring fire, skiing down challenging trails in winter, or sunning on the deck and swimming in a mountain lake in summer, these retreats take you far from the crowd. Breakfast and snacks provided; bring or buy lunch and dinner. Two and a half days/under $100/all levels.

➤**Hungarian Excursion**—Venture beyond the former boundaries of the iron curtain in central Europe and hike in the national forests of Hungary. Canoe and kayak on the Tisza River and tour Budapest. Your multilingual guide is a journalist who focuses on women's and environmental issues. Eleven days/ $1150/all levels.

➤**Snow Trekking**—Archaeological evidence suggests that the snowshoe existed in central Asia some five thousand years ago. Now it's your turn to explore the winter woods by this ancient mode of travel. Two and a half days/ under $200/beginning.

➤**Yoga and Meditation**—Learn to listen to your natural rhythm and become receptive to the energies within. Sessions offer guidance and support to integrate meditation into your everyday life. Two and a half days/under $200/ beginning.

➤**Fly Fishing: the Ultimate!**— Imagine yourself on the banks of an isolated river, swollen with snow melt, whipping your line in long graceful movements and dropping the fly exactly where you want it. Earthwise adheres to the philosophy of catch and release. Groups are kept to a maximum of five women. Fishing gear is provided. Two and half days/$250/beginning.

➤**Maine Coast Sailing**—Learn to sail or simply relax on the *Figaro* in the Penopscot Bay region. Anchor off an island cove and explore the shore. A vegetarian menu accompanies evenings of music, games, or reading beneath a star-filled sky. Seven days/$650/beginning.

Prices include: Meals, accommodations, and group equipment.

Prices do not include: Personal equipment.

Guides: In the Adirondacks: licensed guides; elsewhere: Lesley Nagot.

Training for guides: CPR/advanced first aid, wilderness medicine, group dynamics, an ability to tune into individual needs and capabilities.

Liability coverage: Yes.

Eco-Explorations

P.O. Box 7944
Santa Cruz, CA 95061
408/335-7199 fax: 408/335-3375

Experience the Pulse of the Ocean Realm

Began operating: 1989
Number of trips offered per year: 14–25
Number of all-women's trips per year: 6–12
Usual group size: 6–12
Typical age of participants: 30s–40s
Range of ages of participants: 12–65

Accessible to disabled women: On some programs.
Programs for lesbians
Scholarships available: Work exchange and bartering possible.

Eco-Explorations offers scuba and sea kayaking instruction, guided eco-tours, adventure travel, and women's aquabound retreats. Swimming, snorkeling, kayaking, and scuba programs may be accompanied by optional writing groups. EE believes it is a privilege to explore aquatic eco-systems and recognizes the need to tread lightly to protect natural and cultural resources. Along with its women's programs, EE offers gay and lesbian trips and a volunteer research dive program for experienced divers.

IN THEIR OWN WORDS
"Eco-Explorations is dedicated to ecosystem awareness, safety, and the expansion of one's boundaries through aquatic adventure. Plan to arrive on a program with some personal reserves—learning and exploration is most passionately embraced when you're not completely exhausted and burned out."
— Lori Katz, Owner

HISTORY/BACKGROUND
Lori Katz founded Eco-Explorations in 1989 to share her passion for and knowledge of the aquatic realm. A PADI and NAUI master instructor with over sixteen years of diving experience, Lori has also guided sea kayaking trips for four years. She has studied marine sciences, chemistry, and writing, and her articles and underwater photos have appeared in national publications.

SAMPLE TRIPS

➤**Women's Aquabound Retreat in Monterey Bay or Sea Ranch, California**—Leave the stresses of city life behind for the weekend! Activities include a half-day guided sea kayaking or snorkeling tour, an early morning dive, hot tubbing, and an optional writers' group to integrate these aquatic adventures with your inner journeys. Shared accommodations in a tranquil setting. Two and half days/$300/all levels.

➤**Women's Scuba Extravaganza in Grand Cayman Island, Caribbean**—The Cayman Islands are an underwater photographer's dream—endless wall dives, crystal clear water, prolific reef structures, and spectacular tropical fish. Six days of outrageous unlimited diving includes "Stingray City" and a night dive. Accommodations provided at Coconut Harbour, a dedicated dive resort. Advanced Open Water Diver, Underwater Photographer, and Underwater Naturalist certifications available. Price includes six days' boat diving (two tanks, weights), one "Stingray City" afternoon boat dive, one night boat dive, and unlimited shore diving. Seven days/$900/all levels.

➤**Paddle with the Gray Whales of Magdalena Bay, Baja, Mexico**—Visit the southernmost Baja calving grounds for a once-in-a-lifetime whale-watching experience. There can be as many as thirty-five hundred whales in the bay system at any one time. The group will use a *panga* (small fishing launch) in order to have the best photo opportunities and comply with Mexican government regulations. Paddle top-notch double and single sea kayaks, enjoy tasty vegetarian meals, base camp in style, and relax for two nights at La Concha Beach Resort in La Paz. Seven days/$900/all levels.

Prices include: Some meals, all accommodations, and group equipment.

Prices do not include: Personal equipment, scuba equipment other than tanks and weights, and speciality certifications on dive trips.

Guides: Owner/operator Lori Katz and environmentally responsible local guides, naturalists, or divemasters.

Training for guides: PADI and NAUI scuba instructor's certification, ACA coastal kayaking instructor development training, CPR/first-aid certification, must have excellent judgment, an appreciation of the ecosystems we visit, and a passion for sharing the aquatic realm.

Liability coverage: Yes.

Elakah! Expeditions

P.O. Box 4092
Bellingham, WA 98227
206/734-7270

Kayaking along Baja and the Pacific Northwest

Began operating: 1990
Number of trips offered per year: 35–40
Number of all-women's trips per year: 10
Usual group size: 10
Typical age of participants: 35
Range of ages of participants: 11–74

Multigenerational programs
Scholarships available: A limited number of specific-task barters.

Kayak Washington's Pacific coast in the summer or Mexico's Baja Peninsula in the winter or spring. Venture by sea kayak along Southeastern Alaska's glaciers and fjords. Elakah! Expeditions welcome all levels of experience, always keeping the beginner in mind. No previous experience is necessary as trips introduce paddling and safety skills. One- to ten-day trips combine kayaking and whale watching, spiritual retreats, and mother-daughter tours. Guides share their knowledge of natural history, native uses of plants, storytelling, drumming, and yoga.

IN THEIR OWN WORDS
"It is the perfect excuse to do what I love, and with all the wonderful trappings...azure waves, fireside stories, moonrises, poetry, drumming, silence, whale breath." —Jennifer Hahn, Owner

HISTORY/BACKGROUND
In 1980, while studying environmental law and literature, Jennifer Hahn began kayaking. After ten years of coastal paddling from Alaska to Baja and guiding trips for other outdoor companies, Jennifer established Elakah! Expeditions. She recently completed a one-month solo trip up the Inside Passage of Alaska. A nature illustrator and writer, Jennifer named her company Elakah, which means sea otter in Chinook jargon—a centuries-old trade language of the Northwest Coast native peoples.

SAMPLE TRIPS

➤**Washington San Juan Islands Sea Kayak Tour**—An introduction to coastal kayaking for beginners or a chance for those with paddling experience to explore the more than four hundred coastal islands. Practice paddling techniques, tide and current reading, and navigation. Stroll the beaches, exploring tide pools and watching for marine and bird life. One to four days/from under $100 to $350/all levels.

➤**Wildwoman Sea Kayak**—Rekindle your wild spirit! Kayak along shorelines by day; drum and sing by firelight at night. You will be carried along on the mythic wings of ancient stories as retold by gifted storyteller White Bear Woman. A leisurely pace allows plenty of time for paddling and personal time. Retreat is held at White Bear Woman's Lopez Island home. Indoor or tent space available, hot tub, and outdoor showers. Four days/$400/all levels.

➤**Returning the Balance: Sea Kayak and Yoga Retreat**—Allow the moon, tide, and gentle yoga to bring you into balance. Practice yoga in the morning, kayak past inlets and islands in the afternoon, relax in the rustic retreat house at night. When the moon rises, celebrate with a ceremonial sweatlodge, ritual, and drumming. Led by a certified yoga instructor. Four days/$400/all levels.

➤**Mothers and Daughters: The Sacred Salt**—Mothers and daughters reconnect in this leisurely two-day sea kayak and camping tour of the San Juan Islands. Watch for sea otters, seals, herons, and eagles. Set up camp overlooking the snow-capped Cascades. Two days/$200/all levels.

➤**Of Finwhales and Coyote Tales: Baja, Mexico**—Spend one and a half days traveling overland through cactus plains in bloom followed by six days of kayaking, snorkeling, beachcombing, and camping along desert island shores. Paddle three to seven miles each day, watching for whales feeding alongside you, pelicans, blue-footed boobies, and terns. Stop for a tour of the Museo de Historia y Cultura before the return journey. Ten days/$1000/all levels.

Prices include: In Washington: breakfast and dinner; in Baja: transportation to and from San Diego airport and all meals; group equipment.

Prices do not include: Lunch in Washington; tent; ferry fees.

Guides: Owner Jennifer Hahn co-guides 80 percent of trips.

Training for guides: CPR/first aid, salt water navigation and rescue skills training, apprenticeship, and one to five years' kayak guiding experience.

Liability coverage: Yes.

Equinox Wilderness Expeditions
618 West 14th Avenue
Anchorage, AK 99501
907/274-9087

Alaskan Wilderness Journeys

Began operating: 1986
Number of trips offered per year: 16
Number of all-women's trips per year: 9
Usual group size: 6–8
Typical age of participants: 25–55
Range of ages of participants: 12–75

Multigenerational programs
Programs for older women
Programs for young women
Programs for lesbians

Whether rafting through the largest wilderness in North America, backpacking through the caribou migration, skiing in the shadow of Mount McKinley, or practicing yoga asanas on a sun-bathed Arctic sandbar, Equinox strives to move in harmony with the rhythms of wildlife, water, and weather. Programs emphasize natural history and wildlife observation, minimum-impact adventure, and environmental awareness. These trips are designed for women with previous outdoor experience and a good fitness level. Among Equinox's unique offerings are a sixteen-day ethnobotany exploration, a fourteen-day wildlife safari, and a ten-day ecofeminist seminar and float trip.

IN THEIR OWN WORDS
"In a world where wildlands are shrinking, total wilderness solitude is precious. I love Alaska's unique wild places and the powerful experiences that come from sharing the landscape with small groups of women. "
—Karen Jettmar, Founder

HISTORY/BACKGROUND
Karen Jettmar's twenty years of living in Alaska, including four years as assistant director of the Wilderness Society and a stint as a backcountry ranger, have afforded her intimate knowledge of Alaska's most remote regions.

SAMPLE TRIPS

➤**Yoga, the Inner Dance/Brooks Range Canoeing**—Equinox brings the beauty and serenity of hatha yoga to the Brooks Range. Paddle down the John River with ample time for trekking in the mountains and stretching on river bars. Eight days/$1500 from Fairbanks/moderate.

➤**Heart of the Alaska Range: Ruth Glacier Ski Touring**—Ski and sun in the shadow of Denali, in the deepest mountain gorge in North America. The scenery offers dramatic contrasts of sculpted rock and ice. Glacier ski travel, crevasse rescue techniques, telemarking, rock or snow and ice climbing, and sunbathing are all options. Six days/$500 plus air charter/moderate.

➤**Kenai Fjords Kayaking**—Paddle among jewel-like floes exploring quiet coves and bays, rugged cliffs and the thundering faces of tidewater glaciers. Camp on sandy beaches with the Kenai Mountains towering above. Otter, whale, seal, porpoise, and nesting sea birds inhabit the landscape. No kayaking experience necessary. Seven days/$1200/moderate.

➤**Arctic Wildlife Refuge: Trekking with the Caribou**—Backpack along ancient trails of the Porcupine Caribou herd. Numbering over a hundred and sixty thousand, the herd migrates through mountain passes. With luck, you'll encounter bands of bulls as you trek from the mountains to the arctic coastal plain. You are also likely to encounter grizzlies, wolves, rough-legged hawks, peregrine falcons, and other migratory birds while traversing lands now threatened by oil development. Eight days/$2000/moderate to challenging.

➤**Arrigetch Peaks: Trekking in the Granite Peaks**—These knife-edged, glacially carved granite spires are unique in a region where slowly disintegrating sedimentary mountains are the rule. You backpack into the peaks and explore the towering "fingers of the hand extended," a translation from the Eskimo. Bring your rock climbing shoes and hardware. Nine days/ $2100/challenging.

Prices include: Charter flights from Fairbanks or Anchorage unless otherwise noted, meals, group equipment.

Prices do not include: Personal equipment.

Who guides trips: Alaskan guides and guest experts on speciality trips.

Training for guides: CPR/first aid, Emergency Medical Technician, Alaska natural history.

Liability coverage: Yes.

Et-Then

P.O. Box 607
Yellowknife, Northwest Territories X1A 2N5 Canada
403/873-4940

Canoeing and Dog Sledding in the Northwest Territories

Began operating: 1989
Number of trips offered per year: 5–7
Number of all-women's trips per year: 1–2
Usual group size: 7–10
Typical age of participants: 30–40
Range of ages of participants: 1–80

Accessible to disabled women: Depending on trip and disability.

Fly one hundred and forty miles east of Yellowknife, Canada, to the homestead of Kristen Gilbertson Olesen and Dave Olesen, located on the shores of Great Slave Lake—the eighth largest lake in the world. Their year-round home serves as a base for Et-Then wilderness trips. All-women's canoeing and dog sledding trips set out into the Northwest Territories along the edge of the tundra. Et-Then guides have experience leading disabled wilderness trips and are eager to include a wide variety of women in their programs.

IN THEIR OWN WORDS
"We strive to travel quietly and comfortably. We are small enough that clients feel like friends and are treated like family."
—Kristen Gilbertson Oleson, Co-founder

HISTORY/BACKGROUND
Before establishing an adventure company, Kristen Gilbertson Olesen taught in native Alaskan villages, worked as a camp cook for exploration camps in Canada, led disabled wilderness trips in Minnesota, and led or participated in trips—of up to seventy days—in the Arctic. Kristen is an accomplished photographer and speaks American sign language. She and co-founder Dave Olesen, a commercial pilot and author, are both originally from the U.S. Midwest. They set out to find a remote location to train sled dogs and run an outfitting business. For the past five years, Kristen and Dave have participated in the Iditarod, with Kristen handling the dogs and Dave racing them.

SAMPLE TRIPS

➤**Dog Sled Adventure**—Experience spring in the far north. Travel and snow conditions are still wintry and nights can dip well below zero, but daylight stretches from early morning to late evening. Wildlife is on the move and birds are returning. Setting out from Kristen and Dave's homestead, you'll learn all the basics of mushing, snow camping, and dog team care. Everyone gets a chance to "solo" their own dog team with a loaded sled. Opportunities for snowshoeing and cross country skiing (you must bring your own skis). Camp for four or five nights on the trail in tents heated by small woodstoves. Participants should be in good to excellent physical condition. Eight days/CDN $2250/beginning. Ten days/CDN $2700/beginning.

➤**Canoe Trip, Aylmer Lake**—A summer adventure offering women of all ages a chance to learn to meet the day-to day challenges of Arctic travel. Paddle in twenty-four-foot cedar canoes and explore the nooks and crannies of the upper Lockhart River. Chances for wildlife encounters are excellent: musk oxen, wolves, caribou, and countless bird species thrive in this area in late summer. There are plenty of opportunities for hiking. Good physical condition is a definite asset. Beginning paddlers are welcome. Eight days/CDN $2450/moderate to challenging.

Prices include: Airfare from Yellowknife to homestead, meals, group equipment.

Prices do not include: Personal equipment.

Guides: Co-founder Kristen Gilbertson Olesen.

Training for guides: Previously guided with Wilderness Inquiry, extensive experience participating in and leading wilderness trips in the Arctic.

Liability coverage: Yes.

Firma Hagi

Huiberstraat 8
7412 JR Deventer, The Netherlands
05700-41473

Horseriding Holidays in the Netherlands

Began operating: 1987
Number of trips offered per year: 5–10
Number of all-women's trips per year: All
Usual group size: 5–10
Typical age of participants: 30
Range of ages of participants: 10–50

Multigenerational programs
Scholarships available: Some trips have sliding scale fees, according to income.

Firma Hagi horseriding programs emphasize the pleasure of riding and of working with horses. Set off into the woods or ride onto the beaches. Beginners learn to ride in small groups. More experienced riders can take part in trekkings. Participants stay in summer cottages. Firma Hagi provides a vegetarian menu.

IN THEIR OWN WORDS
"Relaxed learning is a positive way of learning."
— Floor Hijmans, Owner

HISTORY/BACKGROUND
Having worked with horses since her childhood, Floor Hijmans wanted to give other women the opportunity to enjoy riding and so established Firma Hagi in 1987.

SAMPLE TRIPS

➤**Weekends in Holten**—Set out from a stable at the foot of the Holten hills. Ride into the woods or use the inside range in bad weather. Participants can split up into different groups according to skill levels. Trips take place in spring and fall. Children are welcome. No experience is required. Two and a half days/f250/all levels.

➤**Beach Week**—Enjoy the sun, sea, and sand with the horses of the Vaerderij. Horseback ride on the Island of Terschelling. No riding experience necessary. Five days/f500–f600/all levels.

➤**Beach Weekend on Terschelling**—Experience the exhilaration of a free gallop on an empty beach in fall. No riding experience necessary. Two and a half days/f300/all levels.

➤**Trips in Drente**—Enjoy Vanda Oosterhuis's Icelandic horses for a trekking experience in Wapserveen. You work with Vanda in the morning and ride out on the moors with Floor in the afternoon. Includes two days trekking. Some riding experience necessary. Four days/f400–f500/intermediate to advanced.

Prices include: Vegetarian meals, accommodations, and group equipment.

Prices do not include: Personal equipment and boat trip on beach week.

Guides: Owner Floor Hijmans.

Training for guides: Extensive experience leading horse trips.

Liability coverage: No, participants must carry their own insurance.

Hawk, I'm Your Sister

P.O. Box 9109
Santa Fe, New Mexico 87504
505/690-4490

Wilderness Canoe Trips in the U.S., Peru, Canada, and Mexico

Began operating: 1984
Number of trips offered per year: 9
Number of all-women's trips per year: 8
Usual group size: 10–20
Typical age of participants: 30s–50s
Range of ages of participants: 20–75

Programs for young women: Leadership training program.

Learn to feel at home in the wilderness with Hawk, I'm Your Sister. Rise with the sun and paddle for five to eight hours, taking breaks for snacks, stretches, exploration, and lunch along the way. Camp out and eat dinners that include baked chicken and yams, tempeh stir fry, or salmon and baked potatoes. Though trips require strenuous physical effort, programs accommodate all levels of experience, and instruction is provided. Participants have paddled through the Canyonlands of Utah, the White Otter Wilderness of Ontario, and attended canoeing/camping/writing retreats in Baja, Mexico, with with poet Sharon Olds.

IN THEIR OWN WORDS
"Women of all ages, shapes, sizes, and skill levels can enjoy any of the trips. You will experience fatigue, mud, and your own strength. You will thrive on the simplicity of life outdoors and discover you are more capable than you ever imagined." —Hawk I'm Your Sister brochure

HISTORY/BACKGROUND
Founder Beverly Antaeus has guided river trips since 1975. She is a graduate of the Goddard Program of Vermont College and the Bonnie Prudden School of Physical Fitness and Myotherapy in Massachusetts. Between river trips, she and her husband are building a house on a mesa top near Santa Fe, New Mexico. Beverly has also established Sister Hawk, a nonprofit organization supporting raptor (birds of prey) rehabilitation.

SAMPLE TRIPS

➤**Revisioning Personal Power: Emergence from Self-Limitation**—This spiritual journey into the healing powers of water, canyons, mountains, clouds, and trees welcomes women who need a retreat from a too-secular, self-demeaning urban life. Attend to yourself in a community of other women and explore how the laws of nature teach balance. Mornings are time for inward journeying and talk. When the wind is quiet, practice canoeing on Montana's Missouri River. Time to hike, explore, enjoy the company of other women, or experience solitude. Evenings vary according to the group's needs. Nine days/$1900/all levels.

➤**In Search of Sacagawea: Upper Missouri River**—Follow the Lewis and Clark National Historic Trail along 107 miles of this Montana river. Discover more about the person behind the legend, a multilingual Shoshone and skilled forager. The river is gentle and the valley is wide, creating a spacious feeling quite different from canyon and forest rivers. Enjoy panoramas of grass and tree-covered islands and the White Cliffs area, as well as day hikes and wildlife sightings. Nine days/$950/all levels.

➤**Bringing Forth: A Writing Retreat with Sharon Olds**—Camp on the beach, canoe along the coastline in the company of dolphins, and live with the earth's rhythm, remote from the distractions of your life . You can share your dreams and imagination in a space of great safety. Nine days/$1050/all levels.

➤**Of Wizards and Wildflowers: The Lower Canyons of the Rio Grande**— Canoe eighty-seven miles in the Big Bend National Park area of Texas. Paddle through nearly inaccessible desert and canyon country, stop to explore the side canyons, or soak in the hot springs. Flatwater and Class I and II rapids provide initial practice. As the river quickens, experienced paddlers enjoy Class III and IV rapids. Depending on the water level, it may be necessary to line or portage the larger rapids. Beginning canoeists are welcome to come and develop their skills. Ten days/$950/beginning to advanced.

Prices include: Meals and group equipment.

Prices do not include: Personal equipment.

Guides: Beverly Antaeus and guest guides.

Training for guides: CPR/advanced first aid; Beverly Antaeus has studied river rescue techniques with Nantahala Outdoor Center and the Rescue 3 Swiftwater Rescue Seminar.

Liability coverage: Yes.

The Heart of Adventure

P.O. Box 678
Honaunau, HI 96726
808/328-8459 or 310/865-2180

Wilderness Adventure, International Travel, and Healing Retreats

Began operating: 1975
Number of trips offered per year: 3–8
Number of all-women's trips per year: 4 or more
Usual group size: 6–8
Typical age of participants: 25–55
Range of ages of participants: 8–65

Multigenerational programs
Programs for older women
Scholarships available: On an individual basis.

Whether backpacking in Nepal, India, or Colorado, or llama packing in Canyonlands, Utah, the Heart of Adventure emphasizes inner and outer exploration. All trips have a spiritual focus and teach healing techniques. Team up with a group of mothers and daughters for a week's wilderness expedition. Join a group of older women to explore the landscape and life of Bali.

IN THEIR OWN WORDS
"It is powerful to travel in nature with a group of women—it's so full and fun that I can't really call it work in the usual sense of the word. The real work comes from a group of women opening their hearts, strengthening their bodies, aligning with their emotions, and simplifying their minds and lives."
—Debbie Koehn, Founder

HISTORY/BACKGROUND
Debbie Koehn has climbed and skied in the Andes and Rockies, kayaked the rugged Hamakua Coast of Hawaii and trekked in Nepal and India. She speaks Spanish, conversational Indonesian, and Quechua, the Incan dialect. She is a yoga and meditation teacher and has worked as an Outward Bound instructor. In 1982 she and her partner, David, led the first group to summit and then ski down Nevado Ausengate, Peru's highest peak. Her daughter, Alison, travels with them and provided the inspiration for the mother-daughter programs.

SAMPLE TRIPS

➤**Adventures of the Heart**—A healing retreat in Hawaii where you can rest, play, and grow. Experience Spinner dolphins, sea turtles, and fish, explore sacred lava-tube caves, visit the island's active volcano, practice yoga, and sleep out under the stars for a night or two. One week/$1000/easy.

➤**Wise Women Bali Adventure**—Experience Balinese culture and people, its beaches, rainforests, and temples. Your days evolve slowly and rhythmically around nature, movement, food, and market hopping. River raft, snorkel, mountain bike, and sunbathe. Visit rituals, dances, and artisans. Try yoga and Balinese massage. Many nights are spent in local island homes. No experience necessary. Two weeks/$2200/easy.

➤**Red Rock and Ruins in Canyonlands, Utah**—Towering red rock pinnacles, peaceful hidden side canyons, and ancient Anasazi spiritual sites fill your days. Walk two to four hours per day with llamas carrying your gear. Plenty of time to write, relax, and explore. One week/$800/moderate.

➤**Mother and Daughter Backpacking**—Check out Colorado's hot springs and wildflowers. Appropriate for girls aged eight to fourteen. One week/ $800/moderate to challenging.

➤**Colorado Hot Springs Backpacking**—Walk among the wildflowers in summer or the golden aspen trees in fall. This is a powerful time for a vision quest and introspection as well as an opportunity to learn wilderness skills. One week/$800/moderate to challenging.

Prices include: Vegetarian meals, accommodations, and group equipment; on Bali trip: scheduled massage and activities.

Prices do not include: Personal equipment.

Guides: Co-founder Debbie Koehn and an assistant guide on some trips.

Training for guides: Emergency Medical Training; Debbie Koehn has been exploring and guiding for twenty years and has extensive experience in natural healing techniques, herbology, massage, yoga therapy, and hands-on healing.

Liability coverage: Yes.

Her Wild Song

P.O. Box 515
Brunswick, ME 04011
207/721-9005

Exploring the Wilderness within and around You

Began operating: 1991
Number of trips offered per year: 11–13
Number of all-women's trips per year: All
Usual group size: 8–12
Typical age of participants: 35–55
Range of ages of participants: 25–76

Accessible to disabled women
Scholarships available: Payment schedules and work exchange possible.

Her Wild Song invites you to explore the magic and spirituality of living outdoors in a community of women. Whether you're dog sledding or in a deep ecology workshop, taking to the sea in a kayak or exploring your inner wilderness through writing, expect a journey with a feminist perspective as well as an understated Buddhist philosophy. Most programs take place in Maine, with select trips to Montana, Arizona, and Texas. One or two trips each year are co-led by Karen Knight, a founder of Maine Accessible Adventures, who specializes in helping disabled people paddle canoes and kayaks.

IN THEIR OWN WORDS
"Some trips offer particular practice for opening awareness and deepening intimacy. Other trips are more loosely structured and develop according to the mood and rhythm of the women attending. All trips welcome lesbians."
—Anne Dellenbaugh, Founder

HISTORY/BACKGROUND
Anne Dellenbaugh, founder of Her Wild Song, began guiding wilderness trips in 1983. She is a registered Maine guide and a graduate of the National Outdoor Leadership School and the Outdoor Leadership Program at Greenfield Community College. Anne, who holds a master's in theological studies and women's studies from Harvard Divinity School, strives to incorporate the spiritual life of women in Her Wild Song's wilderness programs.

SAMPLE TRIPS

➤**In Celebration of Winter**—These trips are for women who love winter but don't want to be cold. *You will be warm* on these winter adventures, where everyone takes turns mushing the dogs, and you can choose to ski without the burden of a heavy pack. In the evenings, camp beside the frozen lake in canvas-wall tents with portable wood stoves. Five days/$600/beginning.

➤**Jewel Islands in a Bay**—Stay in a seaside country inn while learning to paddle or to paddle more efficiently. Tour Jericho Bay by sea kayak, camping on Maine's coastal islands. An emphasis on island ecology and having fun. Women with disabilities welcome. Six days/$600/beginning.

➤**Discovering Wild Community**—This experimental, deep ecology workshop focuses on the interconnection that links us with the entire natural world. Backpacking in western Maine allows you to study plant and animal communities, learn about weather patterns, enjoy quiet time and meditation, as well as share in the preparation of simple meals. Four days/$400/easy.

➤**Wild Writer/Wild River**—This workshop welcomes the writer in every woman, to give her confidence, skill, and encouragement while enjoying the nature and wildlife of Maine's Penobscot River. Eight days/$700/moderate.

➤**Northern River Journey**—Paddle along a hundred miles of the Allagash Wilderness Waterway, observing abundant wildlife and Maine's striking landscape. Learn or strengthen canoeing and camping skills. Flatwater, Class I and II whitewater, and three short portages. Ten days/$900/challenging.

➤**Mountain Dharma**—Backpack four to seven miles each day on the Appalachian Trail, accompanied by daily meditation, singing, sharing stories, and doing the work/play of community. No previous experience in the outdoors or with meditation is necessary. Nine days/$700/challenging.

Prices include: Vegetarian meals, accommodations on some trips, group equipment, shuttles from local airport.

Prices do not include: First and last night's accommodations on some trips and personal equipment.

Guides: Anne Dellenbaugh and associates.

Training for guides: Wilderness First Responder, outdoor leadership skills training in given activity; familiarity with HWS philosophy, either through an apprenticeship or equivalent experience.

Liability coverage: No.

Herizen: New Age Sailing for Women
Box 4592
Nanaimo, British Columbia V9R 6E8 Canada
604/741-1753

Sailing and Self-Awareness Courses in Canada

Began operating: 1988
Number of trips offered per year: 18
Number of all-women's trips per year: All
Usual group size: 4
Typical age of participants: 40s
Range of ages of participants: 20s–60s

Four-, six-, and eight-day Herizen courses employ a holistic approach that combines personalized sailing instruction with personal development. Join up to three women of varied skill levels aboard a modern, comfortable, and responsive thirty-five-foot sailing yacht. Herizen welcomes participants who have never sailed before as well as women with some sailing experience who want to develop their skills and self-confidence. Trips teach you technical information on how the engine works, leaving dock, setting sail, and dropping anchor as well as various self-awareness techniques.

IN THEIR OWN WORDS
"I can teach the skills, but if you don't believe in yourself, don't feel confident, comfortable, and safe, you won't make use of them. I tailor each course to the client's needs and background. I teach women how to own their reality in a very male-dominated sport."   —Trish Birdsell, Owner

HISTORY/BACKGROUND
Though she owned and lived aboard a thirty-foot sailboat, Trish Birdsell did not have the confidence to take the boat from the dock. Two months after she and her partner separated, she was singlehanding. Rather than having learned new skills, Trish had increased her self-confidence. Trish founded Herizen to help other women develop their sea and personal skills. Singlehanding boats since 1985 and guiding women's trips since 1987, Trish has cruised the South Pacific, Caribbean, Mexico, East and West Coasts of the U.S., and British Columbia. She holds a B.A. in psychology, a B.Sc. in nutrition, and has experience in one-to-one counseling.

SAMPLE TRIPS

➤**Sailing and Self-Awareness**—A hands-on immersion cruise for skill development, confidence-building, and fun. Along with developing your sailing skills, courses introduce you to "inner sailing," where awareness of body, mind, and spirit together with relaxation meditations, affirmation, and focusing techniques promote development of sailing and personal skills. Team with two or three other women and share your experiences. Programs operate from the premise that attending to your emotions, history, and needs as a woman are critical for sailing and personal achievement. Four days/CDN $600/beginning to intermediate. Six days/CDN $1000/beginning to intermediate. Eight days/CDN $1400/beginning to intermediate.

Prices include: Meals on board, accommodations, and tax.

Prices do not include: Meals on shore, if any.

Guides: Owner Trish Birdsell.

Training for guides: Canadian Yachting Association basic and intermediate instructor training; United States Coast Guard captain's licence; American Sailing Association instructor's certifications; Canadian Power Squadron courses for safe boating, seamanship, coastal and celestial navigation.

Liability coverage: Yes.

Himalayan High Treks

241 Dolores Street
San Francisco, CA 94103
800/455-8735 or 415/861-2391

Treks in the Himalayas and on the Tibetan Plateau

Began operating: 1988
Number of trips offered per year: 6
Number of all-women's trips per year: 1–2
Usual group size: 6
Typical age of participants: 30–50
Range of ages of participants: 12–70

Trek through the highest mountains in the world and encounter a living ancient culture. Himalayan High Treks emphasizes respect for indigenous cultures and environmentally low-impact travel that benefits local economies. You trek three to six hours a day with guides fluent in local languages. Most people in good health who exercise regularly are able to enjoy the trips, which always begin slowly in order to acclimatize. HHT provides accommodations in hotels, trekking lodges, and tents. A reference list of past customers is available upon request.

IN THEIR OWN WORDS
"Owning and operating Himalayan High Treks is the most rewarding thing I've ever done. I'm happy to have found my "right livelihood" and appreciate the opportunity to make long-lasting friendships both with local people in the areas we visit and with the people who join me on my treks. We have a policy of inclusion and invite everyone regardless of race, religion, or sexual preference to participate in our trips."   —Effie Fletcher, Owner

HISTORY/BACKGROUND
Out of a love for the Himalayan landscape and an interest in the people and religions of the area, Effie Fletcher founded Himalayan High Treks. She wanted to offer a low-cost alternative to high-end adventure travel; to research, plan, and lead all the trips herself; and to be sure that the programs benefit the local population. For that reason, groups stay in simple accommodations, often family-run hotels, and Effie donates a portion of the profits from each trip to nonprofit foundations working in the area.

SAMPLE TRIPS

►**Langtang & Chitwan**—Langtang National Park is located directly north of Kathmandu on the border of Tibet. The Tamangs, who inhabit the valley, practice a combination of Buddhism and Bon Po, a religion that predates Buddhism. The prayer wheels, mani walls, and many of the customs associated with Tibetan Buddhism are actually from Bon Po. Your trip starts and ends in Kathmandu, with plenty of time for sight-seeing. From the road head (elevation 6,100 feet), you trek for nine days on a circular route through picturesque villages. Follow a spectacular uninhabited river gorge to the monastery at the foot of the Langtang Himal. Visit a yak cheese factory in Kyangjim, your highest camping elevation (12,500 feet), and walk up a 14,000-foot peak for tremendous views. Then spend a day rafting on the Trisuli river en route to Chitwan National Park. The park is located in the Terai, a tropical lowland jungle and grassland. Cross the plain by traditional ox cart, take a canoe down the Rapti River to see crocodiles lazing in the sun, and search for wild rhinos and tigers on elephant back. Watch spectacular sunsets with the Himalayas in the distance. American Marin Johannsson leads the trip along with Ram Lama, a male Sherpa guide. Anyone in good health who enjoys walking should consider this the perfect introduction to trekking. Porters carry your gear and put up your tents; meals are prepared by the camp cook. Twenty-three days/ $1800/moderate.

Prices include: Meals on trek, some meals in hotels; double-occupancy accommodations in hotels (single-occupancy available for additional cost), group equipment.

Prices do not include: Some meals in hotels, personal equipment (some equipment available for rental), tips.

Guides: Owner Effie Fletcher, Marin Johannsson, and local male guides.

Training for guides: First aid and mountain training; guides carry a well-supplied first-aid kit as medical facilities in most areas are limited or nonexistent. HHT offers a 20 percent discount to one doctor or nurse in the hopes that most trips will have medical personnel along.

Liability coverage: No.

Hurricane Creek Llama Treks

63366 Pine Tree Road, Dept. AGC
Enterprise, OR 97828
800/528-9609 or 503/432-4455 (same for fax)

Hiking with Llamas in the Pacific Northwest

Began operating: 1985
Number of trips offered per year: 8–12
Number of all-women's trips per year: 1–2
Usual group size: Up to 10
Typical age of participants: 40–50
Range of ages of participants: 6–79

Hike through the wilderness with Hurricane Creek Llama Treks. You begin the trip by gathering at Chandler's Bed, Bread, and Trail Inn for hors d'oeuvres and beverages to review the plans for the journey. On the trail you can choose to lead a llama or amble along at your own pace. The llamas carry your gear while a llama-packing expert shares her knowledge of local natural history. Llamas are smaller and more docile than horses or mules and not nearly so intimidating to people with little experience handling large animals. Their alert behavior often helps to spot wildlife the group might otherwise miss. These are group participatory trips. You will assist in packing chores, meal preparation, and general camp tending. Meals are a hearty and wholesome assortment of fresh and prepared foods that include garden-grown vegetables and whole-grain breads. Special dietary needs can be accommodated.

IN THEIR OWN WORDS
"Hurricane Creek Llama Treks strives to provide guests with both a connection to the natural wilderness environment and a safe, enjoyable camping experience. The llamas add a unique flavor to the trip, companionably carrying the loads."   —Stanlynn Daugherty, Founder

HISTORY/BACKGROUND
Stanlynn Daugherty started leading llama pack trips in 1985 to share Northwest natural history while using unique pack animals. She began guiding all-women's trips in 1987. A regular contributor to *Llamas Magazine,* Stanlynn is the author of *Packing with Llamas,* the first comprehensive guide to llama packing.

SAMPLE TRIPS

►**Women's Wilderness Llama Trek**—This early summer trip takes you into the Hurricane Creek area of the Eagle Cap Wilderness at a time when the wildflowers are at their peak. You will hike approximately five miles to the base camp, all on a gentle uphill trail. From your base camp (6,000 feet) along Hurricane Creek, you'll have the opportunity to relax as well as hike to your heart's content. On layover days, explore the upper reaches of Hurricane Creek Canyon and perhaps climb up toward Echo Lake (8,350 feet) to see how much is still covered in ice. The area offers expansive views of some of the Wallowa's highest peaks and also a chance to glimpse elk, mule deer, and mountain sheep. Hikers of all ages in good physical condition will enjoy this hike. Five days/$550/easy to moderate.

Prices include: Meals, accommodations the night before and after trek, and group equipment.

Prices do not include: Personal equipment.

Guides: Stanlynn Daugherty and Janet Hohmann.

Training for guides: Extensive backcountry experience, knowledge of natural history, group leadership experience.

Liability coverage: Yes.

Hurricane Island Outward Bound School

P.O. Box 429 Mechanic Street
Rockland, ME 04841
800/341-1744 or 207/594-5548

Sailing, Canoeing, and Confidence Building on the Eastern Seaboard

Began operating: 1965
Number of trips offered per year: 200
Number of all-women's trips per year: 10
Usual group size: 10
Typical age of participants: 14–50
Range of ages of participants: 14–99

Scholarships available: Partial scholarships through financial aid.

An outfit with over twenty-five years' experience in leading wilderness activities, Hurricane Island Outward Bound School now offers all-women's sailing and canoeing courses as well as empowerment workshops for survivors of sexual abuse/assault and for women who have or have had breast or ovarian cancer. Instructors provide close supervision as you learn skills necessary for self-reliance. While prior outdoor experience is not necessary, HIOBS does ask you to bring a sense of adventure, love of the outdoors, a desire to learn wilderness skills, and a willingness to stretch both physically and emotionally.

IN THEIR OWN WORDS

"Our mission is to develop self-esteem, self-reliance, concern for others, and care for the environment through safe adventure-based courses. We help people discover and act upon their strengths through demanding courses, primarily in wilderness settings. These courses challenge you to develop personal resources and form new perspectives through cooperating with others."
—Hurricane Island Outward Bound School brochure

HISTORY/BACKGROUND

Since 1965, Hurricane Island Outward Bound School has provided outdoor adventures on the seas, rivers, and mountains of Maine, Maryland, and Florida. They also have a large array of coed courses including one for people with rheumatoid arthritis and one for people with diabetes. HIOBS custom designs courses for teachers and administrators.

SAMPLE TRIPS

➤**Sailing for Women: 30 and Up**—This course provides a dynamic and open environment for women to focus on self-empowerment in personal relationships at work and with family, while learning basic sea skills and navigation. Florida trips also include swimming and snorkeling, while Maryland programs offer the additional challenges of rock climbing, rappelling, and high ropes. Eight days/$900/beginning. Eleven days/$1110/beginning.

➤**Canoeing for Women: 18 and Up, 30 and Up, or 40 and Up**—Canoe the vast network of lakes and streams at the headwaters of Maine: the Kennebec, St. John, Allagash, and Penobscot. Courses teach all the paddling and camping/ outdoor skills necessary to travel safely along the lakes and streams used for hundreds of years by Abenaki Indians. Rock climbing and day hikes are also included. Eight days/$800/beginning. Twenty-two days/$1600/beginning.

➤**Challenges from Within: For Survivors of Sexual Abuse/Assault**—Canoeing, camping, and adventure activities in Maine aim to assist the process of personal growth as you work at your recovery. In addition, you will have a great time. Move through limiting beliefs to new possibilities in the powerful healing and learning environment of nature. Focuses include: self-confidence, self-esteem, body image, trust, risk taking, and setting and achieving goals. Leaders are Margie Parsons, a clinical social worker who has worked with trauma survivors since 1979, and Linda S. Cooper, a social worker and outdoor adventure guide since 1970. Seven days/$1100/moderate.

➤**For Women Who Have or Have Had Breast or Ovarian Cancer**—The goals of this Florida program are to teach skills that women can use in setting and achieving personal goals in the presence of cancer and to instill personal confidence to help women change their perception of the disease and enable them to resume control of their lives. Canoeing in the Okeefeenokee, ropes-course activities, soloing for a night or an afternoon. Five days/$500/moderate.

Prices include: Meals, group equipment, all specialized and camping equipment, including sleeping bags and foul-weather gear.

Prices do not include: Personal equipment.

Guides: Outward Bound instructors.

Training for guides: Over forty staff trainings each year in first-aid, rescue, and outdoor skills. All instructors have advanced first-aid skills and some are EMTs.

Liability coverage: Yes, and participants are required to carry medical insurance.

Inside Outside Adventures

800 Monroe Street
Oshkosh, WI 54901
414/231-5020

Basketmaking to Backpacking in Upper Michigan & Minnesota

Began operating: 1987
Number of trips offered per year: 75
Number of all-women's trips per year: Approximately half
Usual group size: 6–12
Typical age of participants: 30s–40s
Range of ages of participants: 20–76

Accessible to disabled women: By special arrangement.
Scholarships available: Work exchange may be possible.

Whether it's a weekend of outdoor photography or a week of Boundary Water canoeing, Inside Outside Adventures invites beginning and experienced outdoorswomen to join them for a wilderness excursion. Most trips are based out of your guide's home in the Upper Peninsula of Michigan, a toasty-warm log cabin more than a hundred years old, located on Sandpiper Lake. Hike, backpack, ski, or snowshoe. Choose a weekend of sketching and watercolor to learn new skills or hone your technique. Three-day experience-based workshops for professionals and therapists are offered for those who want to develop their leadership and team building skills. All trips cater to the needs and desires of each group.

IN THEIR OWN WORDS

"I enjoy the multidisciplinary nature of our programs, which are educational, recreational, motivational, and therapeutic. We blend beginners and advanced folks in fun learning experiences."   —Lin Peterson, Founder

HISTORY/BACKGROUND

Since childhood, Lin Peterson has wanted to guide outdoor trips. Inside Outside Adventures gives her the opportunity to share twenty-five years of outdoor experience. Many of IOA's specially contracted trips involve victims of violence and low-income women, and have included trips for mothers on welfare. Current trips focus on the working woman.

SAMPLE TRIPS

➤**Cross Country Ski and Snowshoe**—Evergreens laden with snow line the trails of the Northwoods. Travel beside gurgling river water and ice shoves. Lessons are available for beginners. Hearty homemade meals and camaraderie top off these winter weekends. Two and a half days/$150/all levels.

➤**Basket Making**—Learn to weave baskets in a rustic environment next to a private lake. Whether this is your first basket or your thirty-first, acquire new techniques from local craftswomen. Two and a half days/$150/all levels.

➤**Wildflowers, Birds, Wildlife**—Hike trail hikes with guidebooks and binoculars in tow. Nesting eagles, herons, osprey, and many other birds dot the sky by day. At night, gaze at stars, and perhaps get a glimpse of the northern lights. Over a hundred and fifty varieties of native wildflowers grow in this area of Michigan. Plenty of time to wander, swim in the lake, read, write in a journal, or just listen to the breeze whisper through the pines. Two and a half days/$150/all levels.

➤**Autumn Trails Hiking**—Walk on trails and old logging roads in Upper Michigan with vistas of pine forests, maples, birches, and gentle hills. Hear the honking of ducks and geese flying south and keep a lookout for whitetail deer and wild turkey. Two and a half days/$150/all levels.

➤**Backpack Lake Superior**—Thunderous sounds of waterfalls fill the air as the Black and Presque Isle Rivers tumble over glacial terraces to Lake Superior. Wide trails provide pleasant hiking and vistas. Daily distances are short, leaving time to explore and relax. Four days/$300/all levels.

➤**Boundary Waters Canoe Area**—No one needs to be an expert to enjoy this trip. Paddle by day and relax around the campfire at night. Hike the old fur traders' trails as you portage from lake to lake. First night's accommodations are at a lodge near Grand Marais, Minnesota. Eight days/$600/all levels.

Prices include: Meals, accommodations, group equipment, and backpacks.

Prices do not include: Personal equipment.

Guides: Selected by IOA founder Lin Peterson, most are professional working women in their 30s and 40s who schedule time to guide outdoor trips.

Training for guides: Minimum of one-week training every year to cover policies, emergencies, safety, navigation, skill training, group facilitation skills, CPR/first aid, communication, and the needs of special populations.

Liability coverage: Yes.

Jennifer Smith Fly Fishing Guide Service

P.O. Box 132
Bozeman, MT 59771
406/587-5140

Fly Fishing in Montana

Began operating: 1988
Number of trips offered per year: Daily, May through September
Number of all-women's trips per year: 2–3
Usual group size: 1–2+
Typical age of participants: 30–70+
Range of ages of participants: 12–70+

Jennifer Smith, a professional fly fishing guide and casting instructor, specializes in instructing women and couples, from beginning to experienced fly fishers. She guides mother/daughter and mother/son trips and customizes fly fishing courses and excursions for groups of any size. Trips take place on the Gallatin, Madison, and Yellowstone Rivers near Bozeman, Montana.

IN THEIR OWN WORDS

"Fly fishing is the perfect sport for women. It requires finesse and timing, and it's intellectual and aesthetic. It is a sport women can enjoy and participate in their entire life."   —Jennifer Smith, Founder

HISTORY/BACKGROUND

Jennifer Smith, who has been fly fishing since she was twelve, is a licensed Montana and Yellowstone National Park guide. She has written for *Fly Rod & Reel*, *Fly Tackle Dealer*, the *Scientific Angler Guidebook* and is a contributing author to the anthology *Uncommon Waters: Women Write About Fishing*. Jennifer has appeared on "CBS This Morning," "Fishing the West," and Swedish National Television. A guest speaker and casting demonstrator at national trade shows, her fishing travels have taken her to the Florida Keys, Canada, Alaska, Norway, Mexico, and Argentina. In 1992 Jennifer taught the first all-women's fly fishing school in Sweden.

SAMPLE TRIPS

➤**Fly Fishing in Montana**—On your first day, learn how to fly cast and tie knots before fishing on a favorite trout stream in the afternoon. Spend the second day on one of Montana's famous rivers. The emphasis is on fly fishing techniques, fly and leader selection, reading the water, insect identification, and wading safety. On the third day, continue to develop your skills. For one or two people. Price includes stream-side lunch. Two or three days/$250 per day/all levels.

➤**Montana Weekend**—This cooperative effort by four Montana women guides provides you with a fly fishing school and vacation along the banks of wild trout streams. A day of basic instruction on fly casting, knot tying, and the use of equipment is followed by a guided walk/wade trip on the Gallatin River. Learn about reading the water, wading safety, line control, insects and insect hatches, fly selection, hooking, landing, and releasing. Float down the Yellowstone River on your last day and cast for rainbows, browns, and cut-throats. Enjoy stream-side picnic lunches each day. Some meals are included. Three days/$750/all levels.

➤**Cutthroats and Cowgirls**—Gather at the Gallatin Gateway Inn in Bozeman for a day's instruction on fly casting, knot tying, and the use of equipment before setting out into the backcountry to practice your skills. Horses pack in your gear, a camp cook prepares meals, and roomy tents assure a comfortable stay. Fish for colorful cutthroats in Slough Creek while Jennifer Smith and Lars Olsson instruct you in casting, line control, knot tying, reading the water, fly selection, hooking, landing, and releasing fish. Special stream-side entomology courses and fly tying demonstrations are included. Plenty of time to fish and to explore the beauty of Yellowstone Park. Some meals are included. Five days/$1800/all levels.

Prices include: On pack trip: some meals, group equipment, fishing gear, sleeping bags, and rain gear; on Montana weekend: fishing gear.

Prices do not include: Some meals, accommodations, personal equipment, fishing gear on some trips (fly rods, reels, lines, and waders can be rented from a local Bozeman fly shop); waders on pack trip and Montana weekend (available for rental), fishing license, gratuities.

Guides: Founder Jennifer Smith and professional co-guides.

Training for guides: Licensed Montana guides.

Liability coverage: Yes.

Journeywell
2418 Sherwood Hills Road
Minnetonka, MN 55305
612/544-3986

Retreat along Minnesota's Lake Vermilion

Began operating: 1987
Number of trips offered per year: 3
Number of all-women's trips per year: All
Usual group size: 10–12
Typical age of participants: 40s–50s
Range of ages of participants: 23–80

Programs for older women: Retreats for women in midlife and older.
Scholarships available: One or two usually available.

Retreats are held at a wilderness cabin, accessible only by boat. Programs focus on personal renewal and finding a balance of body, mind, and spirit. Participants include women who have experienced recent life losses as well as those who want to further their self-awareness. Hear the sound of the waves lapping on the ancient rocks, listen to the call of the loon, witness sunsets, smell the birch and cedar burning in the stone fireplace. Swim, canoe, kayak, or sail, or enjoy a sauna and a massage. The focus of each retreat varies.

IN THEIR OWN WORDS
"We provide opportunities for people to better understand and appreciate themselves. The retreats help women connect with each other by sharing their stories, and connect with the earth through various activities. It is a non-hierarchical structure; the leaders participate also. We practice balancing skills, sing, dance, and share tears and laughter."   —Trish Herbert, Founder

HISTORY/BACKGROUND
Trish Herbert has her Ph.D. in psychology and gerontology. She began Journeywell to provide in-service education for professional caregivers, including nurses, social workers, and clergy, then expanded it and developed programs specifically for women. Trish's co-leaders have included a visual artist and teacher, a mind/body therapist, and Judith Guest, novelist, screenwriter, and author of *Ordinary People.*.

SAMPLE TRIPS

➤**Celebrate Your Womanspirit**—Retreats generally focus on transition and methods of self-care. Listen deeply to one another's stories and take turns attending to one another. Practice the art of "being still" and listening to your own inner wisdom. Participants are encouraged to relearn how to play and appreciate the simple, to walk with reverence and joy, and to live more lightly on the earth. The group ponders the preciousness and precariousness of life and the constant need to struggle for balance. This is an opportunity to pause and reflect on where you are now and where you want to be, to experience your feelings and "let go" of what holds you back. Five days/$400/all levels.

Prices include: Meals, accommodations, group equipment, and massage.

Prices do not include: Personal equipment.

Guides: Founder Trish Herbert and co-leaders.

Training for guides: Professional training of various kinds.

Liability coverage: Yes.

Lois Lane Expeditions
8933 Northeast Wardwell Road
Bainbridge Island, WA 98110
206/842-9776

Skiing and Climbing in the U.S., Canada, and Nepal

Began operating: 1992
Number of trips offered per year: 10
Number of all-women's trips per year: All
Usual group size: 3–8
Typical age of participants: 25–62
Range of ages of participants: 7–60+

Multigenerational programs

Out of Superman's shadow emerges Lois Lane Expeditions, leading women on weekend and week-long ski tours, river rafting and climbing explorations, as well as extended international treks. Enjoy yurt-to-yurt skiing or try a "Northwest Sampler" that combines various outdoor activities. Trip sites include Colorado, Montana, the Washington Cascades, the Canadian Rockies, and the Nepali Himalayas. LLE provides a vegetarian menu and is willing to accommodate special diets.

IN THEIR OWN WORDS
"People love Lois Lane Expeditions because Superman is out of the picture! We believe in creating fun, safe, and challenging trips for women, and making *all* women comfortable on them." —Priscilla McKenney, Co-founder

HISTORY/BACKGROUND
Priscilla McKenney and Rachel da Silva started Lois Lane Expeditions to offer women a chance to explore exciting places, learn new skills, and share adventure in the company of other women. Priscilla has been teaching and guiding skiing and climbing trips since 1978. Her guiding has taken her all over the western U.S., Canada, Alaska, and Nepal. She is certified by the professional ski instructors of America (PSIA). Rachel is the editor of *Leading Out: Women Climbers Reaching for the Top*. She has guided skiing and climbing trips for the past five years and has been associated with Women Climbers Northwest since 1985.

SAMPLE TRIPS

➤**Northern Yellowstone Ski Tour**—Skiing and telemarking among Yellowstone's bubbling aquamarine pools and abundant wildlife. Participants must bring telemark skis. Seven days/$700/all levels.

➤**Canadian Rockies Ski Week**—The Banff area, known for its mountain scenery and light powder snow, is host to backcountry and lift skiing from Lake Louise to Mt. Victoria. Daytrips to glaciers and mountain passes. Accommodations in two local hostels. Seven days/$650/all levels.

➤**White Pass Ski Weekend**—Split up to make the most of your skiing options from track to skating to telemark, on and off groomed slopes. Rendezvous in the evening for a home-cooked dinner. Two and a half days/$150/all levels.

➤**North Cascades Moms and Kids**—A trip designed to lighten everyone's load. Lois's steeds carry your gear while you venture through the Pasayten Wilderness. Seven days/$700 (plus $500 for first child, $350 for second child)/easy.

➤**River Rafting in the North Cascades**—Lois guides you down a beautiful river that carves its way through Washington's Cascades. No experience is necessary. Two days/$200/easy.

➤**Labyrinth Canyon, Green River, Utah**—Canoe down one of the most spectacular rivers in the Southwest. Five days/$550/easy.

➤**Mera Peak Trek and Climb, Nepal**—Acclimatize with an eight-day trek to Thangboche Monastery, traveling through local villages in the company of Sherpani women. The twelve-day approach and climb of Mera Peak (21,247 feet) will take you through some of the wildest areas of the Himalayas. Extensive climbing experience is not required, but you must be in good physical shape, have basic ice axe skills, and a readiness for adventure. Twenty-eight days/$2600/challenging.

Prices include: Meals, accommodations, group equipment.

Prices do not include: Personal equipment.

Guides: Co-founders Priscilla McKenney and Rachel da Silva.

Training for guides: Extensive guiding experience and training.

Liability coverage: Yes.

Maggie Merriman Fly Fishing Schools
P.O. Box 775
West Yellowstone, MT 59758
406/646-7824 (in summer) 818/282-3173 (in winter)

Fly Fishing Instruction in the Western U.S.

Began operating: 1971
Number of trips offered per year: 30–40 schools
Number of all-women's trips per year: 8–10 schools; 3–6 trips
Usual group size: 1–20 on schools; 1–8 on trips
Typical age of participants: 30s–40s
Range of ages of participants: 20–65

Maggie Merriman brings twenty-five years' experience to fly fishing instruction. Attend a one- or two-day school on running water, learning to problem-solve or spend a week on Alaskan territory strengthening your skills. Enjoy the outdoors, learn new skills, and meet new friends while fishing. Courses emphasize a respect for nature, and an understanding of the fish, water, and natural surroundings.

IN THEIR OWN WORDS
"Anyone at any age can learn fly fishing. It's not just a sport for men; it is for people who like to be outdoors communing with nature. It is a learned sport and does not take great strength." —Maggie Merriman, Founder

HISTORY/BACKGROUND
Although Maggie Merriman had enjoyed fly fishing all her life, she knew of no women guides and just one woman instructor. As an example to other women, Maggie acquired her teacher's training and opened a school in Montana. With a notable demand in the western U.S., her courses have thrived. In addition to her instructing, Maggie has designed and manufactured a fly fishing vest for women that is not presently available but may be again in the future.

SAMPLE TRIPS

➤**Fly Fishing Schools in the Western States**—Maggie teaches techniques on running water. Skills covered include casting techniques, drag-free drifts, streamside entomology, matching the hatch, how to select the correct fly, and how to approach various fishing situations. Course locations vary. Fly fishing shops or clubs often sponsor these schools. One to two days/$75–$200/beginning and intermediate.

➤**Fly Fishing in West Yellowstone**—Explore the legendary fishing rivers of West Yellowstone Park and the surrounding area. Each day is spent on a famous trout river exploring the various ways to fish and develop one's fly fishing techniques. Each client is evaluated at her level of expertise and taught accordingly. Skills covered include casting, drag-free drifts, selecting the right fly, entomology, and how to fish various situations. One to three days/$150–450/beginning to advanced.

➤**Fly Fishing in Alaska**—Fly from Anchorage to King Salmon and stay at a river lodge in the Alaskan wilderness. Fish for the magnificent Alaskan rainbow, char, and greylin on a river of over three hundred miles. Each day, a lodge guide takes you by jet boat up the river for a full day of fishing. Accommodations are comfortable and the food is excellent. One week/$3200/intermediate to advanced.

Prices include: For Alaska trip: airfare to and from Anchorage and lodge, meals, accommodations, rods and reels, boats if needed; for schools: rods and reels.

Prices do not include: For trips: additional fishing equipment including vest and waders; for schools: meals, accommodations; additional fishing equipment.

Guides: Founder Maggie Merriman.

Training for guides: Over forty-seven years of personal fly fishing experience and over twenty years of teaching fly fishing.

Liability coverage: Yes.

Mahoosuc Guide Service

Box 245 Bear River Road
Newry, ME 04261
207/824-2073

Dog Sledding, Canoeing, and Mountaineering in Maine

Began operating: 1991
Number of trips offered per year: 40
Number of all-women's trips per year: 10
Usual group size: 6–8
Typical age of participants: 30–40
Range of ages of participants: 5–68

Mahoosuc guides are equally comfortable poling a canoe up the Allagash as they are driving a dog team across the ice of Hudson's Bay. Co-founders Polly Mahoney and Kevin Slater build their own cedar-canvas canoes, ash dog sleds, and maple paddles, finding traditional equipment and materials durable, functional, and preferable to today's high-technology outdoor equipment. In line with their interest in Native American culture, MGS also employs local Inuit, Cree, and Quechua guides on its coed cross-cultural trips.

IN THEIR OWN WORDS
"I particularly enjoy women's trips—the supportive atmosphere created and the empowerment women often feel during and after a trip. We have a philosophy of respecting nature and working with it, not competing against it. There are many lessons to be learned in the wilderness if people are receptive and willing to experience them."   —Polly Mahoney, Co-founder

HISTORY/BACKGROUND
Polly Mahoney and Kevin Slater started Mahoosuc Guide Service in 1991 after working together at Hurricane Island Outward Bound School. Both felt that sharing outdoor experiences with others was a great way to make a living. For ten years, Polly lived a subsistence lifestyle in the bush of the Yukon Territory. Her Alaskan huskies were essential to survival, hauling wood and water, and providing transportation in winter. Polly and her huskies were featured in the movie, *Never Cry Wolf*. Kevin, a former program director for Outward Bound, has climbed and guided in Alaska, Peru, Scotland, and the Rockies. Both have a variety of canoe experience in the U.S. and Canada.

SAMPLE TRIPS

➤**Dog Sledding Weekend**—Spend one night at a local bed and breakfast (special rates available for MGS guests) viewing an instructional video. Then head out with the huskies. While on the trail, you'll sleep in canvas-walled tents heated with wood stoves. Three days/$900/beginning.

➤**Canoeing Weekend**—Paddle five to seven miles a day up the Magalloway River to Umbagog Lake and the mouth of the Rapid River. Camp near a bald eagle's nest. Three days/$900/beginning.

➤**St. Croix Canoe Trip**—Guides teach beginning whitewater strokes and maneuvers to negotiate rapids along the U.S./Canadian border. Some canoeing experience necessary. Six days/$900/beginning.

➤**Whitewater Workshop**—The river is your playground as you start in flat water, progress to moving water, and then continue on to beginners' level whitewater. No experience necessary. Three days/$900/beginning.

➤**Rock Climbing Day**—A day for women to experience rock climbing. Learn knots, proper climbing techniques, belaying, and rappelling. One day/under $100/beginning.

➤**Empowerment Weekend Paddling at Aziscohos Lake**—The wilderness is an excellent environment for women to feel our own power. This weekend gives women an opportunity to try new things, learn skills, and share with others some of their own personal experiences. Three days/$900/beginning.

Prices include: Meals; group equipment; specialized personal equipment, including sleeping bags, packs, winter parkas, and boots.

Prices do not include: Accommodations in a bed and breakfast.

Guides: Co-founder Polly Mahoney.

Training for guides: Maine guide training, winter guide training, experience leading and teaching given skill.

Liability coverage: Yes.

McNamara Ranch
4620 County Road 100, P.O. Box 702
Florissant, CO 80816
719/748-3466

Ranch Adventures in Colorado

Began operating: 1989
Number of trips offered per year: Operates May through October
Number of all-women's trips per year: 90%
Usual group size: 1–3
Typical age of participants: 32–52
Range of ages of participants: Varies

McNamara Ranch is located in Saddle Mountain's valley. With just one to three guests, this small working ranch designs visits according to your interests. Enjoy unlimited horseback riding in Colorado's wilderness. Ascend peaks fourteen thousand feet high. Help move the ranch's sheep to different pastures. Spend a day rafting, hiking, fishing, or visit the sites, shops, and rodeos in the area. Take a horse and carriage ride or explore the area for deer, elk, bighorn sheep, and antelope.

IN THEIR OWN WORDS
"Our guests feel like they are visiting a friend in beautiful Colorado. We provide individual attention and plan the rides just for you."
　　　　　　　　　　　　　　　　　　　—Sheila McNamara, Founder

HISTORY/BACKGROUND
Founder Sheila McNamara is a single parent, horse trainer, and ex-Maryland fox hunter (now she hunts coyotes). She and her daughter run McNamara Ranch, which raises sheep rather than cattle. Sheila does all the shepherding of their band of fifty sheep, from shearing to marketing.

SAMPLE TRIPS

➤**Ranch Visits**—Saddle up and explore thousands of acres of Colorado's wilderness. Take a side trip to Cripple Creek, Florissant Fossil Beds, Pikes Peak, Garden of the Gods, or the Royal Gorge. Visit the rodeos or take advantage of the area's fishing and rafting opportunities. The ranch's owner guides you on trips designed according to the guests' interests and skill levels. One day to one week/$98 per day/all levels.

Prices include: Meals, accommodations, and riding.

Prices do not include: Hauling horses to different trail heads, side trips.·

Guides: Founder Sheila McNamara.

Training for guides: Sheila McNamara is an experienced ranch owner and horse handler.

Liability coverage: Yes.

Mariah Wilderness Expeditions

P.O. Box 248
Point Richmond, CA 94807
510/233-2303 fax: 510/233-0956

River Trips in North and South America

Began operating: 1982
Number of trips offered per year: approximately 150
Number of all-women's trips per year: 15
Usual group size: 20–30
Typical age of participants: 30s–40s
Range of ages of participants: 20–75

Accessible to disabled women
Multigenerational programs: At least one trip per year.
Programs for lesbians

Raft rivers in California, Oregon, Colorado, Utah, Costa Rica, or Ecuador. Future travel sites include Australia's rainforests and Great Barrier Reef, the Honduran rainforests, and Mayan ruins. Mariah's Adventure Program for Women organizes at least one all-women's river trip a year on each of the rivers they raft. With trips ranging in length from one to thirteen days, Mariah welcomes women of all ages and degrees of experience. Trips may be operated by, or in coordination with, affiliate outfitters.

IN THEIR OWN WORDS
"We have a commitment to providing a safe, supportive and well-organized adventure travel program in which women can be inspired to continue exploring and developing their skills and self-confidence, increase their awareness of the beauty and fragility of the environments and cultures they visit with us, have fun, and return home feeling a fuller connectedness with nature."
—Mariah Wilderness Expeditions brochure

HISTORY/BACKGROUND
A rafting guide and enthusiast for twenty-two years, Donna Hunter founded Mariah Wilderness Expeditions. She and Nancy Byrnes now co-own the company and have operated the Adventure Program for Women for thirteen years. MWE also organizes a Gay and Lesbian Program.

SAMPLE TRIPS

➤**Costa Rica: Tropical Whitewater and Beaches**—An active adventure vacation in Costa Rica. Raft three different rivers from Class II to Class IV and enjoy warm water rapids, lush vegetation, and wildlife. Explore sandy and rocky beaches, estuaries, and tiny rock islands by sea kayak at your own pace. Accommodations in a beach motel where the jungle meets the sandy beaches, in a private retreat located in the lowland tropical rainforest, and one night of camping. Take a horseback ride, riverboat tour, or guided trail hike. Eleven days/$2000 (includes airfare from Los Angeles) or $1850 (includes airfare from Miami)/all levels.

➤**Galapagos and Ecuador**—Mariah's eighty-foot yacht takes you to places in the Galapagos Islands off-limit to larger tour ships. Land tours, river rafting, scuba diving, snorkeling, sea kayaking, and visits to Indian marketplaces, artists' studios, and rainforests. Crew to passenger ratio of three to four. Fourteen days/$2800/all levels.

➤**Rogue River Rafting in Southern Oregon**—Mariah's annual trip on the Rogue travels through a gorge in the Siskiyou National Forest, along evergreen forests, large sandy beaches, fern grottos, and side canyon waterfalls. No experience necessary. Four days/$600/moderate.

➤**Cataract Canyon Rafting**—If you don't have time for a thirteen-day Grand Canyon trip, try Mariah's newest offering. Raft a stretch of the Colorado River that cuts through Canyonlands National Park in Utah. See three hundred million years of rock history and abundant wildlife. Begin with an easy two-day float past mesas, monuments, and sheer cliff walls, followed by the challenge of Class II–IV rapids. Five days/$800/moderate to challenging.

Prices include: Airfare on some trips, meals, accommodations (sometimes includes the night before the trip), group equipment.

Prices do not include: Airport departure tax, tips, personal equipment.

Guides: A Mariah owner or representative accompanies professional guides.

Training for guides: Professional certification.

Liability coverage: Yes.

Nantahala Outdoor Center

13077 Highway 19 West
Bryson City, NC 28713
704/488-6737   fax: 704/488-2498

Canoeing and Kayaking Instruction in North Carolina

Began operating: 1972
Number of trips offered per year: 250 courses
Number of all-women's trips per year: 8
Usual group size: 5–10
Typical age of participants: 30s
Range of ages of participants: 16–80

Accessible to disabled women: For women with mobility impairment.
Scholarships available: Free whitewater instruction for local Appalachian youth
  through Parks and Recreation Department.

Entering their third decade of outdoor programs, the Nantahala Outdoor Center offers all-women's courses in canoeing and kayaking. Programs emphasize effective paddling techniques, personal and group safety, and how to play on the water. Most courses begin on flatwater, giving beginners time to learn basic strokes necessary to control the canoe or kayak, and intermediate and advanced paddlers the opportunity to fine-tune their techniques. Once on the river, all courses focus on increasing your river-running proficiency. Evening activities may include videos, short "chalk talks" to review a day's videotaping session, or other material. Day-care facilities are available.

IN THEIR OWN WORDS
"We are an employee-owned company, so the consequences of our interaction with our guests are immediate and real. Our continued success depends on their satisfaction with what we do and how we do it."
>   —Gordon Black, Head of Instruction Program

HISTORY/BACKGROUND
NOC began with a handful of staff and the purchase of a hotel on the Nantahala River. The original purpose was to create a community of outdoor-oriented individuals. Today NOC employs an average of three hundred fifty staff members per year, ninety to a hundred of whom work year-round.

SAMPLE TRIPS

➤**Beginner Canoe Course**—For those who have paddled less than five times on whitewater, are not comfortable with boat leans, or are switching from kayak to canoe. Three days/$450/beginning.

➤**Beginner Kayak Course**—For those who have paddled less than five times in a kayak, are not comfortable with wet exits, or waiting underwater for an Eskimo rescue, or are switching from canoe to kayak. Two days/$300/beginning. Three days/$450/beginning.

➤**Beginner/Intermediate Kayak Course**—This program is suitable for participants who have paddled five to ten times on whitewater; can paddle in a straight line without problems; can execute basic ferries, peel-outs, and eddy turns; and would like to develop a reliable lake roll. Three days/$450/beginning to intermediate. Five days/$700/beginning to intermediate.

➤**Intermediate Kayak Course**—Suitable for kayakers who have paddled on Class II whitewater more than ten times; can execute eddy turns and peel-outs; control the ferry angle in Class II currents; accelerate the boat across eddy lines; surf small waves and holes; are comfortable with self-rescue on Class II water; have a 90 percent effective lake roll; and want to work on a river roll. Three days/$450/intermediate.

➤**Advanced Kayak Course**—For experienced kayakers who are comfortable performing the aforementioned skills on Class III waters, assisting in rescues, catching one- or two-boat eddies on Class III water, and would like to work on off-side and hand rolls. Five days/$700/advanced.

Prices include: Meals, accommodations (discount if you lodge elsewhere), group equipment (discount if you bring your own equipment).

Prices do not include: Personal equipment.

Guides: NOC guides including Eileen Ash (first alternate boat in 1992 Barcelona Olympics), Frances Glass (Grand Canyon guide and instructor), and Bunny Johns (NOC president and several-time national and world champion paddler).

Training for guides: CPR/advanced wilderness first aid, American Canoe Association whitewater certification.

Liability coverage: No.

The National Outdoor Leadership School

288 Main Street
Lander, WY 82520
307/332-6973   fax: 307/332-1220

Wilderness Living, Guide Training, and Leadership Development

Began operating: 1965
Number of trips offered per year: 135
Number of all-women's trips per year: 2
Usual group size: 8–17
Typical age of participants: 19
Range of ages of participants: 14–65+

Accessible to disabled women: Contact NOLS admissions office with questions.
Scholarships available: Some specifically for women, based on financial need and
  merit (what the student intends to do with her education).

Outdoor organizations worldwide are actively seeking female staff. Because
women may find it easier to assume a leadership role or practice outdoor skills
in an all-female setting, NOLS now leads all-women's kayaking and rock
climbing courses. To promote diversity, NOLS actively seeks minority students. Special scholarships are available to women, local Native Americans,
and foreign nationals in countries where NOLS operates branch schools (i.e.,
Kenya, India, Mexico, and Chile).

IN THEIR OWN WORDS
"We are more than a school, we are a community united by common ideals
and goals, and haven't changed our philosophy since we began in 1965. We
are actively seeking women both as students and staff. Although 50 percent
of the population is female, 40 percent of our student base is female. We would
love to see this change in the future."
—Tim Wilson, Recruitment Coordinator

HISTORY/BACKGROUND
Paul Petzoldt founded NOLS as a nonprofit organization dedicated to teaching wilderness and leadership skills that protect the user and the environment.
Among their more recent developments is the NOLS Outdoor Education Program, which guides Kenyan youth and adults on outdoor adventures.

SAMPLE TRIPS

➤**Mexico Sea Kayaking**—An introduction to the NOLS core curriculum, with an emphasis on developing leadership and technical kayaking skills. After a day's introduction to kayaking, paddle each day in the Sea of Cortez near Bahía Concepcíon. A midday siesta allows time for required classes, skills practice, and personal time. Classes cover basic wilderness living skills, minimum-impact camping, travel techniques, map reading, safety and hazard evaluation, environmental studies, outdoor baking, and basic first aid. Group dynamics and leadership theory are integral parts of the curriculum. Observe coastal wildlife, snorkel, and hike in the Sonoran desert. Learn coastal navigation skills, rescue skills, trip planning, and gear repair. You may have the opportunity to visit with local fisherman and ranchers living along this rugged coast. Twenty-one days/$2100/intermediate to advanced.

➤**Rock Climbing Leadership Seminar**—A course for female instructors and instructors-in-training to practice technical skills (protection placement, anchor construction, top-rope management, and lead theory) and to discuss issues involving women leaders in the outdoors. This course is open only to individuals who have passed a rigorous screening process. Five days/$200/advanced.

Prices include: Meals and group equipment.

Prices do not include: Personal equipment (most personal items, including sleeping bags, are available for rental).

Guides: Usually senior staff.

Training for guides: Sixty percent are NOLS graduates; supplementary training sessions offered each year range from technical skills to interpersonal communications and teaching; advanced first aid; First Responder or Emergency Medical Technician certification.

Liability coverage: Yes.

New Dawn

Box 1512
Vieques 00765 Puerto Rico
809/741-0495

Caribbean Retreat and Guest House

Began operating: 1986
Number of trips offered per year: 1 or 2
Number of all-women's trips per year: Nearly all
Usual group size: 5–15
Typical age of participants: 35
Range of ages of participants: 15–75

Designed for people who like to go barefoot and don't need all the comforts of home, New Dawn's retreat on the Isle of Vieques, is just a ferry ride from mainland Puerto Rico. Choose from volleyball, horseshoes, croquet, horse and bicycle riding, snorkeling, and massage. Located on five acres of the Pilon hillside, looking out on a display of hibiscus, bougainvillea, and grazing horses. The decor includes Guatemalan textiles, woven palm lampshades, windows open to the trade winds, and decks with swings and hammocks. Six private rooms, a bunkhouse, and tent sites are available. In the future, New Dawn may offer a week-long bicycle tour of Puerto Rico.

IN THEIR OWN WORDS
"New Dawn was built by women for women of all lifestyles and ages, offering safe, affordable, and comfortable surroundings. After Hurricane Hugo blew us away we had to rebuild, and now we're open to all, but focus on women."   —Gail Burchard, Founder

HISTORY/BACKGROUND
Gail Burchard worked as a flight attendant for American Airlines, which frequently brought her to Puerto Rico. After earning her pilot's license and leading sailing trips in the Caribbean, Gail Burchard decided to build a retreat house on Vieques with the help of women carpentry students. No longer leading trips except locally, Gail now focuses on New Dawn's retreat and guest house. In 1989 Hurricane Hugo dramatically altered the course of New Dawn, as did delays in disaster relief. In 1991, Gail's own resources and the help of friends financed New Dawn's revival.

SAMPLE TRIPS

➤**Vieques Sun Tour**—Just arrive on the island, relax in the sun, and enjoy. Your trip can be as vigorous or relaxed as you want to make it. Rent a bike, sailboard or kayak, horseback ride, or go to the beach. Visit the town of Esperanza or take a ferry to Fajardo on the main island of Puerto Rico to hike through the only tropical rainforest in the U.S. Learn about the history of Vieques, take a lesson in palm weaving, or study tropical plants. End your week with a farewell dinner and salsa dance. One week/$500/easy.

Prices include: Meals; accommodations; planned activities such as palm weaving, rainforest trip, snorkeling instruction, and guided tours of the island.

Prices do not include: Personal equipment and optional activities such as horseback riding, bicycle rental, and windsurfing.

Guides: Women knowledgeable about and experienced in the area.

Training for guides: Basic leadership, first aid, on-the-job training for two months or more.

Liability coverage: Yes, for the guest house and guests.

North Carolina Outward Bound School

121 North Sterling Street
Morganton, NC 28655
800/554-5375 or 704/437-6112

Women's Leadership Courses in North Carolina

Began operating: 1965
Number of trips offered per year: 80
Number of all-women's trips per year: 3
Usual group size: 8–12
Typical age of participants: Varies
Range of ages of participants: 21+ and 30+

Scholarships available: Financial aid and no-interest loans.

The North Carolina Outward Bound School offers eight-day courses in the southern Appalachians for women who want to develop wilderness and leadership skills. Programs combine physical challenge, personal reflection, group cooperation, and community service and are often useful for participants in transition who want to restore their sense of self or stretch themselves in new directions. NCOBS promotes diversity through marketing, recruiting, staff recruitment and development, and changes in course curriculum.

IN THEIR OWN WORDS
"We use challenging outdoor adventure as a vehicle for students to learn more about themselves. Courses combine the physical challenge of living and traveling outdoors with the interpersonal challenge of living in a small community of fourteen people. We hope you will leave with a better understanding of your personal and physical abilities, and your relationship to the larger community of home, business, municipality, and world."

—Holly Wiemers, Guide

HISTORY/BACKGROUND
NCOBS has been teaching outdoor education since 1965. The Atlanta Outward Bound Center, an extension of NCOBS, is located in metropolitan Atlanta. The Center's staff works in partnership with Atlanta city schools, Decatur city schools, Georgia Tech, and Georgia Cities in Schools/Exodus to provide inner-city youth with opportunities for personal growth and positive change.

SAMPLE TRIPS

➤**Women's Leadership 21+ and 30+**—Backpacking, rock climbing, rappelling, canoeing, caving in winter, a ropes course, and mini-marathon are combined with leadership development. Explore the traditional aspects of leadership: communication skills, decision making, conflict resolution, and goal setting. Address the leadership roles of women in your own life, community, business, and family. You will use group discussion, personal sharing, and journal writing to clarify your experiences. Eight days/$900/beginning to intermediate.

Prices include: Meals, group equipment, sleeping bags, backpacks, rain gear, and limited medical insurance.

Prices do not include: Personal equipment, required physical exam, and application fee.

Guides: Seasoned outdoor educators with skill and experience in outdoor adventure and group facilitation; average age of thirty-one.

Training for guides: Minimum requirement of Wilderness First Responder certification (first-aid training) and extensive experience in outdoor education.

Liability coverage: Yes.

OceanWomyn Kayaking
620 11th Avenue East
Seattle, WA 98102
206/325-3970

Sea Kayaking in Washington, Alaska, Mexico, and British Columbia

---

Began operating: 1984
Number of trips offered per year: 10–15
Number of all-women's trips per year: All
Usual group size: 6–8
Typical age of participants: 30–55
Range of ages of participants: 21–65

Programs for lesbians
Scholarships available: Sliding fee scale.

OceanWomyn Kayaking takes you on an intimate encounter with the sea at the desert, rainforest, glacier, or jungle edge. Paddle three to four hours each morning and spend your afternoons beachcombing, snorkeling, hiking, bird watching, or photographing. One- and two-week programs are designed for the beginning and the experienced kayaker. You'll learn paddling technique, wind, wave and tide dynamics, navigation and chart reading, marine weather forecasting, and natural history. Guides facilitate group decision making to determine the pace, activities, and style of your expedition. Groups are kept small to preserve the wilderness experience, facilitate learning and cohesiveness, and to maintain safety at sea. After completing a seven-day trip, participants receive a 10 percent discount on all future trips. OWK serves vegetarian fare and can accommodate diet restrictions with advance notice.

IN THEIR OWN WORDS
"Sea kayaking, OceanWomyn style, is noncompetitive, gentle, and community building. Our trips are oriented primarily, though not exclusively, to lesbians."
—Jesse Fenton, Founder

HISTORY/BACKGROUND
Founder Jesse Fenton has led over one hundred and twenty all-women sea kayaking trips and explored thousands of miles of the Pacific Coast. Claire Schwartz, senior guide and beloved cook, has led programs since 1986.

SAMPLE TRIPS

➤**British Columbia Kayaking**—Kayak among hundreds of miniature, uninhabited islands. Explore sandy beaches, ancient fern-filled rainforests, and paths once scouted by the Nootka Indians, a people who not so long ago paddled the Pacific for whales. One week/$600/beginning.

➤**San Juan Islands Kayaking**—This archipelago of two hundred islands supports deer, seal, river otter, and over two hundred species of birds. Broaden your sea skills during the day and camp on islands of sandy beaches, rocky coves, and fern-filled forests at night. Six days/$550/beginning.

➤**Baja Kayaking**—The coast of Baja, where the Sonoran desert's rugged cactus-studded landscape meets the brilliant blue Sea of Cortez, was the legendary home of an Amazon tribe rich in gold. Paddling through the Loreto-Mulege region and along the Sierra de la Giganta mountains, you may encounter pods of leaping bottlenose dolphins or gray, fin, and blue whales. Explore the barren islands and sculpted volcanic shorelines, searching for giant fossils, ancient Indian middens, and rare seashells. Hike in the desert, create rituals on the beach, snorkel, swim, and learn basic desert survival skills. One week/$775/beginning. Two weeks/$1300/advanced.

Prices include: Meals, group equipment (discount if you bring your own kayak), camping fees.

Prices do not include: Personal equipment and tent.

Guides: Founder Jesse Fenton and senior guide Claire Schwartz.

Training for guides: Nineteen years' experience guiding all-women sea kayaking trips.

Liability coverage: No.

Olivia Cruises and Resorts

4400 Market Street
Oakland, CA 94608
800/631-6277 or 510/655-0364   fax: 510/655-4334

Lesbian Cruises and Resort Vacations Worldwide

Began operating: 1990
Number of trips offered per year: 4–6
Number of all-women's trips per year: All
Usual group size: 600
Typical age of participants: 35–55
Range of ages of participants: 22–80

Accessible to disabled women: Most trips are accessible, however some vessels and resorts are not as accessible as others.
Programs for lesbians

Olivia Cruises and Resorts charters entire ships and resorts for week-long vacations during which lesbians of all ages, both singles and couples, can sightsee, socialize, play, and relax. Activities range from music and comedy to snorkeling and horseback riding, meditation and sunbathing to midnight buffets and dance lessons. Daily twelve-step meetings are available. Cruises may stop at popular lesbian and gay destinations like Provincetown and Key West. You can be as active or as relaxed as you choose. Future trip sites include Alaska, Hawaii, the Caribbean, the Galapagos, and Africa.

IN THEIR OWN WORDS
"We offer the 'Olivia Experience'—fun, adventure, luxury, and romance with a healthy dose of relaxation. It's about the personal freedom to do what you want and be who you are every minute of the day. Women receive the very best when they place their vacation dreams in Olivia's hands."
—Judy Dlugacz, President

HISTORY/BACKGROUND
Olivia Records has been producing and distributing music by and for women since 1973. In 1989, a concert goer remarked, "Wouldn't this be wonderful on the water?" Within a year, Olivia chartered a five-hundred-fifty-passenger ship, offering their first cruise.

SAMPLE TRIPS

►**Western Caribbean Cruise**—Sail from Miami to Playa del Carmen, gateway to the Yucatán. Explore ancient ruins in Chichen Itza and Tulum, take a daytrip to Isla Mujeres—the "island of women"—and check out the shops and beaches of Cancún. Spend a day on the tropical island of Cozumel, snorkeling on the three-mile-long Palancar Reef or visiting the Mayan ruins at San Gervasio. Swim, snorkel, scuba, or sunbathe. Return with a visit to Key West. Seven days/$1000–$1800/easy.

►**Playa Blanca Resort**—Located a hundred and twenty miles south of Puerto Vallarta in Mexico, this Club Med resort offers swimming, snorkeling, horseback riding, basketball, volleyball, tennis, a circus workshop, scuba school, rock climbing (on an artificial wall), games, entertainment, and lots of fun. Seven days/$1000–$1050/easy.

►**New York to Montreal Cruise**—Sail from New York to Provincetown, where you can celebrate the Fourth of July. Continue on to Maine, Nova Scotia, and the St. Lawrence Seaway. Wander through Quebec City and Montreal. The cruise ends in Montreal, but Olivia is planning special excursions and hotel packages for those who wish to extend their vacations in Canada. Seven days/$1200–$2600/easy.

►**Sonora Bay Resort**—The high desert meets the sea at this Club Med resort on the northwest coast of Mexico. Scuba dive, snorkel, sail, windsurf, water ski, or swim in the Sea of Cortez. Enjoy tennis, golf, horseback riding, and more. Seven days/$1000–$1100/easy.

Prices include: For cruises: meals, accommodations, entertainment, ship's activities, commitment ceremonies, theme parties; for resorts: meals, beverages with meals, entertainment, most resort activities, gratuities, commitment ceremonies, theme parties.

Prices do not include: Alcoholic beverages, port taxes and gratuities (billed in advance for cruise vacations), optional shore excursions.

Guides: Olivia's senior management coordinate daily operations of vacations; CEO, Cruise and Resort Director, Special Events and Hospitality Director, and Information and Product Manager handle daily activities; twenty to forty trained staff members; shore excursions guided by local women whenever possible; naturalists and specialists contracted for adventure vacations.

Training for guides: Detailed job description and comprehensive meeting for program staff; experienced crew assists in training new personnel; and all program staff are evaluated on their performance at the end of each trip.

Liability coverage: Yes, additional optional travel insurance available.

Onn the Water

P.O. Box 173
Gig Harbor, WA 98335
206/851-5259

Day- and Week-Long Sails on Washington's Puget Sound

Began operating: 1993
Number of trips offered per year: 3
Number of all-women's trips per year: All
Usual group size: Up to 6
Typical age of participants: 30s
Range of ages of participants: 13–60

Set sail on a thirty-foot Catalina for a day's sailing instruction, dinner sail, overnight, or week-long excursion. Onn the Water invites women with sailing experience as well as those who have only dreamed of embarking on such a trip. OTW emphasizes safety and comfort and asks you to bring an adventurous spirit as environmental conditions can add an element of unpredictability to your journey. OTW is also available to skipper your boat or charter boat anywhere you want to go.

IN THEIR OWN WORDS
"I'm familiar with Puget Sound and know the local area. I gear classes and excursions to the participants, allowing them to learn as much about sailing as they want or simply sit back and relax. We concentrate on cruising, comfortable sailing, and the beauty of the Puget Sound Pacific Northwest area."
—Nicki DeBoard, Founder

HISTORY/BACKGROUND
Recognizing the need for more women sailing instructors, sailor, songwriter, and freelance writer Nicki DeBoard founded Onn the Water. A sailor since 1986 and boat-owner since 1990, Nicki earned her Coast Guard license in order to guide other women who have dreamed of sailing.

SAMPLE TRIPS

➤**Day Sails**—Sail South Puget Sound with stops at nearby islands. Instruction or relaxation. Three to eight hours/$30–$80/all levels.

➤**San Juan Islands**—Depart Friday Harbor and sail island to island, exploring, shopping, and dining in the scenic San Juans. Seven days/$750/all levels.

➤**Gulf Islands**—Depart Victoria, British Columbia, and watch for whales and dolphins in Harro Strait en route to quiet anchorages and the quaint town of Sydney. Seven days/$750/all levels.

➤**Desolation Sound**—Depart Powell River, British Columbia, and sail north to views of majestic mountains from warm water anchorages. Seven days/$750/all levels.

➤**South Puget Sound**—Depart Gig Harbor, Washington, and discover points of interest, keeping an eye out for dolphins and eagles. Seven days/$750/all levels.

➤**Overnights**—Destinations include Blake Island, Quartermaster Harbor, Longbranch, Jerrel's Cove, and Poulsbo. Two days/$150–$300/all levels.

➤**Dinner Sails**—Have a private barbecue on board, or dock and dine at a nearby waterfront restaurant. Three to eight hours/$30–$80 (not including dinner)/easy.

➤**Sailing Instruction**—Learn on OTW's boats or your own. Three to eight hours/$15–$20 per hour/beginning to advanced.

Prices include: At least two meals a day on week-long trips, accommodations, and group equipment.

Prices do not include: Personal equipment, some meals, on-shore entertainment.

Guides: Founder Nicki DeBoard.

Training for guides: U.S. Coast Guard certification; A.S.A. certification.

Liability coverage: Yes.

Orvis

Historic Route 7-A
Manchester, VT 05254
800/235-9763   fax: 802/362-3525

Fishing Schools in Wyoming, Colorado, and Vermont

Began operating: 1967
Number of trips offered per year: 60
Number of all-women's trips per year: 4
Usual group size: 10–36
Typical age of participants: 45
Range of ages of participants: 7–80

Learn to fly fish or improve your technique in a two-and-a-half-day Orvis course. Classes are taught on Orvis casting ponds, in indoor classrooms, and on the Battenkill trout stream. Use your choice of an Orvis rod, reel, line, and leader. On the last morning of each class, catch and release beautiful rainbow and brook trout on stocked trout ponds. Special lodging rates are available at Equinox, a restored nineteenth-century inn, though participants may also choose to camp.

IN THEIR OWN WORDS
"My staff and I will get you well past the initial intimidating stage of fly fishing. You will leave our school with a solid foundation of skills to build on. We also welcome 'old pros,' because we know our instructors will teach you enough new skills to make your session worthwhile."
—Rick Rishell, School Director

HISTORY/BACKGROUND
Established in 1856, Orvis is America's oldest mail-order company. They sell a wide variety of fly fishing and hunting products. In the spring of 1967, Orvis organized their first fly fishing school and have since added women's programs to their schedule. Orvis shooting schools began in 1973. Women make up 25 percent of the enrollment in coed schools.

SAMPLE TRIPS

►**Fly Fishing Schools**—Learn the forward cast, roll cast, side cast, roll-cast pickup, and how to false cast and shoot line. Familiarize yourself with the essential knots for tying on a fly and for making and repairing leaders as well as how to select the right flies for trout, bass, panfish, salmon, steelhead, and saltwater fish. Instructors teach you to "read" a trout stream and find out where the fish live and where they feed, find and identify the basic trout stream insects, wade a trout stream safely, manipulate your line in tricky currents, play, land, and release fish, and select the proper equipment. Illustrated lectures and hands-on practice.
Jackson Hole, Wyoming: Two days/$350/beginning and intermediate.
Evergreen, Colorado: Two and a half days/$400/beginning and intermediate.
Manchester, Vermont: Two and a half days/$400/beginning and intermediate.

Prices include: Lunch, fishing equipment, fishing license, *The Orvis Fly Fishing Guide.*
Prices do not include: Breakfast and dinner, and accommodations.
Guides: Female and male Orvis staff.
Training for guides: Yes.
Liability coverage: Yes.

Outdoor Leadership Training Seminars
P.O. Box 20281
Denver, CO 80220
800/331-7238 or 303/333-7831

Utah Canyon Quest

Began operating: 1973
Number of trips offered per year: Varies
Number of all-women's trips per year: 1
Usual group size: 10–15
Typical age of participants: 40
Range of ages of participants: 25–55

Outdoor Leadership Training Seminars sponsors a series of workshops called "Breaking through Adventures." Included is a women's wilderness quest that explores the relationship between personal growth and outdoor experiences. Learn how to gently expose and transform self-limiting behaviors and beliefs. Celebrate your interdependence with other people and the earth. Enjoy some moderate backpacking, desert exploration, ritual, and celebration. Practice tai chi meditation, set out on a short solo quest, and learn outdoor and leadership skills. Coed programs include rock climbing, backpacking, mountaineering, rafting, and backcountry skiing.

IN THEIR OWN WORDS
"We offer quality programs that emphasize personal growth, leadership training, and ecological consciousness. Our programs draw upon a wide range of contemporary psychological, philosophical and educational strategies to bring insight and appreciation of the outdoor lifestyle to the personal and professional lives of our participants."   —Rick Medrick, Executive Director

HISTORY/BACKGROUND
The Outdoor Leadership Training Seminars train instructors and guides in a transformational approach to outdoor learning they call "New Age Wilderness Leadership." This experiential process integrates outdoor skills training, personal awareness, community building, ceremony and ritual, and social and environmental action. OLTS offers five- and eight-month leadership courses, five-week intensives, and five- to ten-day workshops. Their Whitewater Training School trains river guides and individual boaters.

SAMPLE TRIPS

►**Women's Canyon Quest**—Join a celebration of spring in the Canyonlands of Utah. Enjoy the warmth of sun on painted sandstone, the desert in bloom, and the companionship of other women. Share experiences of modern womanhood, explore the essence of basic feminine nature, and further your awareness and appreciation of your unique contribution to "the tribe." Backpack a short distance to your base camp and learn the skills necessary to live comfortably and walk softly on this sacred land. Ceremony, ritual, tai chi, chanting and singing, and a short "solo" enhance your awareness of the land and yourself. Your guides include Dolores LaChapelle, wilderness scholar and author of *Earth Wisdom* and *Sacred Land, Sacred Sex*, and Penny Woodward, an outdoor instructor, rafting guide, and occupational therapist who has worked extensively with handicapped children and their families. Eight days/$650/ all levels.

Prices include: Meals and group equipment.

Prices do not include: Personal equipment and tent.

Guides: Dolores LaChapelle and Penny Woodward.

Training for guides: Extensive training and many years of experience.

Liability coverage: Yes.

Outdoor Vacations for Women over 40

P.O. Box 200
Groton, MA 01450
508/448-3331   fax: 508/448-3514

Worldwide Adventures from Skiing to Sailing

Began operating: 1983
Number of trips offered per year: 25
Number of all-women's trips per year: All
Usual group size: 12–14
Typical age of participants: Late 50s
Range of ages of participants: 40–83

Multigenerational programs: Participants must be eighteen or older.
Programs for older women

Programs accommodate women of varying abilities and range from a weekend of cross country skiing in New Hampshire to a seventeen-day journey to New Zealand. Visit three Hawaiian Islands, enjoy inn-to-inn hiking in New England, or bicycle through Holland. Hike, canoe, and fish in the Pacific Northwest or whale watch and camp in Baja, Mexico. Weekend and weeklong multigenerational trips welcome mothers, daughters, grandmothers, granddaughters, aunts, and nieces to hike, sail, or simply sun. Lodging varies from country inns, chateaus, and rustic lodges to sailboat bunks and sleeping bags under the stars. Food ranges from gourmet to country fare.

IN THEIR OWN WORDS
"Women who participate in our trips love the outdoors. They are primarily beginners at whatever the activity is. All women over forty are welcome."
—Marion Stoddart, Founder

HISTORY/BACKGROUND
Marion Stoddart's goals were traveling, being active in the outdoors, learning new skills, meeting new people, and providing a service to older women like herself. So began OVWOF in 1983. An experienced outdoorswoman and conservationist, Marion received the United Nations Environment Programme's Global Award in 1987. In 1993, National Geographic featured her heroic and successful river restoration efforts for conservation and recreation.

SAMPLE TRIPS

➤**Cross Country Ski Weekend in New Hampshire**—Instruction for first-time and intermediate skiers. A view of White Mountain National Forest and its peaks greets you as you set out from a New England inn. Trails lead to state forests, scenic streams, and ponds. Evening meals, a cozy pub, fireside companionship, and comfortable lodgings complete the day. Two and a half days/ $350/beginning and intermediate.

➤**Rafting in Idaho**—An eighty-mile journey on the Salmon and Snake Rivers. Mountain ranges are visible on both sides. At some places along the route, you can look up to points over a mile above the river. Opportunities to paddle inflatable kayaks, swim, walk, and relax. Six days/$1700/easy to moderate.

➤**Hike, Canoe, and Fish in the Cascade Mountains**—Washington's snowcapped volcanic cones, with their Alpine meadows, lakes, and streams, will delight you. Tour Mt. Rainier National Park, hike in subalpine meadowlands, canoe on Bumping Lake, and receive fly fishing instruction. Accommodations at a small mountain lodge. Six days/$1800/easy to moderate.

➤**Walking in France**—Meander through the Loire river valley past small villages and fields of wheat, corn, and bright orange poppies. Visit historic sites, cave dwellings, chateaus, and inns. A day's hike at a leisurely pace averages ten miles. Stay in Paris for the last three nights. Accommodations in a small hotel on the Left Bank, a guided tour of the city, and time for individual exploration. Baggage is carried separately and transport is available if you want to skip a day's walk. Nine days/$3100/easy to moderate.

➤**Inn-to-Inn Hiking in New Hampshire**—Streams, ridges, forests, and mountaintops are in sight as you hike five to seven miles daily along the Metacomet/Monadnock and Wapack Trails. Hike in the morning, enjoy the villages and inns in the afternoon. Baggage is carried separately and transport is available if you want to skip a day's walk. Four days/$1050/moderate.

Prices include: Meals, accommodations, group equipment, and gratuities.

Prices do not include: Personal equipment and alcoholic beverages.

Guides: Rangers, naturalists, and instructors who have gained their experience from Professional Ski Instructors of America, Outward Bound, NOLS, American Canoe Association, and American Red Cross; guides are women 99 percent of the time.

Training for guides: Experience leading trips, CPR/first aid, naturalist interests.

Liability coverage: No, however rafting outfitter provides insurance.

Pacific Crest Outward Bound School

0110 Southwest Bancroft Street
Portland, OR 97201
800/547-3312 or 503/243-1446   fax: 503/274-7723

Developing Leadership and Self-Confidence in the Wilderness

Began operating: 1966
Number of trips offered per year: 175
Number of all-women's trips per year: 12
Usual group size: 8–10
Typical age of participants: 14–25
Range of ages of participants: 14+

Accessible to disabled women: On a case-by-case basis.
Scholarships available: "Do not let the cost of the programs deter you from
applying"; scholarships exceed $500,000 annually.

The aim of Pacific Crest Outward Bound School is to teach respect for self, concern for others, and care for the environment through backpacking, mountaineering, rafting, canoeing, kayaking and sailing. Programs emphasize wilderness skills, safety and judgment, reflection and evaluation, expedition leadership, environmental and natural history studies, and service ethics. Women's courses are for adults twenty-one and older and are designed with the newcomer in mind.

IN THEIR OWN WORDS
"We believe that a wilderness adventure provides a tangible and dramatic way to deliver our mission. A long ridge climb up a mountain demands commitment and perseverance. Linking a series of moves on a climb requires concentration and courage. Preparing a meal for your companions during a rain storm requires sacrifice, no more, no less. These essential values speak directly to the quality of our lives." —Pacific Crest Outward Bound School brochure

HISTORY/BACKGROUND
The Pacific Crest Outward Bound School began with twenty young men who gathered at Three Sisters Wilderness. Students slept on boughs of fir, cooked over open fires, and learned to use a double-bitted ax. Though much about the courses has changed, the precepts remain the same.

SAMPLE TRIPS

➤**Canoeing and Backpacking**—Spend four days canoeing and four days backpacking into the lush and rugged alpine wilderness of the North Cascades. Glaciated peaks rise abruptly from Ross Lake, where you will learn basic canoe skills and safety before canoes are launched. Ample time to practice basic and advanced paddling skills. The backpacking section is fast paced, with frequent stream crossings and significant elevation loss and gain. Curriculum also includes campcraft, backcountry navigation, natural history, and ecology. Evening discussions provide insight into leadership styles and teamwork. Eight days/$1000/easy to moderate.

➤**Desert Exploration and Rock Climbing**—Experience the diverse landscape of Southern California's Joshua Tree National Monument, its rock formations, desert wildflowers, and unique geological features. The seemingly barren earth is, in fact, a delicate and complex habitat for a variety of plants and animals. You will cross through several ecological zones, from ridges of dense pinyon pine to arroyos of creosote. The climbing curriculum begins with a thorough introduction to the basics of movement and safety. Then proceed at your own pace, with climbs selected according to your group's aspirations and abilities. Between climbs, backpack through the desert and learn to pick your route by using topographic maps. Eight days/$900/moderate.

➤**Alpine Mountaineering**—This alpine expedition in California's High Sierra is a multidisciplined course. Acquire skills necessary to safely and responsibly travel through sensitive alpine environments, and develop judgment, self-confidence and a willingness to accept responsibility. General mountaineering skills include: snow climbing, rock climbing, off-trail hiking, backcountry navigation, minimum-impact camping, and first aid. Exact activities may vary by area and by season, but all courses include a basic curriculum involving technical skills, leadership, natural history, and service. Expect a demanding course; days are typically long and busy. Eight days/$1000/challenging.

Prices include: Transportation to and from airport; meals; group equipment; specialized equipment, including backpacks, sleeping bags, and rain gear.

Prices do not include: Personal equipment and required medical exam.

Guides: Wilderness professionals with extensive personal expeditions and Outward Bound training.

Training for guides: Advanced first-aid or Wilderness First Responder certification; personal expertise in a given outdoor activity; initial PCOBS training; additional skill training each year to help staff with ongoing development.

Liability coverage: Yes.

Pack, Paddle, Ski

P.O. Box 82
South Lima, NY 14558
716/346-5597 (same for fax)

Kayaking, Canoeing, and Bicycling in New England

Began operating: 1983
Number of trips offered per year: 250
Number of all-women's trips per year: 20–30
Usual group size: 12
Typical age of participants: 38–40
Range of ages of participants: 20–70

Pack, Paddle, Ski offers women one-day paddling and bicycling tours and three- and four-day river trips. Courses may take place in the Adirondack wilderness or on the rolling hills along Lake Ontario. Develop outdoor skills, learn about plants, wildlife, geology, and local history. Meet new people and enjoy the splendor of the outdoors.

IN THEIR OWN WORDS
"We are still a family business. This means that *you* are special to us."
—Pack, Paddle, Ski brochure

HISTORY/BACKGROUND
Pack, Paddle, Ski founder Randy French is a former boy scout and eagle scout. After traveling around the U.S., Randy decided to make a living taking people into the outdoors. Pack, Paddle, Ski began by offering a few weekend canoe trips and has grown to support five staff members, of which three are women.

SAMPLE TRIPS

➤**Adirondack Foliage Canoe**—Revel in fall colors as you paddle an Adirondack river to a small rapid. One day/under $100/all levels.

➤**Bike around the Bay**—A thirty-five-mile bike ride through rolling hills, along the shore of Lake Ontario, and through the quaint village of Sodus Bay. After lunch at Chimney Bluffs State Park, take in the sights around the bay. Must provide your own bike and helmet. One day/under $50/beginning.

➤**Introduction to Kayaking**—After a morning of flatwater practice and a good lunch you'll be ready to experience a small rapid and learn basic whitewater technique. One day/under $100/beginning.

➤**Beginning Kayak Tour**—Practice kayak skills at the evening session and then head for Ganargua Creek. Small rapids allow you to develop your ferrying, eddy turns, and surfing skills. One and a half days/under $100/ beginning.

➤**Solo Canoe Tour**—Paddle your own canoe on the quiet waters of a creek near Sodus Bay while enjoying a landscape of wetlands, cliffs, drumlins, streams, and landlocked bays. One day/under $50/beginning.

➤**Pickeral River**—Paddle along the rocky shore of this Canadian river. Explore hidden coves and passages to secret lakes. Relax for five days in open, scenic, pine-covered campsites. A leisurely pace with no portages. This is a great trip for women new to canoeing as well as those veterans searching for new places to explore. Five days/$350/easy.

➤**Algonquin**—One of PPS's most popular women-only courses. Experience the beautiful wilderness of Canada's Algonquin Park, complete with loons and moose. Some portages. Includes wilderness skills instruction. Three days/ $200/moderate.

Prices include: Meals (lunch only on daytrips), group equipment, camping or lodging fees, licenses.

Prices do not include: Personal equipment and tent.

Guides: One of four guides/owners or three additional trained guides.

Training for guides: Advanced first-aid, basic life support, and life guard certification; New York State guide's license; participation in all leader training programs and reconnaissance of trip areas.

Liability coverage: Yes.

Paddling South

4510 Silverado Trail
Calistoga, CA 94515
707/942-4550 fax: 707/942-4904

Sea Kayaking, Mulepacking, and Natural History Hikes in Baja

Began operating: 1983
Number of trips offered per year: 20
Number of all-women's trips per year: 2 (another 5 booked by other agents)
Usual group size: 9
Typical age of participants: 30s–40s
Range of ages of participants: 13–69

Programs for older women: An "Over 40" trip is being planned.

Miles of coves and beaches, blue water, and red rock ridges characterize Baja California, home to Paddling South. Kayak and mulepacking trips for the beginner or intermediate participant vary in length from five to fourteen days. Day-long natural history hikes require only your sense of inquisitiveness. Close cultural contact with friends and families in the areas visited add to these wilderness adventures. An afternoon hike to Chita's palm-thatched kitchen to make tortillas or share a cup of campfire coffee with panga fishermen is often a highlight for guests. Daily mileage ranges from seven to ten miles on the average paddling trip; up to fifteen miles a day may be covered on the two-week trips. There are layover days included on most paddling trips.

IN THEIR OWN WORDS
"Because we live in Baja nine months each year, it is home and not just a travel destination. Familiarity with the people and politics of a small remote town adds value to our place in the local economy, and over 50 percent of our clients' tourist dollars support the local and regional community."
—Trudi Angell, Founder

HISTORY/BACKGROUND
Paddling South owner Trudi Angell organized and led twenty private paddling expeditions on the Baja coast from 1976 to 1983 before starting her own company. Paddling South began with a beach base camp, soon moving to a house in Loreto. Trudi calls her mulepacking trips "Saddling South."

SAMPLE TRIPS

➤**Sea Kayaking**—Slip away from shore in two-person kayaks to explore Baja's islands, shores, and reefs. Excursions reveal 163 species of plants, 16 species of seabirds, and an abundant animal life that includes jack rabbits, coyotes, ringtailed cats, lizards, and whale and dolphin sightings. Six days/$800/beginning. Nine days/$900/beginning. Fourteen days/$1500/beginning to intermediate.

➤**Mulepacking**—Join Trudi, local Mexican cowboys, and Barquito and Tequila—two fuzzy-gray pack burros—on an adventure into the mountains of Baja. Riding mules or horses, or on foot with just your daypack, you explore historical trails that wind along rocky desert ridges, through cactus garden valleys, and into lush palm springs. Glimpses of traditional ranch life, little changed since early Spanish settlement, highlight these trips. No prior riding experience is needed but good physical condition is necessary. Five days/$600/beginning. Seven days/$800/beginning to intermediate.

Prices include: Meals (mostly vegetarian) and group equipment.

Prices do not include: Personal equipment and alcoholic beverages.

Guides: Women and men with knowledge of Baja and Spanish-language ability.

Training for guides: Firsthand training while interning and assisting on trips; first-aid certification; most guides have previous experience in other outdoor leadership positions.

Liability coverage: Yes.

PeerSpirit

P.O. Box 550
Langley, WA 98260
612/898-2221

Outdoor Exploration, Women's Spirituality, and Earth Activism

---

Began operating: 1991
Number of trips offered per year: 6
Number of all-women's trips per year: All
Usual group size: Varies
Typical age of participants: 40s–50s
Range of ages of participants: 29–75

Accessible to disabled women: Depending on location of program.
Scholarships available: Work exchange is also possible.

Whether backpacking in Arizona or visiting ancient goddess sites in England, PeerSpirit's "Women and the Planet" wilderness seminars emphasize reconnecting with one's elemental sources of power through nature. Seminars begin with a sacred circle in which women relearn the skills of council and living in a community. The focus of circles is to help women make spiritually-based changes in their lives. Participants explore the natural world individually and as a group, using rites of passage as a path to personal and shared transformation. Women can call circles in their own community and invite PeerSpirit to guide those seminars.

IN THEIR OWN WORDS
"We feel that teaching the skills of holding circle or council is basic to the formation of new culture; the skills we teach are applicable to all parts of women's lives, whether they be about holding circle or connecting to the planet."
—Ann Linnea, Co-founder

HISTORY/BACKGROUND
Christina Baldwin is the author of *Life's Companion, Journal Writing as a Spiritual Quest* and *Calling the Circle: The First and Future Culture* and has taught journal writing since 1979. Ann Linnea is the coauthor of *Teaching Kids to Love the Earth* and has been a teacher of environmental consciousness since 1979. Ann's upcoming book, *Superior Spirit*, focuses on her circumnavigation of Lake Superior by sea kayak, a story of a midlife transformative journey.

SAMPLE TRIPS

►**Dog Sledding on the Winter Solstice**—Women and the Planet joins forces with Wintermoon for an exploration of the winter woods. Travel to the boreal forest of northern Minnesota, where the simple, rustic lifestyle of log cabins, sauna, wood heat, and solar power await you. Four days/$400/all levels.

►**Ropes Course in Minnesota**—Stay at Wolf Ridge Environmental Learning Center, located on the hills overlooking Lake Superior. Explore the hills, lakes and forests during this ropes course, a rite of passage for individual challenge and group bonding. Three days/$200/all levels.

►**Ocean Kayaking in British Columbia**—Convene circles at the base of five-hundred-year-old cedar trees, on tidal flats, or at the site of ancient medicine stones. From your base at Hollyhock Farm on Cortes Island, Canada, set out by foot and kayak. Planned during the full-moon week, seminars include "Drumming the Heartbeat" and "Maiden, Mother, Crone: Finding Inner Voices of Archetypes." Play, perform, and learn together. Leaders for the week include PeerSpirit's founders as well as drummer Barbara Borden and actress Naomi Newman. Camping and limited cabin space available. Price does not include meals and accommodations. Six days/CDN $450/all levels.

►**Visiting Ancient Goddess Sites in England**—Wiltshire County, England, home to such goddess sites as Silbury Hill, Avebury Stone Circles, and Windmill Hill, sets the scene for this seminar. Housed in the Braeside Education and Conference Center with its Tudor architecture, participants explore the deepest roots of women's spirituality in the company of American and British women. Five days/$650/all levels.

►**Backpacking Sacred Arizona Canyon**—Convene a circle among red sandstone walls and still canyon pools. Return to the simplicity of earlier times. Hiking and packing distances are short; a base camp in a secluded canyon provides a place for meditation, writing, and drumming. Five days/$500/all levels.

Prices include: Meals and accommodations except on kayak trip, group equipment, journal.

Prices do not include: Personal equipment.

Guides: Co-founders Christina Baldwin and Ann Linnea and various other guides.

Training for guides: Fifteen years' teaching experience; PeerSpirit is in the process of designing facilitator training seminars.

Liability coverage: Yes, when programs take place at centers.

Portuguese Princess Whale Watch

P.O. Box 1469
Provincetown, MA 02657
508/487-2651   fax: 508/487-6458

Whale Watching and Moonlight Cruises from Provincetown

Began operating: 1983
Number of trips offered per year: 500
Number of all-women's trips per year: 30+
Usual group size: 10–150
Typical age of participants: 30–60
Range of ages of participants: 1 month–103 years

Accessible to disabled women: Encouraged to participate; PPWW will assist.

A marine biologist describes the bird and marine life as you cruise the waters off the Massachusetts coast. The *Portuguese Princess,* a hundred-foot-long cruiser, sails seven miles to and from Stellwagen Bank, a rich feeding ground for humpback and finback whales. A narrow eight-foot pulpit juts out from the boat so you can walk out over the water. Though it can seat two hundred and seventy passengers, PPWW limits their trips to a hundred and fifty women, leaving room on some trips for a band and dancing.

IN THEIR OWN WORDS
"We are a women-owned business with a ten-year history and a 99.7 percent whale-sighting record. We are a gay-friendly business and support many women's organizations."   —Suzanne Carter, Founder

HISTORY/BACKGROUND
A registered nurse and single parent of a multiply challenged, blind daughter, Suzanne Carter started Portuguese Princess Whale Watch with the hopes of earning enough money to provide for her daughter's special needs. Though discouraged by town officials and bank officers, Suzanne persevered and ultimately obtained a court order to continue her whale watch trips, designed her own boat, and developed a successful business. The name Portuguese Princess Whale Watch refers to the Portuguese fishing village in Provincetown where Suzanne was born. PPWW is currently helping a longtime employee through college.

SAMPLE TRIPS

➤**Whale Watch**—Three to four hours/$15–$18/easy.

➤**Moonlight Cruise**—Two to three hours/$8–$15 (depending on entertainment provided)/easy.

➤**Sightseeing Cruise**—One and a half hours/$8–$10/easy.

➤**Longpoint Beach Fun Day**—Takes place on a secluded beach. Price includes box lunch. Three to four hours/$15/easy.

Prices include: Whale-sighting guarantee on whale watch excursions.

Prices do not include: Meals unless otherwise noted.

Guides: A naturalist (usually a marine biologist) on whale watch excursions and sightseeing cruises.

Training for guides: Background in marine science, training by PPWW head naturalists, and ongoing trainings.

Liability coverage: Yes.

Poseidon Services / Izarra Cruises

2442 Northwest Market, Suite 467
Seattle, WA 98107
206/789-2175 fax: 206/784-2141

International Sailing Adventures and Sail Training Courses

Began operating: 1991
Number of trips offered per year: 16
Number of all-women's trips per year: 14
Usual group size: 3–4
Typical age of participants: 44
Range of ages of participants: 16–72

Scholarships available: By special arrangement; work exchange also available.

Familiarize yourself with points of sail, tides and currents, navigation and chart interpretation, docking and anchoring, and safety procedures. Learn to care for a boat's engine, tie knots, and use a VHF radio. Take leadership roles in all aspects of life aboard. Physical strength is not a prerequisite for these one- and two-week courses and sailing adventures in the U.S., Canada, the South Pacific, and Turkey. Trips focus on local and Native American culture, wildlife encounters, and traveling at "nature's pace." Joan Gottfried encourages contact with local residents whenever possible. Poseidon Services/Izarra Cruises grants discounts to returning participants.

IN THEIR OWN WORDS

"I try to propose cruises that not only teach sailing but also stress sensitivity to our natural environment and place emphasis on treasuring and preserving it. Cruising emphasizes the need to conserve energy, water, and food, and I believe that women return to their 'normal' lives with a greater appreciation for these commodities."   —Joan Gottfried, Founder

HISTORY/BACKGROUND

Joan Gottfried has lived in England, France, Egypt, the Persian Gulf, and Germany. She began sailing in the 1960s on California's High Sierra lakes. Tahiti, Tonga, Alaska, Grenada, and New Zealand have been among her sailing destinations. After teaching with an adventure company for six years, Joan founded Poseidon Services, using her custom-outfitted boat, *Izarra*.

SAMPLE TRIPS

➤**Victoria and Canadian Gulf Islands**—Sail into historic Victoria harbor and explore this charming town as well as the gorgeous Canadian Gulf Islands. One week/$900/easy to moderate.

➤**San Juan Island Sampler**—The San Juan Islands are just across Haro Strait from Canada and provide pristine marine parks for anchorages and exploration. Visit quaint harbors along the way. Wildlife sightings of whales, dolphins, and bald eagles are common. Stretch your legs on several nature walks. One week/$900/easy to moderate.

➤**Barkley Sound, B.C. Exploration**—Sail out the Strait of Juan de Fuca to the Pacific side of Vancouver Island. You are rewarded with excellent fishing opportunities, oysters and warm water temperatures. Swimming is possible. Some sailing skills are necessary. Two weeks/$1600/moderate.

➤**Desolation Sound, B.C.**—Voyage through the Gulf Islands, across Georgia Strait to a magnificent marine park. Hike to lakes for swimming. Enjoy seafood delights; vegetarian palates are respected, of course. Cruisers will travel one way by seaplane service. Two weeks/$1600/moderate.

➤**Southeast Alaska**—You can join this expedition during three different segments: San Juan Island to Pt. McNeill, B.C. (330 miles); Pt. McNeill to Ketchikan, Alaska (450 miles); or Ketchikan to Sitka (375 miles). Features include navigational challenges, several short, open-water crossings, frequent wildlife encounters, spectacular scenery. Visit hot springs, Native American heritage sites, and water-accessible cities and villages in Alaska and British Columbia. Two weeks/$1600/moderate.

➤**Turkey's Turquoise Coast**—Board fifty-foot yachts and sail along the (southwest) Turquoise Coast of Turkey. Plenty of time to explore the Greco-Roman antiquities and visit the famous Lycian rock tombs—Ephesus, Ismir, and Troy. Dine at night in local tavernas. Two weeks/$2500/moderate.

Prices include: Airfare on international trips, transfers, breakfast and lunch, hotel and yacht accommodations, port guides if necessary.

Prices do not include: Dinner in Turkey, personal equipment.

Guides: Founder Joan Gottfried.

Training for guides: U.S. Coast Guard license, thorough experience with boats and their systems, knowledge of cruising areas.

Liability coverage: Yes; PSIC requests a swimming-skills statement from participants.

Prairie Women Adventures and Retreat

Homestead Ranch, Box 2
Matfield Green, KS 66862
316/753-3465 fax: 316/273-8392

Ranch Work and Renewal in the Flint Hills of Kansas

Began operating: 1985
Number of trips offered per year: Operates eleven months per year
Number of all-women's trips per year: 99%
Usual group size: 8
Typical age of participants: 30s–40s
Range of ages of participants: 22–65

Accessible to disabled women: Bunkhouse is wheelchair accessible.

Spend time on a six-thousand-acre working ranch owned and operated by women. Work with ranch hands or simply relax on the land—you choose your level of participation. A creek, a garden, alfalfa fields, and tall grass pastures are located near the farmhouse; wildflowers and wildlife inhabit the area. Farmhouse and bunkhouse facilities are simple and comfortable, and Prairie Women Adventures and Retreat provides home-style meals. Dedicated to women's empowerment, PWAR offers a 15 percent discount to groups that work with victims of domestic violence or sexual assault.

IN THEIR OWN WORDS
"We provide an opportunity to experience the unique Kansas Flint Hills unplowed prairies—a serene setting to get away for a while. We believe there is no magic to being a cowhand; all women can share this experience. We are committed to enhancing women's knowledge of where their food comes from."   —Rhea Miller, Director

HISTORY/BACKGROUND
Born into a Kansan ranching family, Jane Koger traveled widely before returning to the prairie. She ranched with traditional cowboys before purchasing land that once belonged to her family and establishing an all-women's operation. On a recent visit to China with the Society of Range Management she exchanged ideas on grassland management with Chinese farmers and ranchers. Jane also holds a pilot's license.

SAMPLE TRIPS

➤**Ranch Adventure and Retreat**—Ride horseback through the grasslands, run a baler, push up calves (into working chutes), drive a tractor, castrate calves, gather eggs, or mend fences. Bike through the prairie, fish the creek, or simply relax on the back deck. Several weekends a year are set aside for cattle work, including vaccinations, pregnancy checks, sorting, and branding. Weekend/$250–$300 (the higher figure applies in May and October when you are working cattle)/all levels. Five days/$500/all levels.

Prices include: Meals, accommodations, horseback riding, hot tub.

Prices do not include: Personal equipment.

Guides: Experienced ranch hands.

Training for guides: Ranch experience.

Liability coverage: Yes.

Rainbow Adventures

1308 Sherman Avenue
Evanston, IL 60201
800/804-8686 or 708/864-4570

Worldwide Adventure Travel for Women over Thirty

Began operating: 1982
Number of trips offered per year: 22
Number of all-women's trips per year: All
Usual group size: Approximately 14
Typical age of participants: 50
Range of ages of participants: 30–80

As you strive to balance home, family, and work, Rainbow Adventures offers opportunities to meet interesting women, learn something new, experience different cultures, challenge yourself in a supportive environment, and get in touch with nature and the outdoors. From whitewater rafting trips through the Grand Canyon to Tanzanian wildlife safaris, programs are designed for a variety of interests and levels of experience. Trip destinations include North America, Central America, the Caribbean, Europe, Africa, Turkey, and Indonesia. The majority of participants are married or have been married, with between one and three children. After the fall of 1994, Rainbow Adventures will be located at 15036 Kelly Canyon Road, Bozeman, MT 59715.

IN THEIR OWN WORDS
"The most essential gear that we ask participants to bring is a sense of humor; the willingness to be flexible, agreeable, and accept situations as they exist (and not as each of us would prefer or expect them to be); and the attitude of a good-natured realist."　　　　　—Susan Eckert, Founder

HISTORY/BACKGROUND
A former biologist and Peace Corps volunteer in West Africa, Susan Eckert founded Rainbow Adventures in 1982. She quit her job and invested $25,000 of savings in this wilderness venture that would give more women the chance to take a break from their homes, families, and work. She felt that women over thirty were in the generation that grew up, got married, and took care of children while their husbands went off fishing and camping. Susan wanted to add wilderness adventures to those women's lives.

SAMPLE TRIPS

➤**Caribbean Windjammer Sailing in the British Virgin Islands**—Board the *Roseway*, a fully crewed windjammer, for sailing, snorkeling, and swimming in these turquoise waters. One week/$1400/easy.

➤**The National Parks of Southeast Utah by Houseboat, Van, Jeep, and Raft**—Salt Lake City to the Canyonlands and Arches National Parks for hiking, rafting, and geologist-guided jeep rides, followed by three days of houseboating in Glen Canyon. No camping. One week/$1300/easy.

➤**Adventurous Belize and Guatemala: Mayans and Meanderings**—Relax, canoe, swim, horseback ride, and explore ancient Mayan archaeological sites before flying to the world's second-largest barrier reef for two days of snorkeling, swimming, and sunbathing. Ten days/$2600/easy to moderate.

➤**Cross Country Skiing and Snowmobiling in Yellowstone**—Ski instruction and a dazzling display of waterfalls, geysers, bison, and elk. Naturalist-guided snowcoach transportation and a one-day snowmobile tour are included. Meals and ski rental not included. One week/$1100/easy to moderate.

➤**Horsepacking in the Canadian Rockies/Banff**—Visit Banff National Park. Includes three nights' hotel accommodations, four nights of camping. No riding experience necessary. One week/$1300/moderate.

➤**Tanzanian Tented Safari**—Visit the Serengeti plains during the wildebeest migration. Thirteen days/$5800/moderate.

➤**Wales: Hiking the Countryside and Pembrokeshire Coast**—Coastal hikes, Celtic sites, an English guide, and a charming hotel in St. Davids. Airfare not included. Ten days/$2500/moderate.

Prices include: International airfare on some trips (from New York or the West Coast), most meals, accommodations, group equipment.

Prices do not include: Airfare on domestic flights, some meals, personal equipment.

Guides: Founder Susan Eckert and ten associates.

Training for guides: CPR/first aid, wilderness skills.

Liability: Yes.

Reel Women Fly Fishing Adventures

P.O. Box 20202
Jackson, Wyoming 83001
307/733-6934

Fly Fishing in Idaho, Wyoming, Montana, and the Bahamas

Began operating: 1992
Number of trips offered per year: 5
Number of all-women's trips per year: All
Usual group size: 8–16
Typical age of participants: 45
Range of ages of participants: 8–85

Accessible to disabled women: On a case-by-case basis.
Multigenerational programs
Scholarships available: Teton County, Idaho, and Wyoming offer in-county
  scholarships to promote guiding and conservation.

Reel Women Fly Fishing Adventures offers trips ranging from the warm salt waters of the Caribbean to their favorite rivers in Wyoming, Idaho, and Montana. Guiding and instruction for anglers of all levels of experience is provided. You can learn basic and advanced fly fishing techniques at a relaxed and enjoyable pace: learn to read water, tie knots, and select the most effective flies. Custom trips for individuals and groups can be arranged.

IN THEIR OWN WORDS

"We both enjoy the opportunity to help women feel more confident and competent in the out-of-doors. Fly fishing is a wonderful medium for inspiring these transformations. We also feel that it is important for women to have female role models in what has been a typically male arena."

—Christy Ball, Co-founder

HISTORY/BACKGROUND

Lori-Ann Murphy and Christy Ball have been professional fly fishing guides since 1989. During the warm season in the Rocky Mountains, they both guide trips for Bressler Outfitters of Jackson Hole, Wyoming. They were inspired by their clients and the success of the women-only fly fishing schools that they teach for Orvis, to offer a variety of fishing adventures designed specifically for the female angler.

SAMPLE TRIPS

➤**Bahama Bonefishing**—Enjoy the tranquility of the Caribbean while learn-ing angling techniques specific to salt water flats fishing. Spend your time on Great Exuma Island with accommodations at Hotel Peace and Plenty. Six days/$1400/all levels.

➤**Montana Trout Fishing**—Classic river fishing in the heart of Montana's big sky country. Stay at the brand-new Crane Meadow Lodge on the banks of the Ruby River. Plenty of opportunity for fishing and floating in these western wa-ters. Five days/$1500/all levels.

➤**Jackson Hole Favorite**—Float twenty-seven miles through the canyon of the South Fork of the Snake River. Overnights at Bressler Outfitters deluxe camp, complete with cabin tents, cots, and a cook. A great trip for first-time campers as well as experienced outdoorswomen. All-women guides on this trip. Three days/$900/all levels. Five days/$1500/all levels.

➤**Wilderness Week in Yellowstone**—Horsepack into the backcountry and fish the pristine waters of Yellowstone. Explore places most visitors never see. Good physical condition is required. Six days/$t.b.a./all levels.

➤**Alpine Lakes Adventure**—Learn techniques for float-tube fishing in the high mountain lakes of Wyoming. Travel by horseback and camping. Good physical condition is required. Five days/$t.b.a./all levels.

➤**Smith River Canyon, Montana**—Get away from it all on this sixty-seven-mile fishing/float trip on one of Montana's most remote and picturesque riv-ers. Five days/$1300/all levels.

Prices include: Transportation to and from the local airport, meals, accommoda-tions, group equipment.

Prices do not include: Personal equipment; extra fishing days are sometimes available at additional cost.

Guides: Co-founders Christy Ball and Lori-Ann Murphy, and hand-picked female and male guides.

Training for guides: All guides have a minimum of three years of experience and are regularly employed by licensed outfitters in Wyoming, Idaho, or Montana.

Liability coverage: Yes.

Rhonda Smith Windsurfing Center

P.O. Box 116
Hood River, OR 97031
503/386-9463   fax: 503/386-6893

Summer Windsurfing Workshops and Winter Vacations

Began operating: 1991
Number of trips offered per year: Daily summer clinics; 2 winter vacations
Number of all-women's trips per year: Half
Usual group size: daily clinics/4; weekend clinics/25; vacations/10
Typical age of participants: 40
Range of ages of participants: 20s–70s

Programs for older women: "Over 40" course is being planned.

Each summer, the Rhonda Smith Windsurfing Center holds day- and week-end-long clinics in Oregon's Columbia Gorge for all skill levels. In the winter, groups travel to the Dominican Republic, Mexico, Costa Rica, Maui, or Aruba for week-long winter vacations. If you're a first-timer, all you need is a sense of adventure. You learn balance and build the strength you need along the way. Advanced programs are available for experienced windsurfers.

IN THEIR OWN WORDS
"Teaching people is a gift that I can give, and I feel honored to be able to do that. Our motto is that every person deserves to have a positive windsurfing experience. People can try to learn by themselves or with friends, and it can be a negative experience. To be involved in the sport you should start with a lesson. It's like parachuting—you wouldn't parachute without a lesson."
—Rhonda Smith, Founder

HISTORY/BACKGROUND
Rhonda Smith is a five-time world champion (with twenty years' windsurfing experience) and a certified instructor. With ten years of World Cup experience, Rhonda has more wins than any other woman. She founded the International Women's Board Sailing Association in 1982 and was awarded the Tudor Watch Contribution to Education Award in 1993. After retiring in 1990, she opened RSWC for the love of the sport. Rhonda works with local teenagers, providing free classes and instruction through the community high school.

SAMPLE TRIPS

➤**Summer Lessons**—Join no more than four other women for a half-day clinic. Classes are videotaped and equipment is provided. Three hours/under $100/beginning to advanced.

➤**Winter Windsurfing Vacations**—Begin each day with a windsurfing warm-up and stretch. Morning and afternoon workshops provide on-the-water instruction, which is videotaped. You can spend the late afternoon practicing or free sailing. In the evenings, enjoy sessions on self-rescue, video reviews, and equipment talks. Spend five days on the water. If you don't have a minimum of three days of wind, you receive a $50 Wind Voucher for future programs. One week/$700–$1100/beginning to advanced.

Prices include: For daily and weekend clinics: group equipment and personal equipment such as wet suits and harnesses; for winter vacations: group equipment and camp fees.

Prices do not include: Meals, and personal windsurfing equipment on winter vacations.

Guides: Founder Rhonda Smith and thirty-seven assistant instructors in the summer, two senior instructors chosen for winter vacations.

Training for guides: National windsurfing certificates, CPR/first aid, Rhonda Smith Windsurfing Center's certification and training.

Liability coverage: Yes.

Robin Tyler Productions and Tours

15842 Chase Street
North Hills, CA 91343
818/893-4075 fax: 818/893-1593

Worldwide Tours, Cruises, and Festivals

Began operating: 1980
Number of trips offered per year: Varies
Number of all-women's trips per year: All
Usual group size: 15–700
Typical age of participants: 30s–60s
Range of ages of participants: 30–80

Producer of the Annual West Coast Women's Music and Comedy Festival in the U.S. and the International Lesbian and Gay Comedy Festival in Australia, Robin Tyler Productions and Tours has also produced week-long U.S. cruises for up to seven hundred women, African safaris, and New Zealand treks. Travel by land and water through ancient and modern Egypt and Israel, attend the World Conference on Women in Beijing, or simply camp out in California for a Labor Day weekend of music, comedy, and camaraderie.

IN THEIR OWN WORDS
"My company is not just a tour company or a cruise company. We are a production company and, as such, we like to take women on tours connected with various events, such as the Annual Sydney Gay Mardi Gras or the International Women's Conference in China."   —Robin Tyler, Owner

HISTORY/BACKGROUND
A professional performer and comic for twenty years, Robin Tyler has been active in the lesbian/gay, progressive and women's movements. In addition to being the main stage producer of the 1979, 1988, and 1993 Marches on Washington for Lesbian and Gay Rights and a keynote speaker at the 1989 Pro-Choice Rally in Washington, D.C., Robin has addressed rallies in England, Canada, France, and Russia calling for an end to violence and discrimination against lesbians and gay men.

SAMPLE TRIPS

➤**Nile Cruise of Egypt and Israel**—Visit the Pyramids, the Sphinx, and the Egyptian Museum of Antiquities while staying at the Cairo Marriott Hotel. Then fly to Aswan to board your private ship. The *M.S. Sun Boat* holds forty-six passengers and offers air conditioning, a swimming pool, restaurant, and twenty-four-hour lounge. Spend three days exploring trade centers, fabled sites, and ancient temples. Return to Cairo to shop at old bazaars. A professional Egyptologist guides your land and cruise tour. If you choose to continue on to Israel, explore Jerusalem's Jewish, Christian, Muslim, and Armenian quarters, traveling by air-conditioned motorcoach. Visit New Hebrew University, Yad Va'Shem Holocaust Memorial, and the Israel Museum. Nine days/$3300 includes airfare from the U.S. or Canada to Cairo ($600 additional for four optional days in Israel)/easy.

➤**Annual West Coast Women's Music and Comedy Festival**—Join two to three thousand women near Yosemite, California, for nonstop entertainment, workshops, sports, fishing, dancing, and a crafts fair. Camping, cabins, and R.V. space available on this private campground with a lake, pool, and river. Three to five days/$150–250/easy.

Prices include: Airfare from U.S. or Canada for Nile Cruise, meals on cruise and at festival, accommodations.

Prices do not include: Meals in Cairo and Israel, personal equipment, optional tours, visas, fees, gratuities.

Guides: Owner Robin Tyler and other professional guides on all international trips.

Training for guides: Training and experience appropriate to individual trip.

Liability coverage: Yes.

RVing Women

201 East Southern
Apache Junction, AZ 85219
602/983-4678

RVing Rallies and Caravans in the U.S. and Mexico

Began operating: 1991
Number of trips offered per year: Over 50
Number of all-women's trips per year: All
Usual group size: 20–30
Typical age of participants: 50
Range of ages of participants: 29–80

Accessible to disabled women: Contact for further information.

Join RVing Women at the Albuquerque Balloon Fiesta or New Orlean's Mardi Gras. Bird watch in Oregon or fish in Washington. Trips range from three days in Georgia to a six-week caravan in Alaska. Rallies and events include seminars for newcomers and returning members, day excursions, potlucks, campfires, sing-alongs, and book swapping. RVW's bimonthly newsletter includes a vast array of information—from recommended service places to how to pack for pets—and includes caravan reports and rally letters from around the country.

IN THEIR OWN WORDS
"RVing Women provides a support network for all women, with an emphasis on having fun and exchanging information. We share experiences and ideas for making RVing as safe, comfortable, and inexpensive as possible. It is not a forum for personal agendas, commercial ventures, or political, sexual preference or religious issues."   —Lovern King, Co-founder

HISTORY/BACKGROUND
Traveling by RV for several years, Zoe Swanagon and Lovern King met few women. A desire to network, share information, and socialize with other RVing women led them to publish a newsletter and establish an organization that has grown to include over seventy rallies, caravans, and events each year. RVing Women has members in every state, most provinces, and Mexico, Germany, Japan, and Italy.

SAMPLE TRIPS

➤**Mississippi River Barge Trip**—Put your rig on a barge, sit back, and float along the southern Louisiana waterways. Explore moss-hung bayous and travel deep into the swamps. Listen and dance to Cajun music and enjoy plenty of fine food. Tour antebellum plantations, the Tabasco pepper plant, and the Kon-rico rice plantation. The tour ends in New Orleans with two nights tied up on the waterfront, dinner, entertainment, and a free transit pass to wander the city on your own. The barge has hookups, washers and dryers, and a patch of grass just for pets. Ten days/$3000/easy.

➤**Mexico Caravan**—Drive to Puerto Penasco, Sonora, Mexico, and enjoy beachfront spaces. Check out the "friendly hours," potlucks, and shopping trips. Local vendors bring fresh shrimp, oysters, baked goods, and trinkets by your rig, so you can shop on your own steps. Bask on the beach or make arrangements for a fishing trip. The campground has very clean showers, laundry facilities, and a small store. At the end of the week, guides escort you back to your starting point. Seven days/$300/easy.

➤**James Island Rally**—Gather on the first night for dinner and a two-mile tour of lights. The following day, caravan/carpool to Boone Hall Plantation for a tour and Civil War reenactment before continuing on to Palmetto Islands County Park. Marsh boardwalks, pedal boats, and canoes are available for rental. Rent a bicycle or bring your own for miles of nature and bike trails. Take a shuttle to downtown Charleston. Enjoy the Holiday Festival of Lights, unrestricted fishing, grills and fire rings, crabbing, trolley tours, the Naval and Maritime Museum, and more. An open discussion on various RVing subjects takes place on the last day, followed by a catered seafood dinner or meal at a local restaurant, depending on your preference. Three days/under $100/easy to moderate.

Prices include: At rallies: continental breakfast, seminars, and workshops; on caravans: space rental, some meals, and some tours.

Prices do not include: Meals at rallies; some meals on caravans.

Guides: Experienced RVing Women rally leaders.

Training for guides: Observation by experienced leaders; one-on-one training.

Liability coverage: No.

Sacred Sedona

P.O. Box 3661
Sedona, AZ 86340
602/204-2422

Half-day Hikes and Horseback Rides in Arizona

Began operating: 1994
Number of trips offered per year: Varies
Number of all-women's trips per year: All
Usual group size: 4
Typical age of participants: 35–40
Range of ages of participants: 25–75

Programs for older women
Scholarships available: Work exchange and barter.

Sacred Sedona guides half-day hikes and horseback rides through canyons and wildflowers, taking you to natural arches and Indian ruins. Programs may include drumming, singing, storytelling, plant identification, or explorations of Indian ruins. Visit the Toozigut National Monument, walk along the Vultee Arch Trail, or view elk in the Bismark Lake Elk Preserve. All walks are either easy or moderate. Some trips can include meals and accommodations if you choose to stay over. Sacred Sedona can inform you about all-women's accommodations in the area.

IN THEIR OWN WORDS
"My tours are intimate and supportive because they are so small."
—Susan Riebel, Founder

HISTORY/BACKGROUND
Susan Riebel was a U.S.P.T.A. tennis professional and instructor of physical education at several colleges before moving to Sedona in 1993. An avid hiker and explorer, Susan guides half-day hikes for women to share the beauty of Sedona, an understanding of its red rock formations, and the history of the Sinagua Indians.

SAMPLE TRIPS

➤**Coconino National Forest Horseback Ride**—Price includes two meals and accommodations. Three-hour ride/under $100/easy.

➤**Palatki Indian Ruins**—Explore the extensive remains of Indian ruins, petroglyphs, and pictographs dating from approximately 3000 B.C. to the early 1900s. Three and a half hours/under $50/easy.

➤**Red Rock Plants and Birds**—This is an opportunity to see mountain bluebirds and the century plant in her red-and-yellow blossoms. Identify animal tracks and scat as well as plants used medicinally by Indians. Three hours/ under $50/easy.

➤**Crone Hiking, Storytelling, and Writing**—On your way past Lizard Head Rock, take time for storytelling or writing. On your return, make a crone talking-stick from wood gathered along the way. Three hours/under $50 (under $100 includes two meals and overnight accommodations)/easy.

➤**Devil's Bridge**—Located in West Sedona not far from Boynton Canyon Vortex, Devil's Bridge is reached after a gradual ascent. Sit on top of the steep arch and sing or play small flutes provided by your guide or feel the power of the place during a short meditation. Three hours/under $50/moderate.

➤**Fay Canyon Hike**—Walking in a fairly narrow canyon amid yucca, agave, sage, oaks, and sycamores, you come to a path that takes you to an incredible Indian ruin and arch. Three hours/under $50/moderate.

Prices include: Occasional meals and some accommodations.

Prices do not include: Most meals and some accommodations.

Guides: Founder Susan Riebel.

Training for guides: Susan Riebel holds a master's degree in physical education and has thirty-five years of hiking experience.

Liability coverage: Yes.

Sea Safari Sailing

4815 Busch Boulevard, Suite 201B
Tampa, FL 34654
800/497-2500 or 813/985-6565

Multihull Sailing and Getaway Cruises in Florida and the Caribbean

---

Began operating: 1990
Number of trips offered per year: 52
Number of all-women's trips per year: 12
Usual group size: 6
Typical age of participants: 50
Range of ages of participants: 24–72

Set sail from Florida's coast for a getaway cruise or a week of sailing instruction and confidence building. Sea Safari Sailing courses teach all the skills you need to command your own yacht, from proper terminology and "rules of the road" to ship systems and electronic navigation. Time is available for snorkeling, sunbathing, beachcombing, and viewing marine and bird life. Dock and dine on the waterfront and sleep on board. Sea Safari Sailing specializes in training the timid and the novice.

IN THEIR OWN WORDS
"We teach women how to take control of a vessel (and their lives). We know they can master sailing and have fun doing it. All our trips are a learning adventure. All-lesbian trips can be arranged with a minimum of four participants."   —Laurel Winans, Founder and Captain

HISTORY/BACKGROUND
Owner, captain, and chief instructor Laurel Winans founded Sea Safari Sailing so that women could learn the pleasure of sailing, expand their horizons, and build self-esteem. Laurel has delivered yachts throughout the Gulf of Mexico, the Caribbean, and the Atlantic, captained naval vessels, and taught sailing for many years. She is writing a book on navigation and coauthoring one on cruising catamarans.

SAMPLE TRIPS

➤**Swashbucklers**—Sail the old pirates route where ships were captured and treasure chests were buried. Visit the beach where DeSoto landed to find gold and explore the mysterious sandy beaches of Old Venice. Voyage along the west coast of Florida aboard the sailing vessel *Inanna* amid sparkling beaches, soft gulf breezes, and sensational sunsets. Seven days/$950/all levels.

➤**Coastal Cruising**—One to two hours of on-boat classroom instruction during your first three days at sea, equips you with sailing terminology, rules, charting, knots, and safety. Take a greater role each day and learn to sail with limited captain assistance. Practice tacking, jibbing, and staged situations. Review and practice are integrated throughout the week and bareboat certification given upon graduation. Seven days/$900/all levels.

➤**Key West and Tortugas**—Sail the crystal clear waters, snorkel the reefs, and watch the sunsets. Learn offshore sailing and coastal skills. Practice navigation, sail trim, and sea skills. Possible stopover at Boca Grande and Venice on the old pirates route. Some previous sailing experience required. Seven days/$950/intermediate.

➤**Blue Water Cruising**—Learn all the basics during your first three days, spending one to two hours in the on-board classroom and the rest of the day practicing your skills. Days four and five include morning reviews and afternoon sailing with limited captain assistance. Practice tacking and jibbing, role-playing staged situations, and emergencies. Day six provides the final hands-on review before tackling the boat single-handedly on your last day at sea. Seven days/ $950/intermediate.

Prices include: Meals on yacht, accommodations; yacht expenses, including fuel and dockage fees; reference manual, and study guide.

Prices do not include: Meals on shore.

Guides: U.S. Coast Guard–licensed captains.

Training for guides: U.S. Coast Guard training and license.

Liability coverage: Yes.

Sea Sense

25 Thames Street
New London, CT 06320
800/332-1404

Sailing and Powerboating School in the U.S. and the Caribbean

---

Began operating: 1989
Number of trips offered per year: 50–80
Number of all-women's trips per year: All
Usual group size: 6
Typical age of participants: 40s
Range of ages of participants: 15–75

At Sea Sense, U.S. Coast Guard captains share their love for sailing in courses of up to eight days. Short courses introduce or help to brush up on basic skills, while longer cruises allow time for developing more advanced skills. Founded and operated by and for women, Sea Sense teaches on board boats that are big enough for comfortable living, yet small enough to handle easily. Summer trips are based in Connecticut, while winter programs set sail from the gulf coast of Florida. Sea Sense also guides trips to Lake Michigan and the British Virgin Islands.

IN THEIR OWN WORDS
"Learn and have fun at the same time. We demystify boating and offer education and an entry into the sport to women who thought they could never do it. We teach women of any age, race, creed, color, and persuasion."
—Captain Patti Moore

HISTORY/BACKGROUND
Captain Carol Cuddyer began boating more than thirty years ago and has spent more time on the water than on land in the last five years. A registered nurse, Carol has been skipper of both a tour boat and a marine research vessel. More than twenty years' experience has taken Captain Patti Moore up and down the U.S. East Coast, to the Caribbean, the Mediterranean, and across the Atlantic. Carol and Patti met while teaching sailing, became friends, and found they'd both been thinking about establishing a women's boating school. Cofounders of Sea Sense, Carol and Patti deliver yachts to a variety of locations as well.

SAMPLE TRIPS

➤**Powerboating**—Take this opportunity to cruise under power in the Long Island Sound, with an emphasis on boat handling. Two days/$500/beginning to intermediate.

➤**British Virgin Islands**—Just the place to sail away your winter blahs. You'll find picturesque, mountainous islands set in a blue sea and warm trade winds for romping sails from harbor to harbor. Snorkeling, swimming, beachcombing, exploration, and relaxation await you at each new cove or port. A great opportunity to learn new sailing skills. Seven days/$1350/beginning to intermediate.

➤**Florida Coastal Cruising**—For three days you can learn or brush up on points of sail, sail trim, navigation, piloting, helmsmanship, docking, and anchoring. Set sail for five days combining instruction and a vacation in Florida's warm waters. Seven days at sea allows time to develop additional skills, such as piloting and navigating in open waters and busy intercoastal waterways, managing boat systems, and preventive maintenance. Three days/$450/beginning to intermediate. Five days/$700/beginning to intermediate. Seven days/$950/beginning to intermediate.

➤**Florida Offshore Sailing**—Take part in planning a four- or five-hundred-mile passage, sailing around the clock for thirty-six to forty-eight hours. The course covers conventional and electronic navigation, helmsmanship, sail handling, lights at night, watch scheduling, offshore safety equipment and procedures. Eight days/$1100/intermediate to advanced.

➤**Circumnavigation of Long Island**—This course encompasses both coastal cruising and offshore sailing. Cruise down Long Island Sound with stops in historic harbors. Plan a passage through Hell's Gate and New York Harbor, with its big ship traffic, ferryboats, and the Statue of Liberty. Sail overnight along the south shore to Montauk or Block Island and pass through the Race on your way back. Seven days/$1100/intermediate to advanced.

Prices include: Meals, boat accommodations; docking and mooring fees.

Prices do not include: Optional dinners ashore and alcoholic beverages.

Guides: Captains Carol Cuddyer and Patti Moore and additional Coast Guard–licensed captains.

Training for guides: U.S. Coast Guard captain's license, in-house training.

Liability coverage: Yes.

Sheri Griffith Expeditions

P.O. Box 1324
Moab, UT 84532
800/332-2439 or 801/259-8229   fax: 801/259-2226

River Journeys in the Sacred Southwest

Began operating: 1971
Number of trips offered per year: 150
Number of all-women's trips per year: 6–10
Usual group size: 12–15
Typical age of participants: 42
Range of ages of participants: 5–80

Scholarships available: Open for discussion.

Sheri Griffith Expeditions takes you to the sights, sounds, and smells of Colorado's rivers and canyons. Enliven your senses with the smell of flowers, sage, and the earth after a desert rain, take part in spiritual journeys, learn about ancient Indian history and geology, and enjoy star-studded nights by the campfire. Five- and six-day river trips combine whitewater adventure and personalized instruction in a variety of techniques that enhance personal growth. SGE's programs encourage a connection with nature and the earth as well as social and environmental responsibility. Coed programs also include family expeditions and international adventure trips.

IN THEIR OWN WORDS
"Our company's goal is to take our guests to a special place and provide an adventure to enrich, broaden and quiet their mind and body, to provide them with a perspective of what is possible and what really matters—out there and within themselves."   —Sheri Griffith Expeditions brochure

HISTORY/BACKGROUND
Four Griffith siblings originally led river expeditions to earn money for college. Later they found that one-day trips in Colorado had become too much like "bumper cars." In 1971 Sheri Griffith purchased a company that already had permits on more-remote river stretches. Sheri Griffith Expeditions now offers trips to locations where limited numbers of people are allowed each day. Many family members are still involved with the company.

SAMPLE TRIPS

➤**Women and Mother Earth: Taking a Ride on the Wild Side**—Sheri Griffith personally escorts trips to Cataract Canyon or Westwater Canyon on the Colorado River. There will be days of sunshine, whitewater, and lazy drifting through canyons, with deer feeding quietly on the riverbank as eagles soar up the canyon walls. Share nights of camaraderie around the campfire, contemplating your opportunities to "touch the earth," both locally and globally. Three days in Westwater Canyon/$400/all levels. Five days in Cataract Canyon/$700/all levels.

➤**Journey for Sacred Space**—Paddle ninety-six miles into the canyons of the Colorado River. Entering Canyonlands National Park on the Green River, you glide between sheer two-thousand-foot walls that reveal three hundred million years of time. Ruins and pictographs from Anasazi and Fremont Indian cultures a thousand years old mark the human heritage of this land. The area is habitat to eagles, hawks, owls, coyote, bobcats, and the largest herds of desert big horn sheep. The journey includes drumming and drum making, tai chi, qi gong and breath work, a sweat ceremony, meditation, storytelling, shamanic counseling, and transformational body work. On your arrival at the confluence of the Green and Colorado Rivers, the river doubles in size and force, tumbling through fifteen miles of Cataract Canyon's two dozen rapids. End with a float out of Lake Powell and a private flight back over this land. Trip leaders include: River, an acupuncturist and drum maker; Michelle Crone, a political activist and mediator; Amylee, Iroquois Medicine Woman Initiate; and Dancing Owl Woman, dancer, drummer, and bodyworker. Five days/$800/all levels. Six days/$1000–$1100/all levels.

Prices include: Charter flights on Green River and Cataract Canyon, meals, group equipment.

Prices do not include: Personal equipment (tents and sleeping bags are available for rental), beverages, gratuities.

Guides: Sheri Griffith–licensed guides.

Training for guides: Guide licence, CPR/first aid, wilderness medicine, river rescue training.

Liability coverage: Yes.

Skadi

High Grassrigg Barn, Killington
Sedbergh, Cumbria LA10 5EW Great Britain
(05396) 21188

Women's Walking Holidays in Northern England

Began operating: 1985
Number of trips offered per year: 18
Number of all-women's trips per year: All
Usual group size: 4–6
Typical age of participants: 40s
Range of ages of participants: 16–78

Scholarships available

Walking adventures are Skadi's speciality. Setting out from your guide's home at Grassrigg Barn, you can explore the Yorkshire Dales' quiet valleys and gray stone villages, or the Lake District and Howgill Fells' craggy mountains and valley lakes. Walks are organized for every day of your stay, though you can easily take a personal day off and enjoy the pleasures of Grassrigg. Skadi offers programs specifically for women of color, and for women who would like to write, practice photography, or learn outdoor map-and-compass skills.

IN THEIR OWN WORDS
"Women together sharing strength and enjoyment in the hills! There is a strong lesbian presence on most holidays."   —Paula Day, Founder

HISTORY/BACKGROUND
Skadi grew out of Paula Day's own enjoyment of walking in the hills of northern England with women friends. In 1987, Paula moved into Grassrigg Barn, which now serves as a base for the trips.

SAMPLE TRIPS

➤**Lunesdale Journey**—If you've ever fancied the idea of an ongoing journey on foot but have been put off by the thought of long distances and a different bed every night, this is the holiday for you. You'll take a circular walk through the valleys of Dentdale, Barbondale, and Lunesdale, then ride a minibus back to the comforts of Grassrigg every evening, returning to the previous day's finish the next morning. Visit tea shops and stroll along market towns and quiet lanes. Three days/£150/easy.

➤**Writing and Walking**—Explore inner and outer landscapes through creative writing workshops in the mornings that may draw on afternoons out walking. Writers of all experience levels are welcome. Five days/£250/easy.

➤**Black Women's Holiday**—This is a chance for black women (defined in Britain as African, African-Caribbean, Asian, Indian, Chinese, mixed-heritage, and other women who define themselves as black) to stride out and boldly reclaim the countryside. Three days/£150/easy.

➤**Landscape Photography**—Develop your photographic skills on tutor-led walks, followed by developing and appraising your color slides. Beginners are welcome. The price includes materials (apart from film and camera). Five days/£250/easy.

➤**Map-and-Compass Course**—Find your way around in the hills using a map and compass. Instruction and practical exercises equip you for a solo walk in a supportive context. Price includes use of maps and compasses. Four days/£200/moderate.

➤**Howgills Journey**—Stay at three different bases during this hill-walking journey in order to see several sides of the fells. Venture among hills and streams, spending one day walking locally or simply relaxing. Five days/£250/challenging.

Prices include: Vegetarian meals, accommodations, sauna.

Prices do not include: Tea en route, personal equipment (boots and rain gear available for rental).

Guides: Founder Paula Day.

Training for guides: Mountain leadership training.

Liability coverage: No.

Skylink

746 Ashland Avenue
Santa Monica, CA 90405
800/225-5759   fax: 310/452-0562

Worldwide Lesbian Travel

Began operating: 1991
Number of trips offered per year: 6–7
Number of all-women's trips per year: All
Usual group size: 20–60
Typical age of participants: 42
Range of ages of participants: 28–68

Accessible to disabled women: Most trips.
Programs for lesbians
Scholarships available: Limited scholarships and interest-free payment plans.

Spend the Fourth of July in Amsterdam, where there is strong lesbian visibility, or a week in the lesbian-friendly locales of Provincetown or Key West. A cattle drive in Montana and a golfing safari in Kenya are among Skylink's programs as well as trips to the Gay Games. Skylink offers both city-based and nature-based tours to Australia and New Zealand. Skylink books a health spa in the Northern California wine country for two all-lesbian weeks. In an effort to include a wide range of women, Skylink conducts outreach to Latina, Asian, and African American communities.

IN THEIR OWN WORDS
"Lesbian travelers are best served by lesbian tours; networking on lesbian tours is invaluable. Our tours are designed for lesbians, but we are happy to have any woman join one of our trips."   —Tracy Michaels, Founder

HISTORY/BACKGROUND
Tracy Michaels worked for a women's wholesale tour company for two years before setting out on her own. Having seen a lot of room for improvement in her previous work, Tracy founded Skylink. She is the only lesbian member of the board of directors of the International Gay Travel Association.

SAMPLE TRIPS

➤**Montana Cattle Drive**—A rowdy range party for riders of all levels. Spend five hot days on the Montana trail and five nights under the stars. Ride a cowpony between sixty and seventy-five miles over varied terrain, covering ten to fifteen miles of the drive daily. Gourmet meals are cooked for cowgirls by an experienced trail cook. Steaks are the pride of the prairie, but vegetarians can be accommodated. Tents are provided; you bring a sleeping bag. Additional two nights' accommodations in a hotel. Seven days/$1400/all levels.

➤**White Sulphur Springs Resort and Spa**—Located on three hundred thirty acres in the heart of Northern California's wine country. The basic spa package includes a massage, body wrap, daily yoga, and tai chi. Enjoy gourmet menus and evening wine hours, speakers, sports, and live entertainment. Five days/$600–$750 (depending on accommodations)/all levels.

➤**African Safari in Kenya**—Experience Africa firsthand with a native-guided photo safari. This safari encompasses all the traditional highlights, including Nairobi, the Serengeti, Aberdare National Forest, the Rift Valley and Lake Nakuru. Traveling by minivan with a pop-up roof and 360-degree exposure, you can view wildlife as close as you care to be. Accommodations include a luxurious tented city in the Serengeti. European-style meals are served except in the Maasai Mara, where the menu features more native foods. Fourteen days/$3600/easy.

➤**Provincetown Women's Week**—Over eight thousand lesbians travel to Provincetown for this entertainment extravaganza. Fresh Maine lobster, end-of-the-year clearance sales, and some of the best musical and comedy acts make this annual fall party a memorable event. Beautiful New England fall foliage and cool temperatures create an ideal setting for Women's Week. Whale watch off the coast, gallop the dunes of the south shores, or enjoy an athletic event or workshop. Price includes roundtrip airfare from Los Angeles and continental breakfast. Six days/$900/easy.

Prices include: Airfare from U.S. on international trips, accommodations unless otherwise noted, escorted land tours, entertainment packages, taxes, porterage.

Prices do not include: Meals unless otherwise noted, personal equipment.

Guides: Skylink staff.

Training for guides: Minimum of one year with Skylink; must accompany experienced guide on at least two tours prior to appointment as guide.

Liability coverage: Yes.

Sylvan Rocks

Main Street, Box 600
Hill City, SD 57745
605/574-2425

Climbing School and Guide Service in South Dakota

Began operating: 1989
Number of trips offered per year: Daily from May to October
Number of all-women's trips per year: 6–10
Usual group size: 3–4 per guide
Typical age of participants: Teens and up
Range of ages of participants: Varies

Programs for older women: "Over 40" trips.

Sylvan Rocks guides novice and experienced climbers in South Dakota's Needles and Devil's Tower. Introductory courses build confidence on steep rocks and focus on safety, knots, belaying, basic anchor systems, and rappelling. Intermediate courses teach protection placement, equalization of multipiece anchors, rope handling skills, and hazard evaluation. Advanced climbers learn multi- and omnidirectional anchors, emergency bailouts, and intricate gear placements, and develop judgment and safety skills necessary for independent climbing.

IN THEIR OWN WORDS
"We are the only nationally accredited rock climbing school owned and operated by a woman. Our programs differ from the assembly line approach of large climbing programs. We believe climbing should be taught in an enjoyable, supportive, and personable environment. Learning skills correctly from the beginning is critical to long-term enjoyment and safety in climbing."
—Susan Scheirbeck, Founder

HISTORY/BACKGROUND
In 1975, friends taught Susan Scheirbeck to climb. It was a terrifying experience. Her companions should not have been climbing alone, much less taking a beginner out. Competent climbers later took the time to teach her correctly. After many years of climbing and teaching, Susan began her own school and guide service in the Black Hills of South Dakota.

SAMPLE TRIPS

➤**Climbing and Camping Trip**—Learn what you need to know to climb Devil's Tower. A maximum of three clients per guide. Four to six days/$375–$600/beginning.

➤**Devil's Tower Weekend**—Over three thousand climbers each year come to Devil's Tower. Experience its rock and crack climbing for yourself. A maximum of three clients per guide. Two days previous experience required, or equivalent (follow 5.7). There is camping and lodging nearby. Unless prearranged, meals are not included. Two days/$250/intermediate.

➤**Rock Camp**—Four Saturdays/$350/intermediate to advanced.

Prices include: Some meals; UIAA-approved helmets, harnesses, and gear; shoes for beginning courses.

Prices do not include: Some meals; camping equipment and tents are available for rental; shoe rentals for intermediate and advanced courses (under $10).

Guides: Sylvan Rocks guides.

Training for guides: American Mountain Guides Association courses and clinics, Sylvan Rocks clinics and seminars, medical and emergency rescue training.

Liability coverage: Yes.

Tours of Interest to Women

1903 Southeast Ankeny
Portland, OR 97214
503/281-2036

Exploring Sacred and Historical Sites in western Europe

Began operating: 1985
Number of trips offered per year: 1–2
Number of all-women's trips per year: All
Usual group size: 12
Typical age of participants: 40
Range of ages of participants: 21–67

Scholarships available: Work exchange possible, usually driving.

Travel to England, Germany, or Ireland to visit ancient sacred sites. Learn about the contributions women have made to culture, spirituality, healing, and social change. Guides point out ley lines along which sacred sites are built, discuss earth energies, and demonstrate the practice of dowsing to detect underground water. Groups travel at a relaxed pace and have included artists and filmmakers as well as a group of witchy women who chant down in barrows and walk three times around sacred wells. Enjoy concerts and workshops in the company of local women. Accommodations are provided in bed and breakfasts, conference centers, and hotels. Trips last ten days, with optional self-directed extensions of up to four days that are planned with the help of your group leader. TIW offers an effective jet-lag-prevention program.

IN THEIR OWN WORDS

"We offer tours to places of great sanctity and mystery off the beaten track, which stimulate the imagination and satisfy the soul in the company of women of good spirits. Groups have a diversity of lifestyle, sexual orientation, and religion." —Chris Arthur, Founder

HISTORY/BACKGROUND

A native of Great Britain, Chris Arthur has had a longtime interest in sacred sites, earth mysteries, and women's spirituality. She takes particular pleasure in introducing other women to the ancient traditions at places our ancestors gathered.

SAMPLE TRIPS

➤**May Morning Tour: West of England**—Visit women's colleges in Oxford to learn about literary legends. Celebrate May Day with mazes, morris dances, feasts, and songs to the Virgin from Magdalene College tower. Explore the neolithic religious monuments in Avebury on the Downs and their relevance to modern women's spirituality. Travel to Greenham Common, a women's peace camp, for an earth healing celebration and then to Glastonbury, where the Arthurian legend, ley lines, sacred wells, and the Tor maze lie. Ten days/ $900/easy.

➤**Harvest Moon Tour: North of England**—Take daytrips from your base in York, an ancient walled city with Roman, Viking, and medieval remains. Among the sites are the Petrifying Well and Cave at Knaresboro, home of the prophetess Mother Shipton, as well as Whitby Abbey, founded by the diplomat and educator St. Hilda. A local herbal practitioner accompanies you to the Lincoln herb gardens and a traditional harvest supper celebrates the harvest moon. Visit Northumbria's sandy beaches, bird sanctuaries, ancient carved stones, and Holy Island of Lindesfarne. Ten days/$900/easy.

➤**Wine, Women, and Song: France and Germany**—Follow the histories of Joan of Arc and Hildegard of Bingen as you wind through the Rhine, Moselle, and Loire valleys. Learn about Hildegard's understanding of medicine, science, politics, theology, and diplomacy and trace Joan of Arc's travels—her military campaigns, triumphant crowning with the king at Reims, capture, trial, and execution. Explore historical symbols of women in religious and secular thinking as well as their modern importance. Relax in vineyards, sample the region's food and wine, and visit local museums. Ten days/$1000/ easy.

Prices include: Two meals per day, double-occupancy accommodations (single-occupancy available at additional cost).

Prices do not include: One meal per day (usually lunch, occasionally dinner).

Guides: Founder Chris Arthur and local guides.

Training for guides: Extensive experience in local history, legends, and culture.

Liability coverage: No, participants are advised to have their own trip insurance.

Travel Walji's

51 Bank Street, Second Floor
Stamford, CT 06901
203/356-0027

Tours and Treks of Pakistan, China, Nepal, and India

Began operating: 1965
Number of trips offered per year: 11
Number of all-women's trips per year: Varies
Usual group size: 16
Typical age of participants: 50+
Range of ages of participants: 50+

Pakistan's cultural and geographical diversity invite many traveling options, from overland touring to China on the old Silk Route to floating down the Indus river in boats reminiscent of Alexander the Great's navy. Trek to the base camp of K-2, the second-highest mountain on earth, or ride by camel along old desert trade routes first used by the Moghuls and later by the East India Company. With a minimum of four participants, Travel Walji's will lead women on seven- to twenty-five-day treks and tours of Pakistan. Trips depart from New York and itineraries can be tailored according to the group's interests. Some tours include visits to China, Nepal, and India. Daily walks or hikes average between four and six hours a day and porters carry your gear.

IN THEIR OWN WORDS
"It is our belief that no matter how beautiful and interesting one's surroundings, one can enjoy the holiday experience only if at ease and relaxed, confident that arrangements have been meticulously made with comfort and safety in mind."   —Mrs. Shirin Walji, Chairperson

HISTORY/BACKGROUND
When Mr. and Mrs. Walji founded Travel Walji's in 1965, Pakistan had no hotels, no communication system, and insufficient roads. But their love for the country's sites, especially the valleys of the north, led them to guide tours nonetheless. (Now Pakistan is much more accessible to tourists.) Initially a travel agency running a bus shuttle between the twin cities of Rawalpindi-Islamabad, Walji's now has a staff of two hundred fifty, with corporate headquarters in Islamabad and representatives in a variety of other countries.

SAMPLE TRIPS

Mysteries of the Indus Civilization—Visit historical sites dating back to 5000 B.C., when the Indus Civilization included over a thousand towns some with populations of over forty thousand people. Explore Karachi, Peshawar, and Chitral, the Kalash village of Bomborut and the Hoper Glacier in the Nagar Valley. Travel days are followed by local tours. Hotel accommodations provided. Seventeen days/$3000/easy.

Ancient Silk Route—Travel from China to Pakistan over Khunjerab Pass. Full days of sightseeing in Beijing, Xian, Lanzhou, and Dunghuang are followed by stops in Turpan and Urumqi. Fly to Kashgar and visit the Sunday bazaar before driving over Khunjerab Pass. Further exploration takes you through Gilgit, Swat, Peshawar, and Lahore. Accommodations in hotels along the way include the Shangri-La Hotel in Beijing and the Marco Polo Inn/Silk Route Lodge in Hunza. Twenty-four days/$3900/easy to moderate.

Marco Polo Jeep Safari—Spend five days traveling from Islamabad to Chitral with hotel accommodations. Enjoy four nights in tents in Mastuj, Phandar Lake, and Gupis. Hotel accommodations and sightseeing resume in Gilgit and Hunza. Take an excursion to the Pakistan/China border before returning to Islamabad. Eighteen days/$2300/challenging.

Nanga Parbat/Fairy Meadows—So named because of local beliefs that fairies inhabit this forested alpine meadow, Fairy Meadows is host to scattered shepherd huts, pine forests, and a view of the north face of Nanga Parbat. Trek for five days and spend eight days sightseeing in such places as Islamabad and Hunza while staying in hotels. Sixteen days/$2100/challenging.

Hunza and Batura Glacier Trek—Nine days' trekking with a rest day at Patundas are combined with visits to Islamabad, Gilgit, and Karimabad. Eighteen days/$2000/challenging.

Prices include: Transportation between airport and hotel, chauffeur-driven private vehicle, meals, accommodations, group equipment on trek/safari, scheduled sightseeing excursions, porterage, entrance fees.

Prices do not include: Personal equipment, airport departure tax.

Guides: Local English-speaking male Pakistani guides, all-male staff.

Training for guides: Full-time employees attend regular seminars.

Liability coverage: No, participants are encouraged to carry private insurance.

Vaarschool Grietje

Prinsengracht t/o 187
1015 AZ Amsterdam, The Netherlands
020-625-9105 (K.v.K 175924)

Dutch Boating School

Began operating: 1984
Number of trips offered per year: 12
Number of all-women's trips per year: 10
Usual group size: 4
Typical age of participants: 30–50
Range of ages of participants: Varies

Scholarships available

Visit Holland and France on a floating houseboat with Vaarschool Grietje. You will learn how to handle a boat, tie up, take off, and travel through bridges, locks (*sluizen*), and tunnels. Vaarschool Grietje will teach you boating rules, and you will earn a practical diploma. On-board accommodations are simple and accomodate four women at a time. Approximately 50 percent of participants are Dutch women, 30 percent are German, and 20 percent are Belgian and French women.

IN THEIR OWN WORDS
"I want to give women a good vacation and teach them how to maneuver a boat."   —Nelly Duijndam, Owner

HISTORY/BACKGROUND
The *Grietje* is a former freight ship built in Muiden in 1921. It is sixteen meters long and three and a half meters wide, with a kitchen, living areas, and sleeping quarters for four.

SAMPLE TRIPS

▶**France by Boat**—This summer boating adventure takes you through the "Biesbosch" and Brabant, into the Belgian Meuse river. Pass through the Arddennen and over the Marne river on your way to the Seine river. Tie up in Paris for a day before traveling back northward via the Oise and the Aisnes rivers. Visit the Champagne area and the French and Belgian Meuse valley along the way. You follow Dutch rivers through Arnhem on your return to Amsterdam. Five and a half days/f800/beginning.

Prices include: Accommodations, lock and harbor fees.

Prices do not include: Meals (you can cook on board), personal equipment.

Guides: Owner Nelly Duijndam.

Training for guides: Experience as boating instructor.

Liability coverage: No.

Venus Adventures

P.O. Box 167
Peaks Island, ME 04108
207/766-5655

Goddess Tours to England, Ireland, and Greece

Began operating: 1988
Number of trips offered per year: 1–4
Number of all-women's trips per year: Varies
Usual group size: 4–15
Typical age of participants: 30s–50s
Range of ages of participants: 20s–80s

Visit the sacred sites of Athena, wise goddess of the law, and Artemis, goddess of the moon, wild animals, and hunting. Explore the sites of Demeter, Persephone and Hecate, the triple goddesses of death and rebirth, and those of even more archaic goddesses in Greece and Crete. Travel to holy wells, sacred womb caves, and stone circles in England, Wales, and Ireland. Explore their spiritual relevance today. Tours allow time for personal exploration, group sharing, and participation in contemporary happenings. Future trip sites may include the southwestern U.S., Hawaii, Egypt, and India.

IN THEIR OWN WORDS
"Your spiritual journey may vary from mine; these sacred sites tell many stories. I invite those who support peace and the web of life and whose spiritual journey includes goddesses to join us on these tours."
—Delores Lanai, Founder

HISTORY/BACKGROUND
Delores Lanai founded Venus Adventures to guide other feminists interested in spirituality to sacred pagan sites. An avid traveler, travel agent, and businesswoman, Delores holds a degree in cultural anthropology. She is a Priestess of Sophia, dedicated to feminist Wicca, a nature spirituality based on cycles and healing.

SAMPLE TRIPS

▶**Mythic Journey to Greece and Crete**—Travel to the temples and sites of ancient goddesses and gods. Explore dreams, myths, stories, and personal experiences. Visit Athens, the Acropolis, Eleusis, the Island of Aegina, Corinth, Delphi, and Crete. Co-leader and mythic astrologer Wendy Ashley helps to identify your own goddess or god and the archetype most prevalent in your own life. Two weeks/$2800/easy.

▶**Journey of the Sacred Female in England, Wales, and Ireland**—Travel backward thousand of years to the stone circles at the Avebury complex, Silbury Hill, Stonehenge, and Drumbeg. Visit the holy Chalice Well and Bath Spa. Enter into the womb caves of West Kennet Long Barrow and New Grange. Read *The Mists of Avalon* by Marion Zimmer Bradley before walking the grounds of Glastonbury/Avalon, a mystical city for Pagans and Christians. After Wales and Ireland, return to England to celebrate Beltane and May Day, ancient pagan rituals. Two weeks/$2800/easy.

Prices include: Airfare from major U.S. and Canadian cities; two meals per day in Greece, one per day in England; accommodations; admission at scheduled sightseeing locations.

Prices do not include: One meal per day in Greece, two per day in England; insurance; optional sightseeing.

Guides: Selected by founder Delores Lanai, based on expertise.

Training for guides: Previous experience in given area.

Liability coverage: No.

Vertical Ventures

P.O. Box 444
Bend, OR 97709
503/389-7937

Guide Service and Climbing Instruction in Oregon

Began operating: 1993
Number of trips offered per year: 5 clinics, 3 trips
Number of all-women's trips per year: 2 clinics, 1 trip
Usual group size: 3–9
Typical age of participants: 20s–50s
Range of ages of participants: 8–70

Learn to overcome obstacles, build trusting relationships, stimulate your physical and mental muscles, and work through fears while rock climbing. In an effort to provide women with positive climbing experiences, Vertical Ventures leads three-day clinics for beginning, intermediate, and advanced climbers at Smith Rock State Park in Central Oregon. Vertical Ventures is working to develop programs accessible to disabled women and specifically for at-risk youth. Vertical Ventures's women's and coed climbing trips take place in the U.S., Mexico, Spain, France, Germany, India, and Pakistan.

IN THEIR OWN WORDS
"We strive to ensure that the participant has an enjoyable and positive experience. Our teaching and guiding philosophy is geared to the learning style and needs of each individual and each group. We believe that climbing is a fun and exciting experience that exercises the entire body, stimulates the brain, and is an incredible vehicle for personal growth. We provide a supportive, nurturing, and encouraging environment that allows the participant to achieve her best." —Cynthia McDaniel, Co-founder

HISTORY/BACKGROUND
Cynthia and John McDaniel founded Vertical Ventures to offer quality climbing adventures and instruction. Having enjoyed introducing others to climbing, Cynthia and John decided to turn their love for climbing, traveling, and teaching into their business. Between them, Cynthia and John have previous professional experience in nursing, engineering, emergency care, event planning, teaching, and wilderness travel.

SAMPLE TRIPS

►**Climbing Clinics**—Beginners learn the basics of rock climbing, including body position, balance, and movement on the rock, belaying, rappelling, and working with the equipment. Intermediate courses teach you to climb longer routes, how to use protection, set anchors, do multiple rappels, and improve your climbing technique. Advanced climbers learn to lead on bolted routes and those that require natural protection, advanced anchor set-up, and advanced climbing techniques such as stemming, flagging, and jamming. Climb for one day or many days. Three days/$200/beginning to advanced.

Prices include: Some meals for clinics, all meals and accommodations for trips, group equipment.

Prices do not include: Some meals and accommodations, personal equipment.

Guides: Qualified guides, primarily co-founder Cynthia McDaniel; the number of guides depends on group size.

Training for guides: CPR/first aid; minimum of five years' climbing experience; demonstrated teaching experience; training in teaching methods and learning styles; environmental awareness and safety.

Liability coverage: Yes.

Voyageur Outward Bound School

111 Third Avenue South, #120
Minneapolis, MN 55401
800/328-2943 or 612/338-0565   fax: 612/338-3540

Backpack, Canoe, and Dog Sled in Montana, Texas, and Minnesota

Began operating: 1965
Number of trips offered per year: 150
Number of all-women's trips per year: 8–10
Usual group size: 8–10
Typical age of participants: 34
Range of ages of participants: 21–60+

Scholarships available

Backpack and rock climb in the Rocky Mountains, or canoe the waters between the United States and Mexico with canyons towering high above. Voyageur Outward Bound School will take you on a cross country skiing and dog sledding trip to develop winter living skills or a wilderness canoeing journey in the evergreen forests of Minnesota. Expeditions begin with an initial training and become increasingly challenging as students increase their skill and comfort levels. Perseverance, flexible management, and teamwork are necessary components to these Outward Bound adventures. Plans are in process for women's courses in the Gila Mountains of New Mexico and kayaking on Lake Superior.

IN THEIR OWN WORDS
"Outward Bound offers an opportunity to travel into a spectacular wilderness area on an environmentally considerate, low-impact expedition. As part of a small group, our students learn new skills such as canoeing, backpacking, sea kayaking, and rock climbing, but it is the challenge of taking on the unfamiliar, taking risks by doing things they've never done, that most students find rewarding."   —Susan Morrill, Director of Marketing and Admissions

HISTORY/BACKGROUND
The Voyageur Outward Bound School received its charter from the Outward Bound Trust in 1964 and began operating courses as a nonprofit educational organization in 1965.

SAMPLE TRIPS

➤**Whitewater Canoeing in Texas**—Join an expedition on the Rio Grande and travel in the Chihuahuan desert's canyons and mountains. Initial instruction takes place in gentle currents before you near the rapids. Acquire skills in whitewater paddling, river rescue, and expedition management. Includes one day of climbing or rappelling. Seven days/$800/moderate.

➤**Northwoods Canoeing in Minnesota**—Paddle by day and camp lakeside under brilliant night stars, traveling deep into the Boundary Waters Canoe Area. Gather canoes for a floating reconnaissance, learn navigation skills as you plot the route, and read the shoreline for signs of hidden portage trails. Take pleasure in wildlife sightings and a display of the northern lights. Rock climbing and rappelling add an exhilarating challenge. Fifteen-day trips provide opportunities to complete the ropes course and experience whitewater. Eight or fifteen days/$800 or $1300/moderate.

➤**Mountain Backpacking in Montana**—While backpacking in the Rocky Mountains, you traverse lowland sage-covered foothills, follow glacier-fed streams, and ascend lush mountain valleys to alpine plateaus. Then add the physical and mental challenge of rock climbing and the ascent of a mountain peak at altitudes of ten to twelve thousand feet. Appropriate for beginning backpackers. Eight days/$1100/moderate to challenging.

➤**Cross Country Skiing and Dog Sledding in Minnesota**—Ski and mush a team of three to six dogs over the snowbound lakes, rivers, and trails of a northwoods winter. Begin with a thorough training in winter skills, skiing, dog sledding, and ice rescue techniques. Living is focused on necessities—chopping ice for water, making shelter and a fire. As night falls, enjoy a hot, high-energy meal, share memories of a challenging day, and camp in a sheltered bay. Eight days/$800/moderate to challenging.

Prices include: Meals, group equipment, sleeping bags, backpacks, rain gear, and specialized winter gear.

Prices do not include: Personal equipment, application fee.

Guides: Instructors with proficiency in the outdoors and demonstrated interpersonal and teaching skills.

Training for guides: Apprenticeship program; ongoing training in course areas; Wilderness First Responder or advanced first-aid certification; lifesaving certification for water-based courses.

Liability coverage: Yes.

Wander Women
136 North Grand Avenue, #237
West Covina, CA 91791
818/966-8857

House and Canal Boating in the Southwest U.S. and Wales

Began operating: 1991
Number of trips offered per year: 4–12
Number of all-women's trips per year: All
Usual group size: 10+
Typical age of participants: 50s
Range of ages of participants: 40+

Programs for older women

Wander Women is a membership organization designed to distribute travel information to women over forty. WW's quarterly publication, *Journal 'n Footnotes*, provides tips, tales, and trip information. All women, including those under forty, are invited to subscribe to WW's newsletter. Houseboating trips in Nevada and Arizona and a canal-boating adventure in Wales offer further opportunities to network with wandering women. WW has also led a ten-day trip to Coast Rica that included rafting, kayaking, boating, birding, and hiking with a naturalist guide. Backpacking, bicycling, golfing, and snorkeling trips are under consideration.

IN THEIR OWN WORDS
"Wander Women gives you ideas for your vacation/travel/adventure and inspires you to 'get going.' WW women are interesting, adventurous women forty years of age or over, currently living in thirty-nine states, Washington, D.C., and Canada."   —Shirley Giesking, Founder

HISTORY/BACKGROUND
The idea for Wander Women emerged on August 23, 1991, and on November 1, the first newsletter was mailed. Founder Shirley Giesking intended for WW to remain a news source for women-oriented companies. But as members began requesting trips, Wander Women expanded its activities. A high school teacher and department chairperson, Shirley leads trips on her vacation time, relies on other members, or hires guides.

SAMPLE TRIPS

➤**Houseboating Lake Mojave**—Motor up the Colorado River with a fishing boat in tow. Fish, hike, swim, and explore. Read, rest, and enjoy the desert scenery. Come early and enjoy the gambling meccas of Las Vegas or Laughlin. Five days/$250/easy.

➤**Houseboating Lake Powell**—Enjoy the beauty of the Arizona desert aboard a houseboat that accommodates ten adults. Fish, hike, explore, water ski, and sunbathe. One week/$550 (for members) or $600 (for nonmembers)/easy.

➤**Canal Boating in Wales**—Begin with three days in London, staying at bed and breakfasts. Then spend a week in Wales on a narrow boat, hiking on tow-paths and visiting pubs along the way. A three-day tour of the Cotswolds by van tops off this trip. Two weeks/$2500 (for members) or $2600 (for nonmembers)/easy.

Prices include: Airfare on Wales trips, some meals on land, all meals and accommodations aboard boats.

Prices do not include: Some meals on land, personal equipment.

Guides: Founder Shirley Giesking, Wander Women members, or a hired naturalist.

Training for guides: Knowledge of country, skill in given area.

Liability coverage: No.

Widjiwagan YMCA Camp

1761 University Avenue
St. Paul, MN 55104
612/645-6605 fax: 612/646-5521

Canoeing and Backpacking for Young Women

Began operating: 1929
Number of trips offered per year: 40
Number of all-women's trips per year: 19
Usual group size: 5
Typical age of participants: 12–18
Range of ages of participants: 12–18

Accessible to disabled women
Programs for older women: Weekend Boundary Waters canoe trips twice each
  summer for women nineteen and older.
Programs for young women
Scholarships available: Dependent upon parent's income.

At Camp Widjiwagan young women canoe the crystal lakes of the Minnesota-
Ontario border and backpack through alpine meadows and snowfields, building confidence and community. Participants gather at the base camp to meet
their counselors and trail mates, enjoy activities such as swimming and singing, plan their route and menu, and receive wilderness trip instruction. Counselors teach everything from paddle strokes to fire-building techniques before
setting out into the wilderness. Trips then vary from six-day introductory
courses to fifty-day expeditions, always concluding with a base camp celebration. A sequence of progressively challenging courses allow participants to
develop their skills and travel more adventurously each year.

IN THEIR OWN WORDS
"The experience is oftentimes incredibly transformational for young girls who
need to get in touch with their self-worth and physical and emotional
strengths."   —Julia Renfro, Guide and Alumna

HISTORY/BACKGROUND
Located at the edge of the Boundary Waters, Camp Widjiwagan has been specializing in wilderness adventure for young people since 1929. Many of the
wood-canvas canoes purchased in the 1930s are still in use.

SAMPLE TRIPS

▶**Introductory Boundary Waters Canoe Area**—These sessions are ideal for the first-time Widji camper. Spend six days "on trail" exploring Minnesota's far north by canoe, viewing waterfalls, picking berries, listing to loons cry, and learning to travel with pack and canoe. Ages 12–14. Ten days/$500/ beginning.

▶**Isle Royale**—A backpacking introduction on Isle Royale National Park. Six days hiking on various trails where wildlife abounds. See moose and fox and hear howling wolves. Ages 12–14. Eleven to thirteen days/$600–$700/ beginning.

▶**Boundary Waters Canoe Area**—Widji's most popular trip is suitable for first-time campers and experienced canoers. Follow the trails of the Native Americans and French Canadian voyagers and explore the far reaches of the Boundary Waters wilderness. Experienced or older campers paddle across the border and travel in the southern areas of Canada's Quetico Provincial Park. Ages 12–16. Fifteen to eighteen days/$700–$850/beginning to advanced.

▶**Bighorn Mountain**—Confident first-time campers and experienced backpackers learn mountain backpacking. Hike for nine days at moderate elevations and enjoy vistas of snow-capped peaks and forested valleys. Ages 13–15. Fifteen to eighteen days/$850–$950/beginning to advanced.

▶**Quetico**—Experienced campers travel along the lakes and trails of Canada's Quetico Provincial Park, learning the basics of expedition-style canoeing. Ages 14 and up. Eighteen to nineteen days/$850–$900/advanced.

▶**Rocky Mountain**—Experienced backpackers hike for twelve days in the rugged terrain of Montana's Rocky Mountains. Traveling above the treeline, you encounter changes in elevation and cross snowfields. Ages 14–18. Eighteen to nineteen days/$1000–$1050/advanced.

Prices include: Meals and group equipment.

Prices do not include: Personal equipment (boots, rain gear, and sleeping bags can be provided if necessary).

Guides: Nineteen- to twenty-seven-year-olds; 75 percent are Widjiwagan alumnae.

Training for guides: CPR/first-aid, lifeguarding certification; Wilderness First Responder for advanced trip leaders, co-lead trip before soloing.

Liability coverage: Yes.

Wild Women Expeditions

P.O. Box 145, Station B
Sudbury, Ontario P3E 4N5 Canada
416/535-0748 or 705/866-1260

Wilderness Canoe Trips & Outdoor Programs in Northern Ontario

Began operating: 1991
Number of trips offered per year: 12
Number of all-women's trips per year: All
Usual group size: 8–10
Typical age of participants: 37–45
Range of ages of participants: 18–70

Explore northern Ontario's landscape by fastwater or a leisurely paddle. Some trips are planned to coincide with the full moon; others follow the paths of native peoples. Wild Women Expeditions hosts three- to eight-day trips through various Canadian lakes and rivers as well as weekend "getaways" and summer outdoor recreation programs at their base camp along the Spanish River. Base camp programs incorporate many aspects of the canoe trips without their strenuous nature. Participants enjoy the use of canoes, evening saunas, and two hundred acres of private forest, meadows, hills, and wetlands to explore as well as miles of rivers to paddle. A massage or shiatsu therapist is available on site. Programs may focus on particular topics such as the ancient medicine wheel or the art of drawing. Trips are relaxed; the group determines the pace.

IN THEIR OWN WORDS
"We operate with the belief that canoe tripping is a part of the Northern American heritage. Our trips are an opportunity to retreat into wild, rugged places in the company and camaraderie of other women and live simply and in profound communion with each other, nature and the elements. We do not see the wilderness as something to 'conquer,' but rather, as a place to live more deeply."   —Beth Mairs, Founder

HISTORY/BACKGROUND
The vision for Wild Women Expeditions came to Beth Mairs in 1988 while on a canoe trip with some friends: "It was a personal strategy to work toward getting out of the city and to spend more time doing what I love most—canoe tripping." Wild Women Expeditions became a reality in the summer of 1991.

SAMPLE TRIPS

➤**Autumn and Solstice Getaways**—Wild Women Expeditions' base camp along the Spanish River, surrounded by forest, meadows, hills, and wetlands, is host to three days of hiking, canoeing, warm fires, good company, and hearty food. Three days/CDN $300/all levels.

➤**Weekend Trips**—Emphasize relaxation and play as you paddle along a peaceful section of the Spanish River and set up camp with ample time to read, explore, fish, practice strokes, sketch—whatever your pleasure. No camping or canoeing experience is necessary, though you need to be able to swim. Two to three days/CDN $200–$300/easy.

➤**Killarney Canoe Trip**—Explore ancient quartzite hills, wild landscapes, and turquoise lakes by canoe and hike up a rocky ridge used by native people for sacred "vision quests." Prior camping or canoeing experience is recommended but not required. Three days/CDN $300/moderate. Five days/CDN $450/ moderate.

➤**North Channel Canoe Trip**—Lake Huron's North Channel is rich in history of native peoples and voyagers. Experience calm channels and big open water, high white rock, protected coves, and beaches as you travel between La Cloche Mountains and Manitoulin Island. Prior canoeing and camping experience necessary. Seven days/CDN $550/moderate to challenging.

➤**Temagami Canoe Trip**—Home to Ontario's oldest remaining pine forest, Temagami provides a vast system of interconnecting lakes and rivers, high cliffs and lookouts, rock paintings, cascading waterfalls, and aquamarine water. Trips trace routes established by native peoples over thousands of years. Previous camping experience necessary. Four days/CDN $350/moderate to challenging. Eight days/CDN $650/moderate to challenging.

Prices include: Meals, accommodations, group equipment, permits, use of sauna.

Prices do not include: Personal equipment.

Guides: Women skilled in group facilitation, outdoor living, and graciousness.

Training for guides: Proven ability to lead canoe trips and work effectively with women; prior guiding experience.

Liability coverage: Yes.

Wilderness Hawaii

P.O. Box 61692
Honolulu, HI 96822
808/967-7131

Outdoor Education in Hawaii

Began operating: 1982
Number of trips offered per year: 2–4
Number of all-women's trips per year: Varies
Usual group size: 6–10
Typical age of participants: teenagers
Range of ages of participants: 13–60

Wilderness Hawaii is an outdoor education program that follows the philosophy of the international Outward Bound schools. Wilderness Hawaii offers wilderness experiences in the varied terrain of Hawaii Volcanoes National Park that can lead to personal empowerment and enhanced self-esteem. The basic format of each program is a backpacking expedition that includes training in wilderness skills and safety, communication, teamwork, and leadership. Previous wilderness experience is not necessary to join a course, only a willingness to face new challenges and an openness to adventure.

IN THEIR OWN WORDS
"People have a lot more gumption than they give themselves credit for. Wilderness Hawaii creates the opportunity to dig a little deeper and discover untapped reserves."   —Shena Sandler, Director

HISTORY/BACKGROUND
Shena Sandler was an employee of the Hawaii Bound School when they declared bankruptcy. She and a partner then purchased the school's gear, took over their applications, obtained insurance and a National Park permit, and established Wilderness Hawaii. After co-directing Wilderness Hawaii for three years, Shena now directs the organization on her own. She resides in the town of Volcano, just outside the entrance to the National Park.

SAMPLE TRIPS

➤**Halape**—Designed to challenge the urban dweller, this hiking trip includes camping, swimming, exploration, and fishing. You begin with a rigorous seven-mile hike carrying full packs three thousand feet down to the coast. Your reward is Halape, hidden at the base of a thousand-foot cliff, where you set up camp for three nights. Two full days are set aside for swimming, snorkeling in the protected lagoon, lounging by the fresh water pond, and investigating a Hawaiian archaeological site. The last day's demanding hike out begins at dawn. This course can function as a means to re-evaluate, motivate, appreciate, or just get away from it all while learning new skills. Four days/$300/challenging.

➤**Mauna Loa**—The world's most massive volcano is named "Long Mountain." A visit to its summit requires strenuous hiking, a willingness to forget the lushness of Hawaii below the clouds, and the perseverance to keep going when you can't see the top. It is humbling, inspiring, and serene. Four to five days/$400/very challenging.

Prices include: Meals, group equipment, camping gear, and supplies, including backpacks and sleeping bags.

Prices do not include: Personal equipment.

Guides: Director Shena Sandler.

Training for guides: Assistant guides are either graduates of WH's summer program for teenagers or former instructors with the Hawaii Bound School.

Liability coverage: Yes.

Wildwise

P.O. Box 299, Darlinghurst
New South Wales 2010 Australia
61-2-360-2099 fax: 61-2-380-5699

From Camel Trekking to Surfing in Australia and New Zealand

Began operating: 1989
Number of trips offered per year: 15–41
Number of all-women's trips per year: 99%
Usual group size: 10
Typical age of participants: 30s–40s
Range of ages of participants: 18–88

Accessible to disabled women: By arrangement.
Multigenerational programs
Scholarships available: Work exchange or professional barter by application.

Whether exploring the rockpools of Kakadu, cross country skiing through a canopy of snow gums, or visiting the Bush College of Pitjantjatjara, Wildwise leads you through Australia's uniquely diverse bush. Farther afield you can "tramp" volcanic regions of New Zealand or trek in the Langtang region of Nepal. Many courses are suitable for first-timers and all strive to facilitate team building, cooperation, and self-knowledge rather than a militaristic approach. Learn a wide variety of new skills, such as rock climbing, mountain biking, kayaking, navigating, or surfing during Wildwise's weekend-long "learn-to" programs. Wildwise also offers adult mother-daughter programs. *Wildwords*, Wildwise's newsletter, provides travel information, bush recipes, and stories about women's experiences and the environment.

IN THEIR OWN WORDS
"Wildwise is committed to regenerating and empowering women through fun, physicality and contact with the land. We employ a leadership philosophy based on respect for the land, the indigenous inhabitants and the women travelers. Our name says it: wild and wise, wilderness and wisdom, untamed and knowledgeable."   —Wildwise Brochure

HISTORY/BACKGROUND
Wildwise was founded and is operated by Deb Collins and Chia Moan.

SAMPLE TRIPS

➤**Women's Surf Safari**—Bring those boogie boards, knee boards, malibus, and standard surfboards for a week of sun and surf. The pace is up to you. Fun for beginner and experienced surfers. Seven days/AUS $600/all levels.

➤**Kakadu Aboriginal Artwalk**—Walk away from the crowds to see Aboriginal art. Seven days/AUS $1000/easy.

➤**Outback Alice**—This is a trip for those who want to enjoy the outdoors without carrying a pack or taking a strenuous trek through the bush. Take day-walks at Gosses Bluff and Ormiston Gorge and a camel ride up the Finke River. Visit the Ipolera aboriginal community, stay overnight at Glen Helen Lodge, and climb Mt. Sonder if you choose. Transport is by four-wheel drive. You sleep in swags under the stars. Ten days/AUS $1750/easy.

➤**Kimberley Walk/Paddle**—Six days canoeing the Ord River followed by seven days bushwalking in the Bungle Bungle. Fifteen days/AUS $1550/moderate.

➤**Cradle Mountain Classic**—Walk through buttongrass moorland into the temperate forests and open plateaus of Tasmania. Led by a Tasmanian guide, you climb among the alpine slopes and valleys and encounter the area's wildlife. Five to six hours of walking each day. Some backpacking experience is recommended. Nine days/AUS $900/moderate to challenging.

➤**Women's Leadership Training**—Using an experiential, feminist model, participate in outdoor activities that develop self-confidence, powers of analysis and perception, and your ability to deal with group dynamics. Courses are relevant to community organizers and business women as well as outdoor leaders. Five days/AUS $750/moderate to challenging. Nine days/AUS $1600/moderate to challenging.

Prices include: Mostly vegetarian meals (special diets with notice), accommodations, group equipment, park fees.

Prices do not include: Personal equipment.

Guides: Full-time Wildwise personnel and local guides.

Training for guides: Participation in Wildwise leadership course, wilderness first-aid certificate, experience in given area and/or skill.

Liability coverage: Yes.

Wintermoon

3388 Petrell
Brimson, MN 55602
218/848-2442

Sled Dog Adventures in the Minnesota Northwoods

Began operating: 1990
Number of trips offered per year: 15
Number of all-women's trips per year: All
Usual group size: 6–8
Typical age of participants: 40
Range of ages of participants: 20–70

Wintermoon is located in the Superior National Forest of Minnesota amid miles of trails for dog sledding, skiing, and snowshoeing. Join Wintermoon guides and their twenty-five Alaskan huskies for three- to six-day mushing adventures. Learn about harnesses, gang lines, sleds, how to care for the dogs, and how to drive your own team. No experience is necessary. In the spirit of a simple and natural setting, Wintermoon includes log cabins, wood heating, solar power, a hand pump for well water, an outhouse, and a sauna.

IN THEIR OWN WORDS
"My philosophy is for women to have fun and succeed at running sled dogs; I respect each woman's personal strengths and goals."
—Kathleen Anderson, Owner

HISTORY/BACKGROUND
Kathleen Anderson founded Wintermoon out of a desire to teach women a nontraditional sport in a comfortable, supportive, and fun atmosphere. Kathleen has been mushing since 1983, was 1987 Beargrease Race Director, has experience as a racing team dog handler, and has raised and trained all of her huskies.

SAMPLE TRIPS

➤**Winter Solstice: PeerSpirit and Dog Sledding**—Though the earth can teach us how to behave, often we don't notice or know how to respond. Offered in cooperation with PeerSpirit, this trip offers you the chance to reconnect your personal energies and insights to the natural world. Combine the inner world of writing and reflection with the outer world of northern forests and dog sledding to foster a connection with the land, develop confidence and discover physical strength. Four days/$400/beginning to intermediate.

➤**Brimson Cabins in the Superior National Forest**—Miles of trails and abundant wildlife in Wintermoon's backyard provide the setting for running sled dogs. In the evening, you enjoy wood heat and hot chocolate while sharing information on mushing, racing, and equipment; or you can relax your muscles in the Finnish sauna. Three days/$300/beginning to intermediate. Four days/$400/beginning to intermediate.

➤**Winter Camping Adventure**—Travel by dog sled and skis to winter camping in the northern wilderness. The late winter sun will be high and warm as you explore and have fun in the snow. Four days/$400/beginning to intermediate.

➤**Dog Sledding II**—For those who have been to Wintermoon and would like to return. Get right out with the dogs, do some longer runs, and experience more mushing. Four days/$400/intermediate.

Prices include: Meals, accommodations, group equipment.

Prices do not include: Personal equipment.

Guides: Owner Kathleen Anderson and assistants.

Training for guides: Pre-season training with dogs.

Liability coverage: Yes.

Womanpower Enterprises

2551 Sumac Circle
St. Paul, MN 55110
800/879-1696 or 612/773-0937

Kenya Safaris

Began operating: 1993
Number of trips offered per year: 13
Number of all-women's trips per year: All
Usual group size: 20
Typical age of participants: 30s–40s
Range of ages of participants: 18–65

Womanpower tours spend seven days on safari, visiting game reserves, and seven days in Nairobi, allowing time to visit women-owned businesses and interact with Kenyan citizens. Tour sites vary and may include a visit to Kazuri, a business that employs one hundred fifty women in the creation and production of ceramic jewelry, and to the Kenya National Theater for a performance. Experience a night game viewing at Aberdare National Park and then relax for a day at Aberdare Country Club. Visit museums and prehistoric sites. Womanpower contracts with Gorretty Ofafa, a university lecturer and a member of the Luo tribe.

IN THEIR OWN WORDS
"I believe that much of the fun and value of travel occurs from connecting with average citizens. I am committed to ecotourism: responsible travel that conserves the natural environment and sustains the well-being of the local people."   —Evelyn Staus, Owner

HISTORY/BACKGROUND
Evelyn Staus first visited Kenya in 1991 to attend the Twentieth Congress of the International Federation of Business and Professional Women. She noticed how easy it would be to go on a safari to game parks, where all the guests were Caucasian like herself, and never encounter a Kenyan who was not either serving or selling her something. As a result, Evelyn began Womanpower Enterprises to provide opportunities where women could meet Kenyan citizens as peers. She has a master's in counseling and has run pre-vocational programs for single mothers and displaced homemakers for state and county agencies.

SAMPLE TRIPS

➤**Kenya Safari**—A drive along the Ngong Hills and into the Rift Valley takes you to a prehistoric site about six hundred thousand years old. Visit the bamboo forests and open moorland of Aberdare National Park and the flamingo feeding grounds at Lake Nakuru. Wildlife abounds in the Maasai Mara, including wildebeest, buffalo, zebras, and giraffes. While in Nairobi, visit Maridadi Fabrics, Kariokor Syondo women's group basket market, and a green-belt movement project. Fourteen days/$1550–$1950/easy.

Prices include: On safari: transportation, meals, and accommodations; in Nairobi: transportation to scheduled events, breakfast, and accommodations; park and museum entry fees; taxes.

Prices do not include: Lunch and dinner in Nairobi, visa fees, airport departure tax.

Guides: Owner Evelyn Staus.

Training for guides: Drivers and guides employed by ground handling tour company.

Liability coverage: No.

Womanship

The Boat House, 410 Severn Avenue
Annapolis, MD 21403
800/342-9295   fax: 410/263-2036

Learning Cruises in Eight U.S. Locations and Worldwide

Began operating: 1984
Number of trips offered per year: 360
Number of all-women's trips per year: All
Usual group size: Maximum of 6
Typical age of participants: 30s–60s
Range of ages of participants: 18–75

Accessible to disabled women
Multigenerational programs

Three- to seven-day learning cruises take place in seven locations around Annapolis and the Chesapeake Bay, Florida, New England, and the Pacific Northwest. International sailing trips and month-long passages drop anchor in the Caribbean, Canada, Greece, New Zealand, and Tahiti. Womanship teaches special clinics for apprehensive sailors through yacht clubs and sailing associations around the United States. Custom "partnership" courses offer the same teaching approach to couples, families, and groups.

IN THEIR OWN WORDS
"In my own mind, the term *womanship* means the fulfillment of oneself as a woman. We are the top-rated sailing school in the U.S. But we are a lot more than a sailing school; we are an educational institution that works with the learner, not just the skills to be learned. We use sailing as a vehicle for personal growth, teamwork, and leadership. The students gave us our motto the very first week of school, which is: Nobody Yells. That truly symbolizes our conducive learning environment."   —Suzanne Pogell, Founder

HISTORY/BACKGROUND
In 1984, its first year, Womanship was named in *Who's Who in Sailing* and given an award by them for "the unique philosophy that confidence and teamwork are as important as the skills learned." In 1991, Womanship was rated the top cruising sailing school by the readership of *Practical Sailor* magazine.

SAMPLE TRIPS

➤**Daytime Classes**—Two days/$250/beginning. Three days/$350/beginning.

➤**Live-Aboard Learning Cruises**—Based on practical, hands-on learning, these programs teach you all you need to know about sailing and skippering a cruising sailboat under varying conditions. Skills include coastal piloting, navigation, getting the boat under way, keeping it sailing, and bringing it to dock or anchor. Three days/$500/beginning to advanced. One week/$1000–$1250 (depending on the location)/beginning to advanced.

➤**Mother-and-Daughter Programs**—Ten- to seventeen-year-old daughters and their mothers learn to sail together at one of four levels. Mothers and daughters bond by learning together. Each also has a chance to learn within her own peer group. Instructors are experienced in working with adults and youth. Programs last from two to seven days. Weekend/$350 (for mother) and $300 (for daughter)/beginning to advanced.

➤**Womanship Around the World: Sailing Trips and Land Tours**—Six trips per year travel to such places as the Galapagos, Denmark, Greece, New Zealand, and Tahiti. You can choose a ten- or fifteen-day tour that includes a seven- or ten-day learning cruise followed by land exploring. Ten to fifteen days/cost varies/beginning to advanced.

➤**Offshore Passages**—Sail from New England to the Virgin Islands or Annapolis to Florida. Sign up for a full month, or a one- or two-week segment. Four weeks/$3500 (or $1000 per week)/advanced.

Prices include: Meals and accommodations for live-aboard cruises, group equipment.

Prices do not include: Personal equipment.

Guides: U.S. Coast Guard licensed and skilled sailing instructors; some instructors have been with Womanship since 1984.

Training for guides: Intensive screening, clinics, and in-service training.

Liability coverage: Yes.

WOMBATS

P.O. Box 757
Fairfax, CA 94978
415/459-0980

Women's Mountain Bike and Tea Society

Began operating: 1986
Number of trips offered per year: 4
Number of all-women's trips per year: All
Usual group size: 20
Typical age of participants: 32
Range of ages of participants: 16–60

Accessible to disabled women: For any woman who can ride; experience with deaf participants.
Multigenerational programs
Scholarships available: Especially for chef/menu planning, ride guide, or brochure layout.

Join the knobby sisterhood for a weekend or week of mountain biking in California, Colorado, or Maine. Beginning, intermediate, and advanced bikers can attain the wisdom of the WOMBATS. A mountain bike champion coaches, feeds, and amuses you along the way. Subscribe to the WOMBATS newsletter and receive tips for the mechanically impaired, reading lists, shopping hints, and more. Become a network member and receive the quarterly newsletter, a bat tea towel, and an embroidered bat badge.

IN THEIR OWN WORDS
"Our motto is: You're Never Totally out of the Woods. Mountain biking is the ideal sport for women, whether they're gnarly or nervous (or neither). We aim to teach, encourage, and entertain newcomers as well as to advise and coach racers."
        —Jacquie Phelan, Founder

HISTORY/BACKGROUND
When Jacquie Phelan began racing, she found an invisible sign tacked to the door that read, No Girls. So the mountain bike champ constructed a new entrance for women. In 1984, she and a friend produced their first mother-daughter campout and ride. There are now over six hundred club members, with close to two thousand belonging at some time since 1986.

SAMPLE TRIPS

➤**Camp Winnawombat**—Ride, eat, and socialize, with your only cares being how to make it over a particularly "technical" arrangement of rocks at the bend in the trail and what the bat-chef-in-residence is making for supper. Plenty of off-bike time to sit by the fire and contemplate the implications of two-wheeled travel in a four-wheel world, or simply stare into space, enjoying the classic post-ride endorphin "cocktail." Two and a half days/$200/beginning to intermediate.

➤**Fat Tire Finishing School**—Tackle the subtleties of uphill riding: position, maintaining traction and rhythm, getting restarted, breath work, and pacing for long climbs. Course covers descending, route planning, wilderness awareness—heck, you can even re-create the experience of getting lost! Bicycle-skill games, proximity practice, and riding the plank bolster your bat skills. One week/$700/beginning to advanced.

Prices include: Meals, accommodations (six participants per room), group equipment.

Prices do not include: Bike, personal equipment, including helmet, patch kit, tube, and pump.

Guides: Founder Jacquie Phelan and assorted "Wombats."

Training for guides: Extensive mountain biking experience.

Liability coverage: No.

Women in the Wilderness

566 Ottawa Avenue
St. Paul, MN 55107
612/227-2284

Joyful Wilderness Trips from the Arctic to the Amazon

Began operating: 1987
Number of trips offered per year: 30+
Number of all-women's trips per year: All
Usual group size: 8–14
Typical age of participants: 35–55
Range of ages of participants: 16–91

Multigenerational programs
Scholarships available: Some work exchange is possible.

Women in the Wilderness programs in Minnesota, Canada, Utah, Peru, and the Virgin Islands (with new destinations to come) include canoeing, rafting, outdoor leadership workshops, dog sledding, snowshoeing, and sailing. Trips are designed both for the beginning and the experienced outdoorswoman. There is no "character building." WITW trusts that you probably like your character just fine already. WITW strives to make many programs accessible to women who are older, not physically strong, or simply seek to relax and get close to nature. Women in the Wilderness also has a mail-order book service.

IN THEIR OWN WORDS
"We focus on fun, freedom, letting women's playfulness and creativity come out, and we put individual wishes and goals high, not letting "the group" run things. We do not create stress and challenge. We always create an atmosphere where lesbians (and non-lesbians) are comfortable being out."

—Judith Niemi, Director

HISTORY/BACKGROUND
Judith Niemi began a woman's program in 1975 because she was meeting so few women in canoe country. It also became a path to two of her goals: reintroducing city people to the natural world and providing a place for women to be powerful and free. Judith is the co-editor of *Rivers Running Free: Canoeing Stories by Adventurous Women* and *Basic Essentials of Women in the Outdoors*.

SAMPLE TRIPS

►**Amazon Rainforest**—Peruvian guides introduce you to pink dolphins, black caimans, and hoatzin birds. Travel by boat one hundred miles up the Amazon from Iquitos, live in a traditional jungle hut at your base camp, take easy daytrips by foot or boat, or choose more strenuous overnight hikes by canoe or raft. Learn about the medicinal uses of plants from a naturalist guide or visit native villages. Fourteen days/$2100 (from Miami)/all levels.

►**Canada's Northwest Territories**—Join in musk ox watching, tundra hiking, and visits to archaeological sites in the beautiful Barrenlands. Nine days/$3000 (from Yellowknife)/easy.

►**Utah Canyon Canoeing or Rafting**—Canoe the Green River, viewing desert sunsets, high red sandstone walls, and petroglyphs. Hike up side canyons and receive a naturalist's introduction to the desert environment. Raft the whitewater San Juan River, through canyons a thousand feet deep, and see cliff dwellings of the ancient Anasazi while an artist and a writer lead you in drawing and travel journal workshops. Eight days/$1000/easy.

►**Dog Sledding in Minnesota**—Learn the lively art of mushing at your teacher's northern Minnesota homestead. Communicate with the team and make exhilarating runs through the wilderness. Four days/$400/moderate.

►**Outdoor Leadership Workshops**—Discussion sessions for professional and informal outdoor leaders concentrate on leadership philosophies and techniques. Includes demonstrations on how to teach outdoor skills. Four or five days/$300/moderate.

►**Nature Study and Canoeing in Canada's Northwest Territories**—Join other experienced canoe women on the legendary Nahanni River, traveling past a waterfall twice the height of Niagara, through deep mountain canyons. Fourteen days/$1750 (from Fort Simpson)/moderate to challenging.

Prices include: Chartered or bush flights in Northwest Territories, round-trip airfare from Miami to Iquitos, meals, group equipment.

Prices do not include: Personal equipment.

Guides: WITW guides and various local guides.

Training for guides: In-service training and leadership workshops, prior outdoor experience and group leadership ability, first-aid training.

Liability coverage: Yes.

Women of the Wilderness Australia

P.O. Box 340, Unley
South Australia 5061 Australia
08-3627591 (same for fax)

Outdoor Adventure in Australia

Began operating: 1990
Number of trips offered per year: 76
Number of all-women's trips per year: All
Usual group size: 6–12
Typical age of participants: 20–50
Range of ages of participants: 20-50

Multigenerational programs
Programs for young women
Scholarships available: Work exchange and bartering are possible.

Join Women of the Wilderness Australia, paragliding, surfing, camel riding, or waterskiing in the Australian landscape.Whether you're interested in bushwalking or rock climbing, caving or horseriding, diving or sailing, Women of the Wilderness Australia will guide you in an outdoor adventure. You can develop your leadership skills or set out on a mother-daughter adventure. Women of the Wilderness Australia's programs include day-long workshops, three-day retreats, and extended wilderness experiences.

IN THEIR OWN WORDS
"We provide a safe, supportive and noncompetitive approach to wilderness adventure travel and believe this approach enhances and develops the potential of every woman."   —Women of the Wilderness Australia brochure

HISTORY/BACKGROUND
Believing that women and girls were in need of a wider variety of outdoor opportunities, Deb Nanschild established Women of the Wilderness Australia in 1990 as an affiliate of Alaska Women of the Wilderness. It received a State Recreation Award in 1992 for increasing the participation of women and girls in physical recreation. In 1994, South Australia's women's suffrage centenary, it conducted a major long-distance trek across the state to celebrate women's achievements.

SAMPLE TRIPS

➤**Wilderness Retreat on Kangaroo Island**—Care for and explore the "soul essence in life form." Explore your inner wilderness and the beauty of the environment around you. Three days/AUS $350/all levels.

➤**Girls' Adventure Camp**—Girls experience the fun and adventure of camping, canoeing, bushwalking, horseriding, and sailing in a safe and comfortable environment. Recommended for ages ten to fourteen. Three days/AUS $100/all levels.

➤**Bushwalking**—Two to eight days/AUS $80–$100 per day/all levels.

➤**Whale Watching**—Eight days/AUS $1000/easy.

➤**Rock Climbing in Victoria**—Two to three days/AUS $300/all levels.

➤**Coorong Sailing and Sea Kayaking**—Three days/AUS $400/all levels.

➤**Caving Expedition**—One to three days/AUS $80–$120 (per day)/all levels.

Prices include: Vegetarian meals, accommodations, group equipment, camp fees.

Prices do not include: Personal equipment.

Guides: Thirty instructors with experience in given field, trained by WOWA.

Training for guides: Outdoor leadership courses, WOWA support for guides in leadership experience and development.

Liability coverage: Yes.

Women on the Water

P.O. Box 502
Key West, FL 33041
305/294-0662

Snorkel Trips and Sunset Sails for Lesbians in Key West, Florida

Began operating: 1982
Number of trips offered per year: Daily
Number of all-women's trips per year: All
Usual group size: 6
Typical age of participants: 35
Range of ages of participants: 20–60

Accessible to disabled women: Some.
Programs for lesbians

Set sail on the waters around Key West on *Waxing Moon,* a thirty-foot trimaran. The boat provides an extra-stable ride. Snorkel during the day, enjoy striking sunsets in the evening. Women on the Water's chartered trips create an easy-going atmosphere for lesbians to experience the wonders of the ocean world. The first mate instructs on deck, while your captain shares her interest in bird and marine life and points out places of interest to women in Key West.

IN THEIR OWN WORDS
"We enjoy providing a space for women to meet each other and spend time in a magical world on the water. It is important for lesbians to have access to a wide variety of activities."   —Kathy Kirkland, Owner

HISTORY/BACKGROUND
Captain Melody Coulter started Women on the Water in 1982 to provide lesbians with a sailing experience in a comfortable environment. Kathy Kirkland joined the company in 1983, and in 1990 Kathy and Leslie Devereux purchased the boat and business from Melody, who bought another boat for her solo crossing of the Atlantic.

SAMPLE TRIPS

➤**Day Sail and Snorkel Trip**—All you need is a lunch, towel, and some sunscreen as you set off to explore the marine world. Snorkeling instruction and gear are provided. Bring a roll of film along and try out an underwater camera. Five hours/$50/beginning.

➤**Sunset Sails**—Women on the Water provides the champagne, other beverages, and hors d'oeuvres for this friendly harbor cruise. Two hours/under $50/easy.

➤**Combination**—Put the two together and you have a day of underwater exploration and an evening of relaxed socializing by sunset. Six hours/under $100/easy.

Prices include: Champagne, nonalcoholic beverages, and hors d'oeuvres on sunset sails; snorkeling equipment and underwater camera on day sails.

Prices do not include: Meals and personal equipment.

Guides: Captain Kathy Kirkland and First Mate Leslie Devereux.

Training for guides: Experience sailing and teaching.

Liability coverage: No.

Women to Women Cross-Cultural Adventures

50 River Road
Grandview-on-Hudson, NY 10960
800/831-1231 or 914/353-0678

An Opportunity for Women to Meet across Cultures

Began operating: 1990
Number of trips offered per year: 12
Number of all-women's trips per year: 12
Usual group size: 7-10
Typical age of participants: 40s
Range of ages of participants: 28-68

Women to Women Cross-Cultural Adventures takes women to Maasailand, the Himalayas, Bolivia, and Costa Rica in order to bring women of different cultural backgrounds together to share experiences. You can join women in their daily activities and spend nights in their homes. The depth of participation depends on your interests. These cultural journeys also include active elements such as wildlife safaris in Tanzania, treks in Nepal and Tibet, and hikes through the rainforests of Costa Rica. Overseas Adventure Travel guides trips throughout Africa, North Africa/the Mediterranean, Asia/Himalayas, the Americas, and the Pacific/Southeast Asia.

IN THEIR OWN WORDS
"These trips offer a cultural and anthropological experience both to the women traveling and to the women who are visited. It is one of the few ways women in 'developing' countries have to share their lives with us. And it offers an unusual opportunity for women in 'developed' countries to learn firsthand from local women. Despite the many fascinating differences, we have a lot in common as women. "   —Judi Wineland, Co-founder

HISTORY/BACKGROUND
Co-founder Carole Angermeir is an anthropologist who has worked to improve women's lives both in the U.S. and internationally. She is the Director of Travel for the Institute of Noetic Sciences. Judi Wineland has extensive experience in every phase of adventure travel planning and has been featured in *The New York Times, Ms., Savvy* and *Working Woman*. They established WWCA in 1992.

SAMPLE TRIPS

►**Land of the Maasai: Tanzania**—Join a fascinating journey to the heart of Maasailand, where you'll have the rare opportunity to live in the world of Maasai women. To bridge the language barrier between the Maasai and you, an educated Tanzanian interpreter involved with women's issues will help everyone share thoughts, impressions, and concerns. Work with Maasai women cooking *ugali* (the Tanzanian equivalent of rice), milking cows, or beading skirts. Set out on a five-day wildlife safari that spotlights Ngorongoro Crater in the Serengeti Plains. Stay with women in their homes or, alternately, sleep under the African skies at a luxury campsite. Two weeks/$4500/moderate.

►**Through a Woman's Eyes: Tibet and Nepal**—Visit Hindu and Buddhist women in Nepal, and Buddhist women in Tibet. The religious diversity provides the opportunity to see a marked contrast in women's lifestyles within a small geographic area. After visiting Kathmandu, trek to Himalayan mountain villages where Buddhist women work the fields, gather wood, wash, cook, and raise their families. The journey culminates in the windswept, high plateau of Tibet. Each night, stay in a woman's home, or sleep in a comfortable campsite or local hotel. Two and a half weeks/$4500/moderate.

►**A New Wave of Women: Bolivia**—Bolivia is host to rugged mountains, a vast, high sun-washed plateau, and the highest navigable lake in the world, Titicaca. Learn how peasant women from a "developing" nation have overcome oppression and marshaled their considerable entrepreneurial skills to create and preside over their own agrarian businesses. Hike to isolated weaving hamlets in the Andes and visit Quechuan women. Then boat to Taquile Island on Lake Titicaca's Peruvian side. Visit some of Bolivia's Incan ruins, as well as museums and galleries in La Paz and Sucre. You are accompanied by expert female Bolivian and Peruvian guides throughout the trip. Two weeks/$3500/moderate.

Prices include: Meals, accommodations, and group equipment.

Prices do not include: Personal equipment.

Guides: Multilingual experienced local guides.

Training for guides: Extensive experience in given location.

Liability coverage: Yes.

Women's Outdoor Adventure Cooperative
P.O. Box 1597
Wolfeboro, NH 03894
603/569-5510

Affordable Adventures in New Hampshire and Beyond

Began operating: 1987
Number of trips offered per year: 12
Number of all-women's trips per year: All
Usual group size: 4–10
Typical age of participants: Late 30s
Range of ages of participants: 18–65

Multigenerational programs
Programs for young women: Some programs specifically for teenagers.
Scholarships available: Sliding-fee scales, work exchange, and barter; part of
  membership fee goes into scholarship fund.

Participants share equipment, knowledge, and companionship on a wide
range of outdoor trips, from one day of hiking to ten days of paddling and
camping. Members pay a one-time membership fee based on .001 percent of
their annual salary, attend meetings, participate in consensus decision making, and contribute to trip coordination, leadership, child care, and newsletter
publication. Members have led trips to the top of the world's highest peaks as
well as afternoon strolls in the White Mountains. Spend one day cross country skiing, snowshoeing, or rock climbing, or a week bicycling.

IN THEIR OWN WORDS
"We are based on the ideals of inclusivity and crossing the boundaries of age,
ability, class, racial and ethnic backgrounds, and sexual orientation. We provide an opportunity to feel a sense of camaraderie with other women, to relax
and vacation without feeling guilty, to feel healthy, adventurous and fit, and
to have fun."   —Women's Outdoor Adventure Cooperative newsletter

HISTORY/BACKGROUND
Recognizing that outdoor adventures are not equally accessible to all women,
WOAC became a reality with the help of a grant from the Ms. Foundation.
Founders Donna San Antonio and Holly Manoogian also serve as guides for
a youth leadership and service organization.

SAMPLE TRIPS

➤**Snorkeling and Sailing in Puerto Rico**—Ten days/$t.b.a./easy.

➤**Mother-Daughter trips**—One to three days/$15–$60/easy to moderate.

➤**Bicycle Touring**—One to six days/$5–$150/easy to moderate.

➤**Hiking**—One day/$10/easy to moderate.

➤**Cross Country Skiing**—One to three days/$15–$60/easy to moderate.

➤**Skijoring with Sled Dogs**—One day/$10–$20/moderate.

➤**Wilderness Canoeing in the Allagash Waterway**—Ten days/$650/moderate.

➤**Introductions to Rock Climbing**—One to two days/$15–$50/moderate.

➤**Outdoor Leadership Training**—Three days/$25-150/moderate.

➤**Canoe Racing Clinic**—One to two days/$25–$50/moderate to challenging.

➤**Mountaineering and Winter Camping**—Three days/$50/moderate to challenging.

Prices include: Meals, accommodations, group equipment, and special clothing.

Prices do not include: Personal equipment.

Guides: Skilled and experienced outdoorswomen.

Training for guides: Leadership training is provided; some trips require Emergency Medical Technician certification and extensive experience in given area; some staff have master's degrees in counseling, environmental education, or other related fields.

Liability coverage: No.

Women's Sailing Adventures

39 Woodside Avenue
Westport, CT 06880
800/328-8053 or 203/227-7413

Sailing in the U.S., New Zealand, and British Virgin Islands

Began operating: 1988
Number of trips offered per year: 40
Number of all-women's trips per year: All
Usual group size: 4
Typical age of participants: 40
Range of ages of participants: 22–80+

Whether participating in a day sail out of Westport, Connecticut, or a week's run in the British Virgin Islands, you can learn to sail with confidence. WSA offers both beginner and intermediate course instruction in: coastal navigation, sail trim, helmsmanship, radio contact, engine maintenance, safety preparedness, shipboard conservation, knots, docking and anchoring, teamwork, terminology, and points of sail. Intermediate and advanced course instruction is offered in: offshore navigation and instruments, weather, sail shape, aero/hydrodynamics, balancing the boat in seaway, heavy-air solutions, electrical systems, provisioning, crew care and morale, teamwork, and self-reliance. Aboard high-performance yachts averaging forty feet in length, you will find the living quarters comfortable and the sailing challenging.

IN THEIR OWN WORDS
"Our sailing groups are small but always compatible. Each group is unique, comprised of women from all walks of life. The common thread is the desire to improve sailing skills through an authentic adventure. We've found that women-only groups foster competence and competitiveness in all aspects of sailing."   —Sherry Jagerson, Founder

HISTORY/BACKGROUND
Sailing instructors Sherry Jagerson and Carol Hayward have more than sixteen years of teaching experience between them. Sherry is a sailmaker and has raced in three Bermuda races and the Trans-Atlantic Race. Carol, First Mate Sea Education Association, has sailed across the Atlantic and in ocean waters from Nova Scotia to Grenada.

SAMPLE TRIPS

►**Stonington, Connecticut Coastal**—Setting out from Stonington, an old seafaring harbor, you look across Long Island Sound analyzing possible destinations based on wind direction, speed, and currents: maybe Fishers Island; Newport, Rhode Island; Narrangansett Bay; Block Island; or Sag Harbor. Seven days/$1100/beginning and intermediate.

►**Penobscot Bay, Maine Coastal**—Navigate between the craggy spruce and granite islands of Penobscot, Jericho, and Frenchman's Bay. Explore jewel-like islands with endless gunkholes and quaint harbors in winds that vary from gentle to exhilarating. Anchor at the end of the day in the calm protected harbors of one of the most beautiful areas of the world. Relax to the sailor's delight of dinner under the stars and a sleep on the water bed of the world. Seven days/$1100/beginning and intermediate.

►**Tortola, British Virgin Islands**—Board the boat in the bustling port of Roadtown. While circumnavigating Tortola, sail through sparkling blue-green water to islands that at a distance appear to melt into the horizon. Enjoy a warm evening breeze over tropical islands with stars and planets so bright you can almost touch them. In the BVIs, the warm trade winds blow a perfect fifteen to twenty-five knots every day. Seven days/$1100/beginning and intermediate.

►**Block Island Race Week**—Race in the famous Block Island Race Week off the coast of Newport, Rhode Island. Meet us on the wind-swept, glacial remnant island via ferry or plane. Stay with the racing fleet in Great Salt Pond and awake every morning to tunes of a Dixieland band serenading the fleet. Post-race, shore-side activities include volleyball and dancing. Racing takes place both around the island and on specially marked courses. While the racing is taken seriously, you will have lots of fun. Seven days/$1200/intermediate and advanced.

Prices include: Meals (except for one meal ashore), accommodations, and group equipment.

Prices do not include: Personal equipment.

Guides: Founder Sherry Jagerson and instructor Carol Hayward.

Training for guides: Veteran sailing instructors Jagerson and Hayward are both USCG-licensed captains.

Liability coverage: Yes.

Woodswomen

25 West Diamond Lake Road
Minneapolis, MN 55419
612/822-3809 fax: 612/822-3814

Worldwide Adventure Travel for Women of all Ages

Began operating: 1977
Number of trips offered per year: 70
Number of all-women's trips per year: 60
Usual group size: 8–12
Typical age of participants: 30–50
Range of ages of participants: 18–70

Multi-generational programs: Ten per year.
Scholarships available: Partial scholarships available.

Woodswomen offers wilderness journeys, adventure vacations, skills trips, and leadership/professional development programs. You can dog sled in Minnesota or bicycle through Ireland, kayak in Washington's San Juans or hike in Costa Rica. Learn to bicycle, rock climb, or cross country ski. Participate in a canoeing and leadership course or an evening of moms and kids fishing. If you become a Woodswomen member, you receive their quarterly newsletter, free personal ads, discounts in the WW General Store, free consultation for your own trip planning, and a copy of the membership directory.

IN THEIR OWN WORDS
"We offer safe, exciting trips for women of all ages, turning trips into events to remember, to cherish, to build on."
—Tammy Dehne, Administrative Manager

HISTORY/BACKGROUND
Woodswomen has been a leader in developing outdoor programs for women since 1977. In 1982, they led the first women's guided descent of the Noatak River in Alaska and in 1988 guided a successful climb of Mt. McKinley with seven women summitting. With a grant from the Emma B. Howe Foundation in 1988, Woodswomen created a women-and-children's program for socially and economically disadvantaged families. In 1990, they developed the first outdoor leadership program for women felons in the U.S.

SAMPLE TRIPS

➤**Mt. Olympus Hiking**—Hike through the Olympic rainforest, along rivers and lakes to Glacier Meadows at the foot of Mt. Olympus to explore alpine flowers and glacial geology. Seven days/$600/all levels.

➤**Africa Climb and Tour**—Explore Ngorongoro Crater, Tarangire Park, and Serengeti Park, climb Kilimanjaro, view lions, giraffes, zebras, and wildebeests. Accommodations in comfortable jungle lodges and tented camps. Eighteen days/$5000/all levels.

➤**New Zealand Bike Tour**—Bicycle with van support among New Zealand's sea coasts and river valleys, when the weather's good and the crowds have thinned. Fourteen days/$2300/all levels.

➤**Roatan: Ocean Lover's Paradise**—Scuba dive and snorkel off the coast of Honduras. Stay at Anthony's Key Resort and dive out your back door. Highlights include swimming with dolphins and horseback riding on a secluded beach. Must be PADI certified to dive. Seven days/$1000/all levels.

➤**Horsepacking in Wisconsin**—Enjoy a long weekend of riding, riverside camping, and delicious campfire food. Three days/$300/all levels.

➤**Galapagos Island Cruise**—Visit islands of giant tortoises and flightless cormorants, swim and snorkel with fur seals, visit old lava flows, the equator, native Indian markets, and the city of Quito. Relax on the ship at night. Price includes airfare from Miami. Twelve days/$3000/all levels.

➤**Boundary Waters Canoeing**—This leadership course begins with a day of rock climbing and sessions on an island retreat. Then paddle along the Boundary Waters as you experiment with leadership styles and decision-making models while refining your wilderness skills. Seven days/$700/challenging.

Prices include: Airfare on some trips, meals, accommodations, group equipment, permits, and camping fees.

Prices do not include: Personal equipment (bike bags, backpacks, daypacks, sleeping bags, and pads are available for rental), climbing equipment for advanced programs, bicycles, skis, and airport taxes.

Guides: Trained Woodswomen guides.

Training for guides: Extensive experience in the particular skill; completion of Woodswomen training program.

Liability coverage: Yes.

NOTES

Introduction

1. Ruth Murray Underhill, "Clarissa and Seraphine on the Canal," from *Rivers Running Free: Canoeing Stories by Adventurous Women,* edited by Judith Niemi and Barbara Wieser (Seattle: The Seal Press, 1987), p. 138.

PART I

What Will It Be?

2. *Women's Sports and Fitness,* published eight times a year, P.O. Box 472, Mt. Morris, IL 61054 (815/734-1116).

Bicycling

3. Susan Weaver, *A Woman's Guide to Cycling* (Berkeley: Ten Speed Press, 1990).

Canoeing, Kayaking, and Rafting

4. Mary Wickham Bond, "The Passionate Paddler," *Rivers Running Free: Canoeing Stories by Adventurous Women,* edited by Judith Niemi and Barbara Wieser (Seattle: The Seal Press, 1987), p. 193.

5. Judith Niemi and Barbara Wieser, eds., *Rivers Running Free: Canoeing Stories by Adventurous Women* (Seattle: The Seal Press, 1987).

6. Constance Helmericks, *Down the Wild River North* (Seattle: The Seal Press, 1988).

7. Jean Aspen, *Arctic Daughter* (Minneapolis: Bergamot Books, 1988).

8. Linda Lewis, *Water's Edge: Women Who Push the Limits in Rowing, Kayaking and Canoeing* (Seattle: The Seal Press, 1992).

9. Lloyd D. Armstead, *Whitewater Rafting in Western North America: A Guide to Rivers and Professional Outfitters* (Chester, CT: The Globe Pequot Press, 1990).

Fishing

10. Holly Morris, ed., *Uncommon Waters: Women Write About Fishing* (Seattle: The Seal Press, 1991), pp. 100–101.

Horse, Mule and Llama Packing, and Ranch Vacations

11. Stanlynn Daugherty, *Packing with Llamas: A Comprehensive Guide to Llama Packing* (Ashland, OR: Juniper Ridge Press, 1989).

12. David Harmon and Amy S. Rubin, *Llamas on the Trail: A Packer's Guide* (Missoula, MT: Mountain Press Publishing Company, 1992).

Mountaineering

13. Janet Robertson, *The Magnificent Mountain Women: Adventures in the Colorado Rockies* (Lincoln, NE: University of Nebraska Press, 1990), p. 3.

14. Ibid., p. 6.

15. Arlene Blum, *Annapurna, A Woman's Place* (San Francisco: Sierra Club Books, 1980).

16. Rachel da Silva, ed., *Leading Out: Women Climbers Reaching for the Top* (Seattle: The Seal Press, 1992).

17. Bill Birkett and Bill Peascod, *Women Climbing: 200 Years of Achievement* (Seattle: The Mountaineers, 1990).

Sailing and Cruising

18. Linda Grant De Pauw, *Seafaring Women* (Boston: Houghton Mifflin Co., 1982).

19. Ibid., p. 84.

20. Jeannine Talley, *Women at the Helm* (Racine, WI: Mother Courage Press, 1990).

21. Ibid., p. 1.

22. Tania Aebi, *Maiden Voyage* (New York: Simon and Schuster, 1989).

Skiing, Snowshoeing, and Dog Sledding

23. Elissa Slanger and Dinah Witchel, *Ski Woman's Way*, (New York: Summit Books, 1979), p. 17.

24. Susanna Levin, "Shredding Inhibitions," *Women's Sports and Fitness*, Vol. 12, Nov/Dec 1990, p. 2.

25. Libby Riddles and Tim Jones, *Race Across Alaska: First Woman to Win the Iditarod Tells Her Story* (Harrisburg, PA: Stackpole Press, 1988).

Snorkeling and Scuba Diving

26. Dennis K. Graver, *Scuba Diving* (Champaign, IL: Human Kinetics Publishers, 1993).

27. Rainbow Divers is a gay and lesbian diving club in Northern California. For more information, call or write 62A Vicksburg Street, San Francisco, CA 94114 (415/252-7870).

Surfing and Windsurfing

28. Lisa Chase, "Room and Board," *Women's Sports and Fitness*, Vol. 12, May/June 1990, pp. 32–35.

Walking, Hiking, Trekking, and Backpacking

29. Stephen Bezruchka, *A Guide to Trekking in Nepal* (Seattle: The Mountaineers, 1991).

30. Lynn Thomas, *The Backpacking Woman* (New York: Anchor Books, 1980).

For Lesbians

31. *Women Going Places*, 141 Praed Street, London W2 1RL, United Kingdom.

32. Ferrari Publications, Inc., P.O. Box 37887 Phoenix, AZ 85069 (602/863-2408).

33. *Out & About*, 542 Chapel Street, New Haven, CA 06511 (800/929-2268).

34. *Our World: International Gay & Lesbian Travel*, 1044 North Nova Road, Suite 251, Daytona Beach, FL 32117 (904/441-5367).

35. Ferrari Publications, Inc., P.O. Box 37887 Phoenix, AZ 85069 (602/863-2408).

36. Ferrari Publications, Inc. See note above for address.

37. Pamela Robin Brandt and Lindsy Van Gelder, *Are You Two...Together?* (New York: Random House, 1991).

For Disabled Women

38. Cindy Lewis and Susan Sygall, *A World of Options for the 90s: A Guide to International Educational Exchange, Community Service, and Travel for Persons of Disabilities* (Eugene, Oregon: Mobility International USA, 1990). P.O. Box 10767, Eugene, OR 97440 (503/343-1284).

39. *Including Women with Disabilities in Development Projects* (Eugene, Oregon: Mobility International USA, 1990). See note above for address.

PART II

Organizing Your Own Group

40. Tracy Johnson, *Shooting the Boh* (New York: Vintage Books, 1992).

41. Kathleen Meyer, *How to Shit in the Woods* (Berkeley: Ten Speed Press, 198).

42. Dale Ward and Dustine Davidson, *Deck with a View: On the Water Vacations in Greece and Turkey* (Ashland, OR: Link International, 1993).

INDEX TO COMPANIES BY LOCATION

Prairie Women Adventures and Retreat
Rainbow Adventures
Sylvan Rocks
Voyageur Outward Bound School
Widjiwagan YMCA Camp
Wintermoon
Womanpower Enterprises
Women in the Wilderness
Woodswomen

ROCKY MOUNTAIN: **COLORADO, IDAHO, MONTANA, NEVADA, UTAH, WYOMING**

Artemis Sailing Charters
Bar H Ranch
Boulder Rock Club
CenterPoint in Aspen
Colorado Outward Bound School
Jennifer Smith Fly Fishing Guide Service
Maggie Merriman Fly Fishing Schools
McNamara Ranch
National Outdoor Leadership School
Outdoor Leadership Training Seminars
Reel Women Fly Fishing Adventures
Sheri Griffith Expeditions

SOUTHWEST: **ARIZONA, NEW MEXICO, OKLAHOMA, TEXAS**

Artemis Wilderness Tours
At the Helm
Hawk, I'm Your Sister
RVing Women
Sacred Sedona

PACIFIC COAST: **CALIFORNIA, OREGON, WASHINGTON**

Adventure Associates
Adventure Women
Ancient Forest Adventures
Backroads
Blue Moon Explorations

Call of the Wild
Cloud Canyon Wilderness Experience
Dirt Roads and Damsels
Earthlodge and Womenspeak Journeys
Eco-Explorations
Elakah! Expeditions
Himalayan High Treks
Hurricane Creek Llama Treks
Lois Lane Expeditions
Mariah Wilderness Expeditions
OceanWomyn Kayaking
Olivia Cruises and Resorts
Onn the Water
Pacific Crest Outward Bound School
Paddling South
Poseidon Services/Izarra Cruises
Rhonda Smith Windsurfing Center
Robin Tyler Productions and Tours
Skylink
Tours of Interest to Women
Vertical Ventures
Wander Women
WOMBATS

ALASKA

Alaska Women of the Wilderness
Equinox Wilderness Expeditions

HAWAII

Adventure Spirit Hawaii
The Heart of Adventure
Wilderness Hawaii

CANADA

Canadian Outward Bound Wilderness School
Et-Then
Wild Women Expeditions
Herizen: New Age Sailing for Women

INDEX TO COMPANIES BY GEOGRAPHIC AREA OF TRIPS OFFERED

Women's Sailing Adventures
Woodswomen

**SOUTH: ALABAMA, ARKANSAS, DELAWARE, FLORIDA, GEORGIA, KEN-
TUCKY, LOUISIANA, MARYLAND, MISSISSIPPI, NORTH CAROLINA, SOUTH
CAROLINA, TENNESSEE, VIRGINIA, WEST VIRGINIA**

Adventure Women
Earthwise
Hurricane Island Outward Bound School
Nantahala Outdoor Center
North Carolina Outward Bound School
Outdoor Vacations for Women over 40
PeerSpirit
RVing Women
Sea Safari Sailing
Sea Sense
Womanship
Women on the Water

**MIDWEST: ILLINOIS, INDIANA, IOWA, KANSAS, MICHIGAN, MINNESOTA,
MISSOURI, NEBRASKA, NORTH DAKOTA, OHIO, SOUTH DAKOTA, WIS-
CONSIN**

Inside Outside Adventures
Journeywell
PeerSpirit
Prairie Women Adventures and Retreat
Rainbow Adventures
RVing Women
Sea Sense
Sylvan Rocks
Voyageur Outward Bound School
Widjiwagan YMCA Camp
Wintermoon
Women in the Wilderness
Woodswomen

**ROCKY MOUNTAIN: COLORADO, IDAHO, MONTANA, NEVADA, UTAH,
WYOMING**

Adventure Associates

Backroads
Bar H Ranch
Boulder Rock Club
CenterPoint in Aspen
Cloud Canyon Wilderness Experience
Colorado Outward Bound School
Dirt Roads and Damsels
Earthlodge and Womenspeak Journeys
Earthwise
Hawk, I'm Your Sister
The Heart of Adventure
Jennifer Smith Fly Fishing Guide Service
Lois Lane Expeditions
Maggie Merriman Fly Fishing Schools
Mariah Wilderness Expeditions
McNamara Ranch
National Outdoor Leadership School
Orvis
Outdoor Leadership Training Seminars
Outdoor Vacations for Women over 40
Rainbow Adventures
Reel Women Fly Fishing Adventures
Sheri Griffith Expeditions
Voyageur Outward Bound School
Wander Women
Widjiwagan YMCA Camp
WOMBATS
Women in the Wilderness
Woodswomen

SOUTHWEST: ARIZONA, NEW MEXICO, OKLAHOMA, TEXAS

Alaska Women of the Wilderness
Artemis Wilderness Tours
At the Helm
Blue Moon Explorations
Call of the Wild
Colorado Outward Bound School
Dirt Roads and Damsels

Earthlodge and Womenspeak Journeys
Hawk, I'm Your Sister
Her Wild Song
Mariah Wilderness Expeditions
PeerSpirit
Rainbow Adventures
RVing Women
Sacred Sedona
Voyageur Outward Bound School
Wander Women
Woodswomen

PACIFIC COAST: CALIFORNIA, OREGON, WASHINGTON

Adventure Associates
Ancient Forest Adventures
Backroads
Blue Moon Explorations
Call of the Wild
Cloud Canyon Wilderness Experience
Dirt Roads and Damsels
Earthlodge and Womenspeak Journeys
Eco-Explorations
Elakah! Expeditions
Hurricane Creek Llama Treks
Lois Lane Expeditions
Mariah Wilderness Expeditions
OceanWomyn Kayaking
Onn the Water
Outdoor Vacations for Women over 40
Pacific Crest Outward Bound School
Poseidon Services/Izarra Cruises
Rhonda Smith Windsurfing Center
Robin Tyler Productions and Tours
RVing Women
Skylink
Vertical Ventures
Womanship
WOMBATS

Women's Sailing Adventures
Woodswomen

ALASKA

Alaska Women of the Wilderness
Call of the Wild
Dirt Roads and Damsels
Elakah! Expeditions
Equinox Wilderness Expeditions
Maggie Merriman Fly Fishing Schools
OceanWomyn Kayaking
Olivia Cruises and Resorts
Poseidon Services/Izarra Cruises
Rainbow Adventures
RVing Women
Widjiwagan YMCA Camp
Woodswomen

HAWAII

Adventure Spirit Hawaii
Alaska Women of the Wilderness
Blue Moon Explorations
Call of the Wild
The Heart of Adventure
Olivia Cruises and Resorts
Outdoor Vacations for Women over 40
Wilderness Hawaii

AFRICA

Olivia Cruises and Resorts
Rainbow Adventures
Skylink
Womanpower Enterprises
Women to Women Cross-cultural Adventures
Woodswomen

ASIA

Adventure Trekking

Alaska Women of the Wilderness
Club Le Bon
The Heart of Adventure
Himalayan High Treks
Lois Lane Expeditions
Rainbow Adventures
Travel Walji's
Wildwise
Women to Women Cross-cultural Adventures

CANADA

Blue Moon Explorations
Canadian Outward Bound Wilderness School
Dirt Roads and Damsels
Et-Then
Hawk, I'm Your Sister
Herizen: New Age Sailing for Women
Lois Lane Expeditions
OceanWomyn Kayaking
Olivia Cruises and Resorts
Onn the Water
Pack, Paddle, Ski
PeerSpirit
Poseidon Services/Izarra Cruises
Rainbow Adventures
Widjiwagan YMCA Camp
Wild Women Expeditions
Womanship
Women in the Wilderness
Women's Outdoor Adventure Cooperative

CARIBBEAN

Club Le Bon
Dirt Roads and Damsels
Eco-Explorations
New Dawn
Olivia Cruises and Resorts
Outdoor Vacations for Women over 40

Rainbow Adventures
Reel Women Fly Fishing Adventures
Rhonda Smith Windsurfing Center
Sea Sense
Womanship
Women in the Wilderness
Women's Outdoor Adventure Cooperative
Women's Sailing Adventures

EUROPE

Adventure Associates
Call of the Wild
Earthlodge and Women Journeys
Earthwise
Firma Hagi
Outdoor Vacations for Women over 40
PeerSpirit
Skadi
Skylink
Tours of Interest to Women
Vaarschool Grietje
Venus Adventures
Wander Women
Womanship
Woodswomen

LATIN AMERICA

Adventure Associates
Adventure Spirit Hawaii
Artemis Sailing Charters
Backroads
Blue Moon Explorations
Club Le Bon
Eco-Explorations
Elakah! Expeditions
Hawk, I'm Your Sister
Mariah Wilderness Expeditions
National Outdoor Leadership School

OceanWomyn Kayaking
Olivia Cruises and Resorts
Outdoor Vacations for Women over 40
Paddling South
Rainbow Adventures
RVing Women
Womanship
Women in the Wilderness
Women to Women Cross-cultural Adventures
Woodswomen

MIDDLE EAST

Poseidon Services/Izarra Cruises (Turkey)
Robin Tyler Productions and Tours (Israel and Egypt)

SOUTH PACIFIC

Alaska Women of the Wilderness
Artemis Sailing Charters
Bushwise Women
Dare You!
Eco-Explorations
Outdoor Vacations for Women over 40
Poseidon Services/Izarra Cruises
Rainbow Adventures
Skylink
Wildwise
Womanship
Women of the Wilderness Australia
Woodswomen

INDEX TO COMPANIES THAT OFFER SCHOLARSHIPS

Adventure Associates
Adventures for Women
Alaska Women of the Wilderness
Ancient Forest Adventures
Appalachian Mountain Club

Blue Moon Explorations
Boulder Rock Club
Canadian Outward Bound Wilderness School
Cloud Canyon Wilderness Experience
Colorado Outward Bound School
Earthlodge and Womenspeak Journeys
Earthwise
Eco-Explorations
Elakah! Expeditions
Firma Hagi
The Heart of Adventure
Her Wild Song
Hurricane Island Outward Bound School
Inside Outside Adventures
Journeywell
Nantahala Outdoor Center
National Outdoor Leadership School
North Carolina Outward Bound School
OceanWomyn Kayaking
Pacific Crest Outward Bound School
Poseidon Services /Izarra Cruises
Sacred Sedona
Sheri Griffith Expeditions
Skadi
Skylink
Tours of Interest to Women
Vaarschool Grietje
Voyageur Outward Bound School
Widjiwagan YMCA Camp
Wildwise
WOMBATS
Women in the Wilderness
Women of the Wilderness Australia
Women's Outdoor Adventure Cooperative
Woodswomen

ABOUT THE COVER ARTIST

The cover art for *Adventures in Good Company* is by Maggie Rudy, an artist who lives in Portland, Oregon. The work is pastel on paper. To achieve the deeply saturated color, she makes her own pastels from pure pigment. She received her B.A. in Fine Arts from Reed College in 1980. Her work has appeared in shows locally and nationally and has won numerous awards. Primarily a fine artist, Maggie Rudy enjoys doing an occasional illustration. She also created the cover art for *A Journey of One's Own*.

ABOUT THE AUTHOR

An experienced international traveler, Thalia Zepatos wrote her first book, *A Journey of One's Own: Uncommon Advice for the Independent Woman Traveler*, to encourage and assist other women to "stop waiting and start traveling." *A Journey of One's Own* was enthusiastically received, quickly becoming *the* book on women traveling internationally, alone or with a partner.

After the publication of *A Journey of One's Own*, Thalia Zepatos organized a group of women to charter a boat for a week in the Greek Isles. Long a solo traveler, she was quickly won over to the great joy of group adventure travel for women. She wrote *Adventures in Good Company: The Complete Guide to Women's Tours and Outdoor Trips*, her second book, in order to make available to more women, information about the burgeoning world of all-women's tours and outdoor trips. She now intersperses her solo traveling with leading women's tours for several adventure companies to a variety of destinations worldwide.

The author lectures and teaches workshops on women's travel issues nationally and regularly contributes travel stories to newspapers, magazines, and anthologies.

ALSO BY THALIA ZEPATOS

A Journey of One's Own

Uncommon Advice for the
Independent Woman Traveler

THALIA ZEPATOS

"Superlatives generally make us suspicious, but we
must say: This is THE best women's travel resource
we've seen, ever.... It's authoritative; it's supportive; it's
amusing; it really does have it all."
—Pamela Robin Brandt, *New York Daily News*

"Sensitive, intelligent and inspirational."
—*San Francisco Chronicle*

"Thalia Zepatos is teacher, spokeswoman and heroine of
sorts to a generation of travelers, both women and men,
who understand travel as more than the periodic recreational migration that out commercial culture promotes.
—*The Seattle Times*

*T*ales of the author's own cross-cultural encounters and self-discovery,
along with stories from a wide array of women travelers, add spice to
expert and detailed advice on practical matters:

- ◆ **dealing with sexual harassment**
- ◆ **staying healthy**
- ◆ **traveling safely**
- ◆ **avoiding theft**
- ◆ **choosing luggage and guidebooks**
- ◆ **finding the cheapest airline tickets**
- ◆ **managing a trip of extended duration**

While encouraging solo travel, the book carefully explores travel with a
partner, or with a group:

- ◆ **trying on solo travel for size**
- ◆ **how to make partner travel work**
- ◆ **traveling with a child**
- ◆ **finding the right group for you**

Particular attention is given to traveling outside the West:

- ◆ **getting acquainted with new cultures**
- ◆ **accepting hospitality**
- ◆ **bargaining**
- ◆ **arranging a homestay**

Thoroughly entertaining and encouraging, *A Journey of One's Own* is
a unique combination of the useful, the imaginative, and the inspiring.

trade paperback ISBN 0-933377-20-7 $14.95
cloth ISBN 0-933377-21-5 $24.95

Available at your local bookstore. To order by mail, send a check including $2.50
($3.50 in Canada) for the first book and 50¢ each additional book, postage and han-
dling to: The Eighth Mountain Press, 624 SE 29th Avenue, Portland, OR 97214.